First published in English in 2022 by Nobrow Ltd. 27 Westgate Street, London E8 3RL.

© Sarbacane, Paris, 2022.

Lucie Bryon has asserted her rights under the Copyright, Designs
and Patents Act, 1988, to be identified as the Author and Illustrator of this Work.

1 3 5 7 9 10 8 6 4 2

Published in the US by Nobrow (US) Inc.

Printed in Lithuania on FSC® certified paper.

ISBN: 978-1-838741-19-8

www.nobrow.net

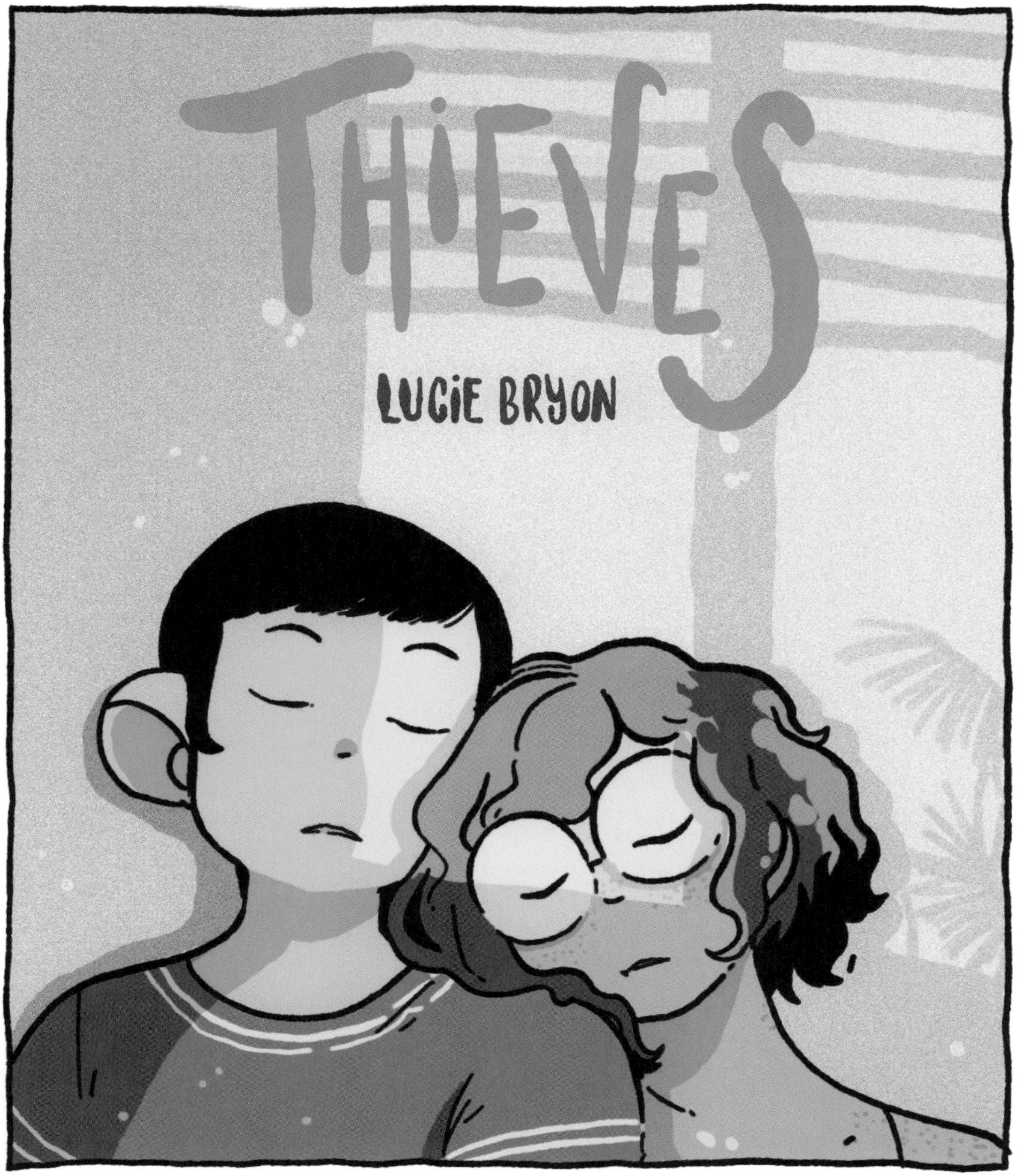
THIEVES
LUCIE BRYON

NOBROW

1

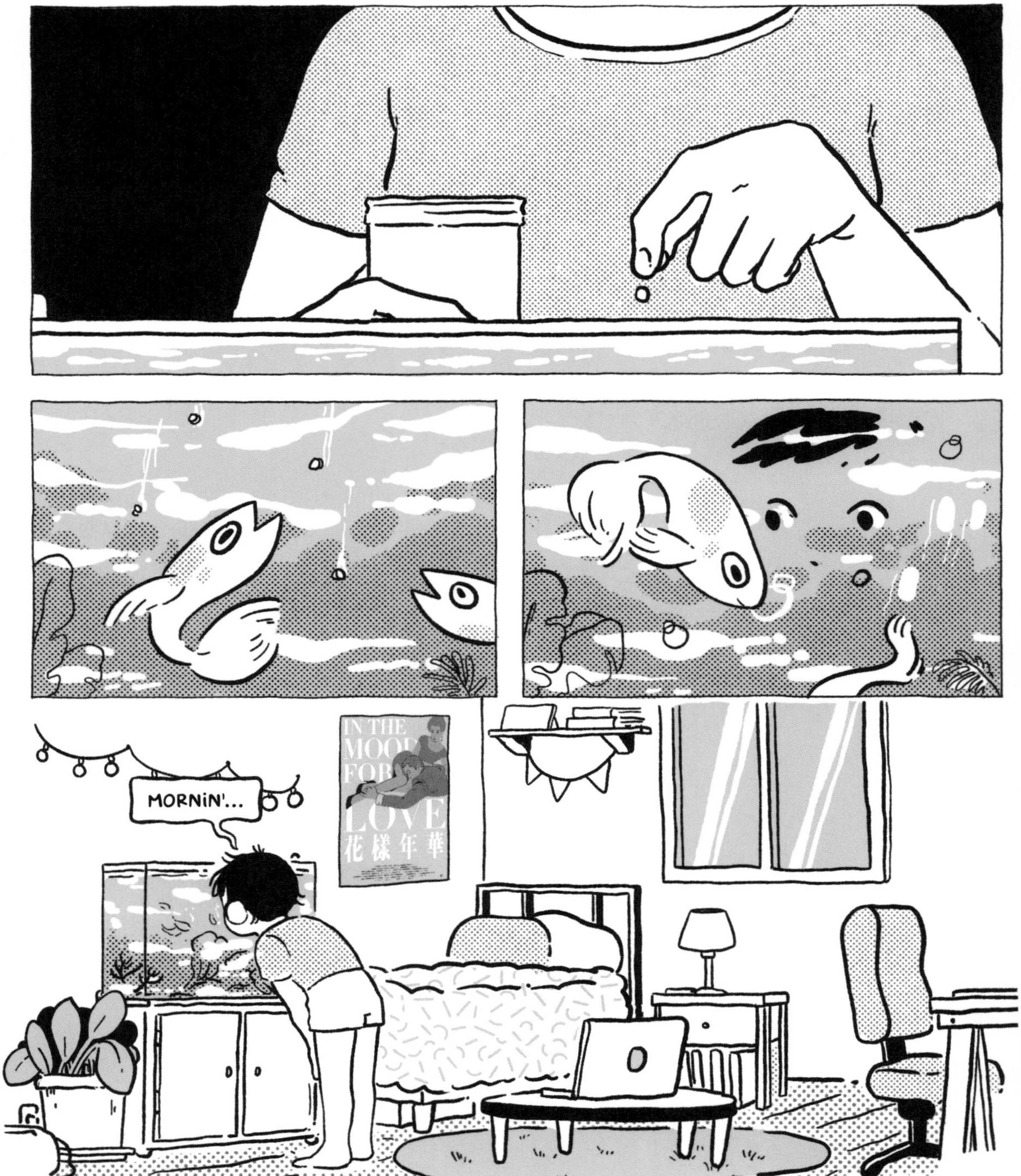
MORNIN'...
IN THE MOOD FOR LOVE
花樣年華

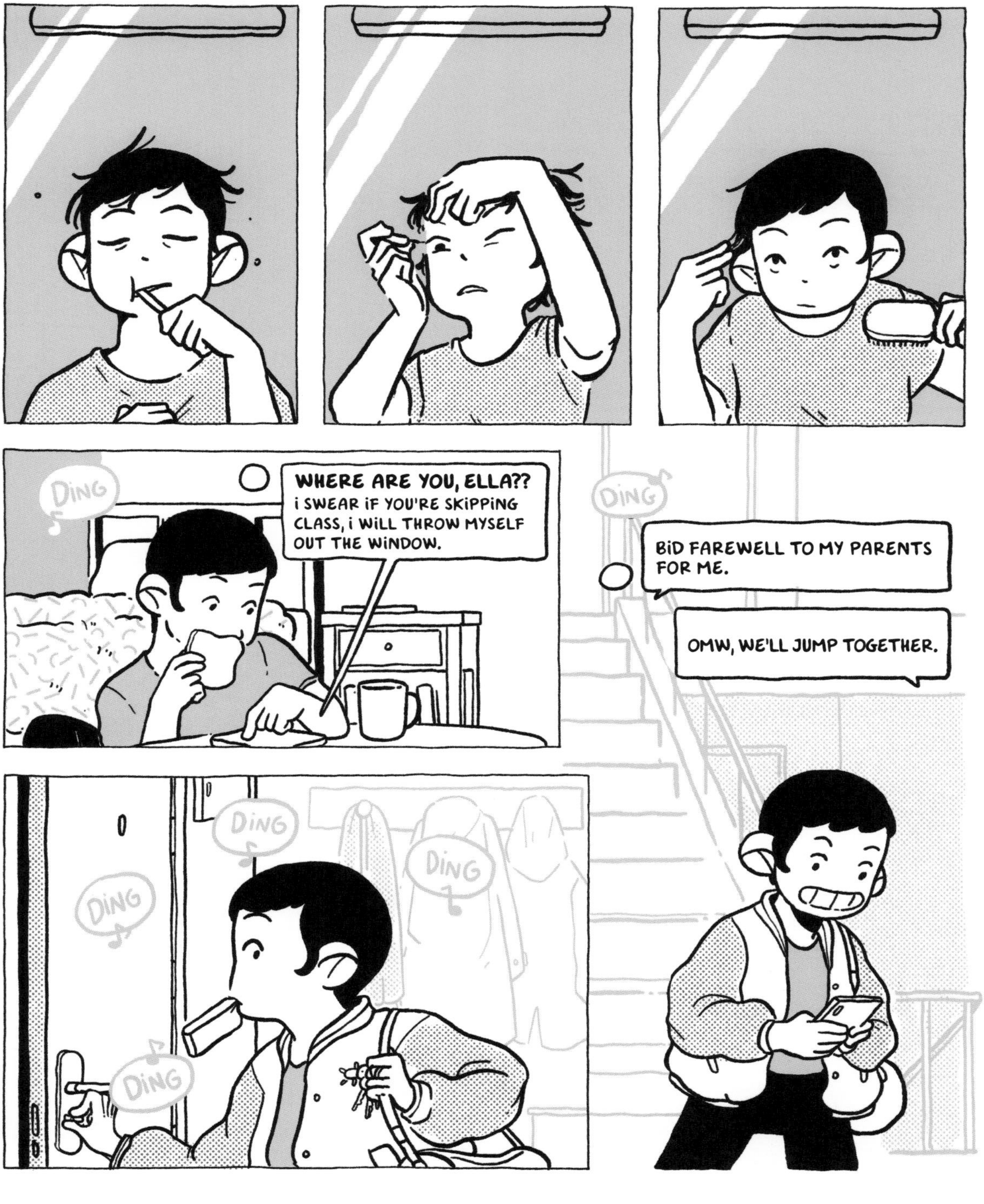
DING
WHERE ARE YOU, ELLA?? i SWEAR iF YOU'RE SKiPPiNG CLASS, i WiLL THROW MYSELF OUT THE WiNDOW.
DING
BiD FAREWELL TO MY PARENTS FOR ME.
OMW, WE'LL JUMP TOGETHER.
DiNG
DiNG
DiNG
DiNG

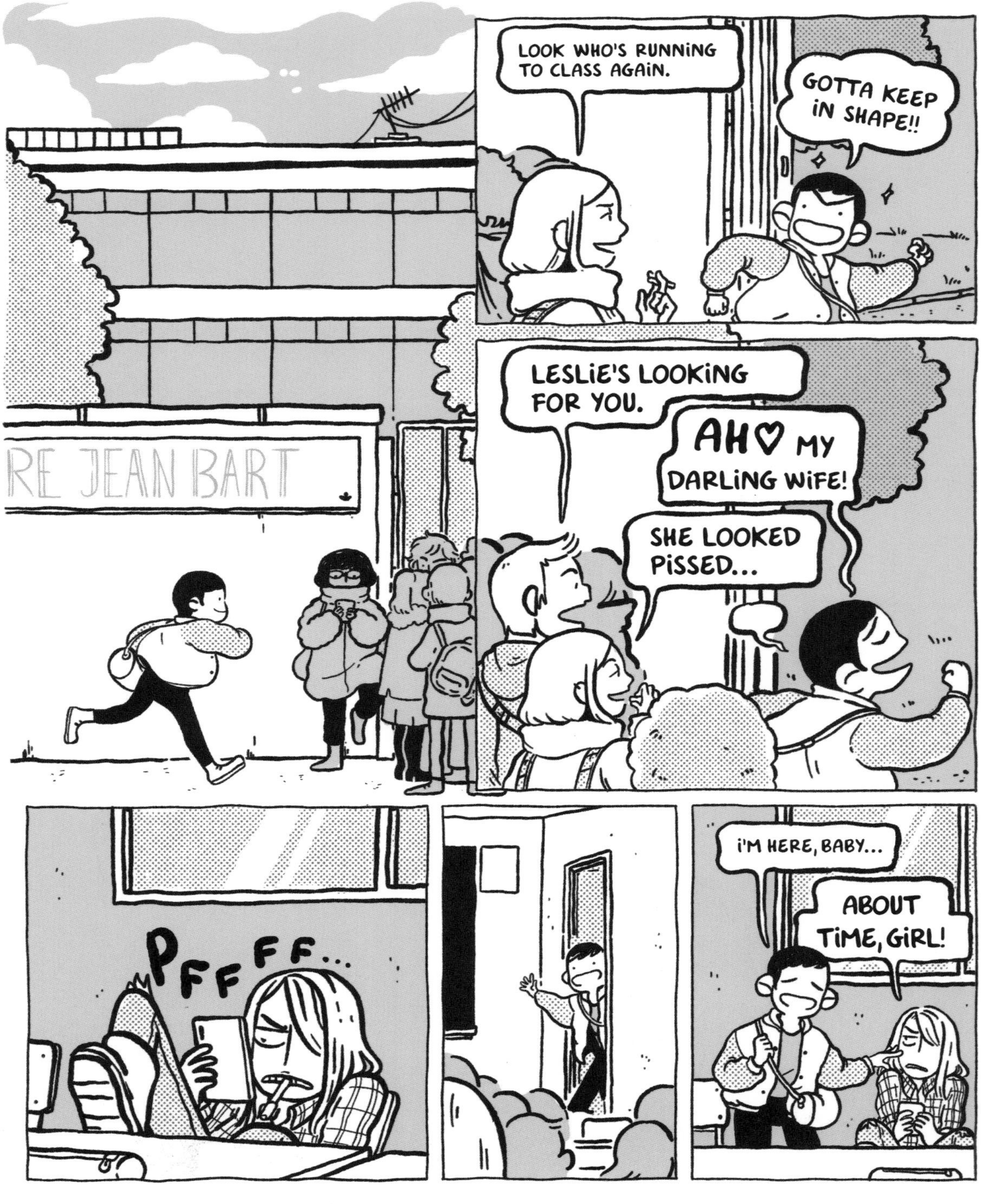

RE JEAN BART
LOOK WHO'S RUNNING TO CLASS AGAIN.
GOTTA KEEP IN SHAPE!!
LESLIE'S LOOKING FOR YOU.
AH♡ MY DARLING WIFE!
SHE LOOKED PISSED...
PFFFF...
I'M HERE, BABY...
ABOUT TIME, GIRL!

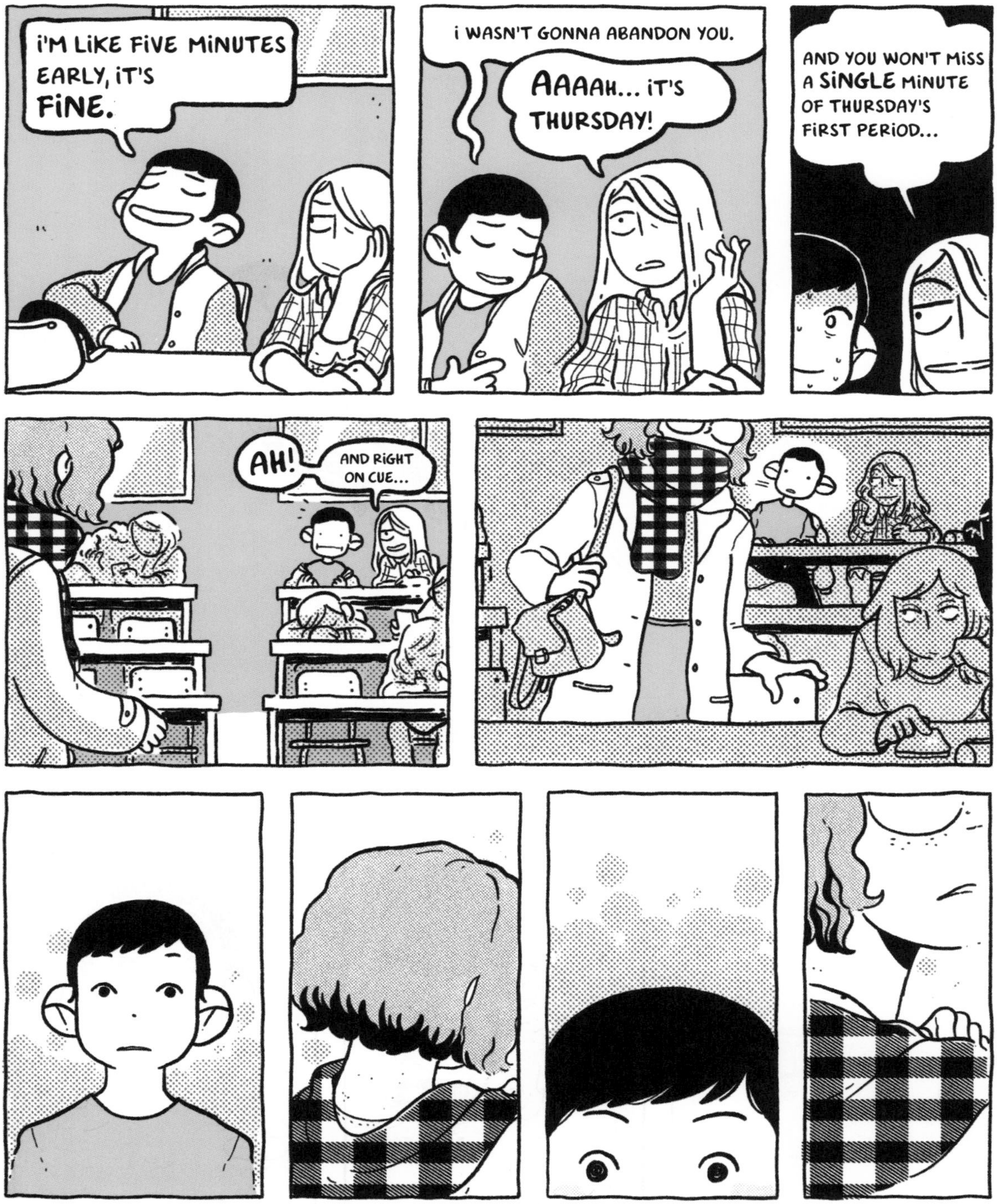
i'M LiKE FiVE MiNUTES EARLY, iT'S FiNE.
i WASN'T GONNA ABANDON YOU.
AAAAH... iT'S THURSDAY!
AND YOU WON'T MiSS A SiNGLE MiNUTE OF THURSDAY'S FiRST PERiOD...
AH!
AND RiGHT ON CUE...

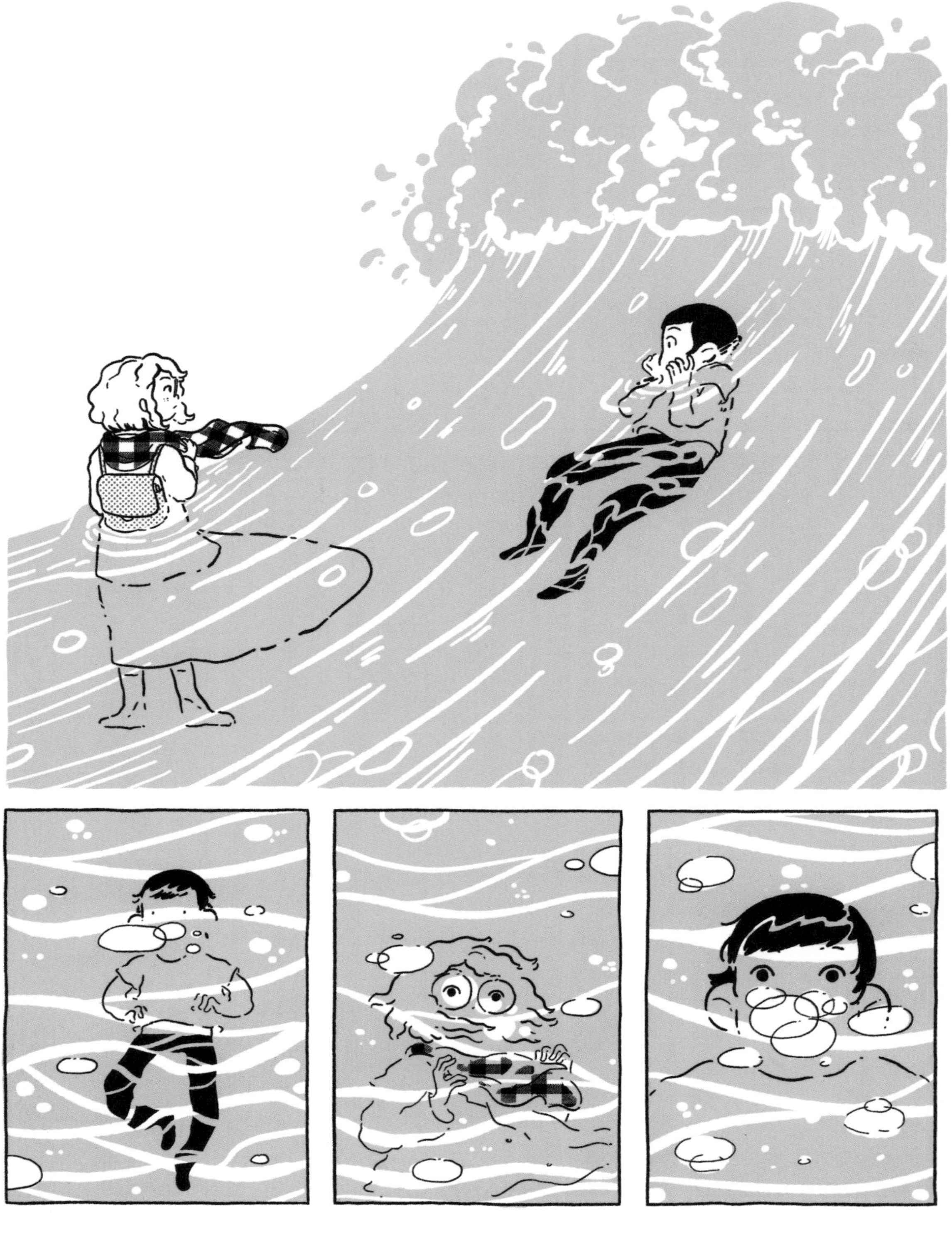

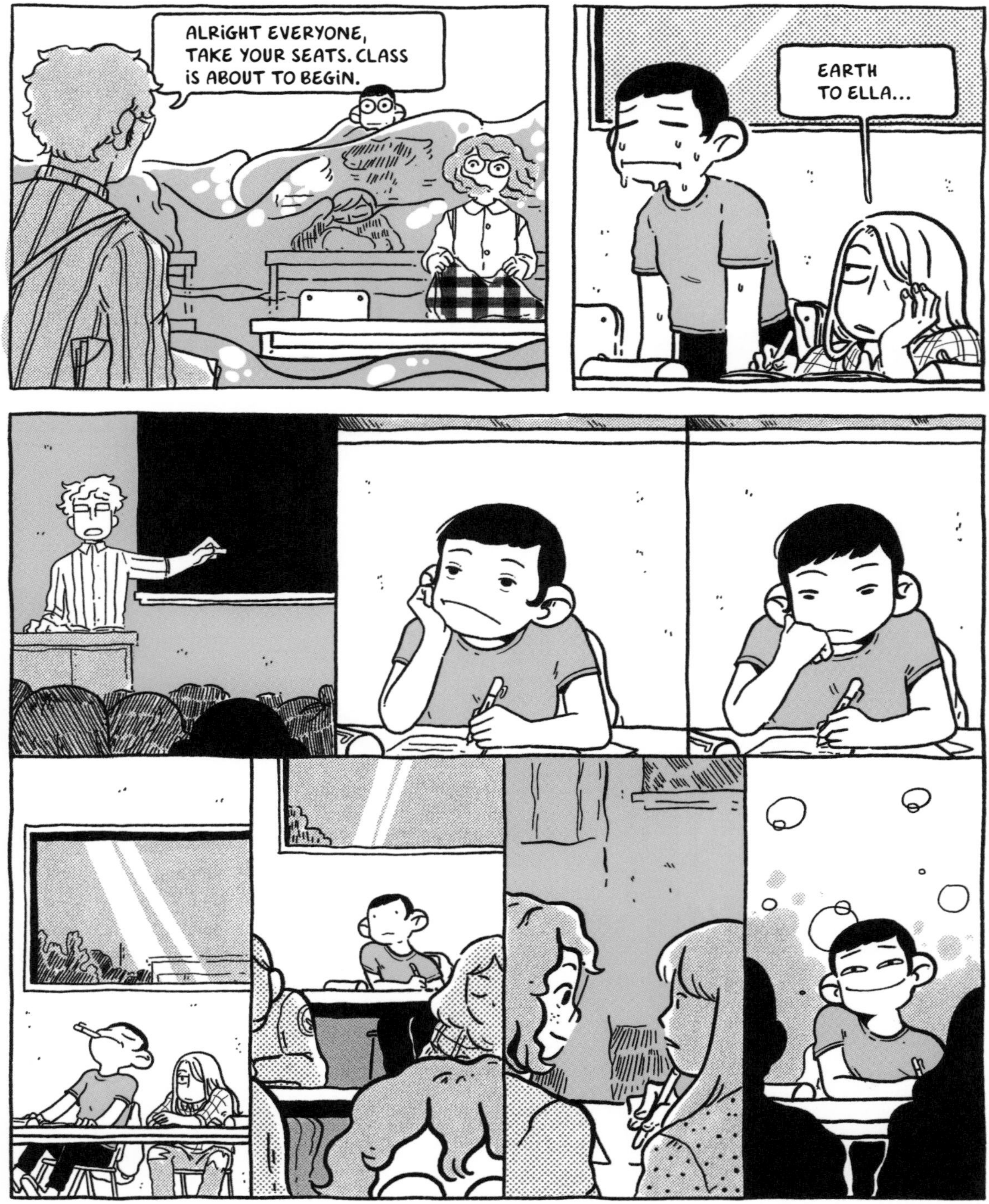
ALRiGHT EVERYONE, TAKE YOUR SEATS. CLASS iS ABOUT TO BEGiN.
EARTH TO ELLA...

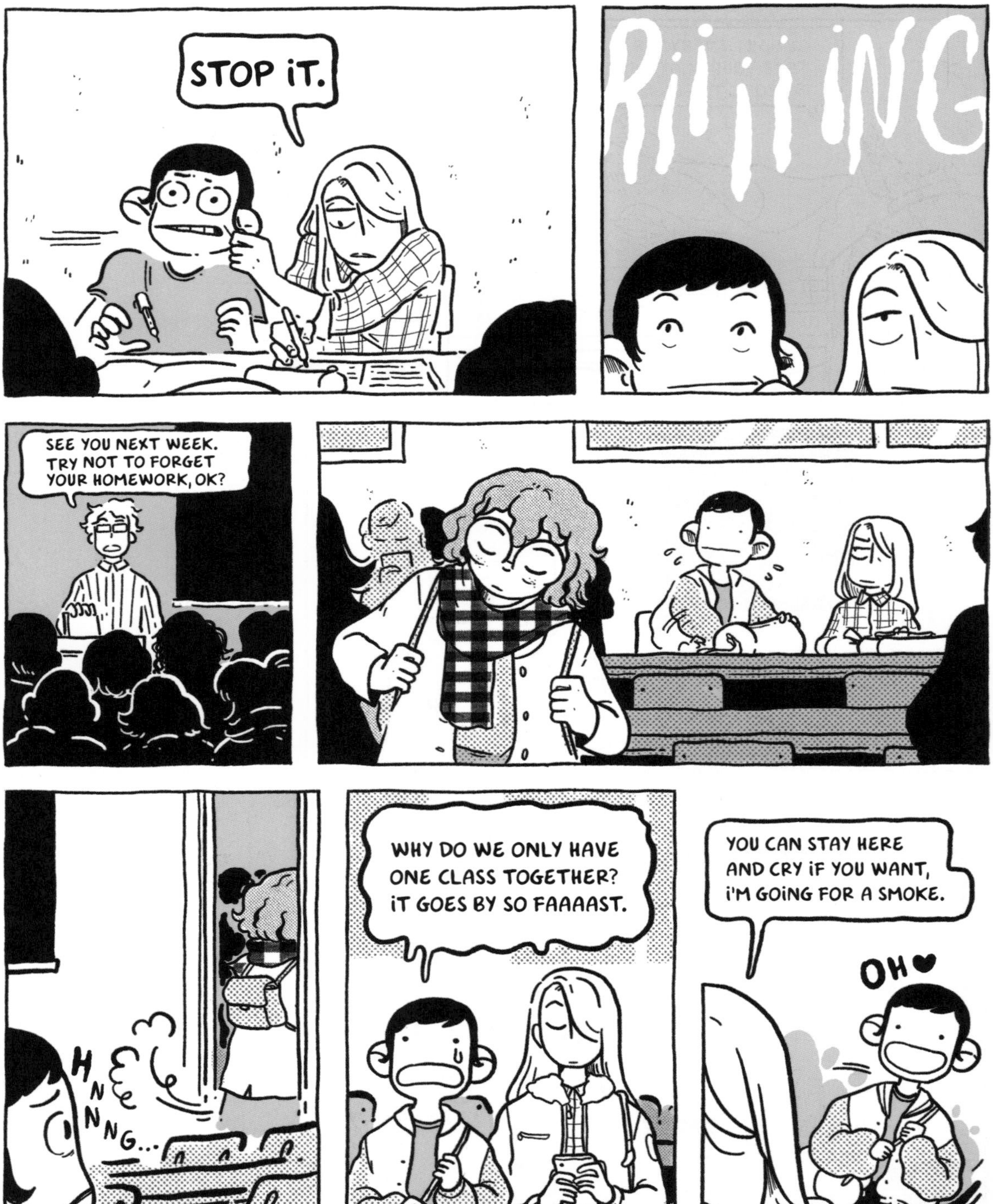
STOP iT.
RiiiiiNG
SEE YOU NEXT WEEK. TRY NOT TO FORGET YOUR HOMEWORK, OK?
HNNNG...
WHY DO WE ONLY HAVE ONE CLASS TOGETHER? iT GOES BY SO FAAAAST.
YOU CAN STAY HERE AND CRY iF YOU WANT, i'M GOiNG FOR A SMOKE.
OH♥

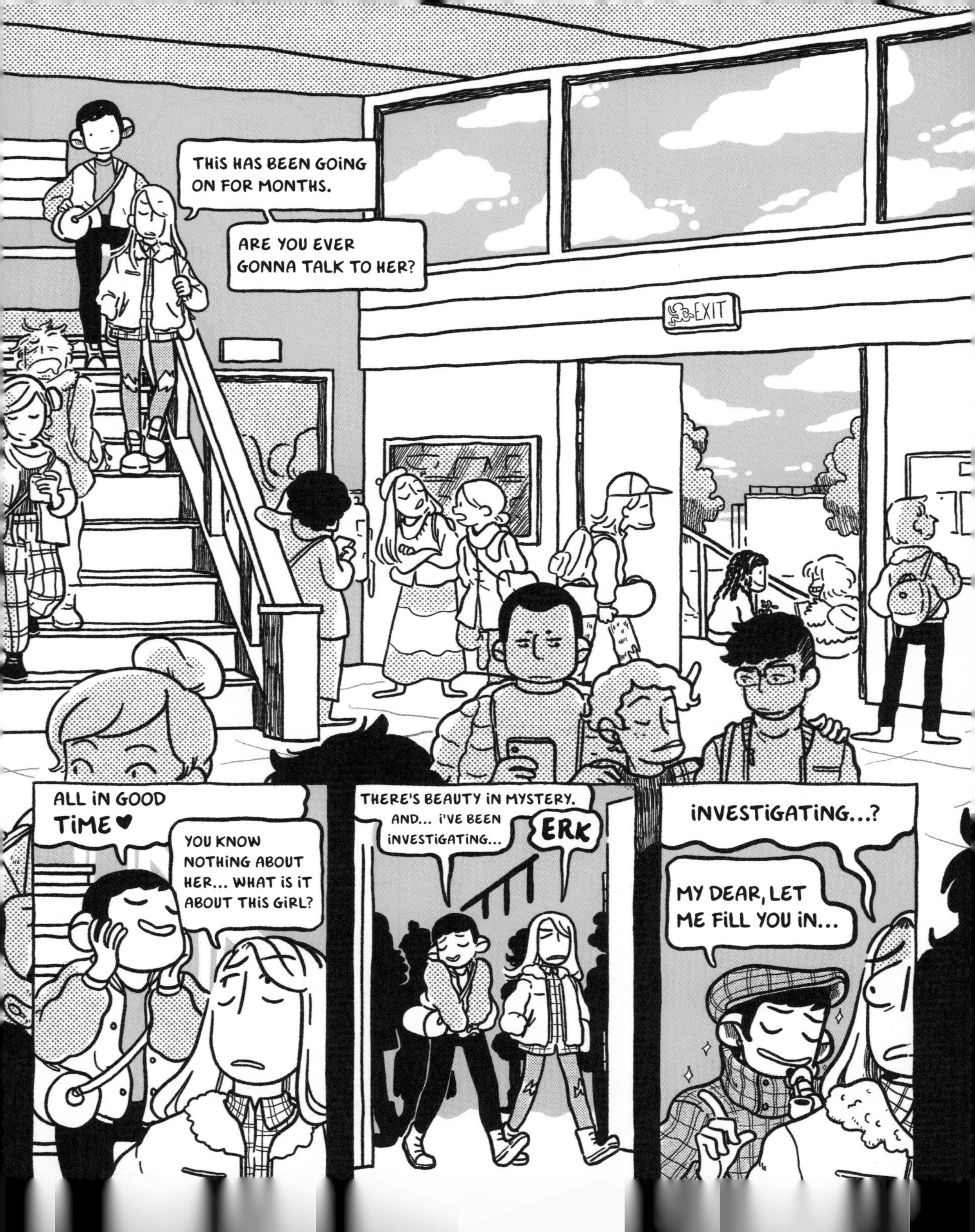
THIS HAS BEEN GOING ON FOR MONTHS.
ARE YOU EVER GONNA TALK TO HER?
EXIT
ALL IN GOOD TIME ♥
YOU KNOW NOTHING ABOUT HER... WHAT IS IT ABOUT THIS GIRL?
THERE'S BEAUTY IN MYSTERY.
AND... I'VE BEEN INVESTIGATING...
ERK
INVESTIGATING...?
MY DEAR, LET ME FILL YOU IN...

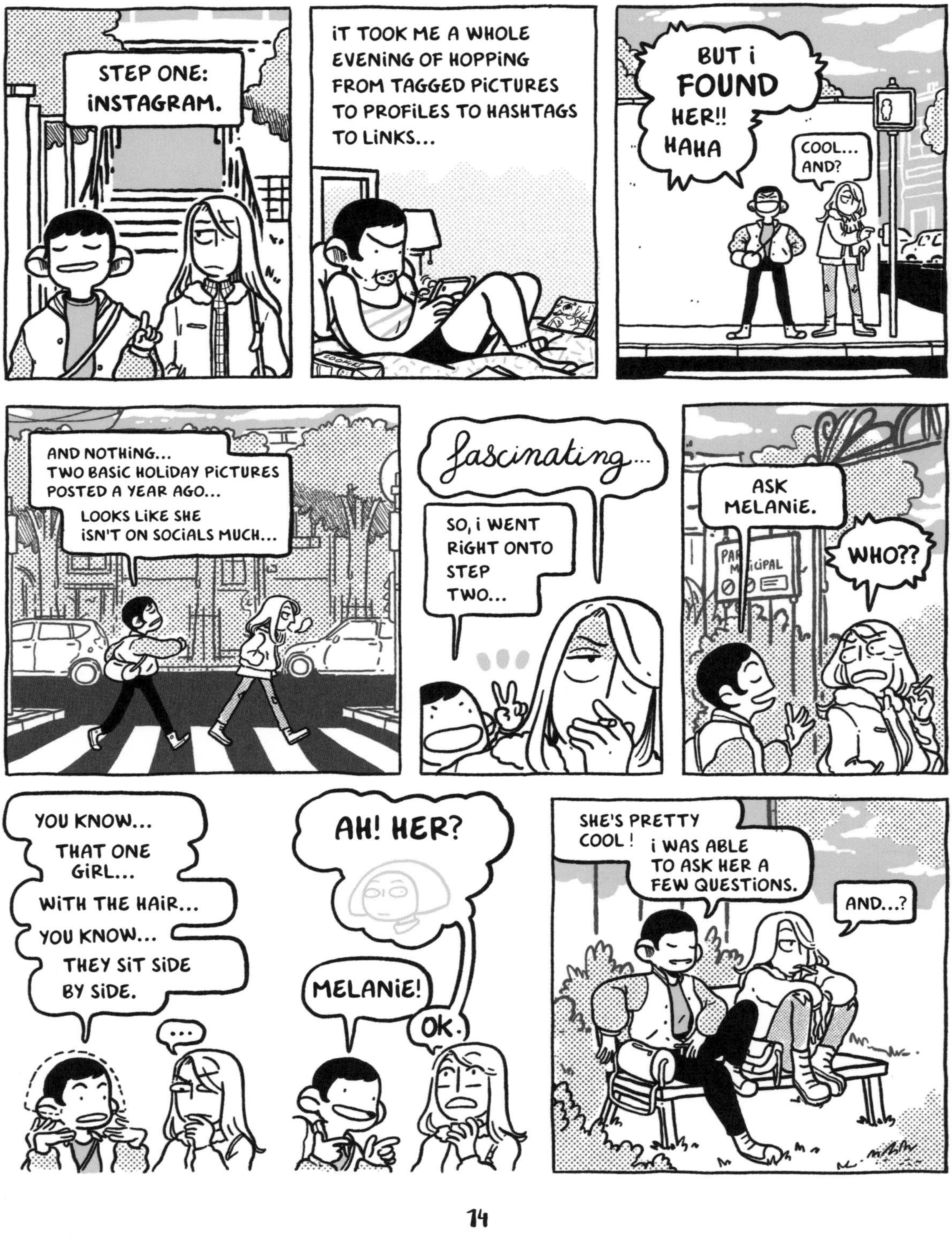

STEP ONE: INSTAGRAM.
IT TOOK ME A WHOLE EVENING OF HOPPING FROM TAGGED PICTURES TO PROFILES TO HASHTAGS TO LINKS...
BUT I FOUND HER!! HAHA
COOL... AND?
AND NOTHING... TWO BASIC HOLIDAY PICTURES POSTED A YEAR AGO...
LOOKS LIKE SHE ISN'T ON SOCIALS MUCH...
fascinating...
SO, I WENT RIGHT ONTO STEP TWO...
ASK MELANIE.
WHO??
YOU KNOW... THAT ONE GIRL... WITH THE HAIR... YOU KNOW... THEY SIT SIDE BY SIDE.
...
AH! HER?
MELANIE!
OK.
SHE'S PRETTY COOL! I WAS ABLE TO ASK HER A FEW QUESTIONS.
AND...?

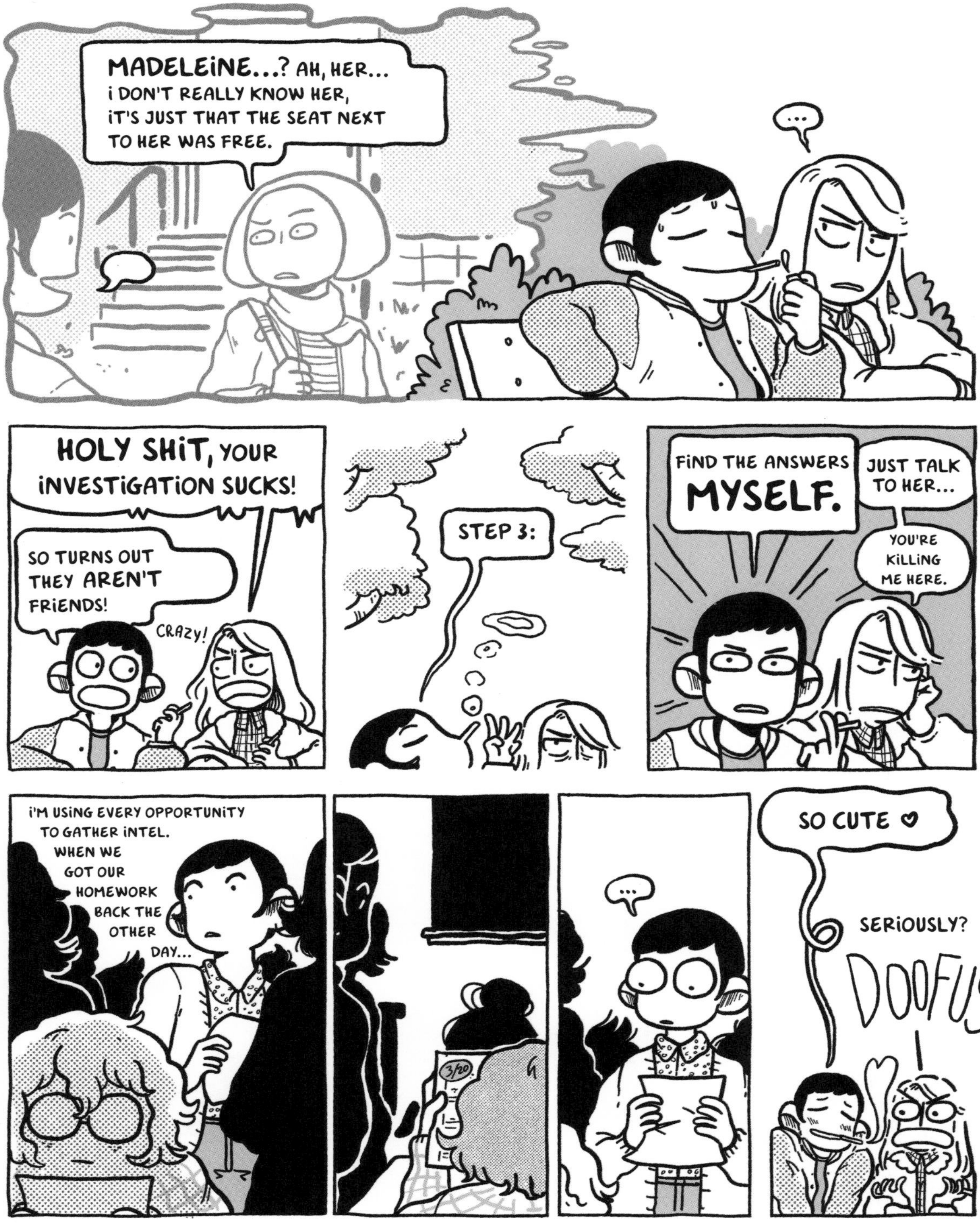
MADELEINE...? AH, HER...
I DON'T REALLY KNOW HER,
IT'S JUST THAT THE SEAT NEXT
TO HER WAS FREE.
...
HOLY SHIT, YOUR INVESTIGATION SUCKS!
SO TURNS OUT THEY AREN'T FRIENDS!
CRAZY!
STEP 3:
FIND THE ANSWERS MYSELF.
JUST TALK TO HER...
YOU'RE KILLING ME HERE.
I'M USING EVERY OPPORTUNITY TO GATHER INTEL. WHEN WE GOT OUR HOMEWORK BACK THE OTHER DAY...
3/20
...
SO CUTE ♥
SERIOUSLY?
DOOFUS!!

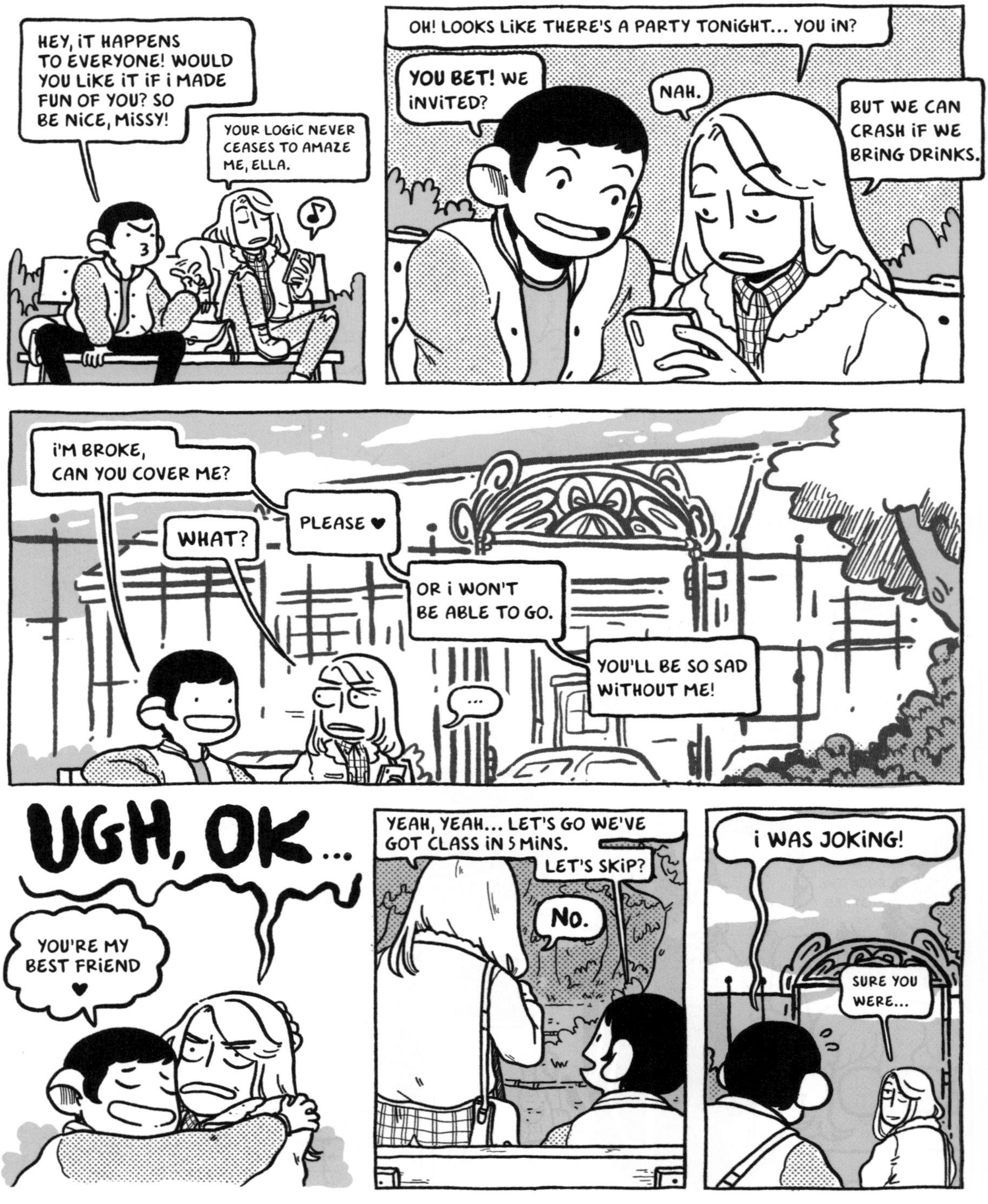
HEY, iT HAPPENS TO EVERYONE! WOULD YOU LiKE iT iF i MADE FUN OF YOU? SO BE NiCE, MiSSY!
YOUR LOGiC NEVER CEASES TO AMAZE ME, ELLA.
OH! LOOKS LiKE THERE'S A PARTY TONiGHT... YOU iN?
YOU BET! WE iNViTED?
NAH.
BUT WE CAN CRASH iF WE BRiNG DRiNKS.
i'M BROKE, CAN YOU COVER ME?
WHAT?
PLEASE ♥
OR i WON'T BE ABLE TO GO.
YOU'LL BE SO SAD WiTHOUT ME!
...
UGH, OK...
YOU'RE MY BEST FRiEND ♥
YEAH, YEAH... LET'S GO WE'VE GOT CLASS iN 5 MiNS.
LET'S SKiP?
NO.
i WAS JOKiNG!
SURE YOU WERE...

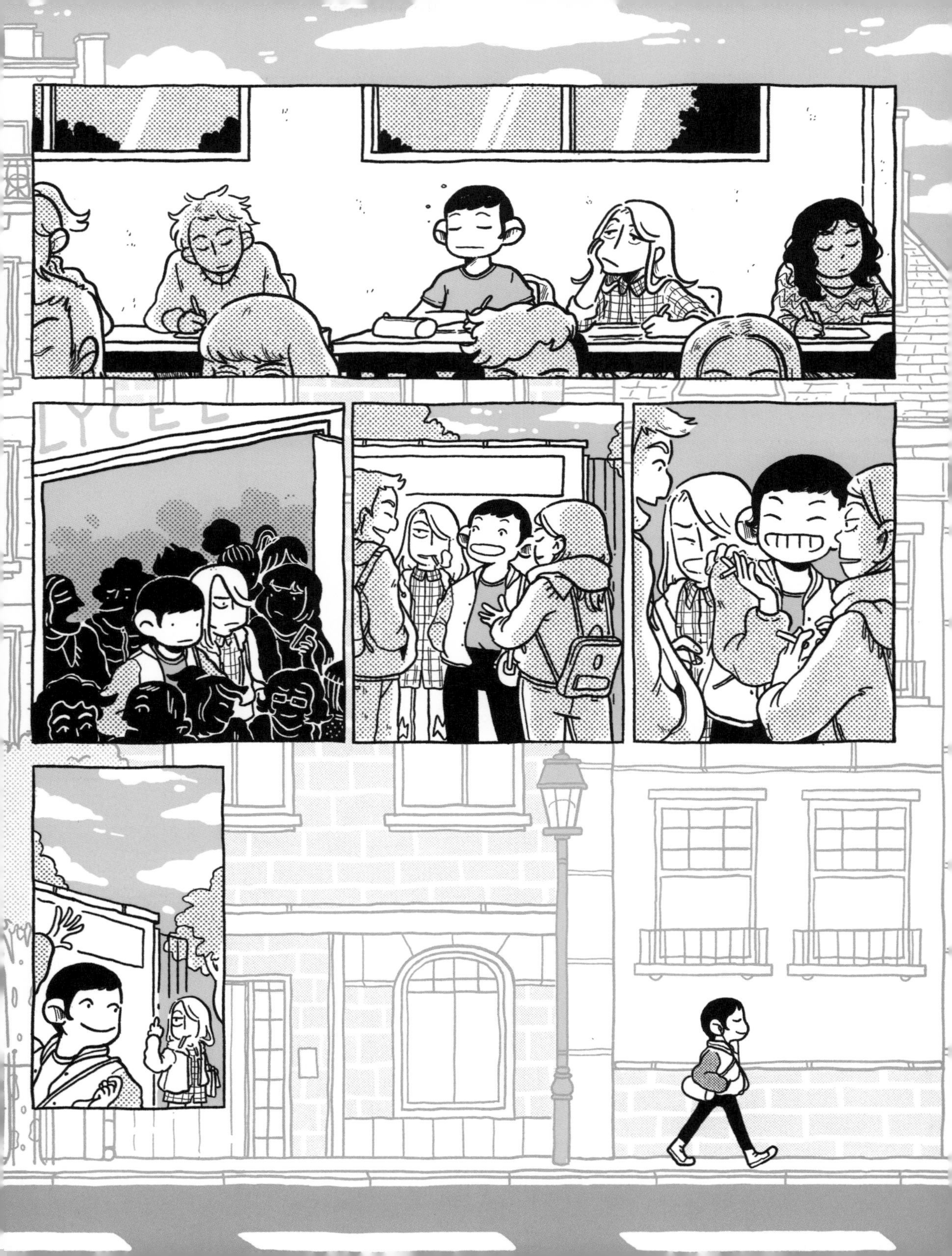
LYCEE

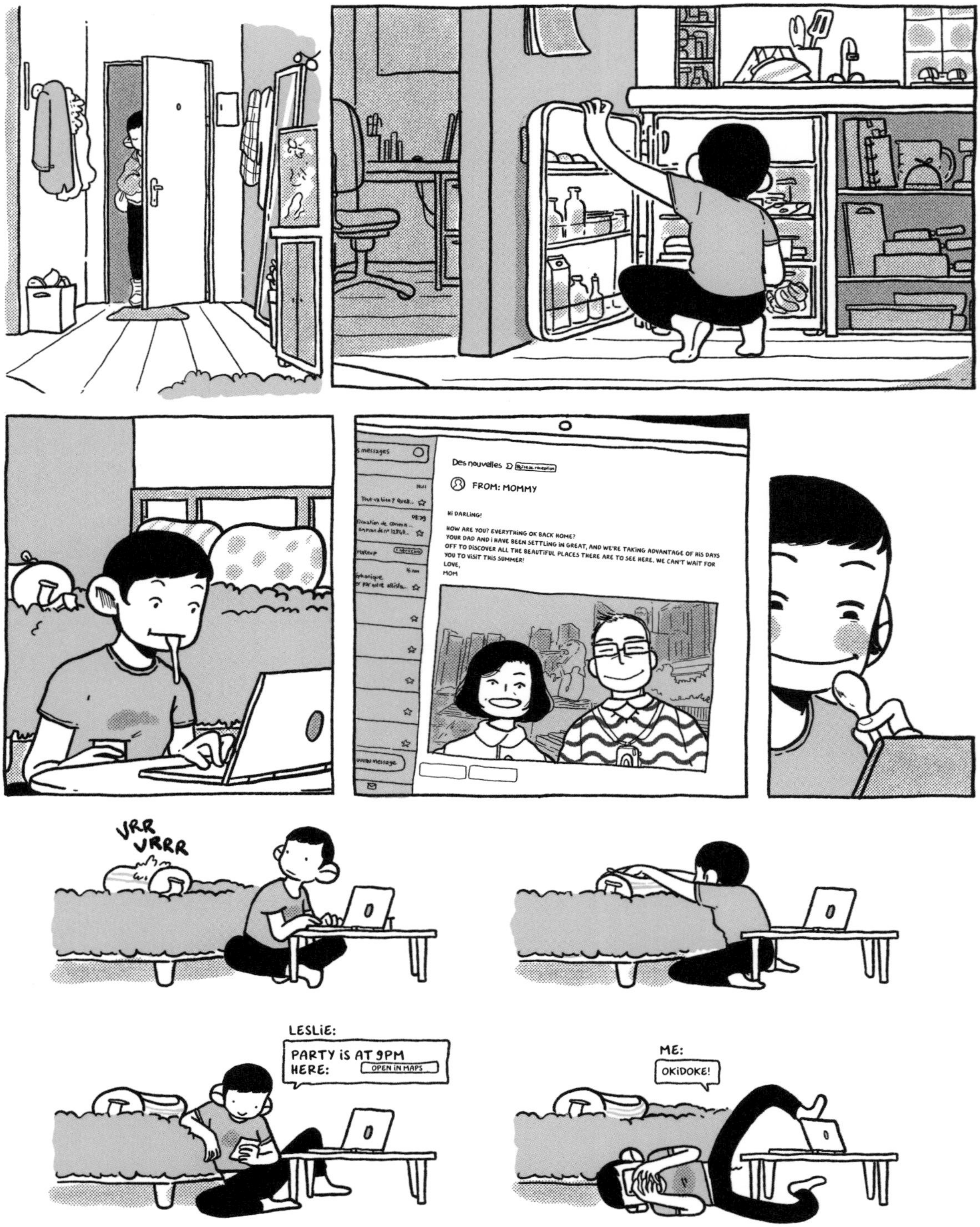
Des nouvelles
FROM: MOMMY
HI DARLING!
HOW ARE YOU? EVERYTHING OK BACK HOME?
YOUR DAD AND I HAVE BEEN SETTLING IN GREAT, AND WE'RE TAKING ADVANTAGE OF HIS DAYS
OFF TO DISCOVER ALL THE BEAUTIFUL PLACES THERE ARE TO SEE HERE. WE CAN'T WAIT FOR
YOU TO VISIT THIS SUMMER!
LOVE,
MOM
VRR
VRRR
LESLIE:
PARTY IS AT 9PM
HERE: OPEN IN MAPS
ME:
OKIDOKE!

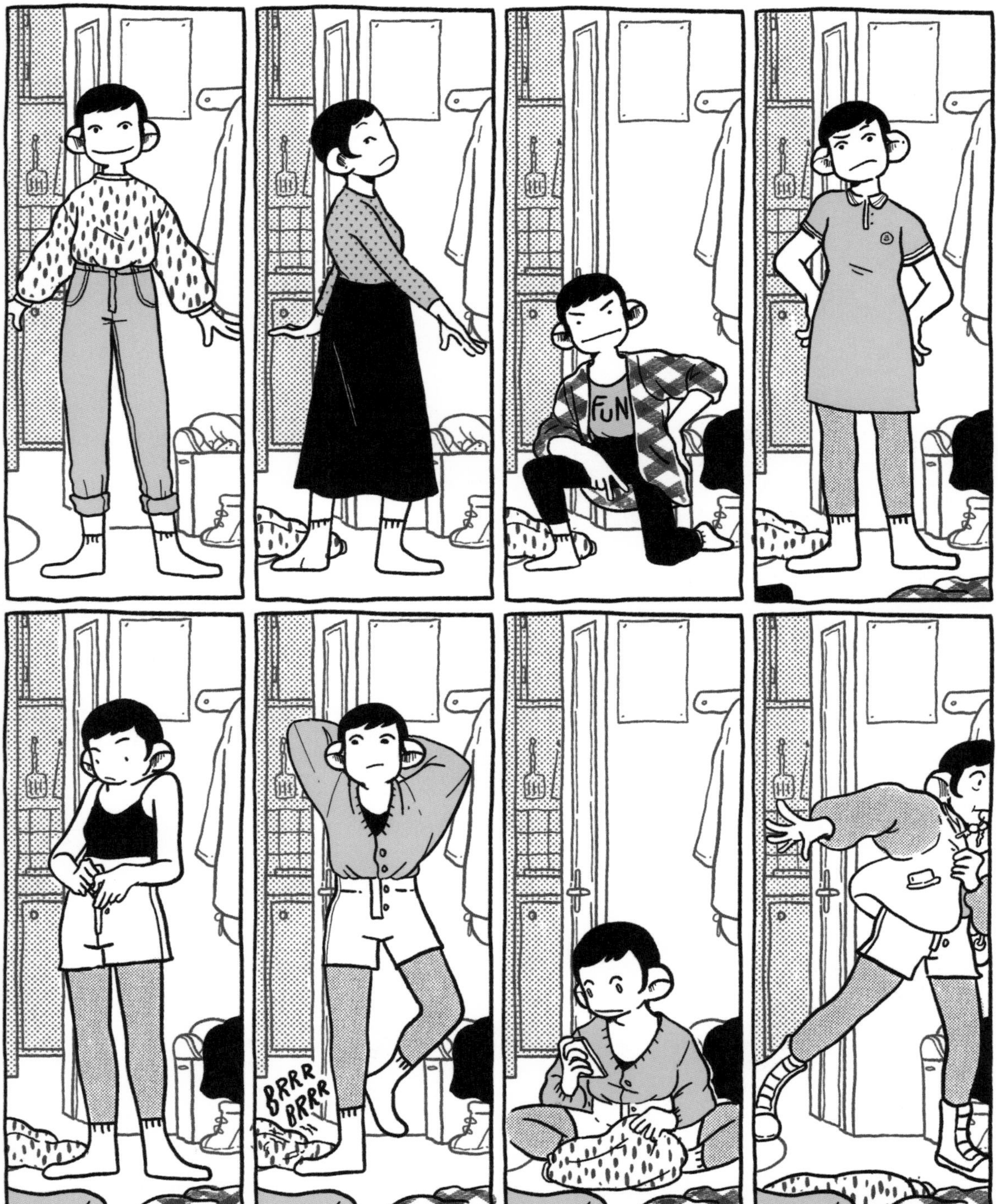
FUN
BRRR
BRRR

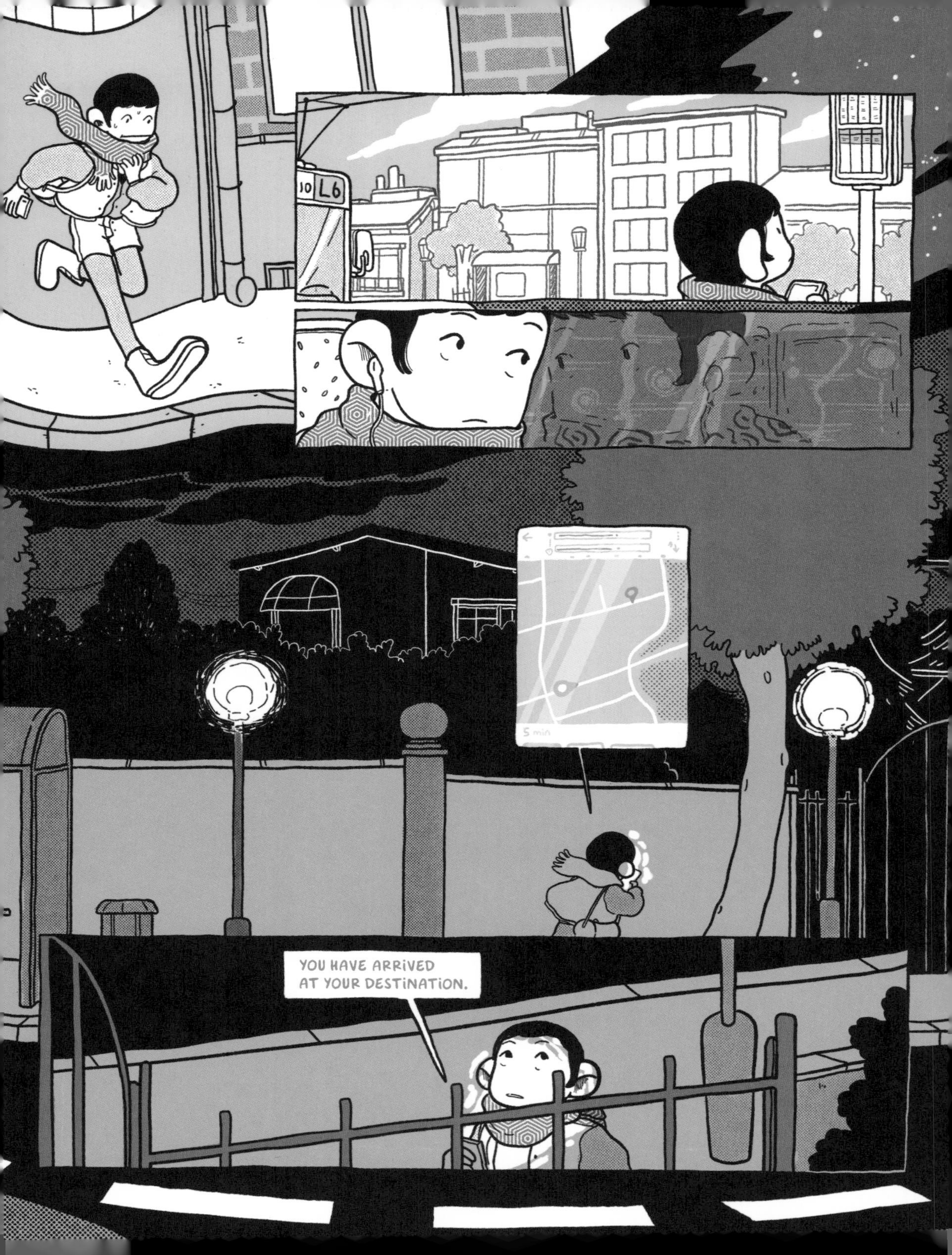
L6
5 min
YOU HAVE ARRIVED AT YOUR DESTINATION.

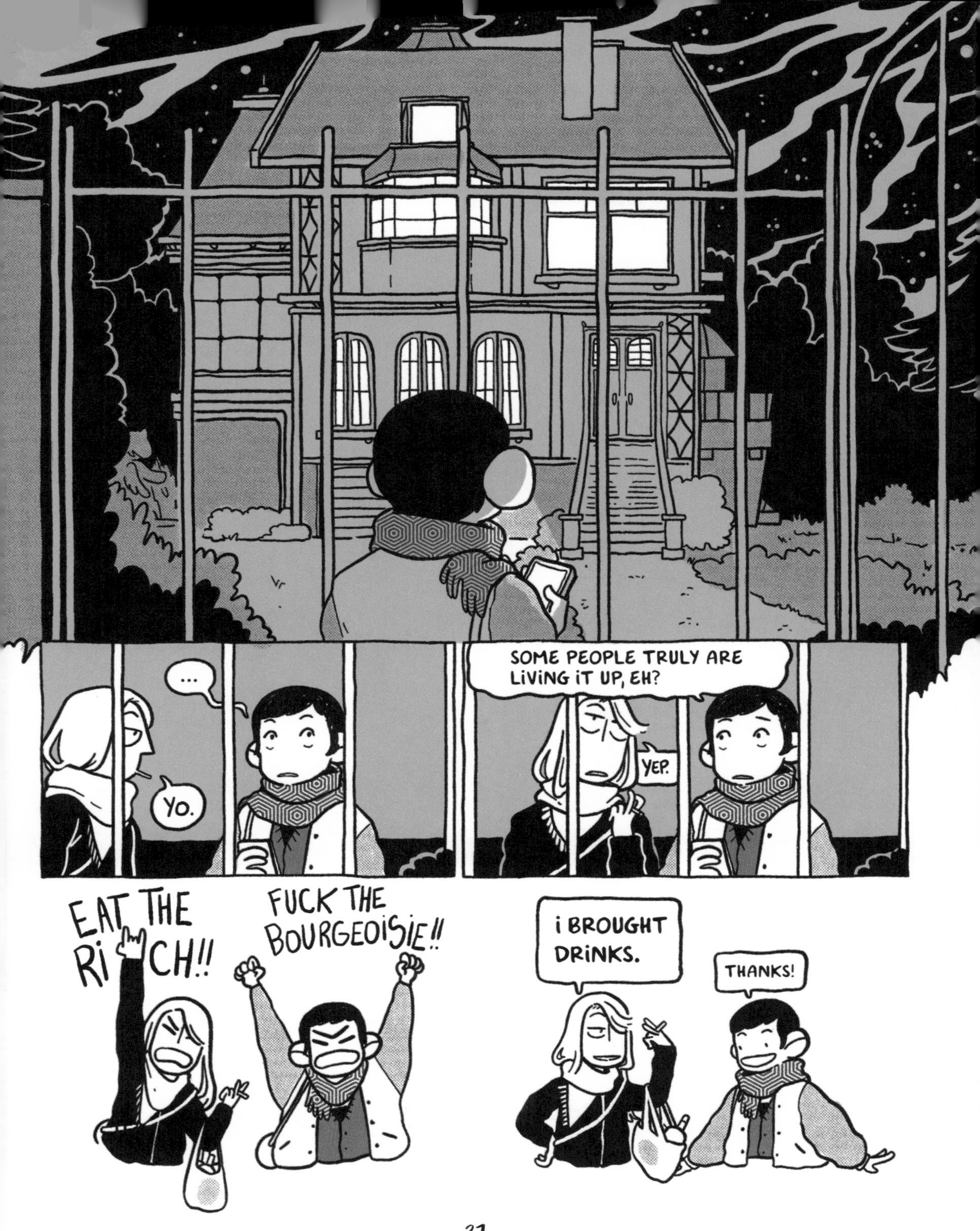
...
YO.
SOME PEOPLE TRULY ARE LIVING IT UP, EH?
YEP.
EAT THE RICH!!
FUCK THE BOURGEOISIE!!
I BROUGHT DRINKS.
THANKS!

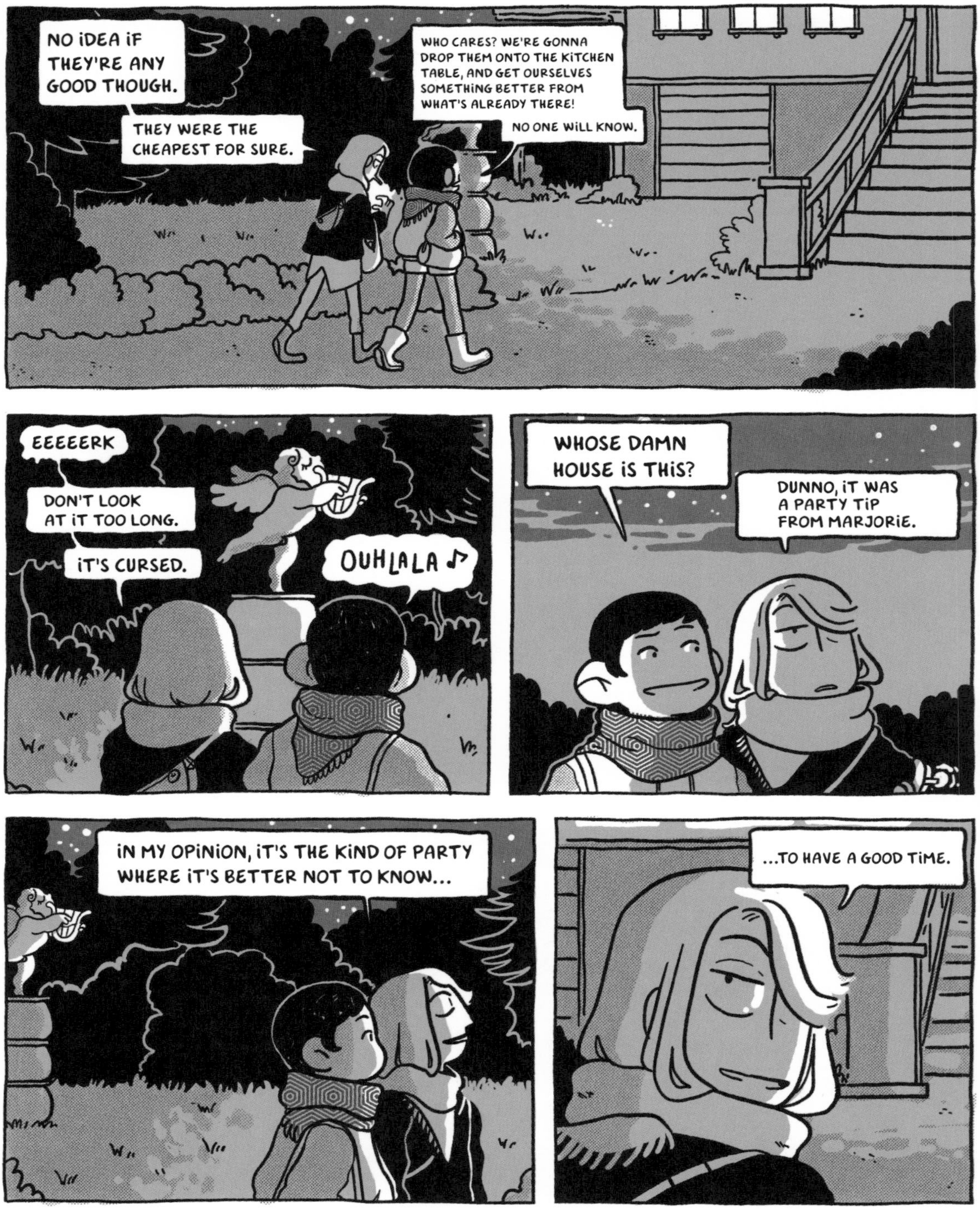
NO iDEA iF THEY'RE ANY GOOD THOUGH.
THEY WERE THE CHEAPEST FOR SURE.
WHO CARES? WE'RE GONNA DROP THEM ONTO THE KiTCHEN TABLE, AND GET OURSELVES SOMETHiNG BETTER FROM WHAT'S ALREADY THERE!
NO ONE WiLL KNOW.
EEEEERK
DON'T LOOK AT iT TOO LONG.
iT'S CURSED.
OUHLALA ♪
WHOSE DAMN HOUSE iS THiS?
DUNNO, iT WAS A PARTY TiP FROM MARJORiE.
iN MY OPiNiON, iT'S THE KiND OF PARTY WHERE iT'S BETTER NOT TO KNOW...
...TO HAVE A GOOD TiME.

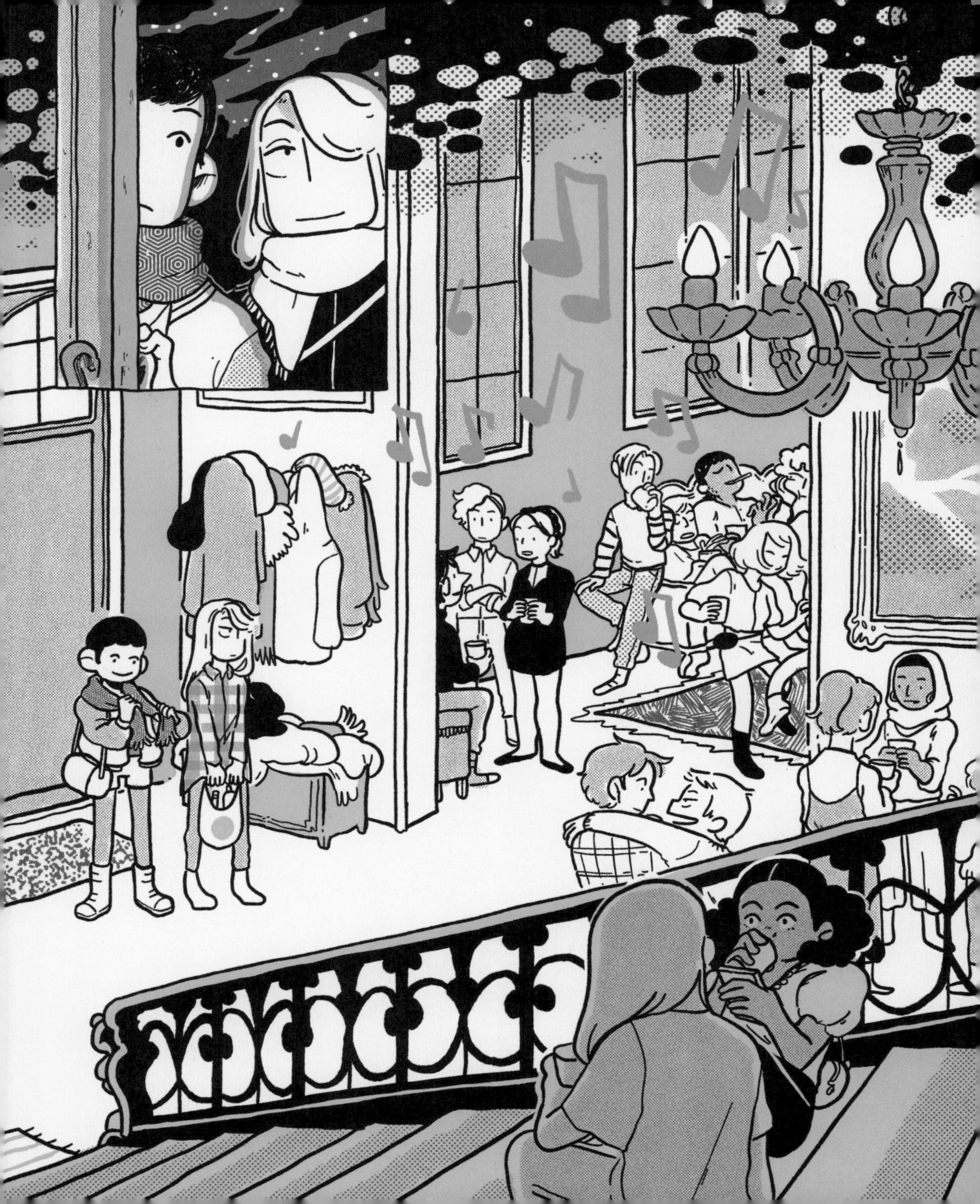

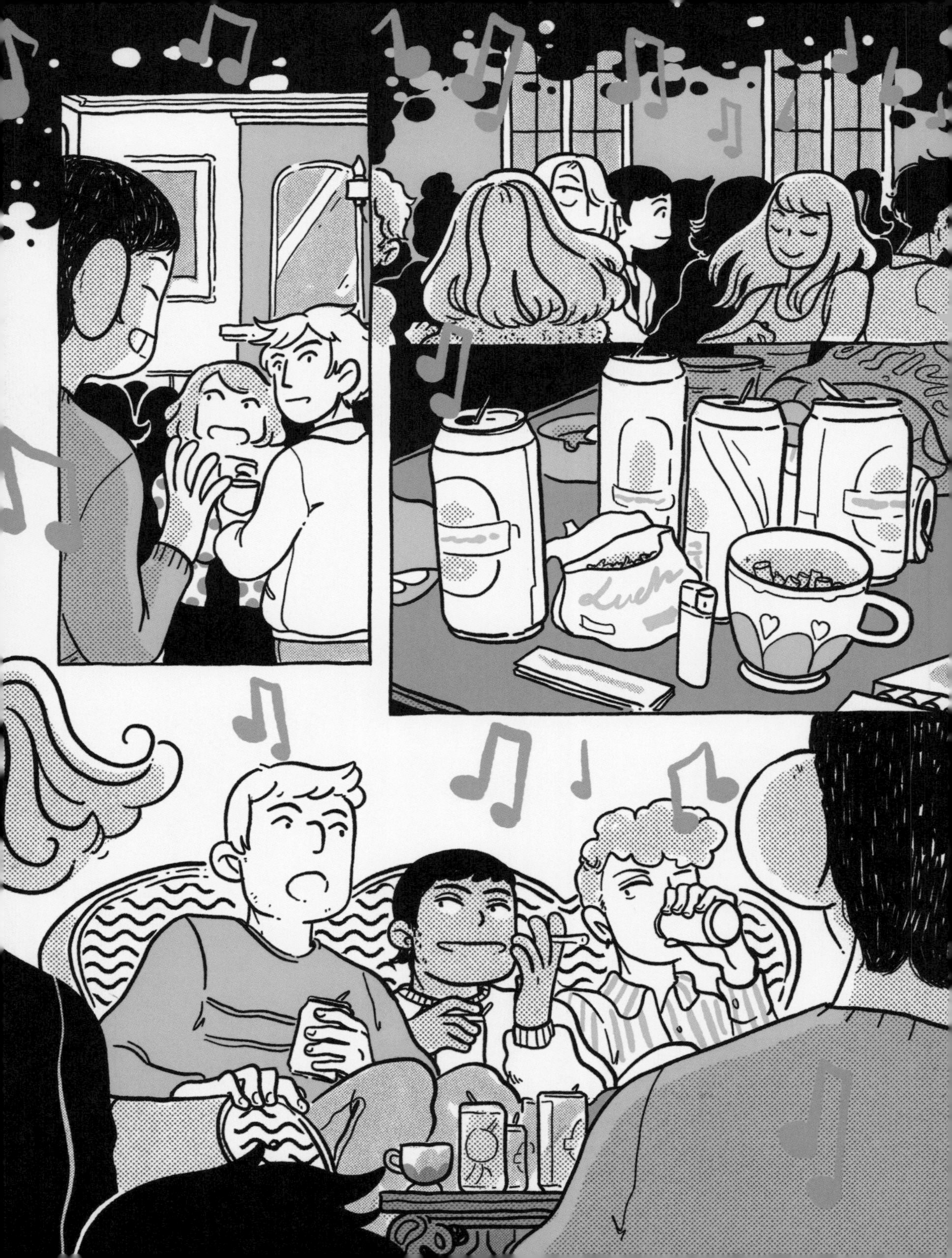

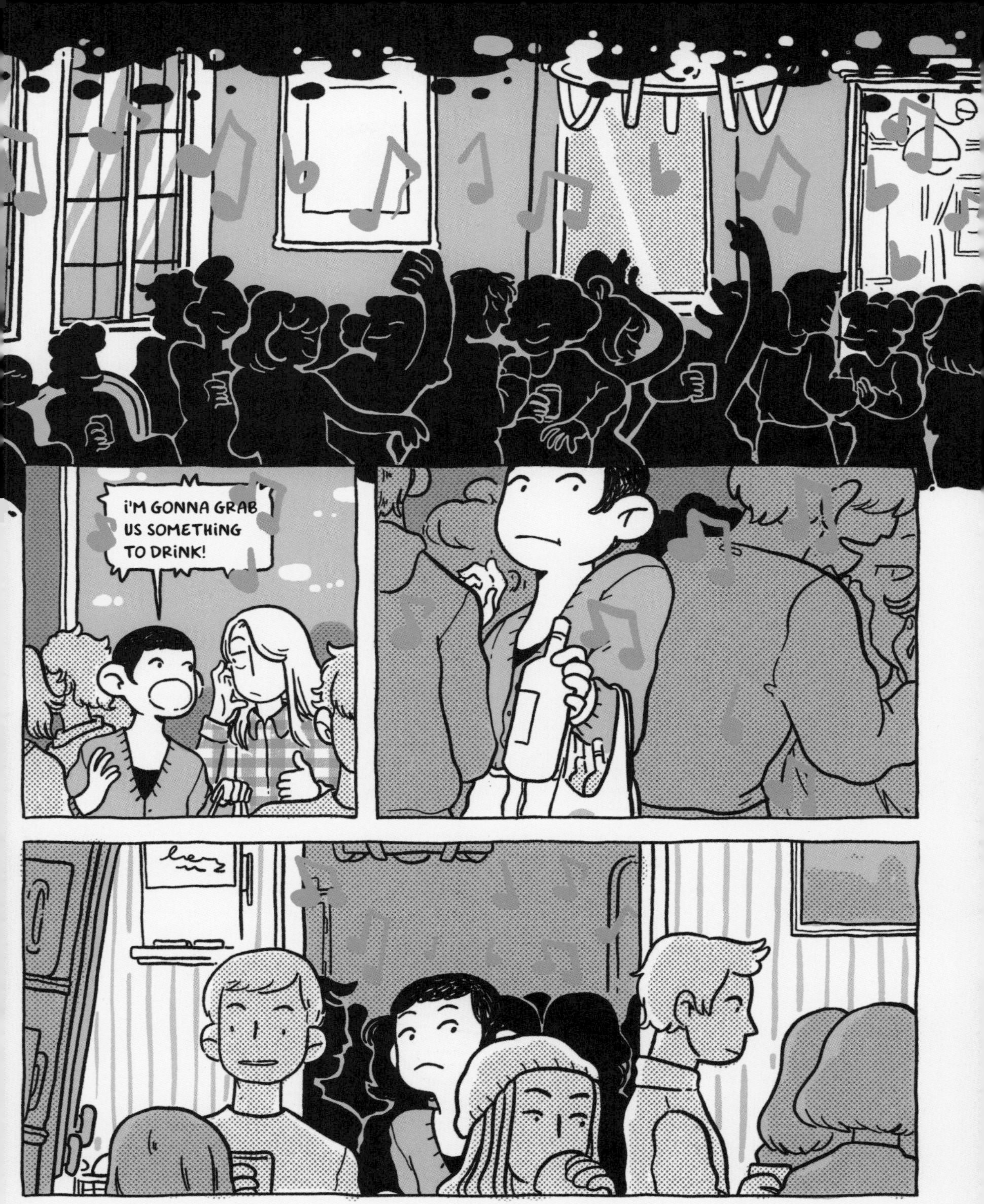

i'M GONNA GRAB US SOMETHING TO DRiNK!

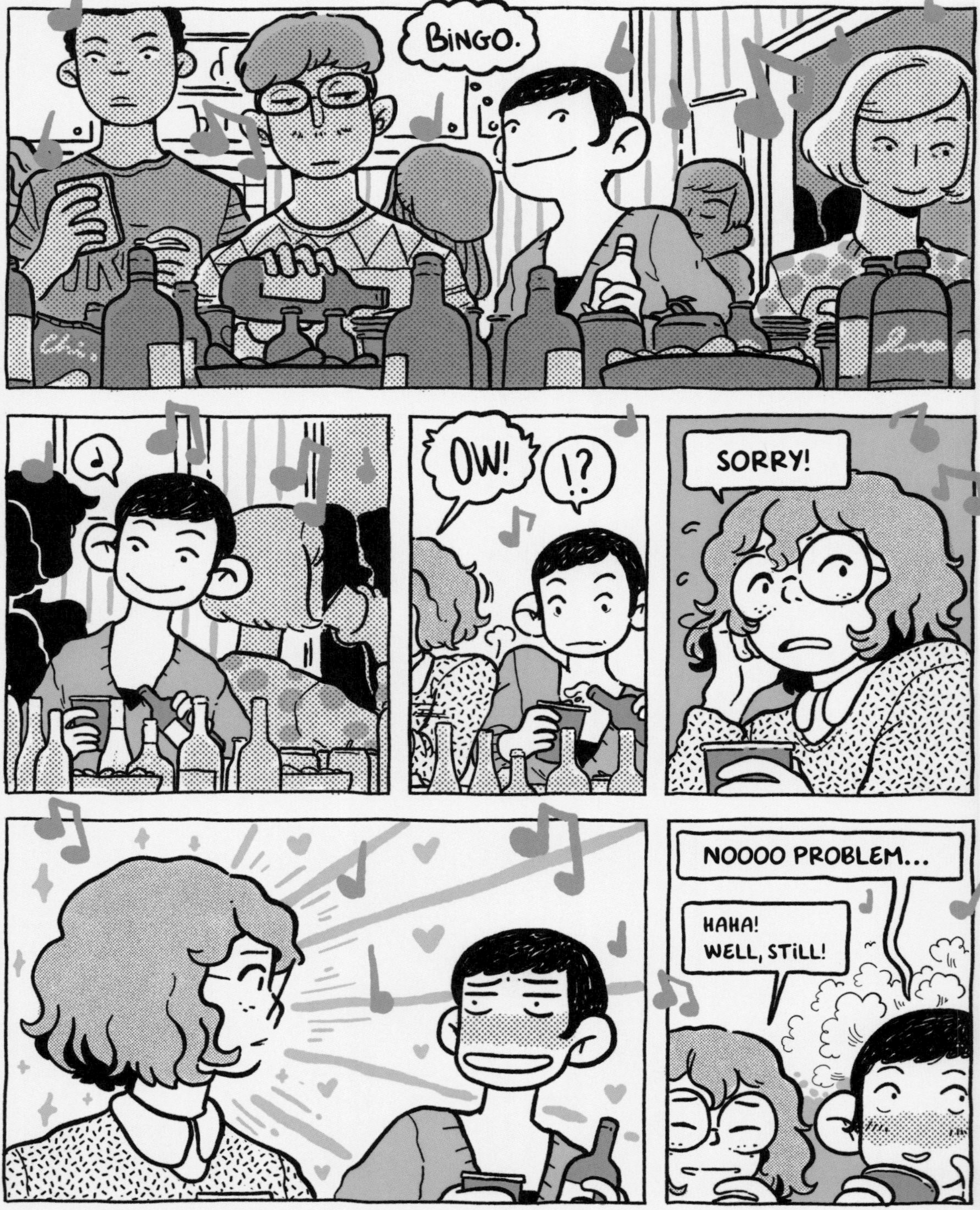
BINGO.
OW!
!?
SORRY!
NOOOO PROBLEM...
HAHA! WELL, STILL!

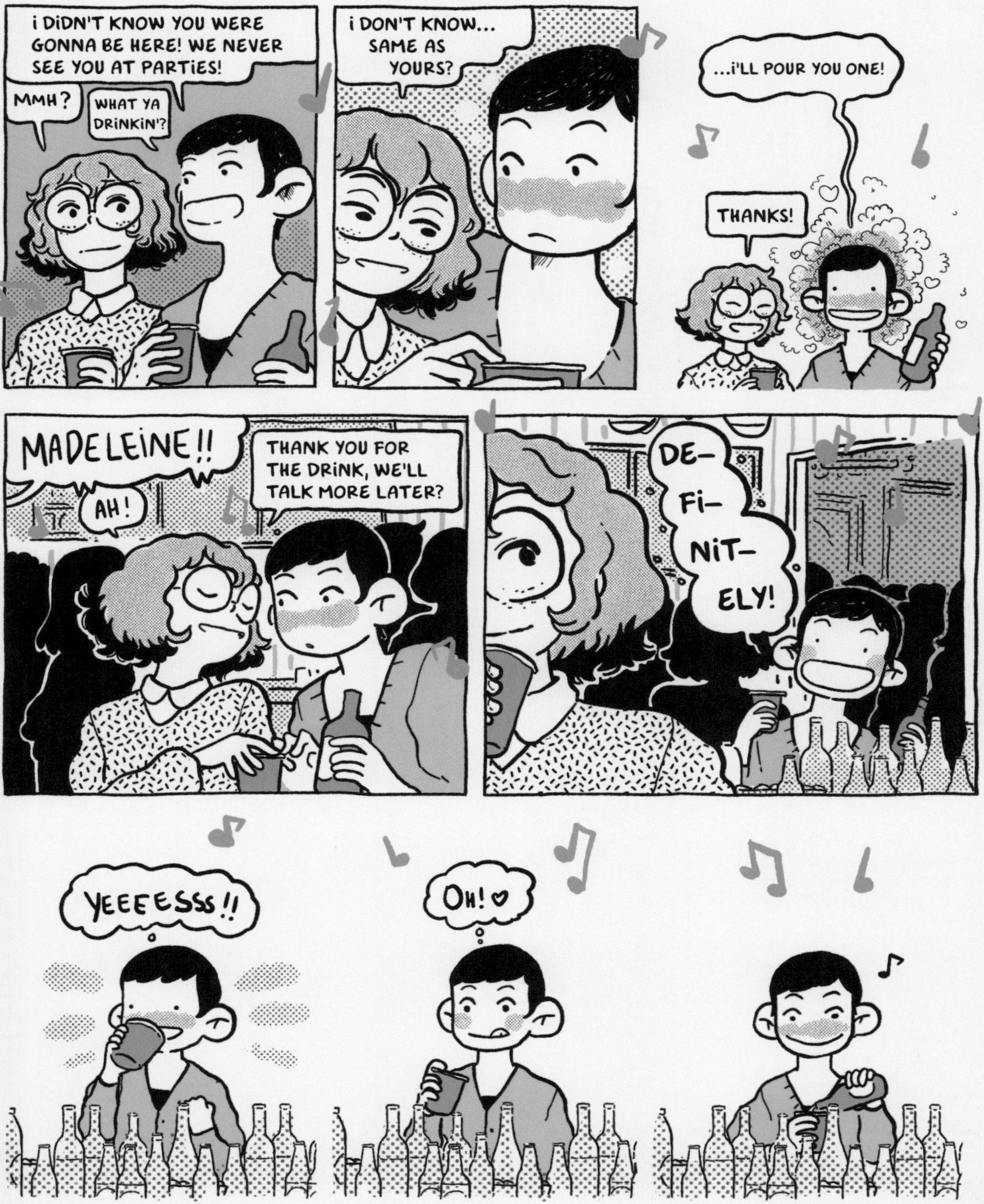
MMH?
WHAT YA DRiNKiN'?
i DiDN'T KNOW YOU WERE GONNA BE HERE! WE NEVER SEE YOU AT PARTiES!
i DON'T KNOW... SAME AS YOURS?
...i'LL POUR YOU ONE!
THANKS!
MADELEINE!!
AH!
THANK YOU FOR THE DRiNK, WE'LL TALK MORE LATER?
DE- Fi- NiT- ELY!
YEEEESSS!!
OH! ♡

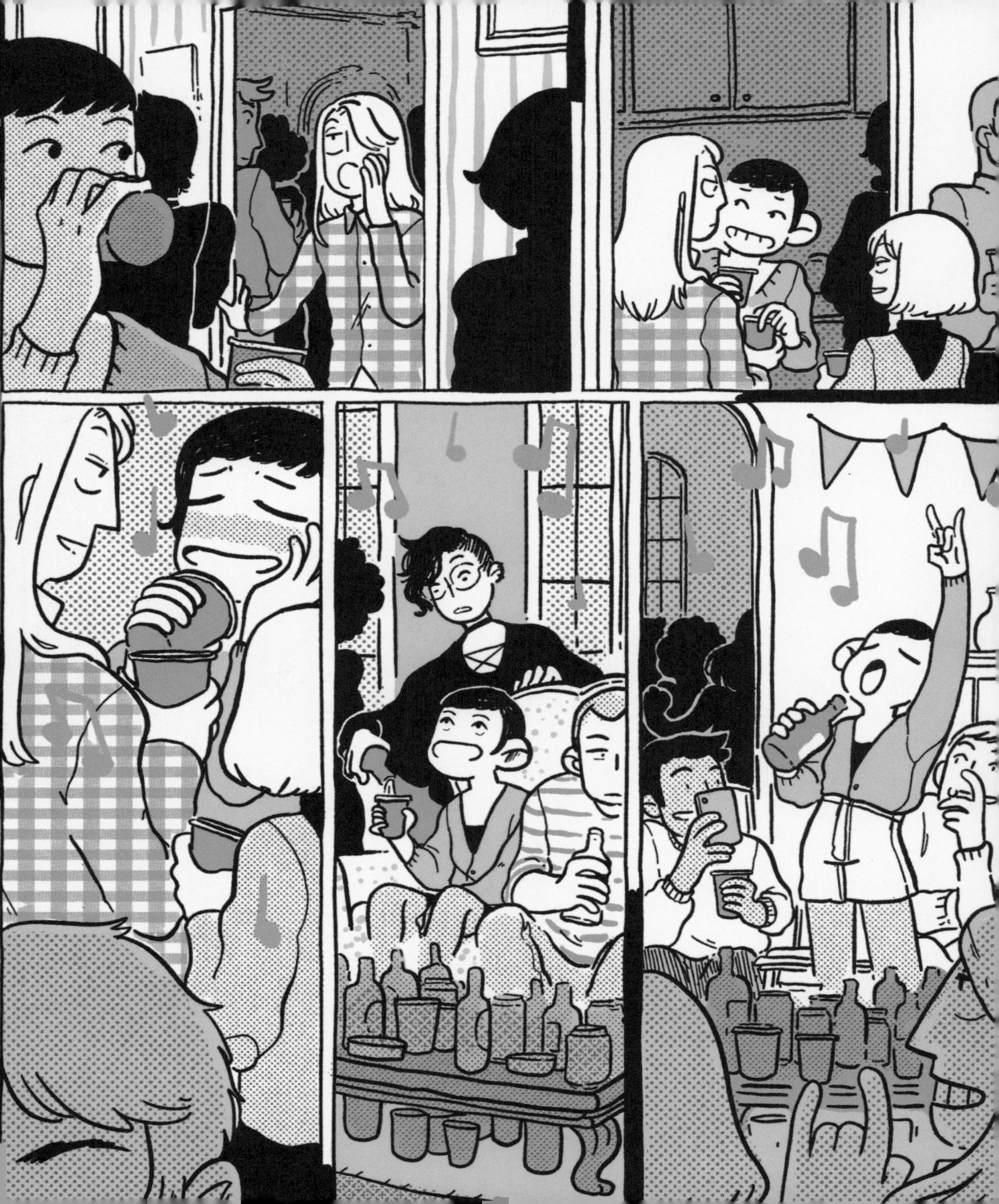

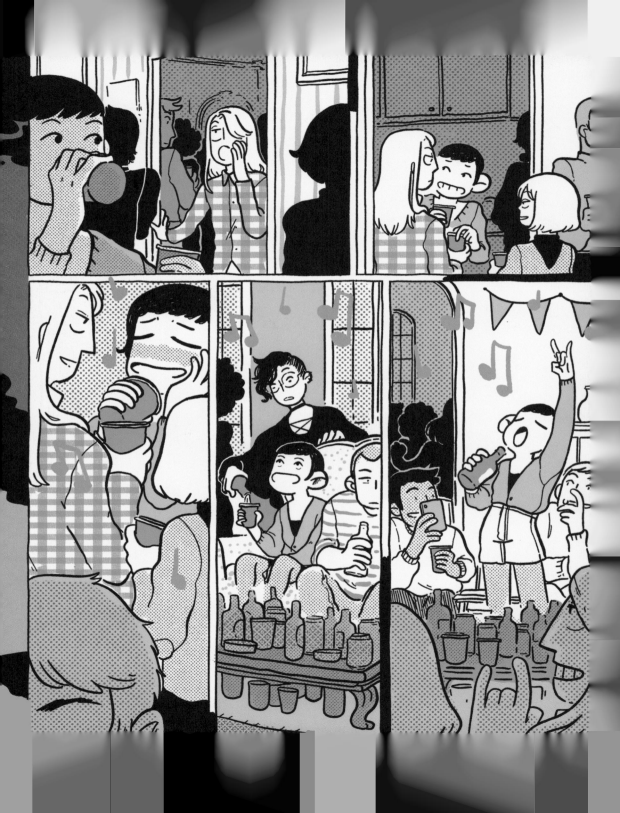

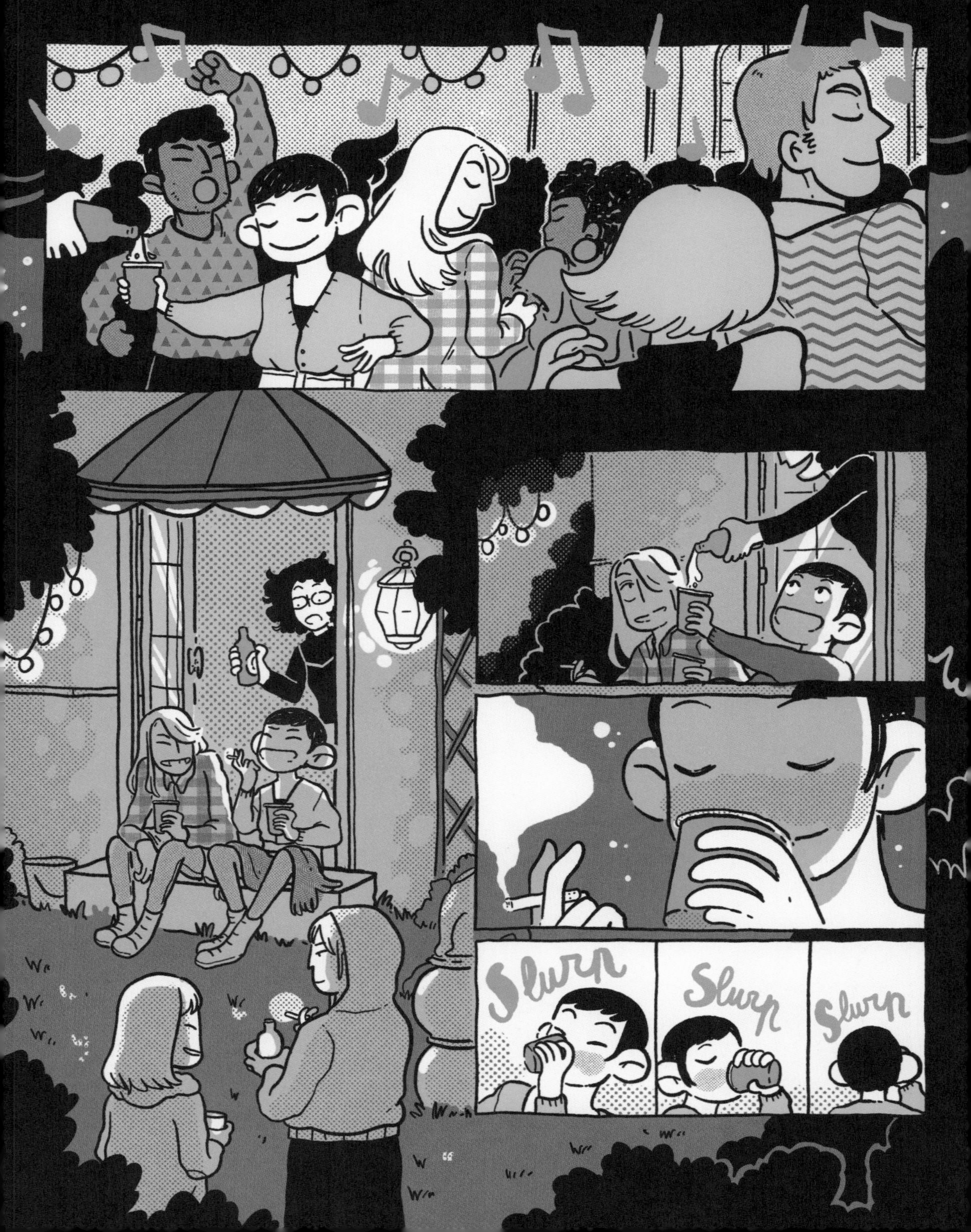
Slurp
Slurp
Slurp

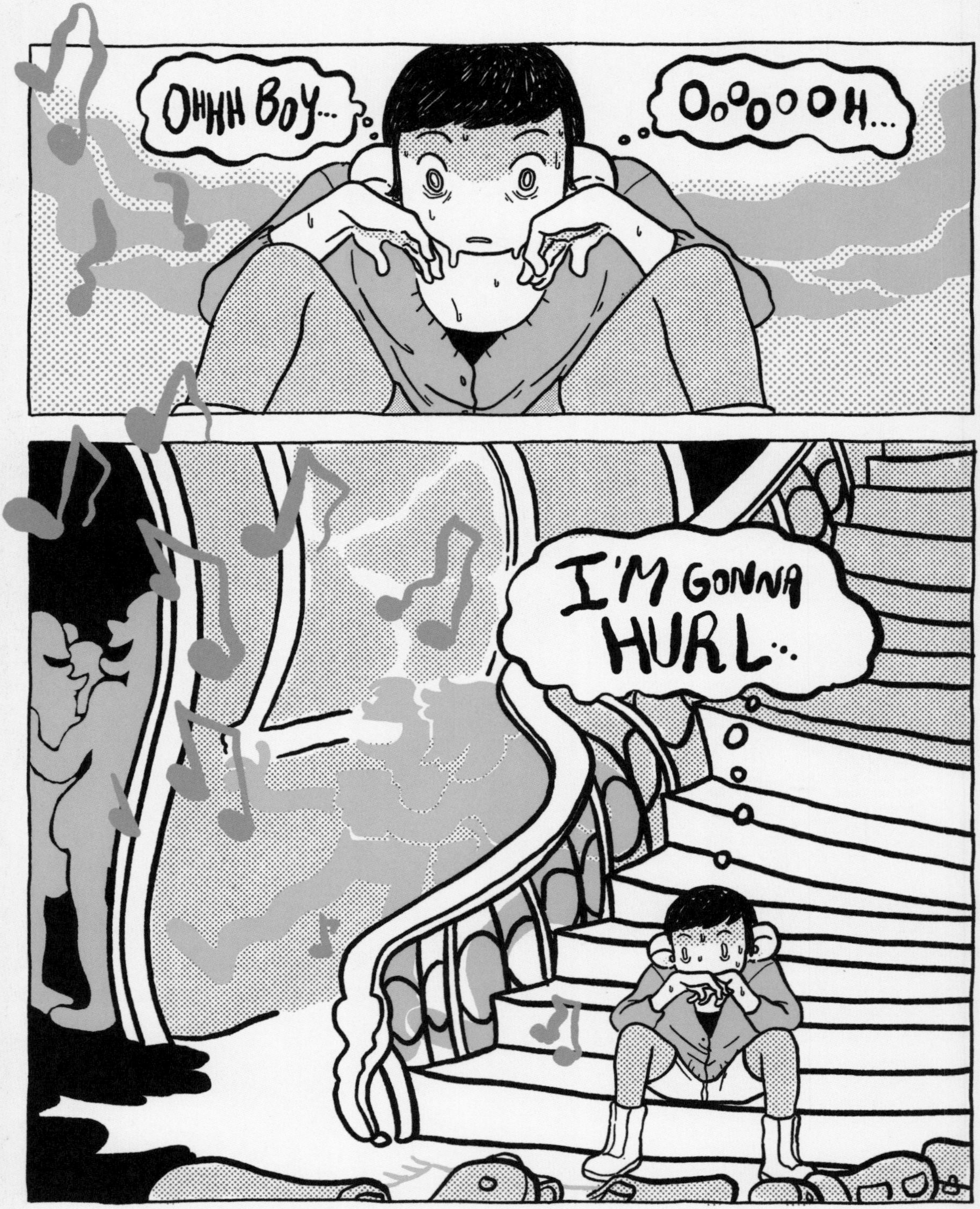
OHHH BOY...
OoOOOOH...
I'M GONNA HURL...

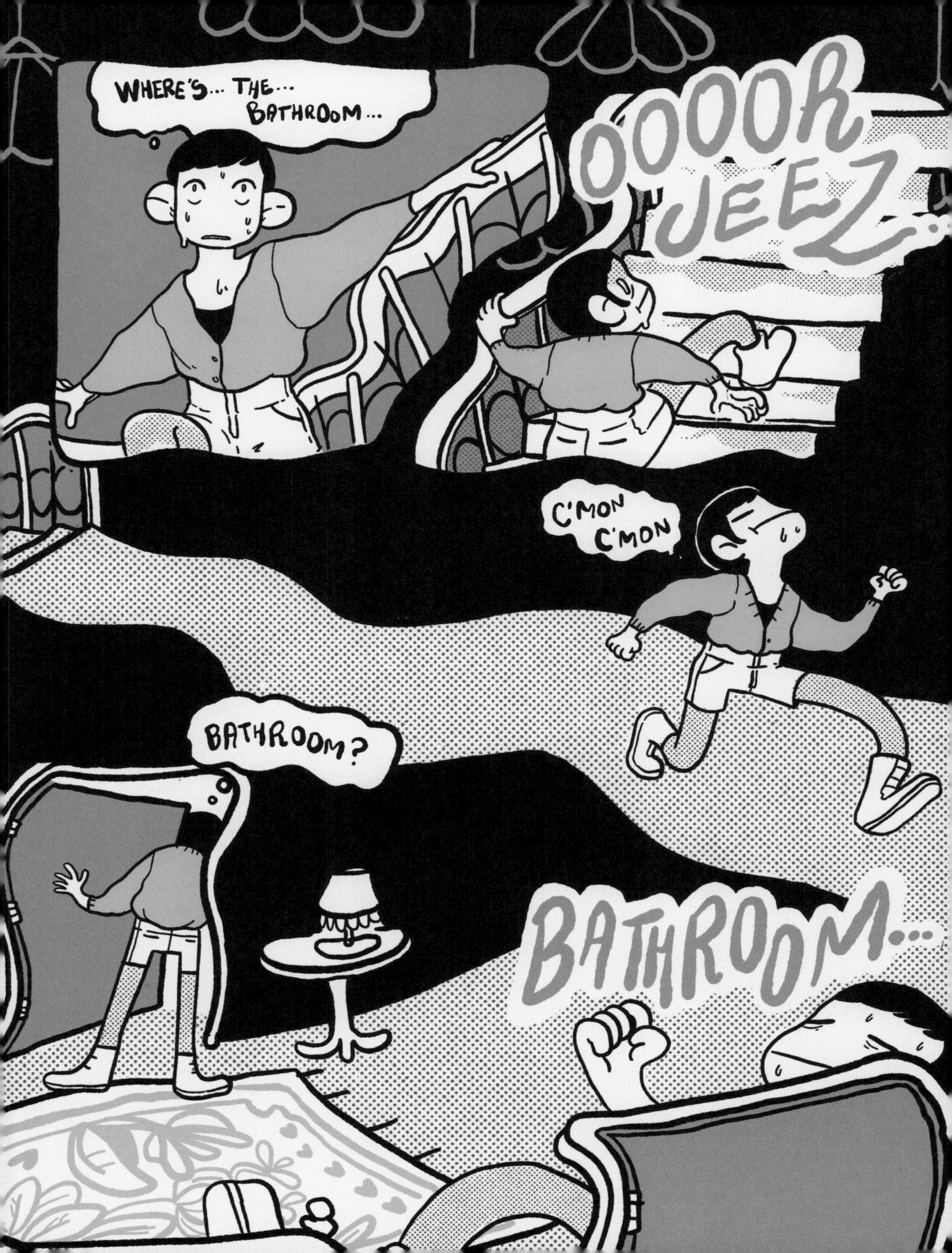
WHERE'S... THE... BATHROOM...
OOOOh JEEZ...
C'MON C'MON
BATHROOM?
BATHROOM...

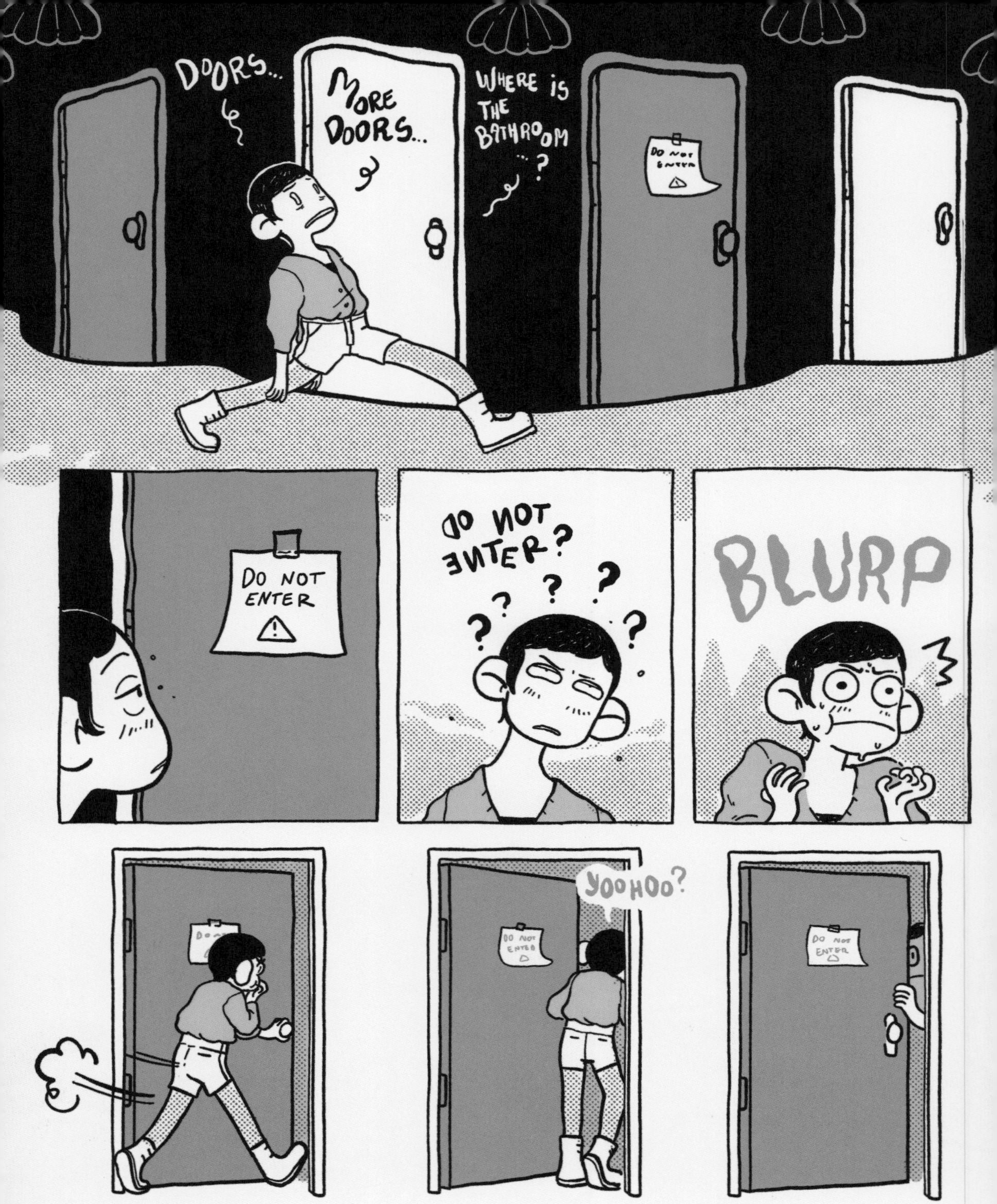
DOORS...
MORE DOORS...
WHERE IS THE BATHROOM ...?
DO NOT ENTER
DO NOT ENTER
DO NOT ENTER?
? ? ? ? ?
BLURP
YOOHOO?
DO NOT ENTER
DO NOT ENTER

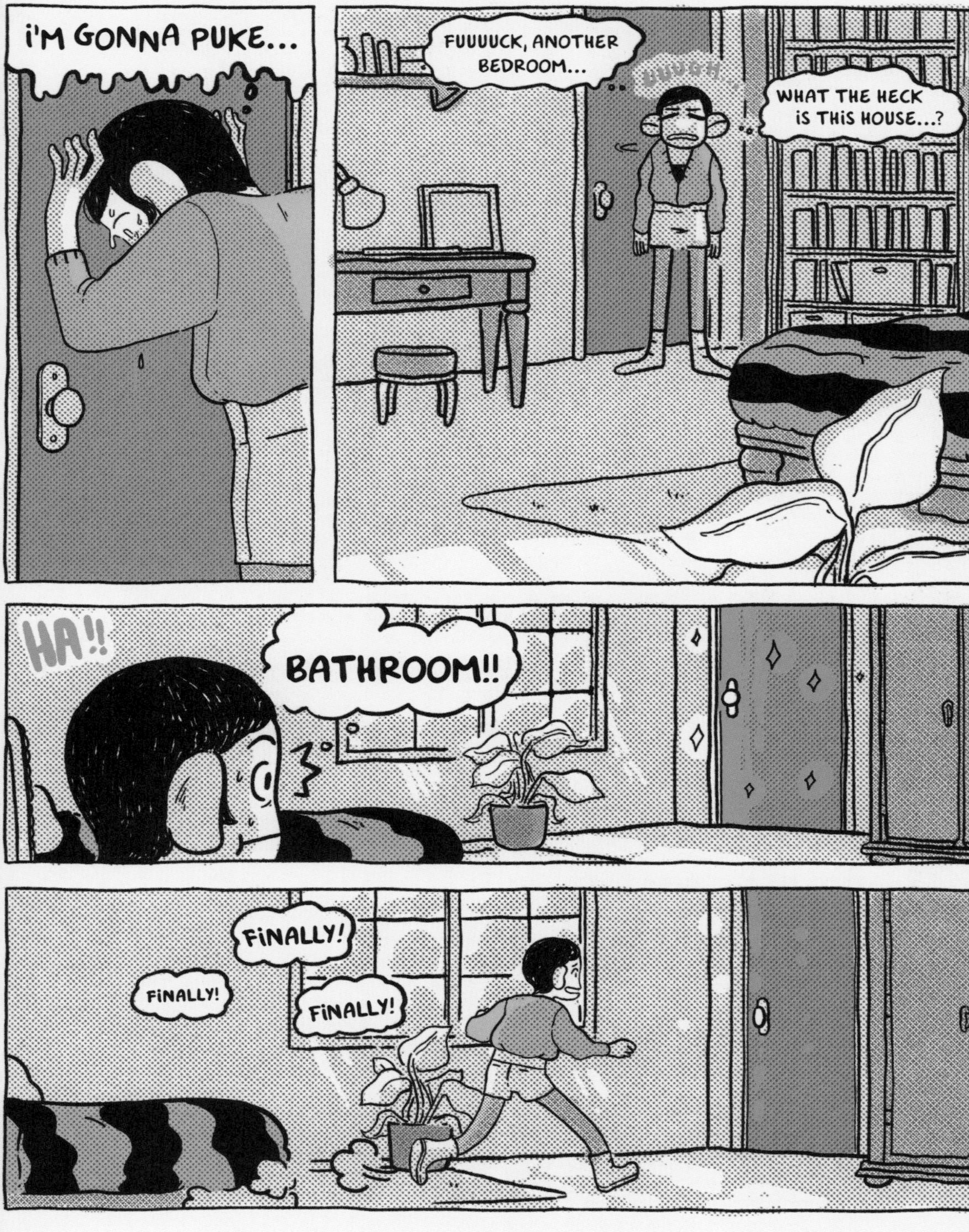

i'M GONNA PUKE...
FUUUUCK, ANOTHER BEDROOM...
UUUGH..
WHAT THE HECK IS THIS HOUSE...?
HA!!
BATHROOM!!
FiNALLY!
FiNALLY!
FiNALLY!

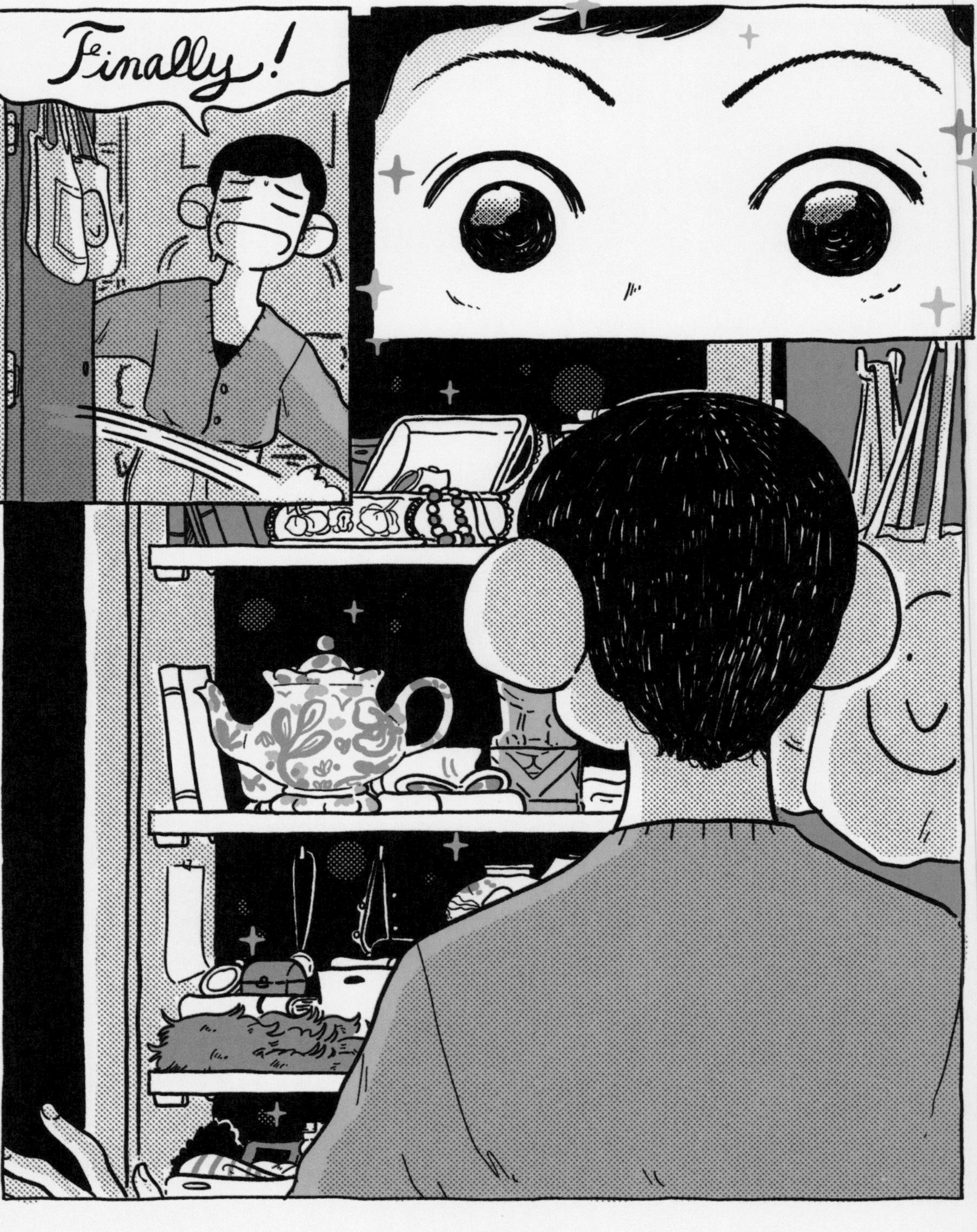
Finally!

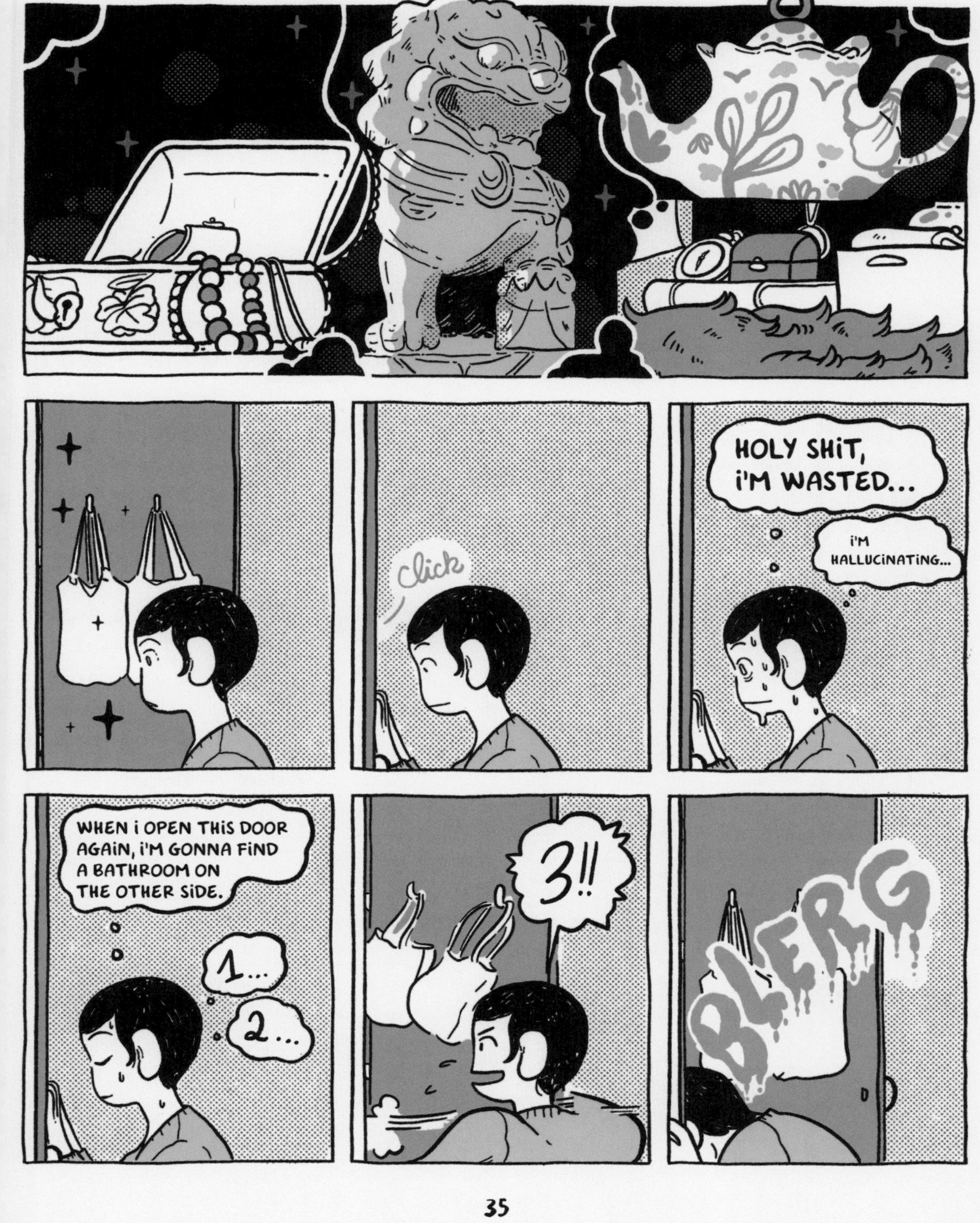
Click
HOLY SHiT, i'M WASTED...
i'M HALLUCiNATiNG...
WHEN i OPEN THiS DOOR AGAiN, i'M GONNA FiND A BATHROOM ON THE OTHER SiDE.
1...
2...
3!!
BLERG

UGH...

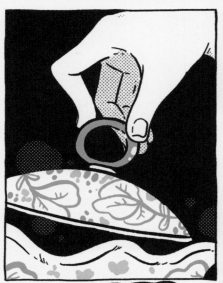

IT'S REALLY PRETTY...

BUT...

IT'S USELESS ♪

RICH PEOPLE LOOOVE USELESS TRINKETS, DON'T THEY...?

BUNCHA IDIO...

OH?

OOOH...!

36

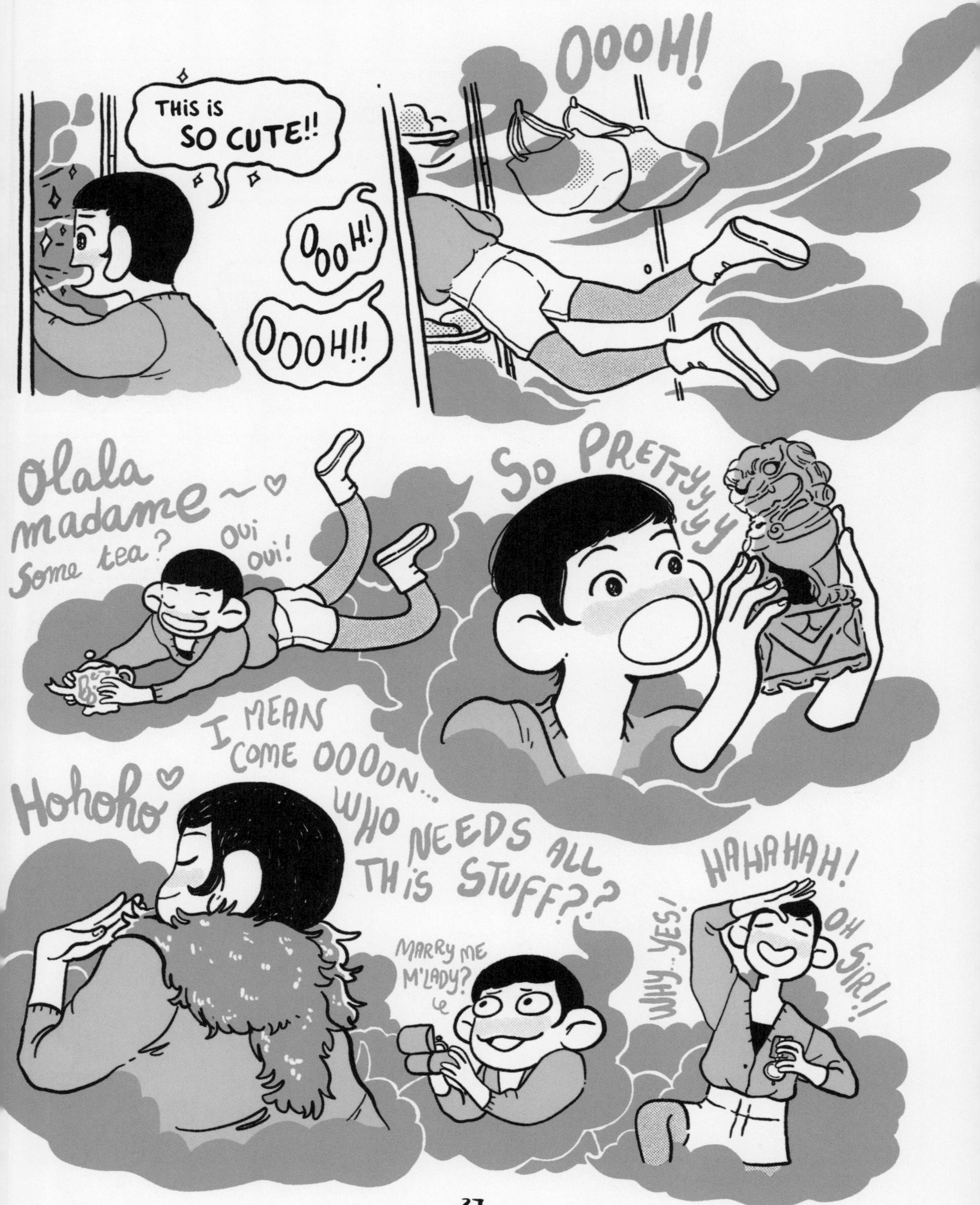
THIS IS SO CUTE!!
OOOH!
OOOH!
OOOH!!
Olala madame~♡ Some tea?
Oui oui!
SO PRETTYYYYY
I MEAN COME OOOON... WHO NEEDS ALL THIS STUFF??
Hohoho♡
MARRY ME M'LADY?
WHY...YES!
HAHAHAH!
OH SIR!!

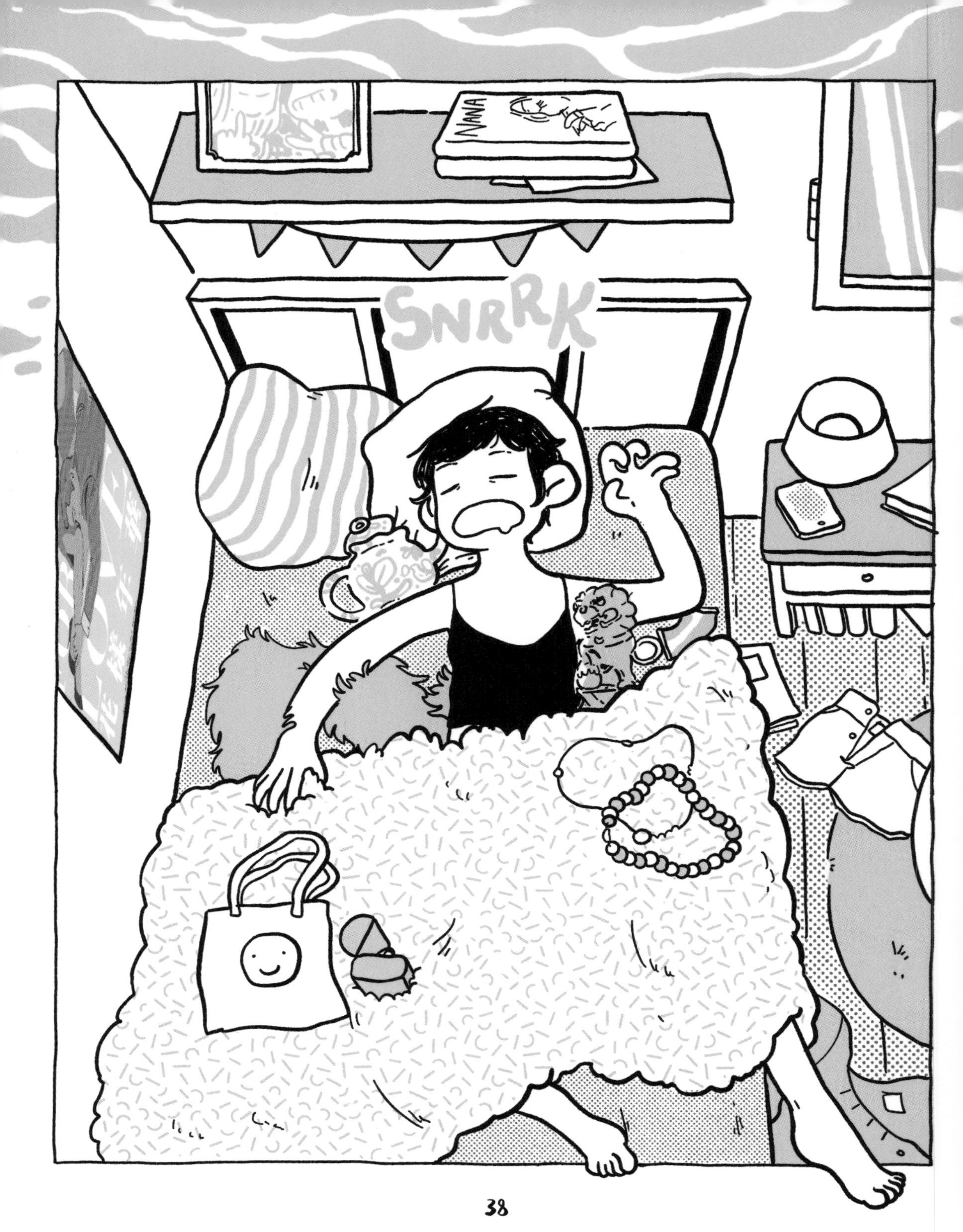
NANA
SNRRK

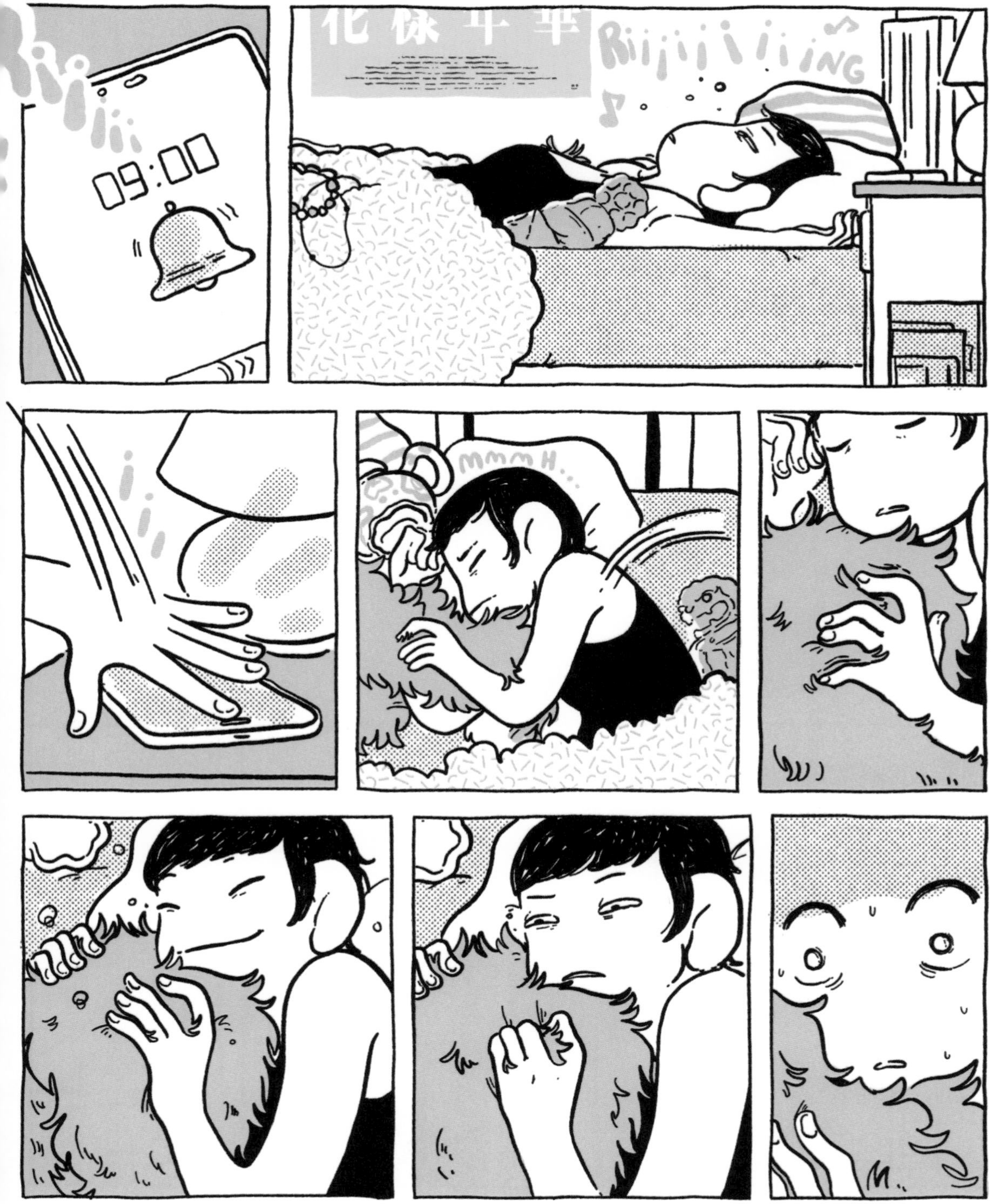
09:00
Riiiiiiiiiiing
MMMH...

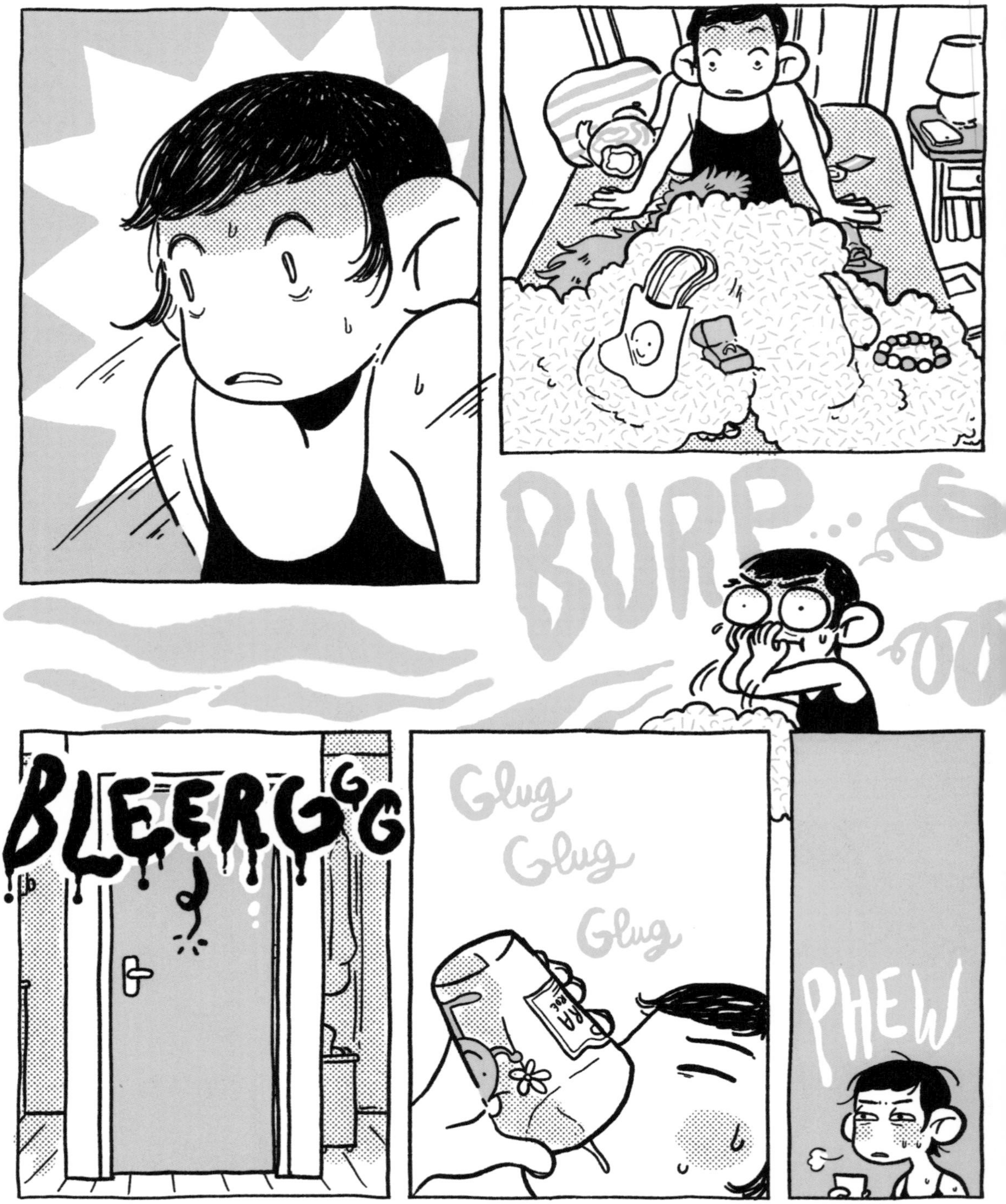
BURP...
BLEERGGG
Glug
Glug
Glug
PHEW

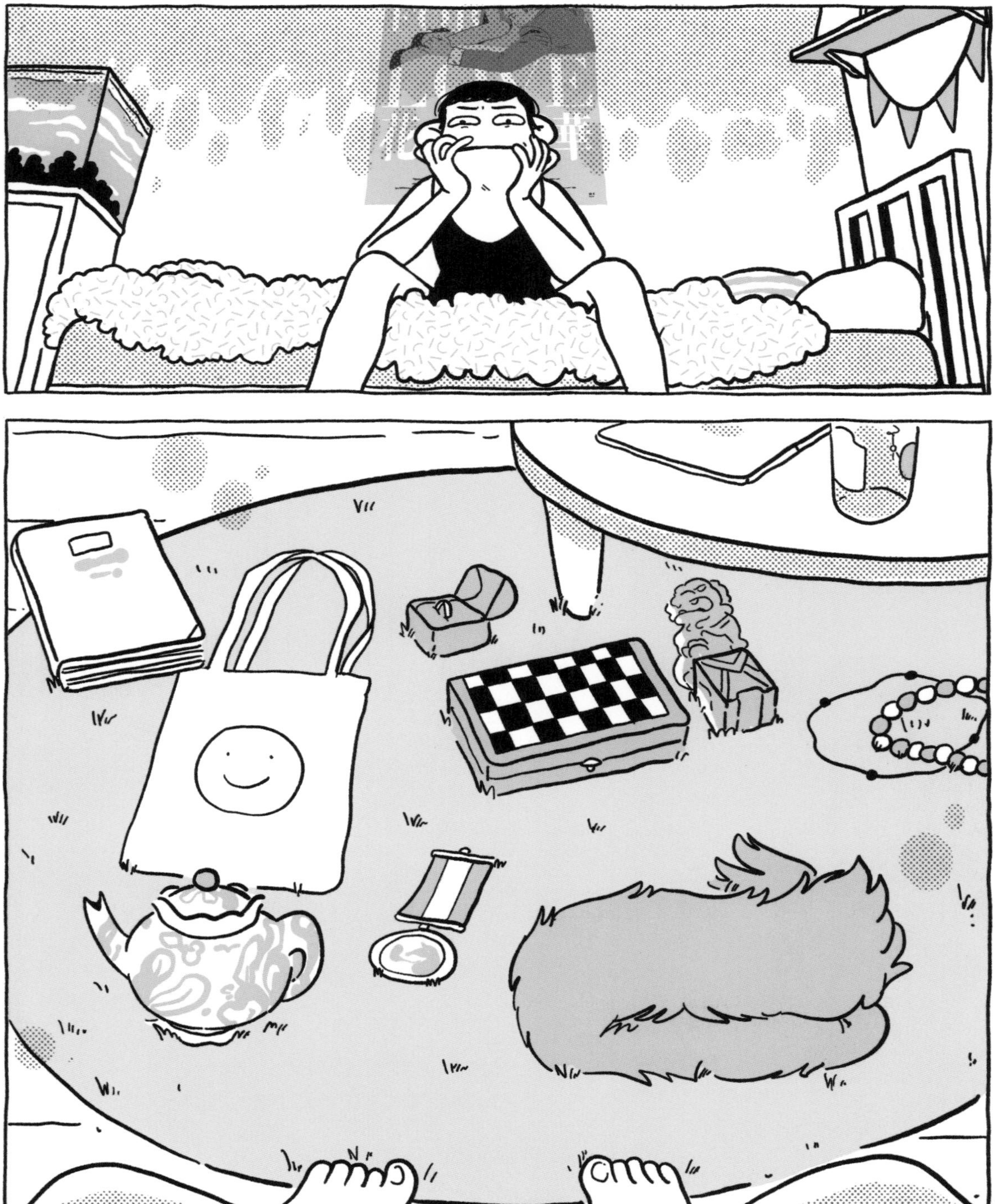

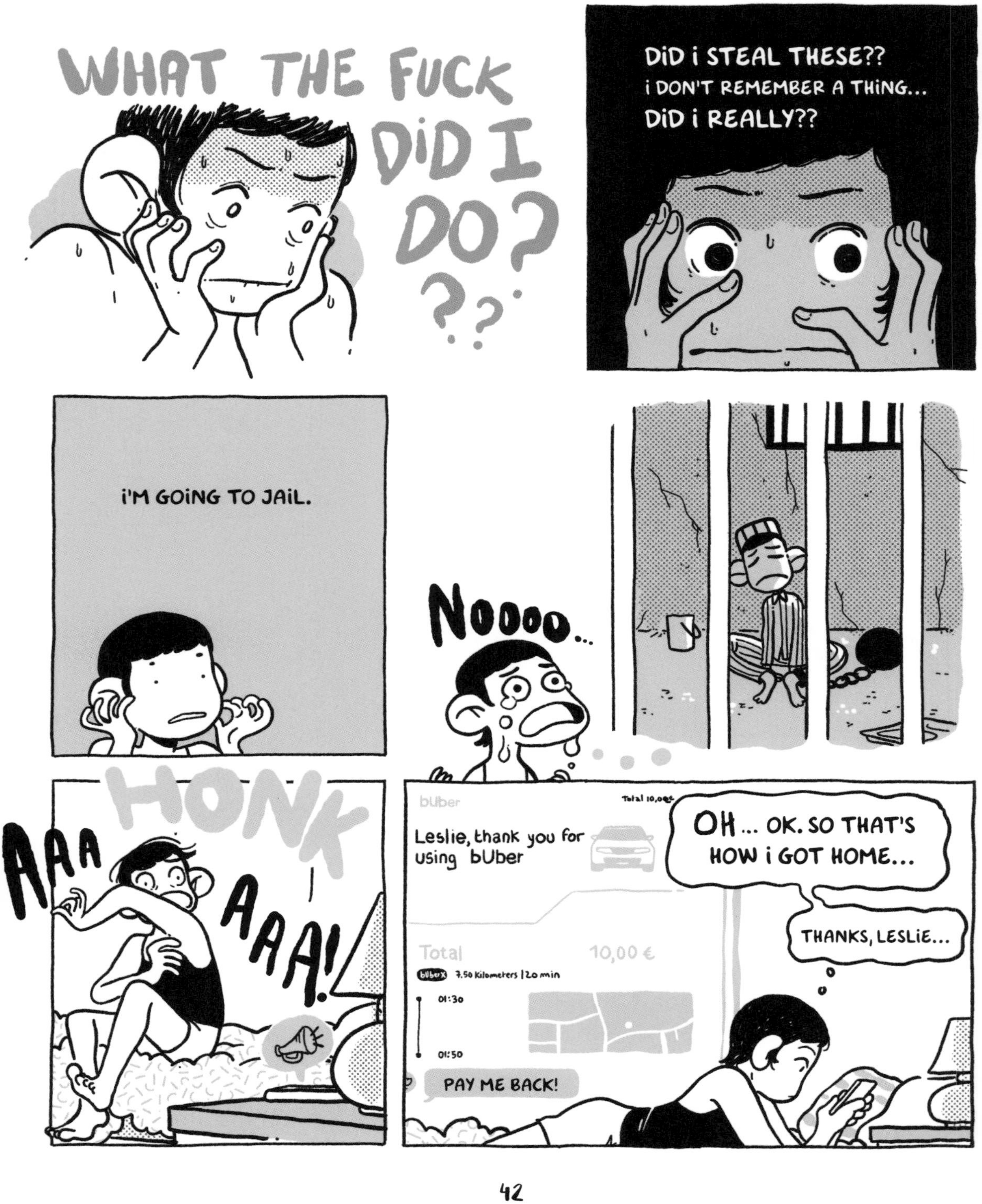
WHAT THE FUCK DID I DO???
DiD i STEAL THESE??
i DON'T REMEMBER A THiNG...
DiD i REALLY??
i'M GOiNG TO JAiL.
NOOOO...
HONK
AAAAAA!
bUber
Total 10,00€
Leslie, thank you for using bUber
Total 10,00 €
bUberX 7.50 Kilometers | 20 min
01:30
01:50
PAY ME BACK!
OH... OK. SO THAT'S HOW i GOT HOME...
THANKS, LESLiE...

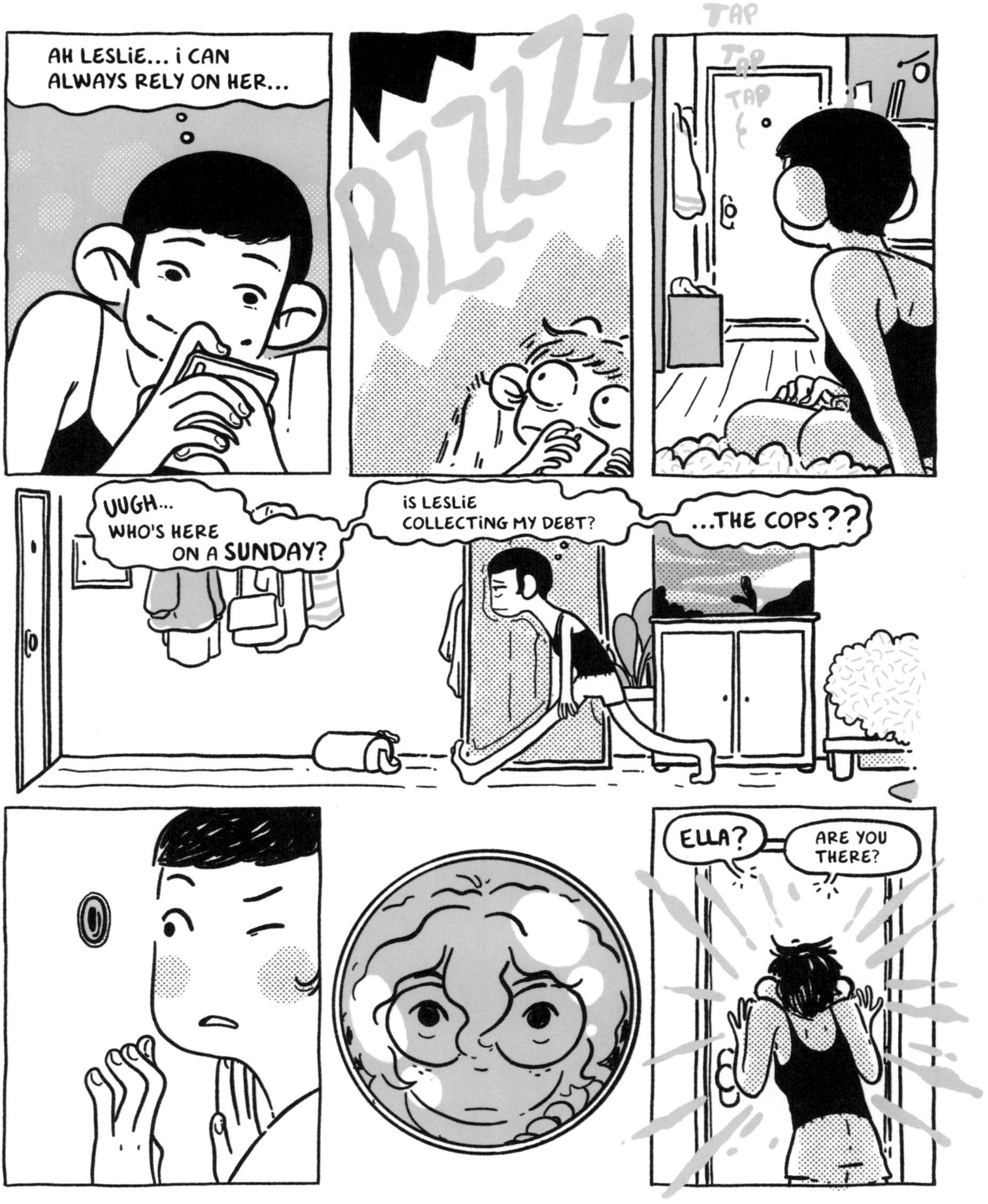
AH LESLIE... i CAN ALWAYS RELY ON HER...
BZZZZZ
TAP TAP TAP
UUGH... WHO'S HERE ON A SUNDAY?
iS LESLIE COLLECTiNG MY DEBT?
...THE COPS??
ELLA?
ARE YOU THERE?

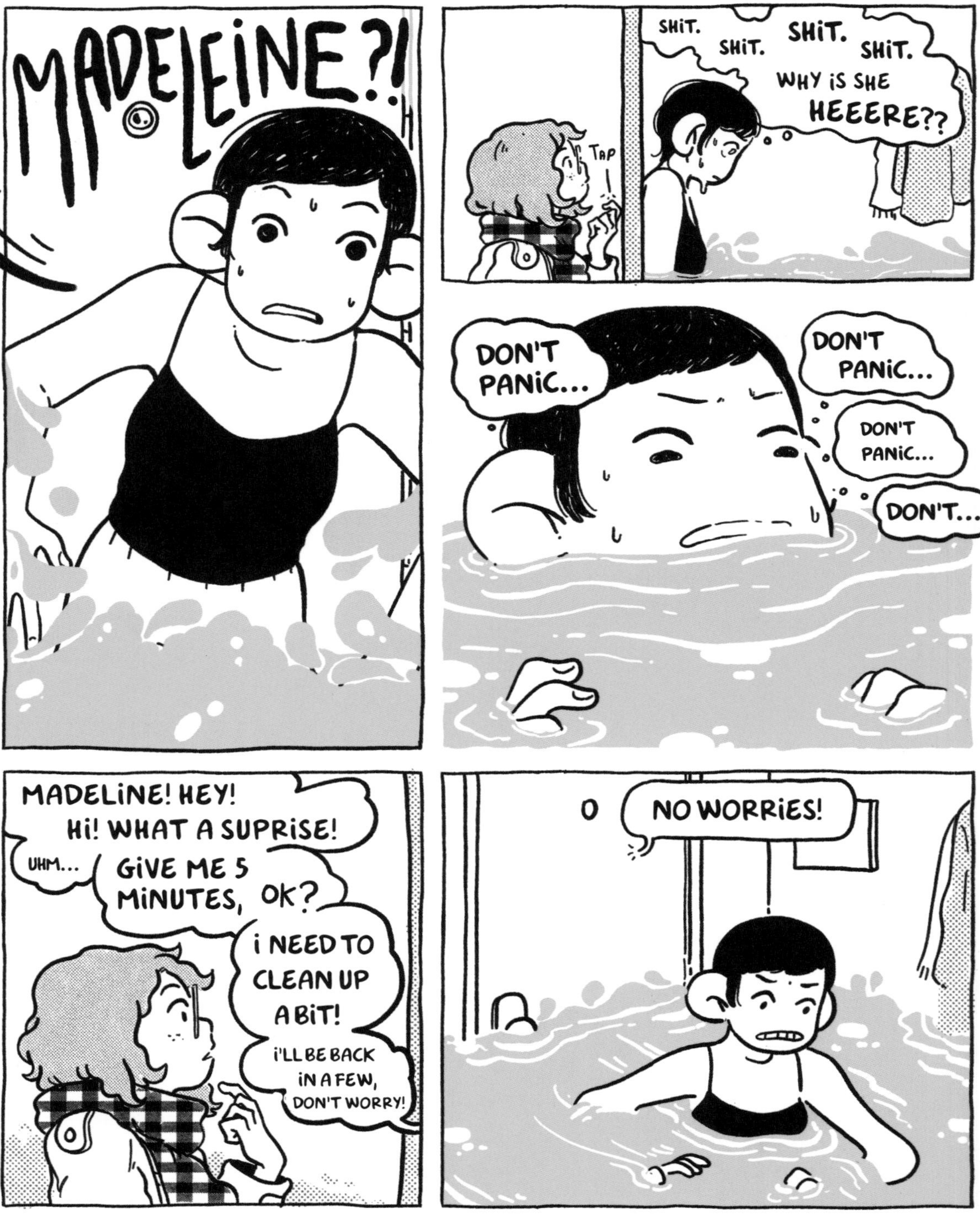
MADELEINE?!
SHIT.
SHIT.
SHIT.
SHIT.
WHY IS SHE HEEERE??
TAP
DON'T PANIC...
DON'T PANIC...
DON'T PANIC...
DON'T...
MADELINE! HEY! HI! WHAT A SUPRISE!
UHM...
GIVE ME 5 MINUTES, OK?
I NEED TO CLEAN UP A BIT!
I'LL BE BACK IN A FEW, DON'T WORRY!
O
NO WORRIES!

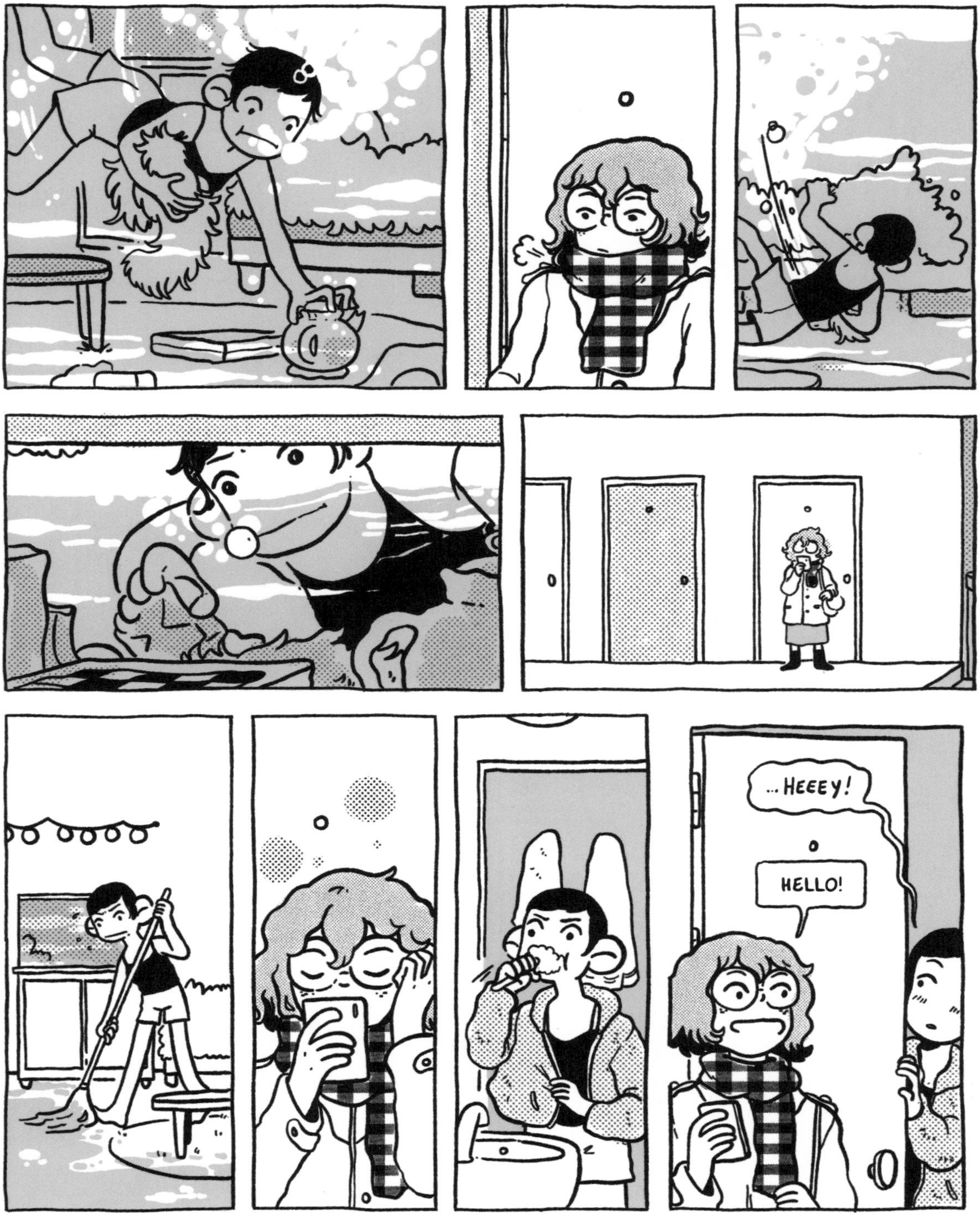
...HEEEY!
HELLO!

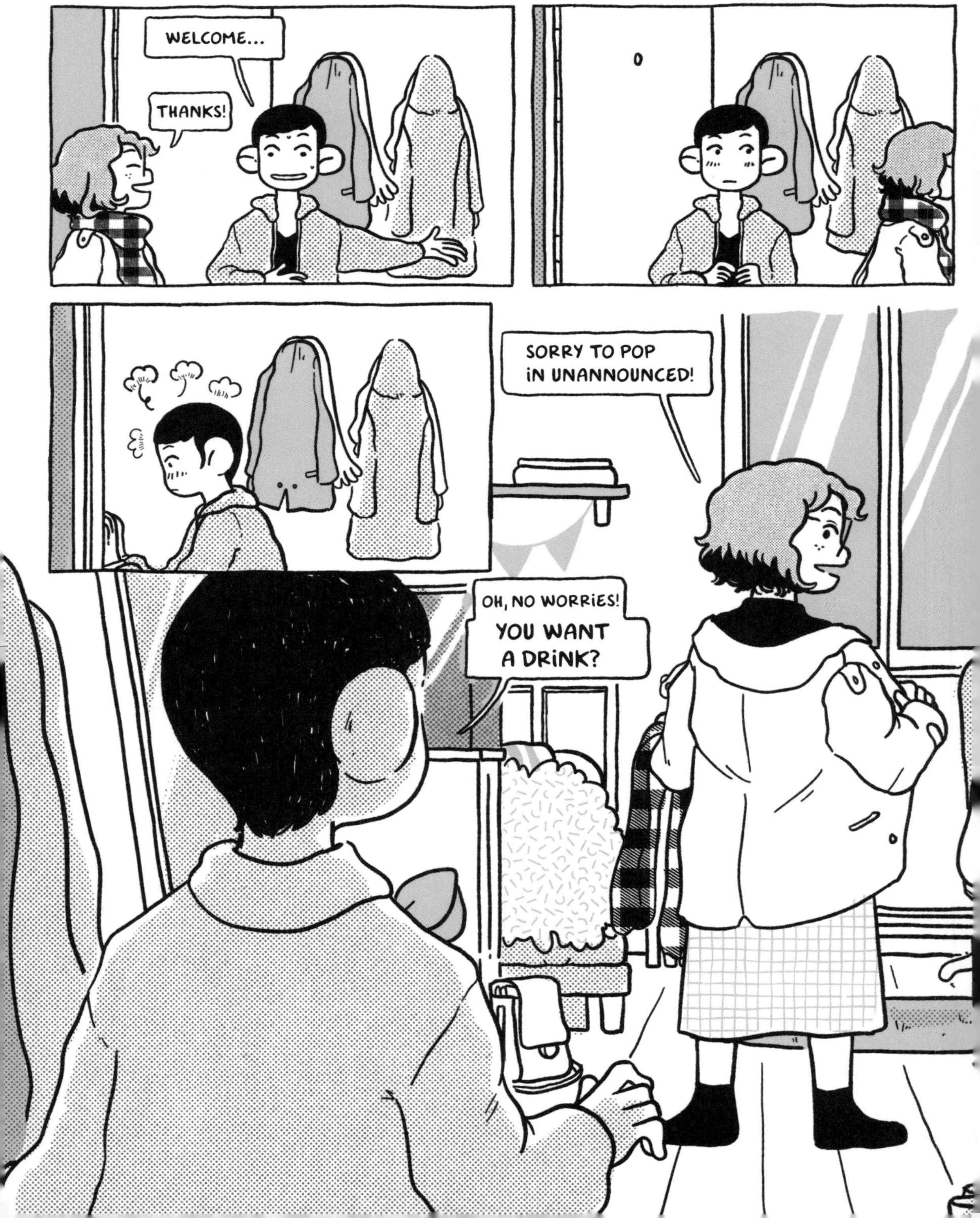
WELCOME...
THANKS!
SORRY TO POP
iN UNANNOUNCED!
OH, NO WORRiES!
YOU WANT
A DRiNK?

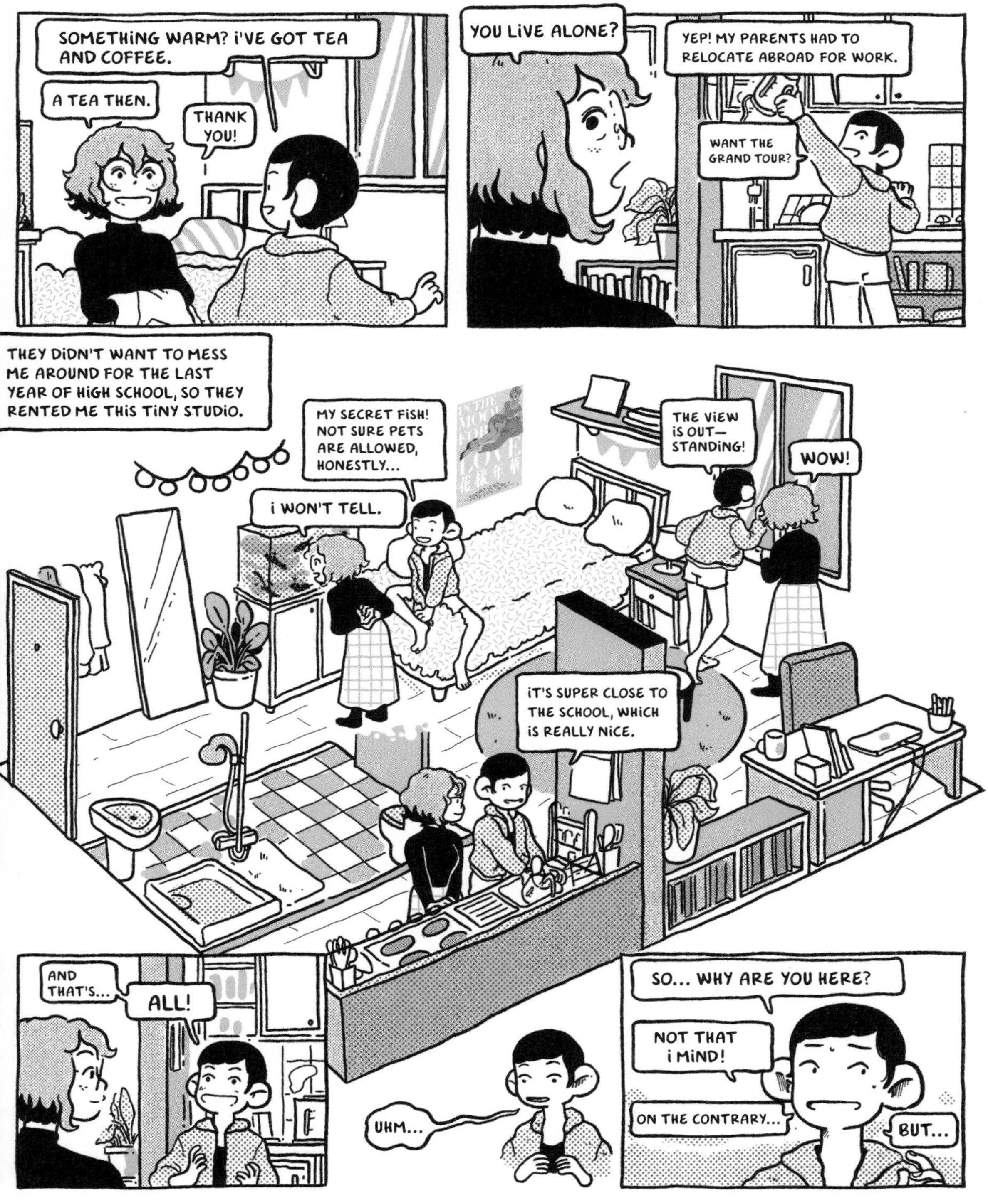
SOMETHING WARM? i'VE GOT TEA AND COFFEE.
A TEA THEN.
THANK YOU!
YOU LiVE ALONE?
YEP! MY PARENTS HAD TO RELOCATE ABROAD FOR WORK.
WANT THE GRAND TOUR?
THEY DiDN'T WANT TO MESS ME AROUND FOR THE LAST YEAR OF HiGH SCHOOL, SO THEY RENTED ME THiS TiNY STUDiO.
MY SECRET FiSH! NOT SURE PETS ARE ALLOWED, HONESTLY...
i WON'T TELL.
IN THE MOOD FOR LOVE
花樣年華
THE ViEW iS OUT-STANDiNG!
WOW!
iT'S SUPER CLOSE TO THE SCHOOL, WHiCH iS REALLY NiCE.
AND THAT'S...
ALL!
UHM...
SO... WHY ARE YOU HERE?
NOT THAT i MiND!
ON THE CONTRARY...
BUT...

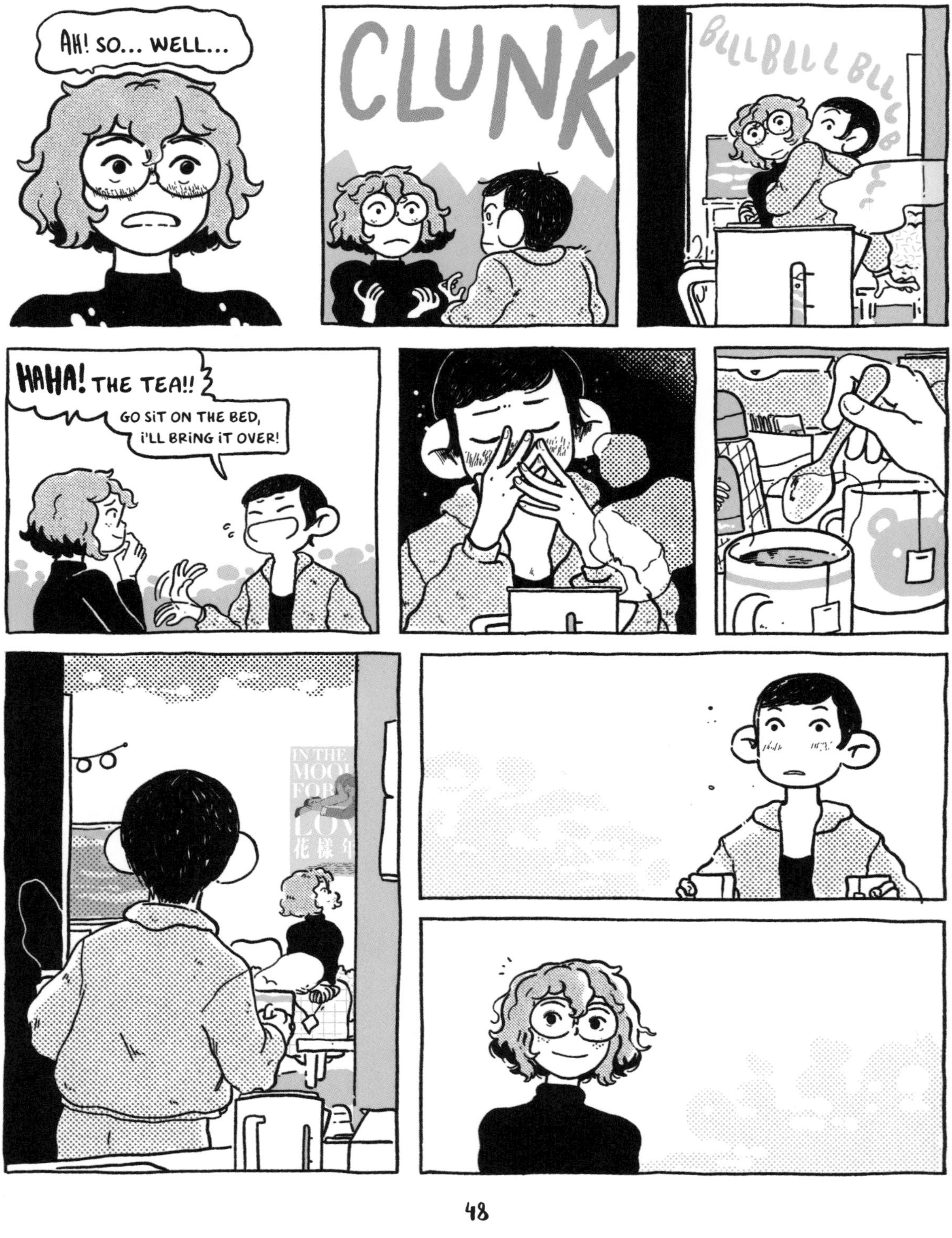
AH! SO... WELL...
CLUNK
BLLLBLLLBLLLBLLL...
HAHA! THE TEA!!
GO SIT ON THE BED, I'LL BRING IT OVER!
IN THE MOOD FOR LOVE
花樣年

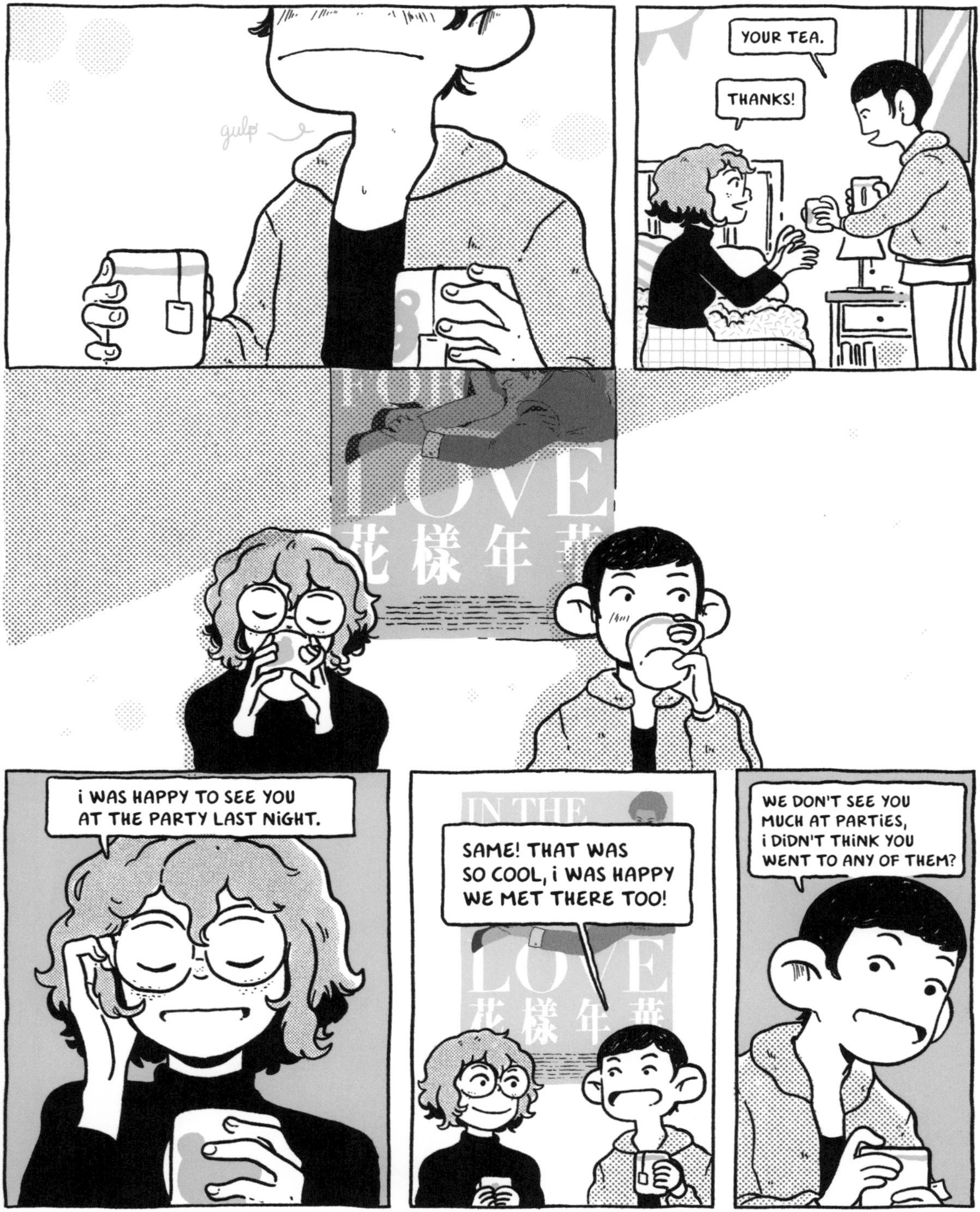
gulp
YOUR TEA.
THANKS!
LOVE
花樣年華
i WAS HAPPY TO SEE YOU AT THE PARTY LAST NiGHT.
IN THE
LOVE
花樣年華
SAME! THAT WAS SO COOL, i WAS HAPPY WE MET THERE TOO!
WE DON'T SEE YOU MUCH AT PARTiES, i DiDN'T THiNK YOU WENT TO ANY OF THEM?

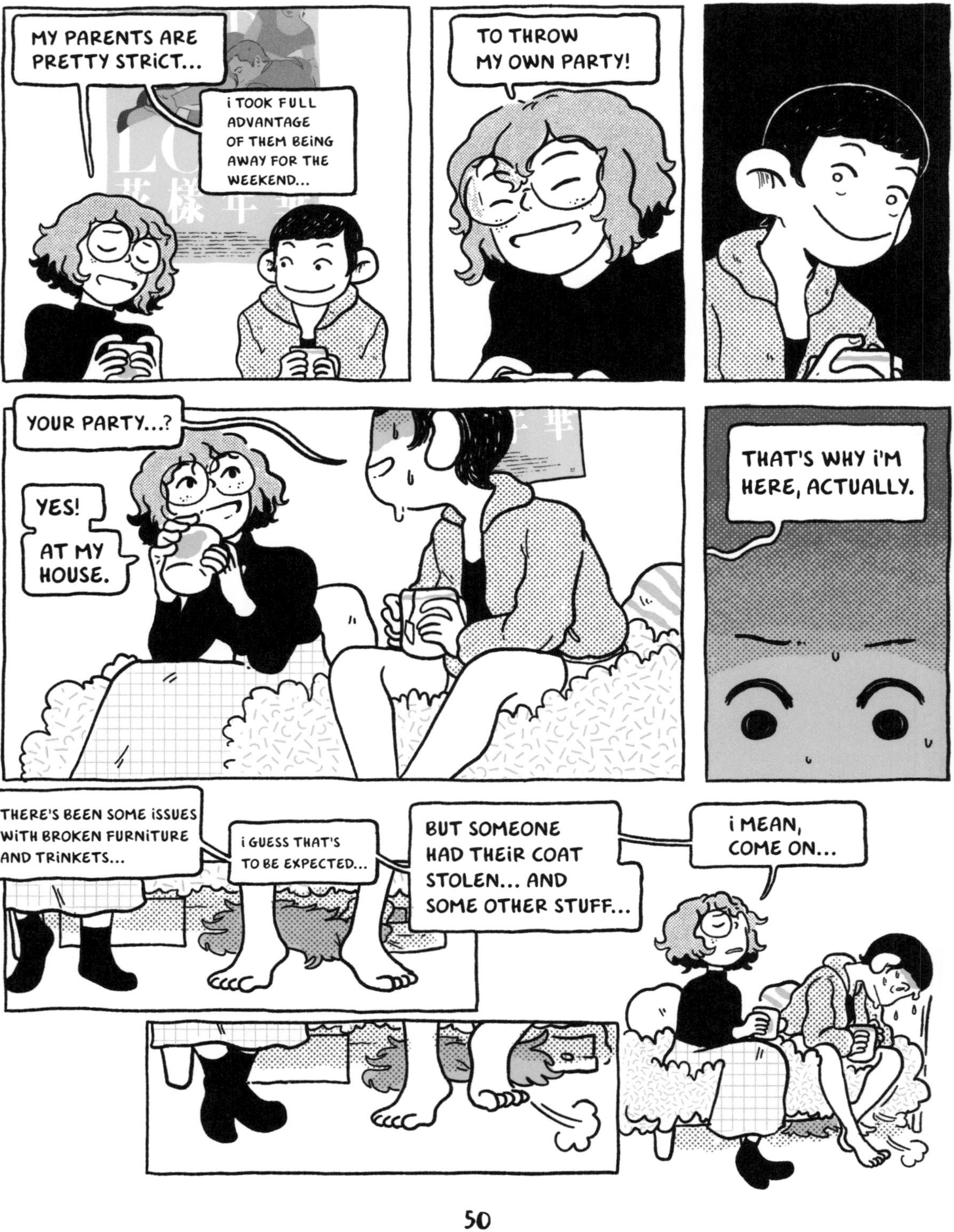
MY PARENTS ARE PRETTY STRiCT...
i TOOK FULL ADVANTAGE OF THEM BEiNG AWAY FOR THE WEEKEND...
TO THROW MY OWN PARTY!
YOUR PARTY...?
YES!
AT MY HOUSE.
THAT'S WHY i'M HERE, ACTUALLY.
THERE'S BEEN SOME iSSUES WiTH BROKEN FURNiTURE AND TRiNKETS...
i GUESS THAT'S TO BE EXPECTED...
BUT SOMEONE HAD THEiR COAT STOLEN... AND SOME OTHER STUFF...
i MEAN, COME ON...

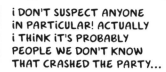 i DON'T SUSPECT ANYONE iN PARTiCULAR! ACTUALLY i THiNK iT'S PROBABLY PEOPLE WE DON'T KNOW THAT CRASHED THE PARTY...

BUT WHO CRASHES A PARTY AND STEALS STUFF? LiKE, iSN'T THAT **CRAZY**??

iT'S NOT THAT BiG OF A DEAL BUT... THAT'S THE FiRST AND LAST TiME i THROW A PARTY AT HOME FOR SURE...

WHEN LESLiE TOLD ME YOU WENT HOME ON YOUR OWN, i WAS WORRiED SOMETHiNG MiGHT HAVE HAPPENED?

YOU KNOW, WiTH EVERYTHiNG YOU HEAR, iT'S ALWAYS A WORRY...

BUT i'M GLAD TO SEE YOU'RE OKAY!

51

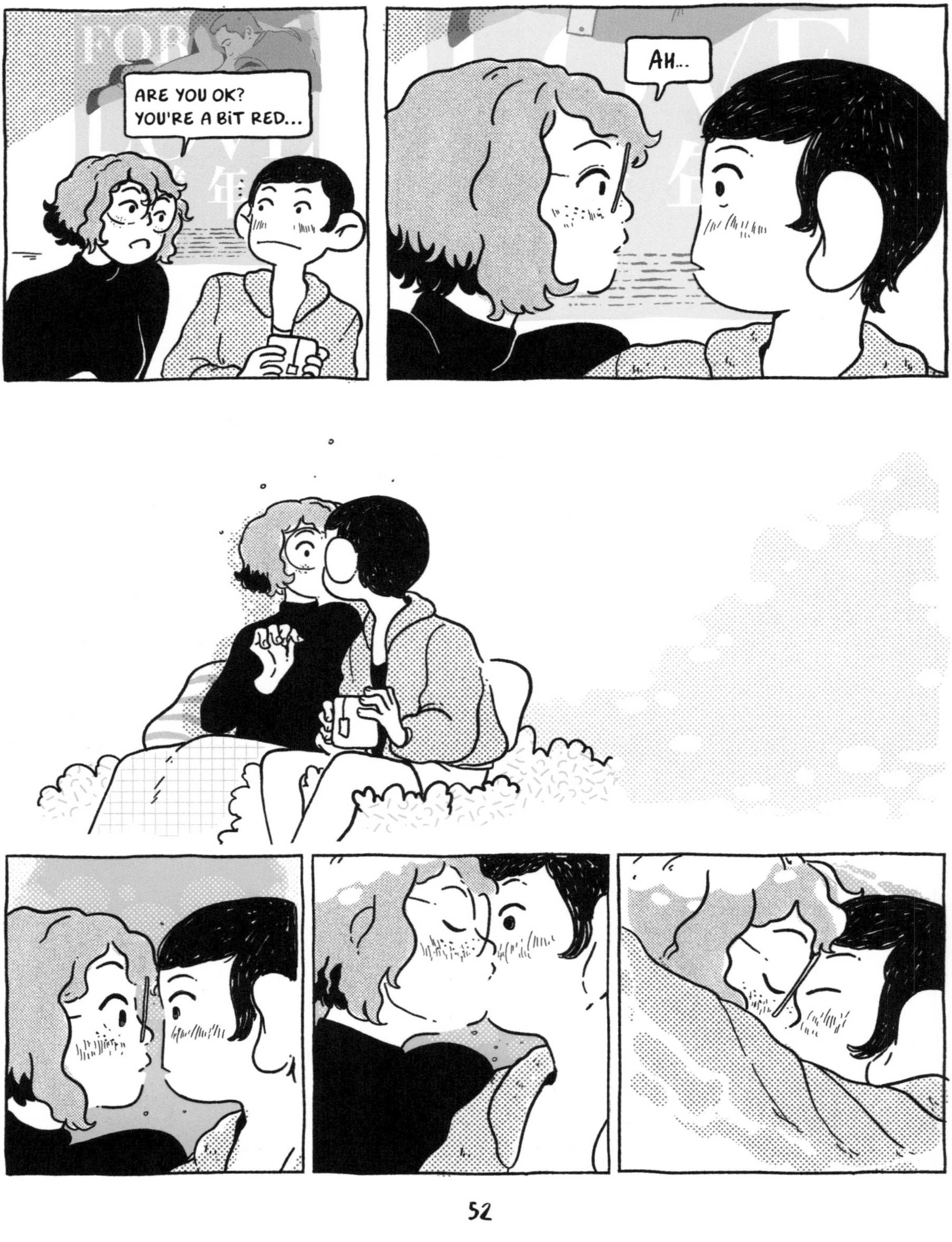
ARE YOU OK?
YOU'RE A BIT RED...
AH...

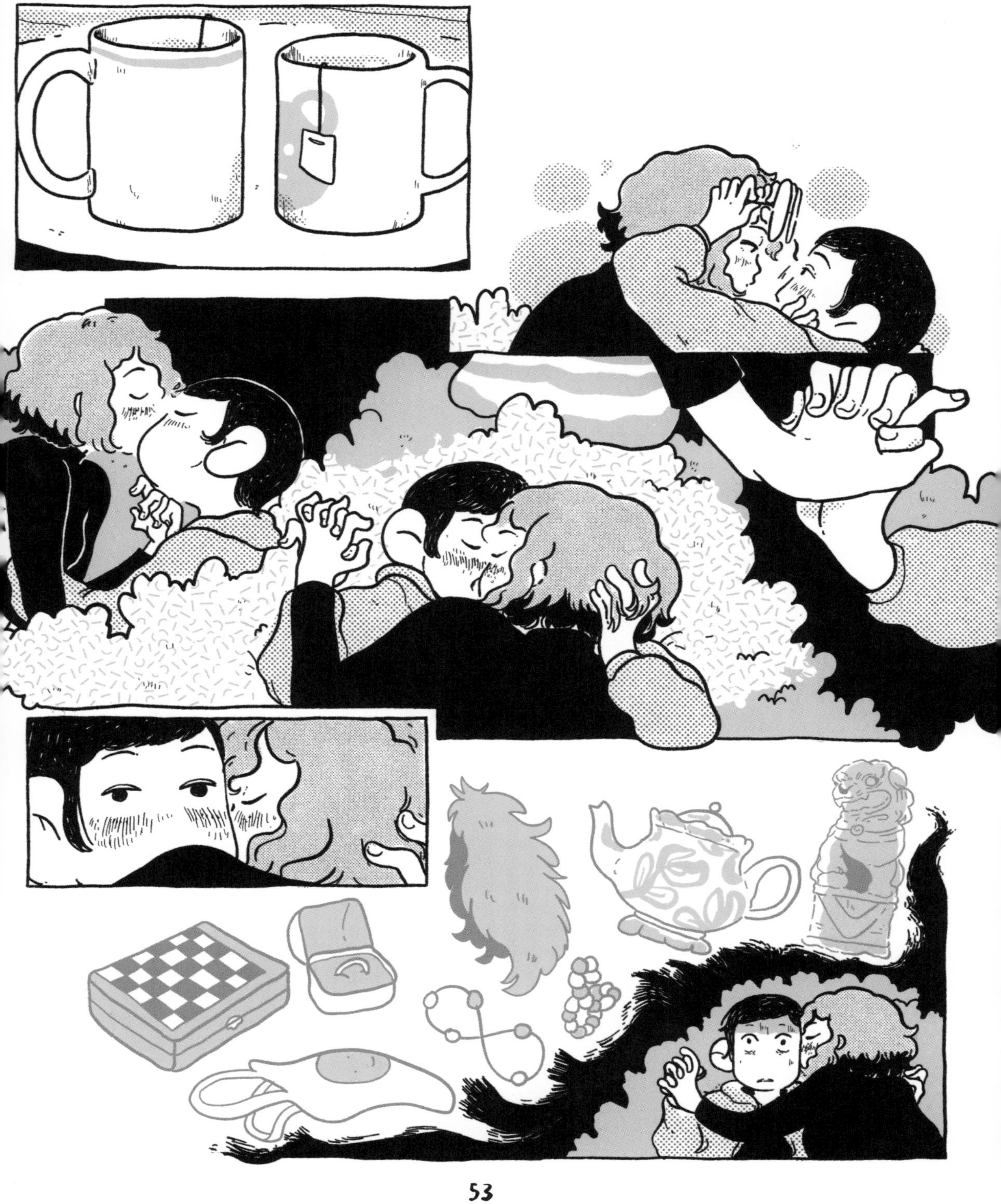

UHHM...

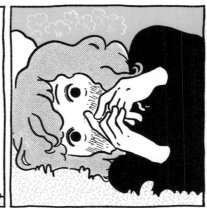

SO UH... i'M LiKE... SO HAPPY... BUUUUT... LET'S NOT GO TOO FAST? NOT THAT i DON'T WANT TO... BUT...

SORRY!!

AAAH DON'T APOLOGiZE!!

THAT WAS AWESOME.

...YES...

i'LL SEE YOU TOMORROW AT SCHOOL?

YES... YEP, YEAH...

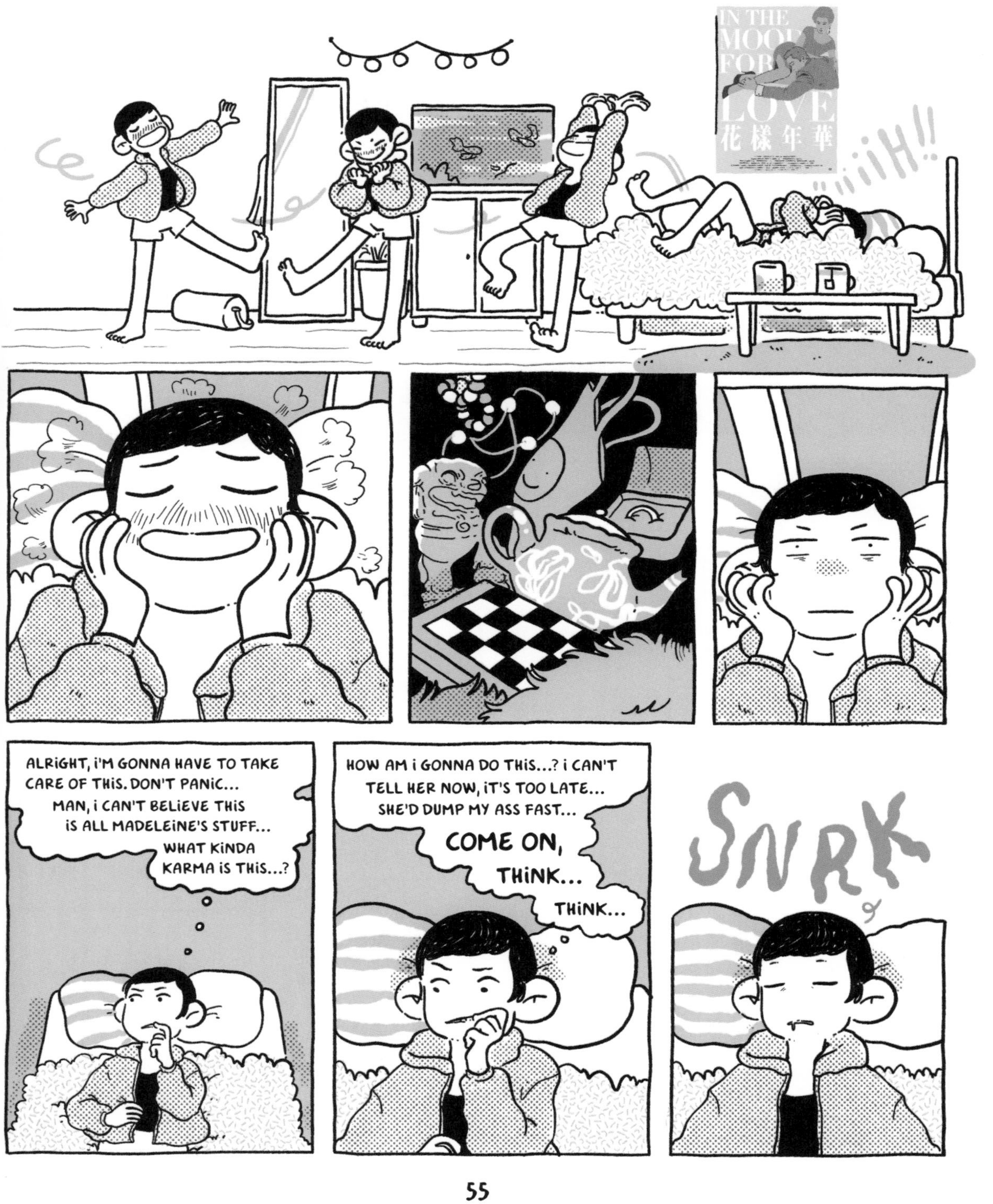
IN THE
MOO
FOR
LOVE
花樣年華
iiiiH!!
ALRIGHT, I'M GONNA HAVE TO TAKE CARE OF THIS. DON'T PANIC... MAN, I CAN'T BELIEVE THIS IS ALL MADELEINE'S STUFF... WHAT KINDA KARMA IS THIS...?
HOW AM I GONNA DO THIS...? I CAN'T TELL HER NOW, IT'S TOO LATE... SHE'D DUMP MY ASS FAST...
COME ON, THINK...
THINK...
SNRK

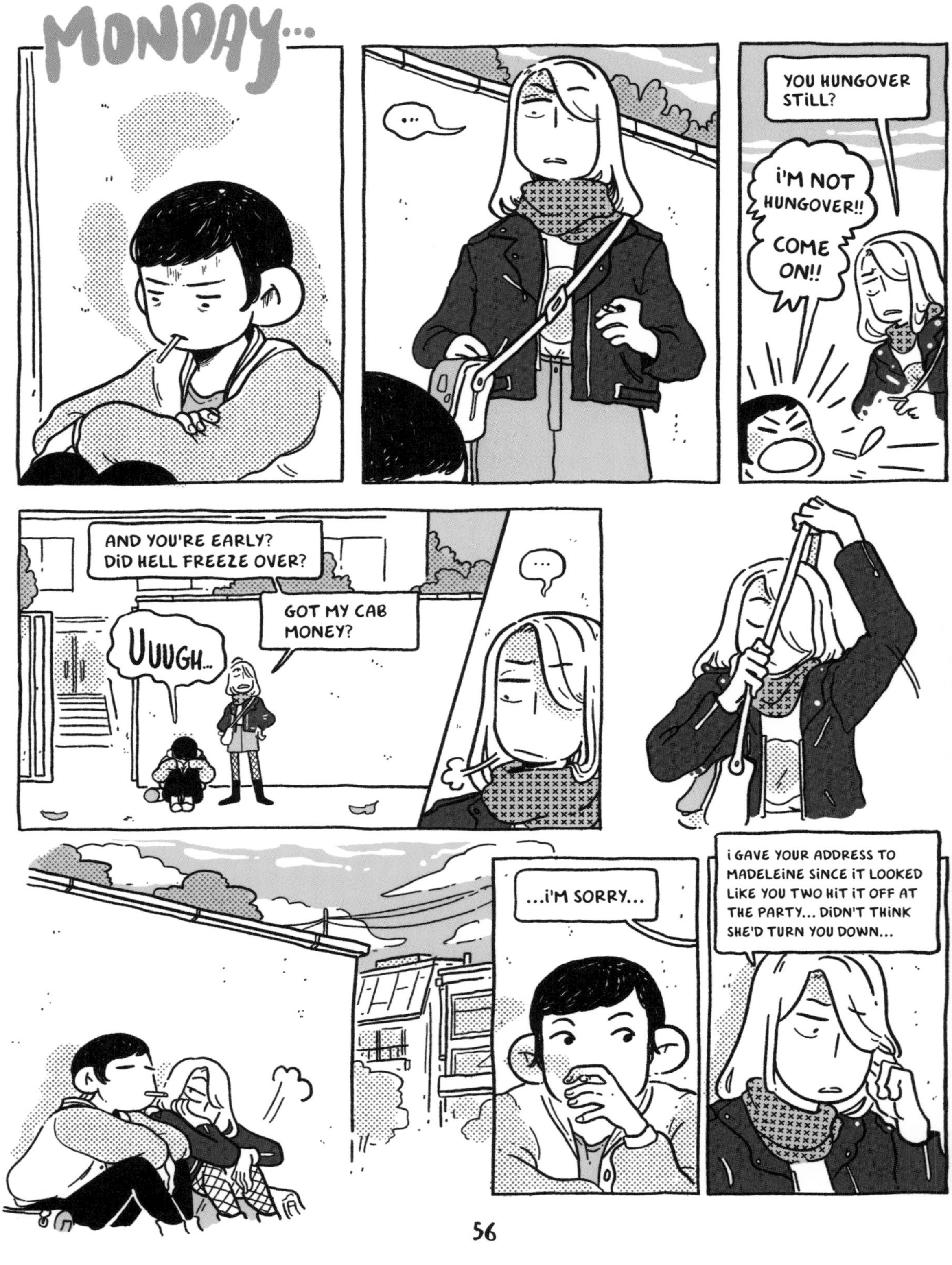
MONDAY...
...
YOU HUNGOVER STiLL?
i'M NOT HUNGOVER!! COME ON!!
AND YOU'RE EARLY? DiD HELL FREEZE OVER?
UUUGH...
GOT MY CAB MONEY?
...
...i'M SORRY...
i GAVE YOUR ADDRESS TO MADELEiNE SiNCE iT LOOKED LiKE YOU TWO HiT iT OFF AT THE PARTY... DiDN'T THiNK SHE'D TURN YOU DOWN...

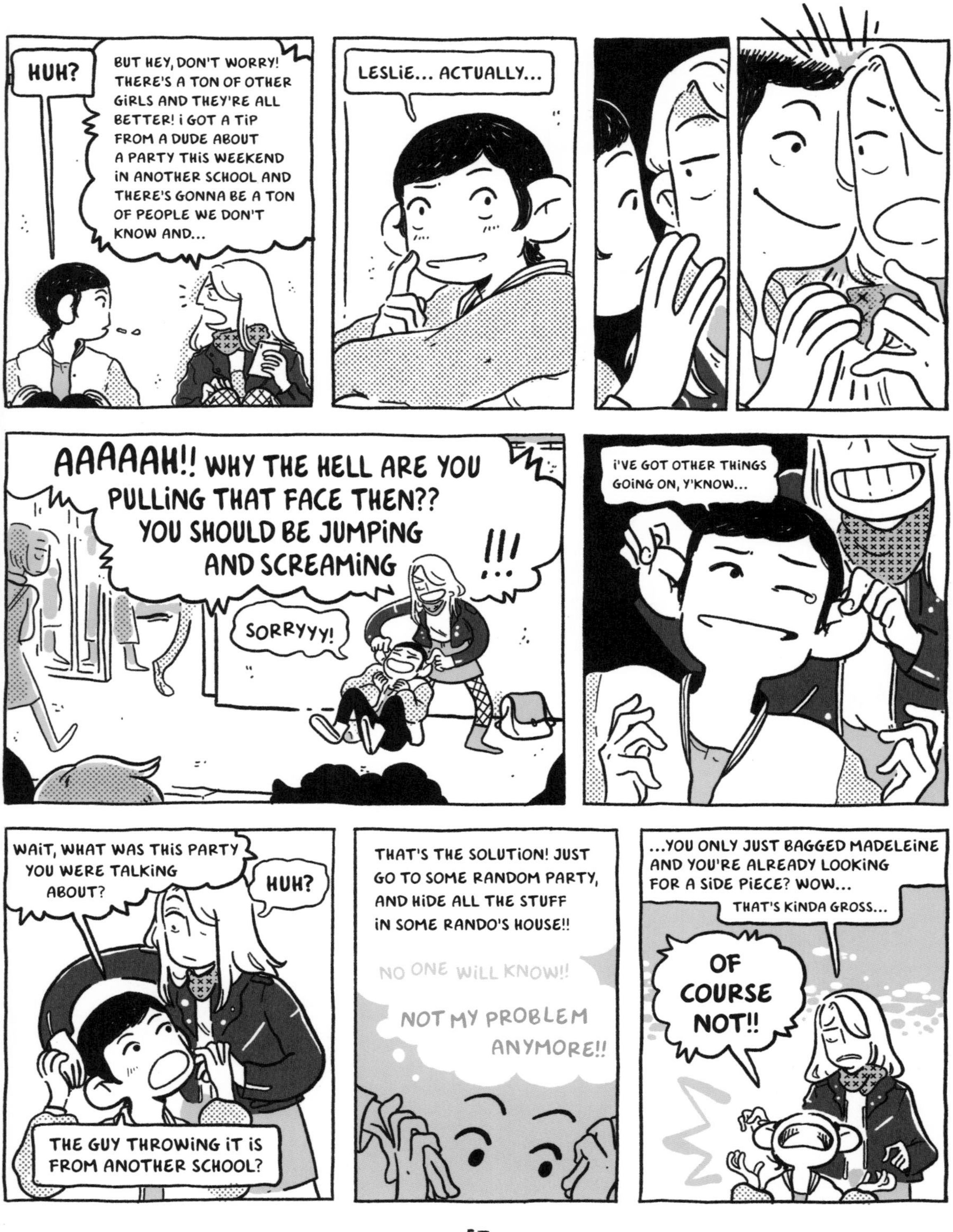
HUH?
BUT HEY, DON'T WORRY! THERE'S A TON OF OTHER GIRLS AND THEY'RE ALL BETTER! i GOT A TiP FROM A DUDE ABOUT A PARTY THiS WEEKEND iN ANOTHER SCHOOL AND THERE'S GONNA BE A TON OF PEOPLE WE DON'T KNOW AND...
LESLiE... ACTUALLY...
AAAAAH!! WHY THE HELL ARE YOU PULLiNG THAT FACE THEN?? YOU SHOULD BE JUMPiNG AND SCREAMiNG !!!
SORRYYY!
i'VE GOT OTHER THiNGS GOiNG ON, Y'KNOW...
WAiT, WHAT WAS THiS PARTY YOU WERE TALKiNG ABOUT?
HUH?
THE GUY THROWiNG iT iS FROM ANOTHER SCHOOL?
THAT'S THE SOLUTiON! JUST GO TO SOME RANDOM PARTY, AND HiDE ALL THE STUFF iN SOME RANDO'S HOUSE!!
NO ONE WiLL KNOW!!
NOT MY PROBLEM ANYMORE!!
...YOU ONLY JUST BAGGED MADELEiNE AND YOU'RE ALREADY LOOKiNG FOR A SiDE PiECE? WOW...
THAT'S KiNDA GROSS...
OF COURSE NOT!!

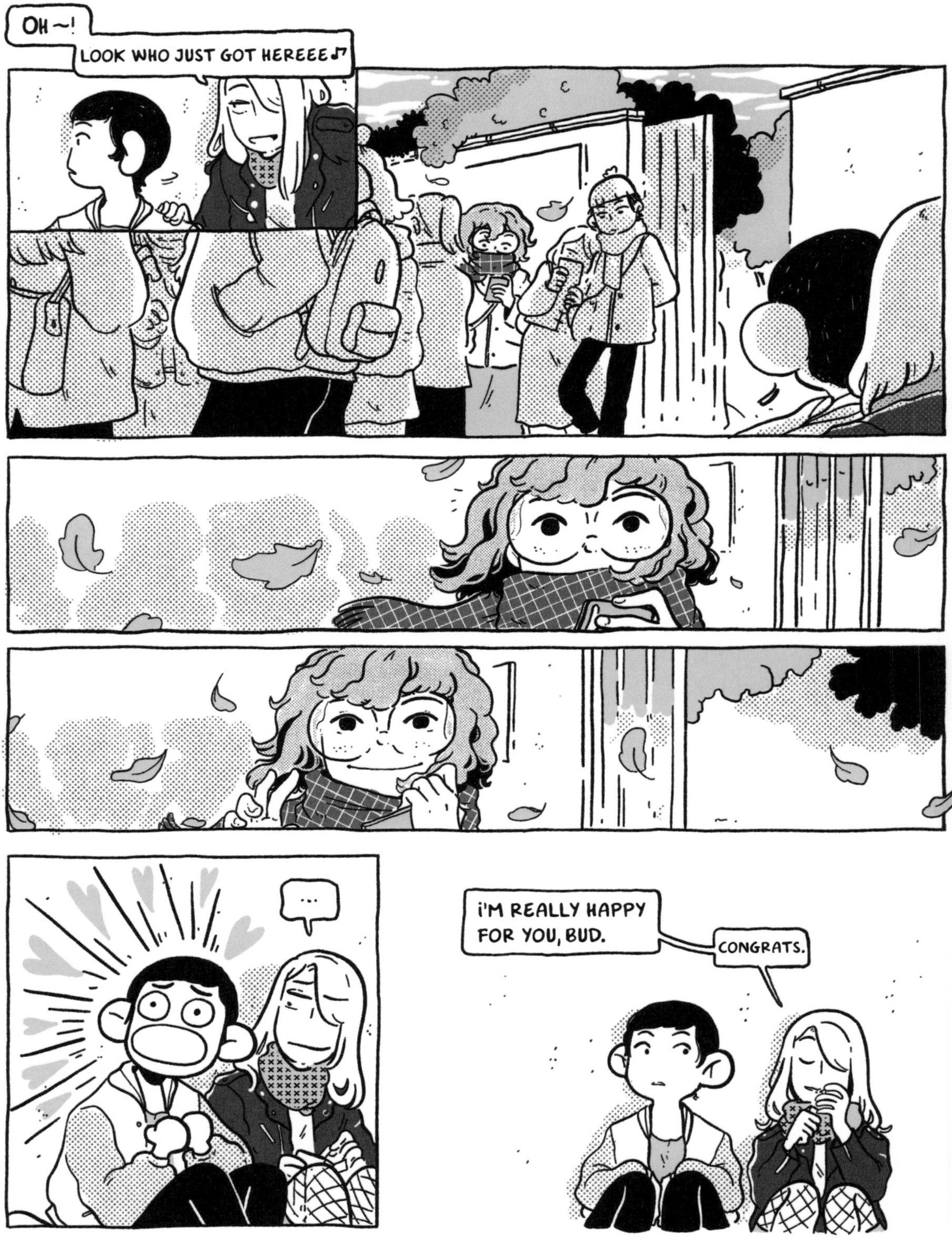
OH~!
LOOK WHO JUST GOT HEREEE♪
...
I'M REALLY HAPPY FOR YOU, BUD.
CONGRATS.

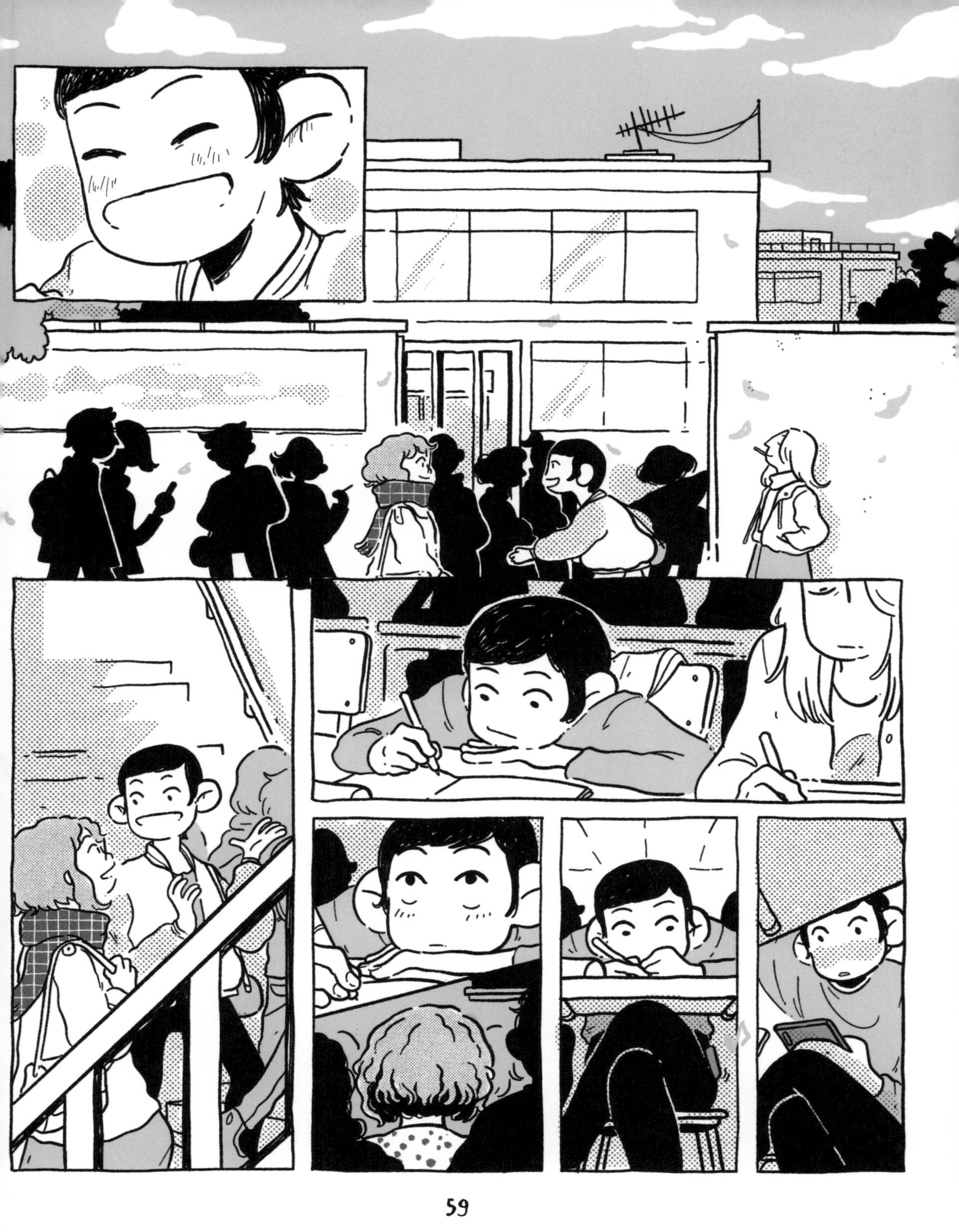

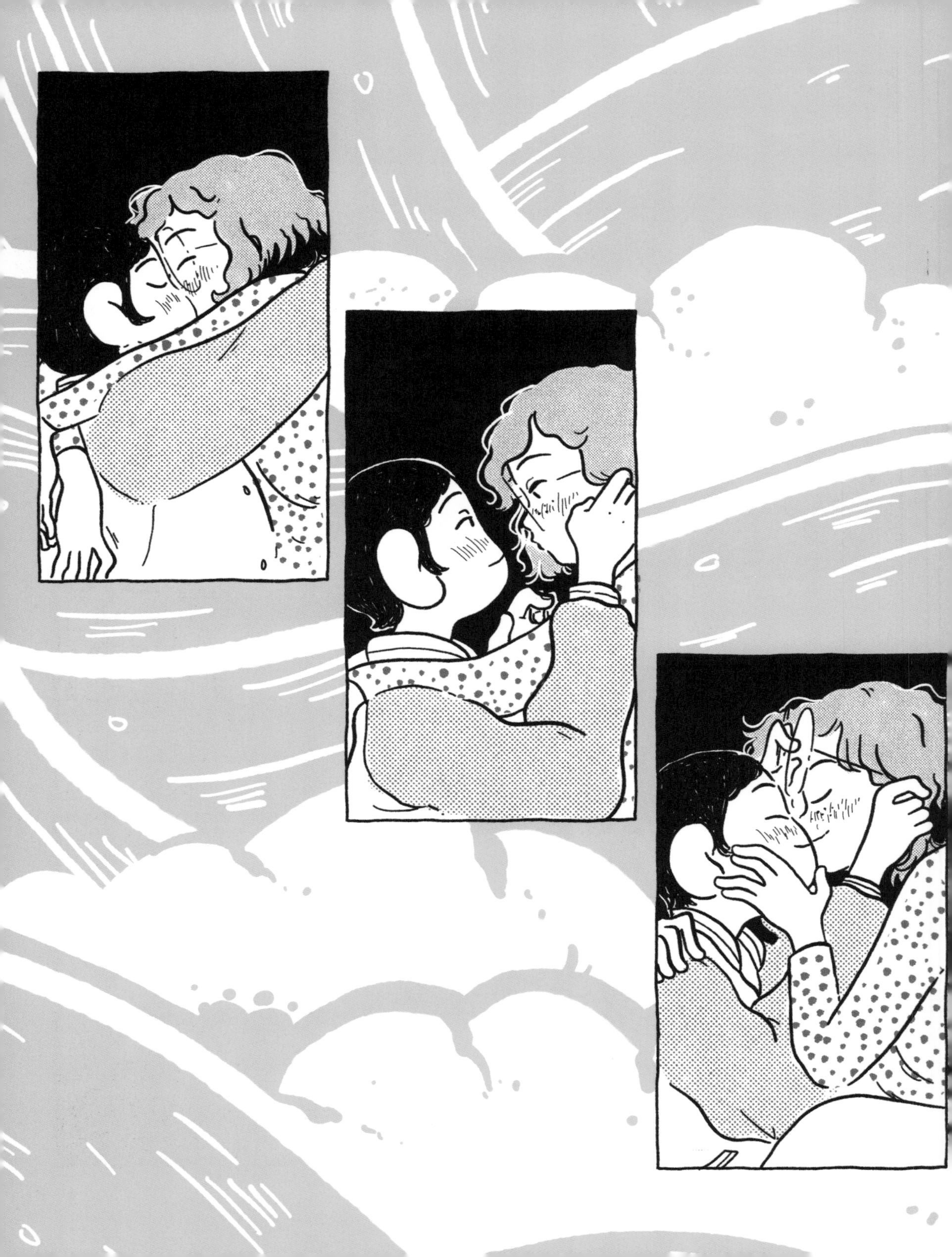

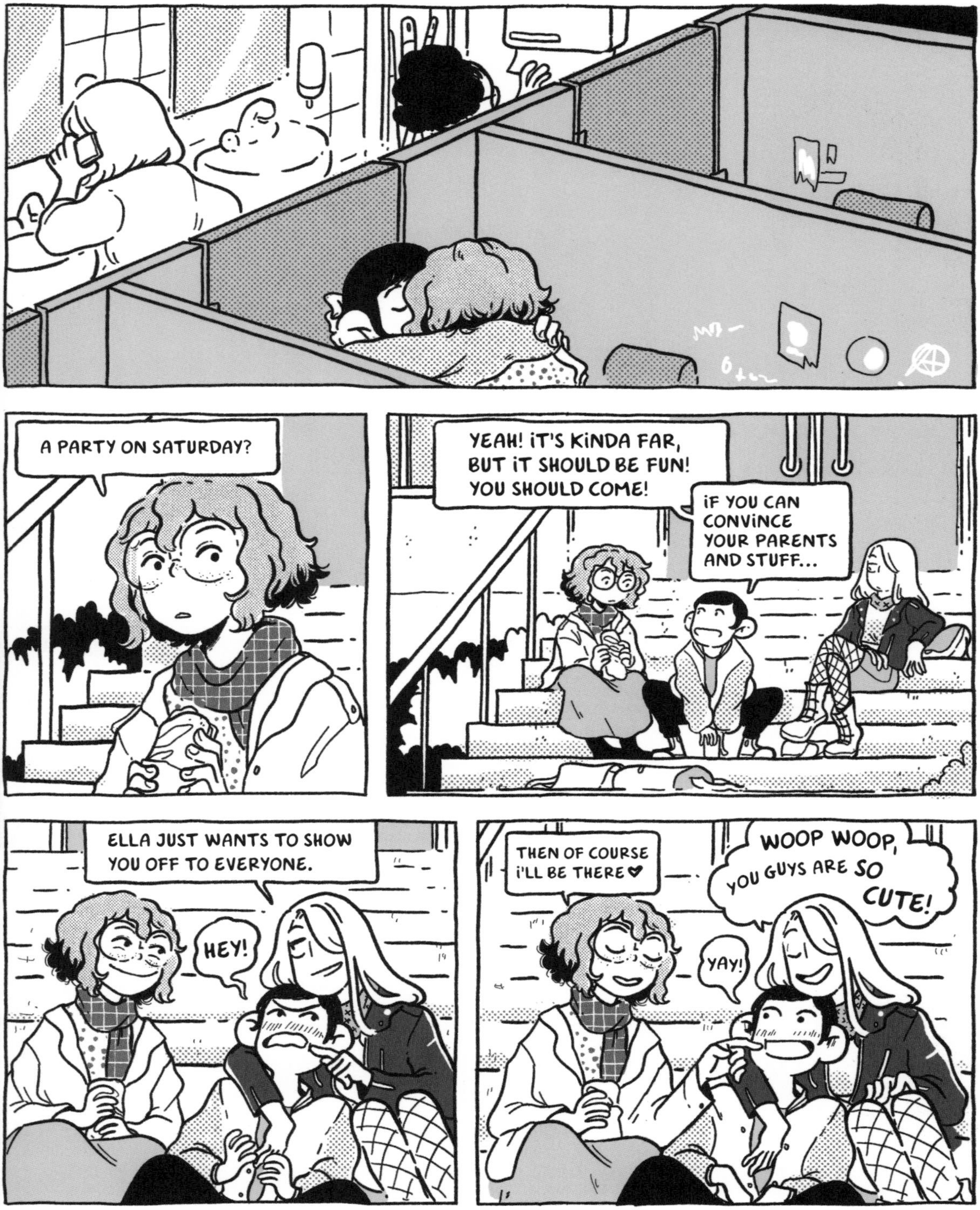
A PARTY ON SATURDAY?
YEAH! IT'S KINDA FAR, BUT IT SHOULD BE FUN! YOU SHOULD COME!
IF YOU CAN CONVINCE YOUR PARENTS AND STUFF...
ELLA JUST WANTS TO SHOW YOU OFF TO EVERYONE.
HEY!
THEN OF COURSE I'LL BE THERE ♥
YAY!
WOOP WOOP, YOU GUYS ARE SO CUTE!

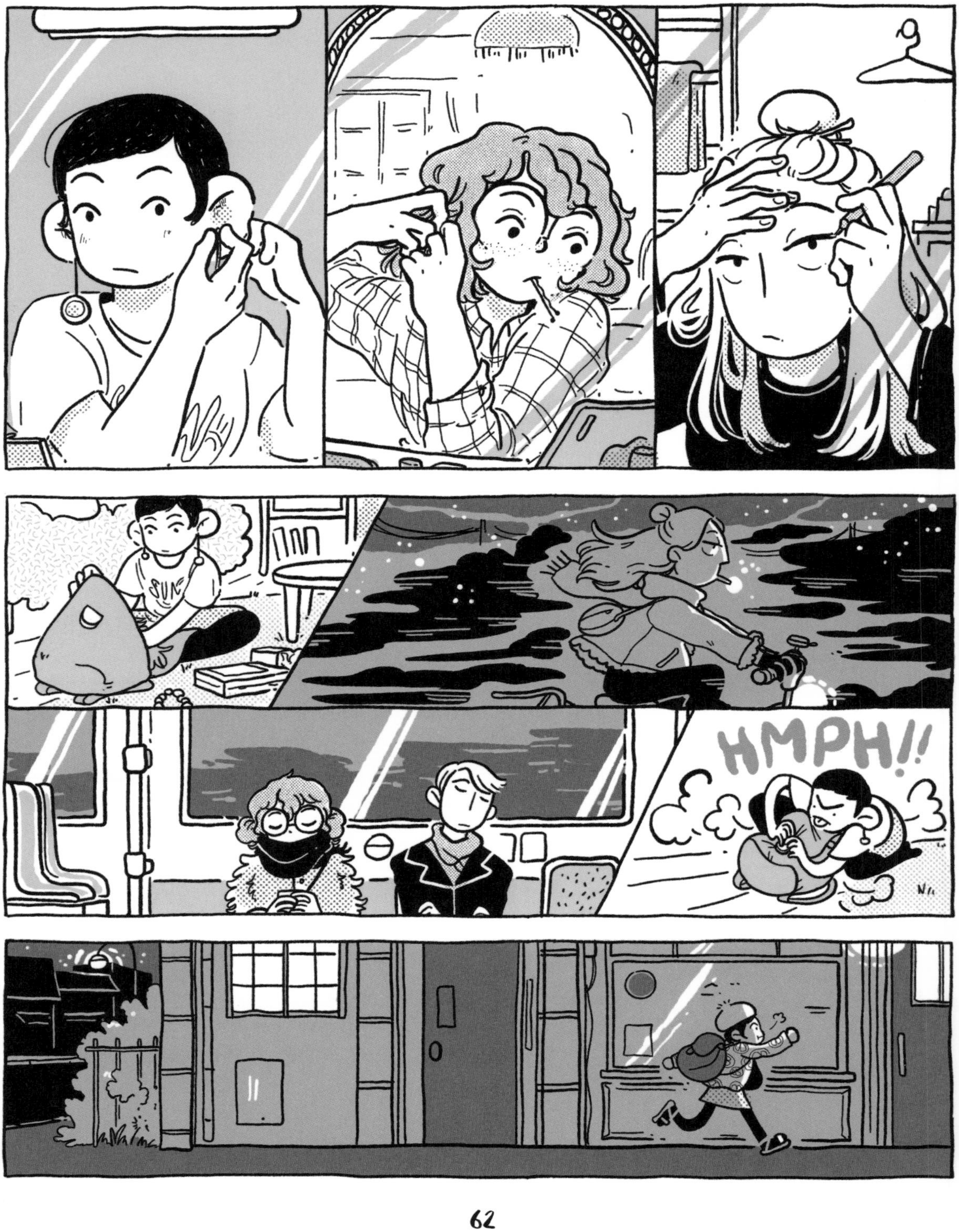
HMPH!!

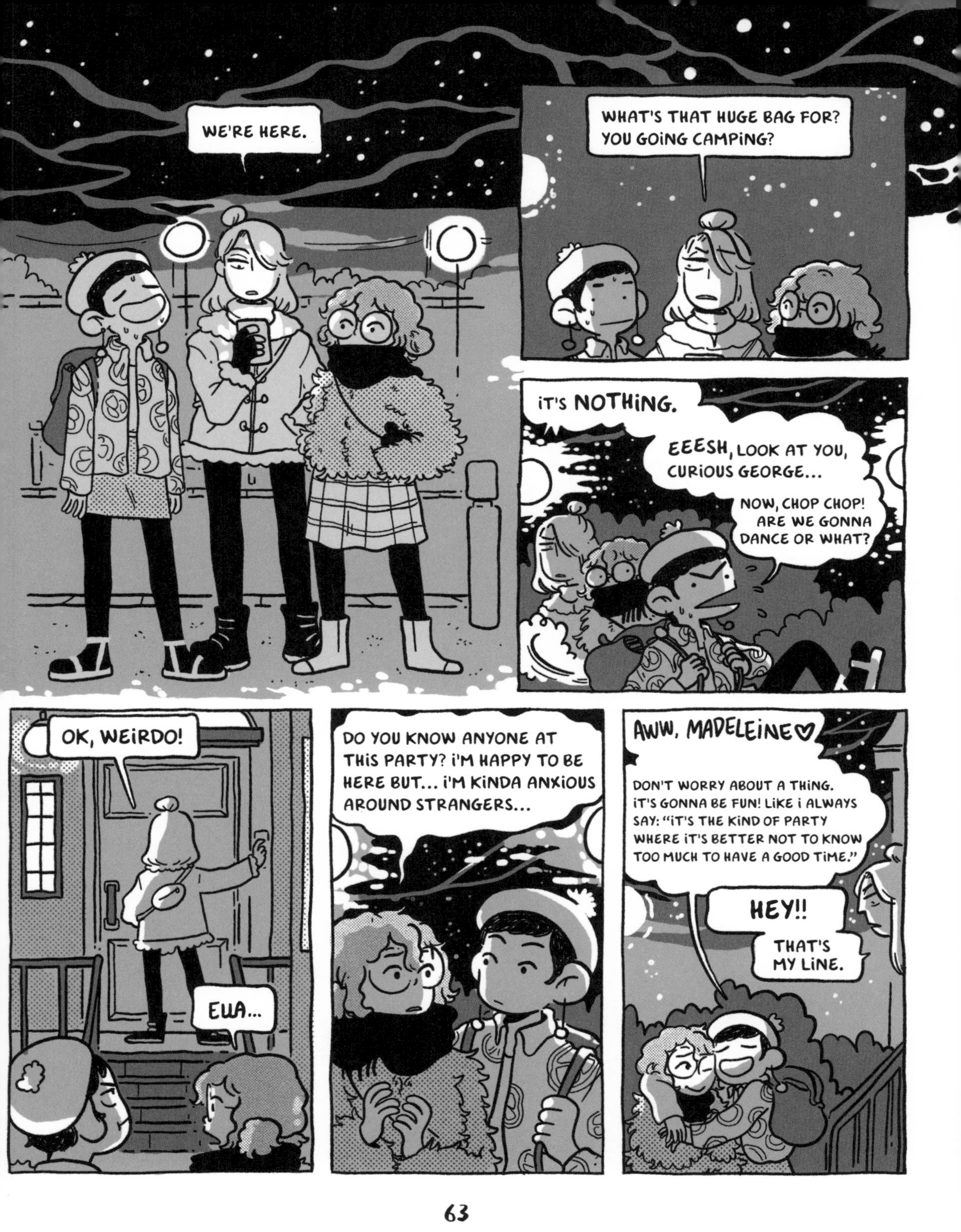
WE'RE HERE.
WHAT'S THAT HUGE BAG FOR? YOU GOING CAMPING?
IT'S NOTHING.
EEESH, LOOK AT YOU, CURIOUS GEORGE...
NOW, CHOP CHOP! ARE WE GONNA DANCE OR WHAT?
OK, WEIRDO!
ELLA...
DO YOU KNOW ANYONE AT THIS PARTY? I'M HAPPY TO BE HERE BUT... I'M KINDA ANXIOUS AROUND STRANGERS...
AWW, MADELEINE♡
DON'T WORRY ABOUT A THING. IT'S GONNA BE FUN! LIKE I ALWAYS SAY: "IT'S THE KIND OF PARTY WHERE IT'S BETTER NOT TO KNOW TOO MUCH TO HAVE A GOOD TIME."
HEY!!
THAT'S MY LINE.

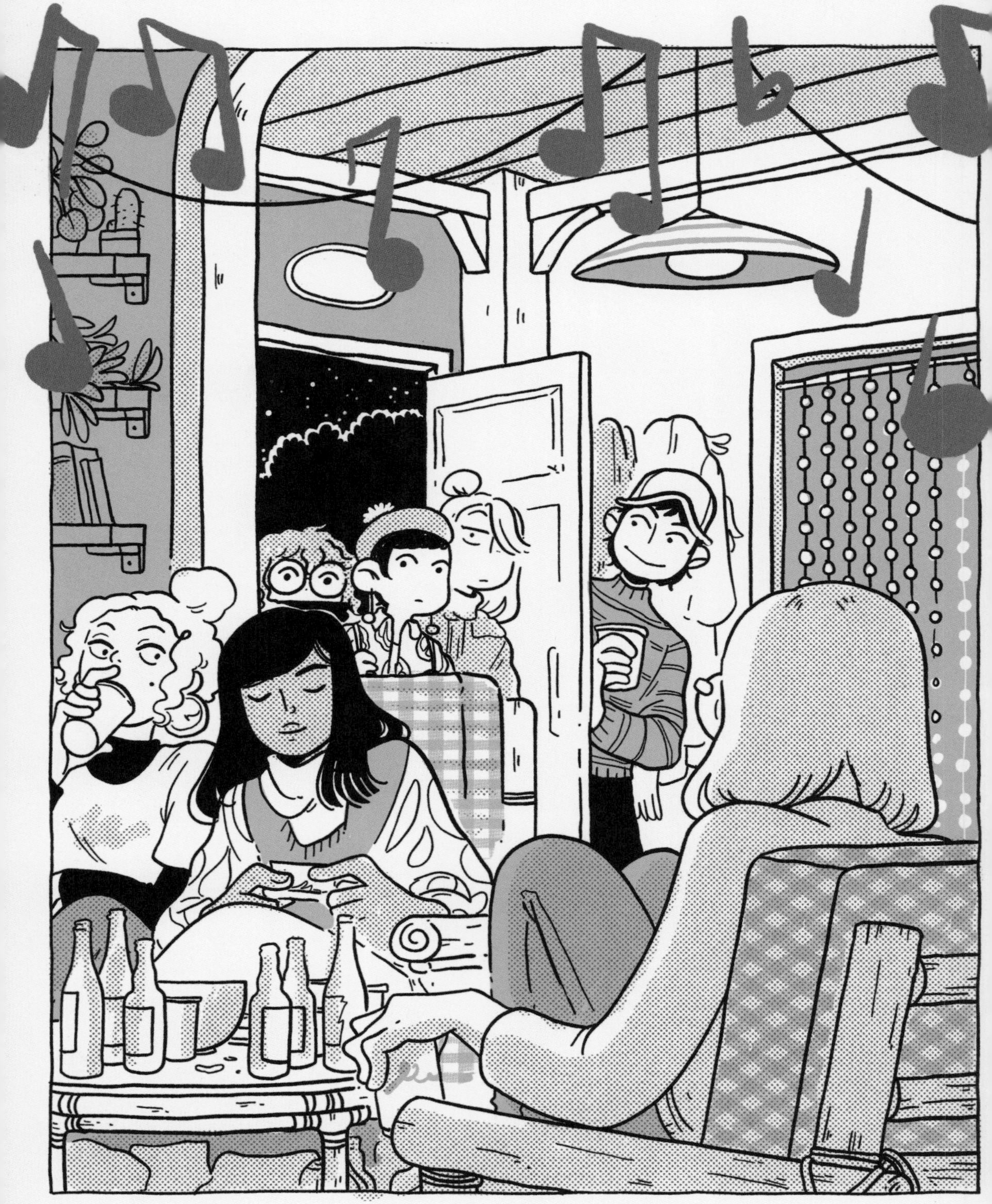

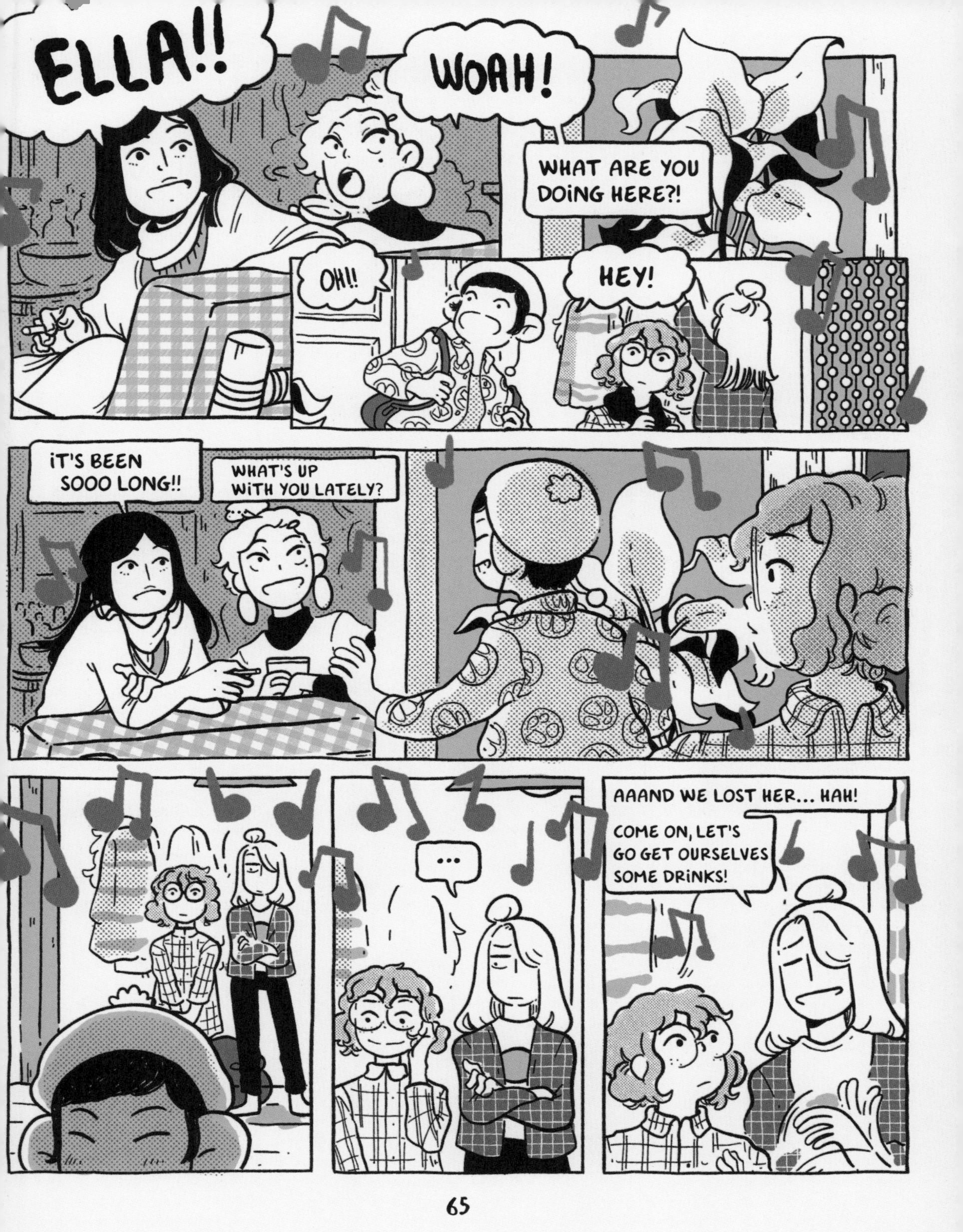

ELLA!!
WOAH!
WHAT ARE YOU DOiNG HERE?!
OH!!
HEY!
iT'S BEEN SOOO LONG!!
WHAT'S UP WiTH YOU LATELY?
...
AAAND WE LOST HER... HAH!
COME ON, LET'S GO GET OURSELVES SOME DRiNKS!

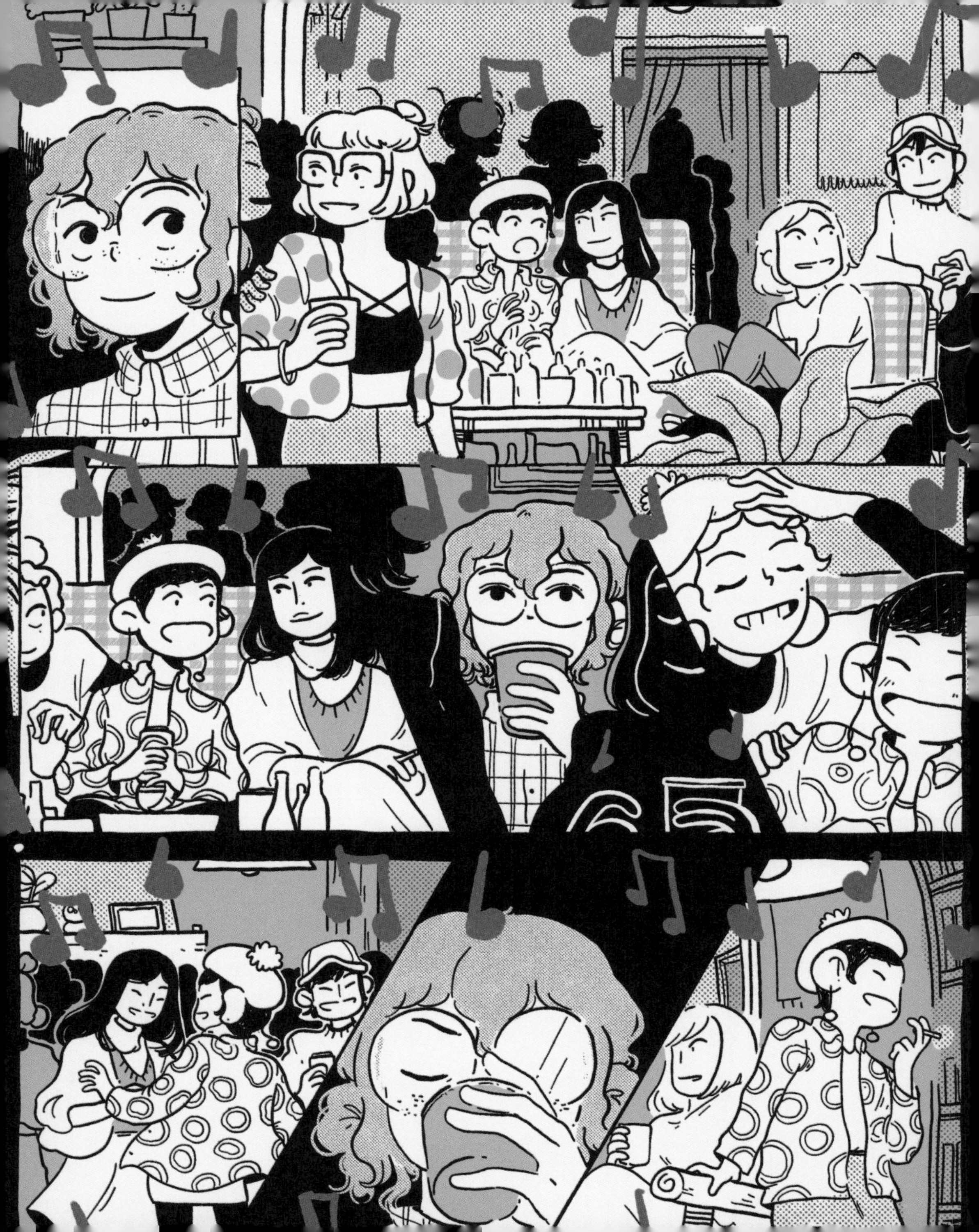

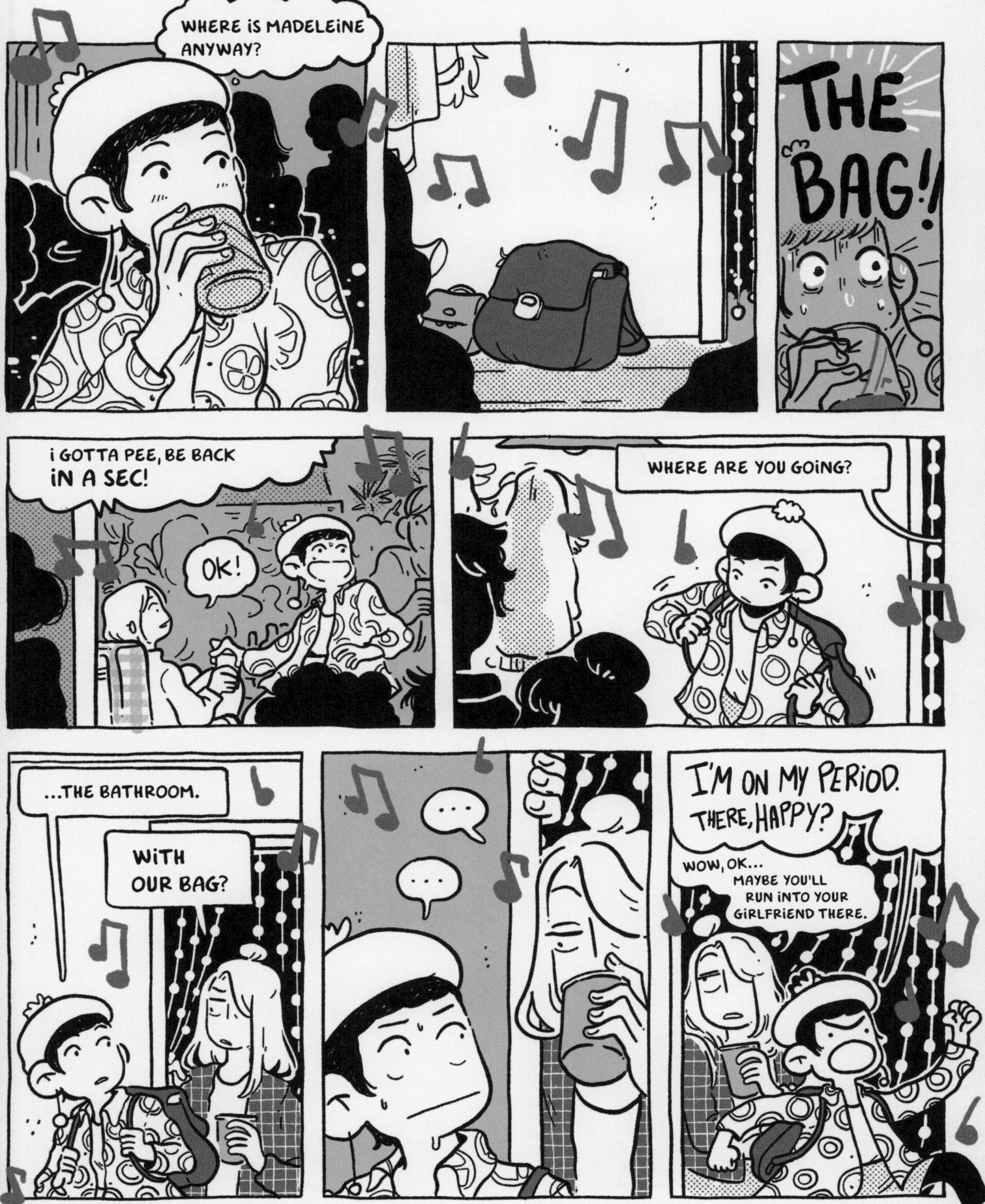

WHERE IS MADELEINE ANYWAY?
THE BAG!!
I GOTTA PEE, BE BACK IN A SEC!
OK!
WHERE ARE YOU GOING?
...THE BATHROOM.
WITH OUR BAG?
...
...
I'M ON MY PERIOD. THERE, HAPPY?
WOW, OK... MAYBE YOU'LL RUN INTO YOUR GIRLFRIEND THERE.

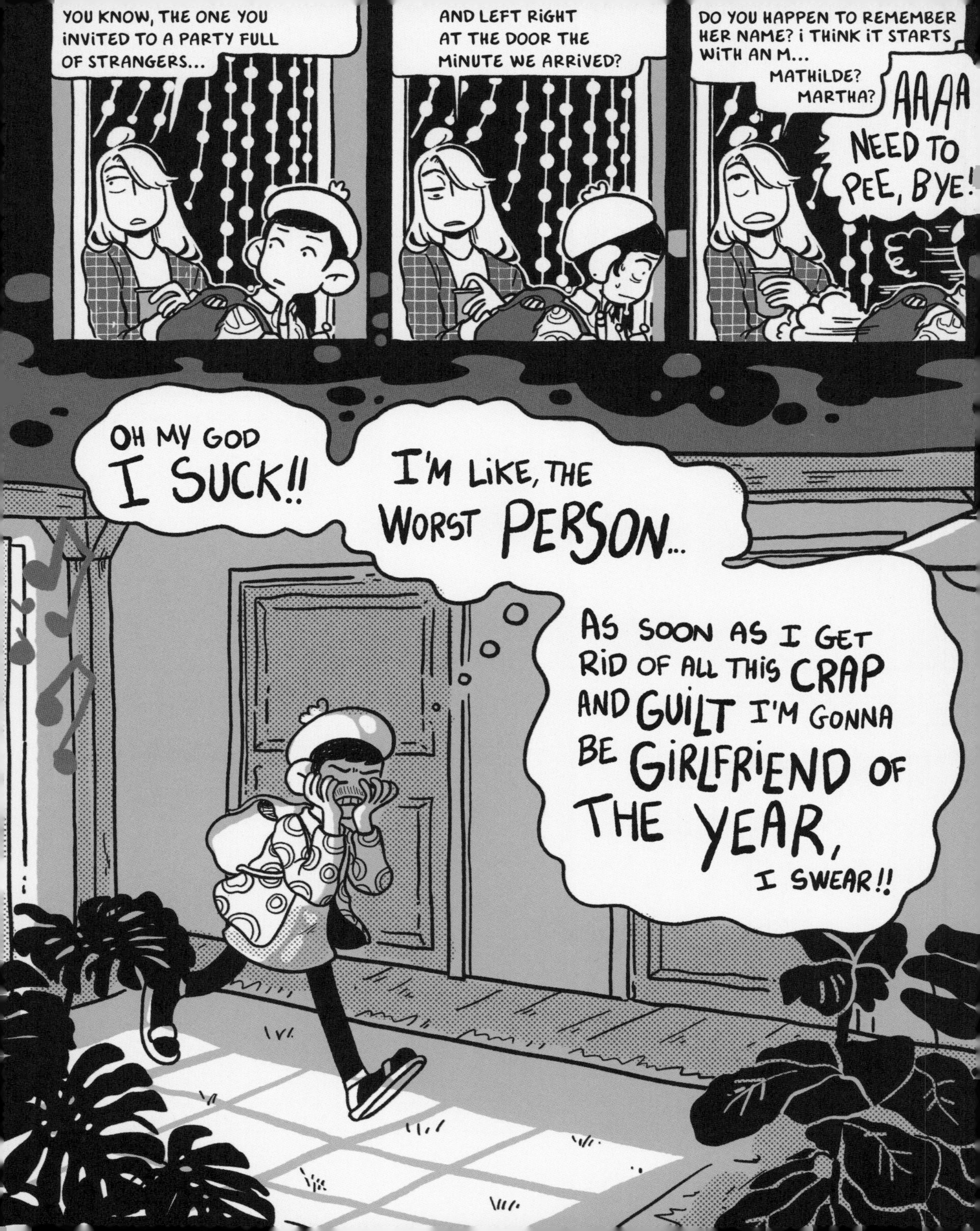
YOU KNOW, THE ONE YOU INVITED TO A PARTY FULL OF STRANGERS...
AND LEFT RIGHT AT THE DOOR THE MINUTE WE ARRIVED?
DO YOU HAPPEN TO REMEMBER HER NAME? I THINK IT STARTS WITH AN M...
MATHILDE? MARTHA?
AAAA
NEED TO PEE, BYE!
OH MY GOD I SUCK!!
I'M LIKE, THE WORST PERSON...
AS SOON AS I GET RID OF ALL THIS CRAP AND GUILT I'M GONNA BE GIRLFRIEND OF THE YEAR,
I SWEAR!!

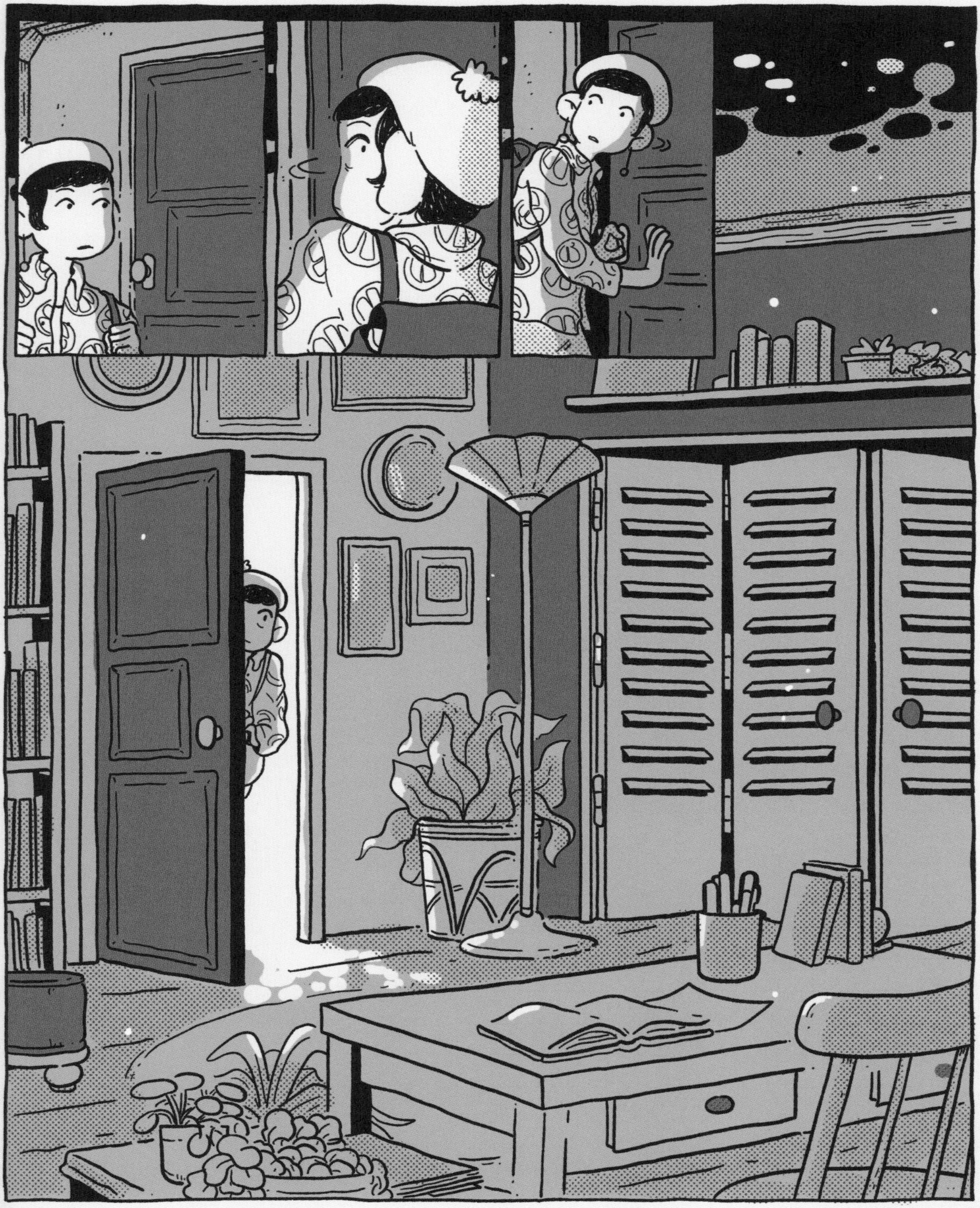

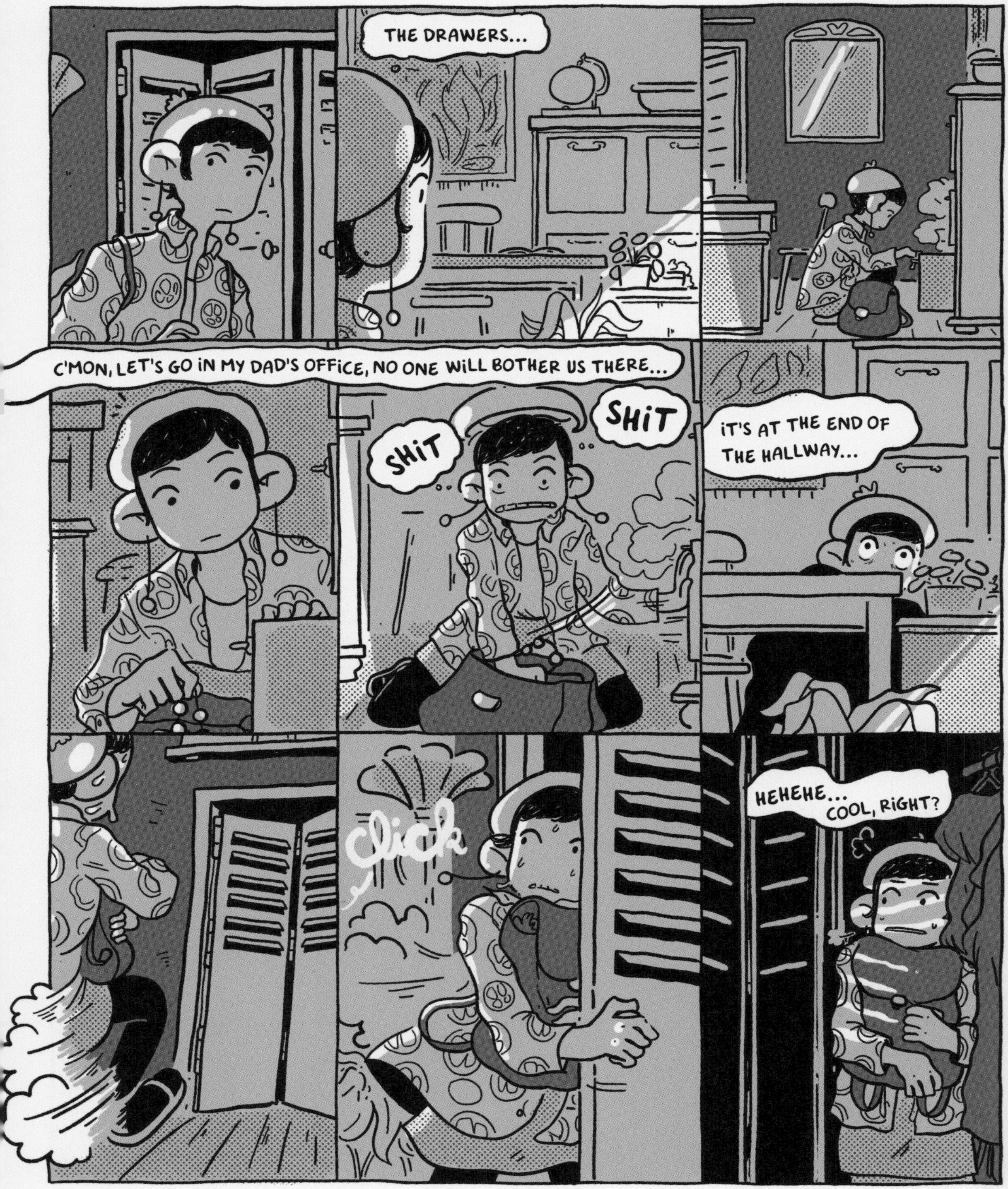
THE DRAWERS...
C'MON, LET'S GO IN MY DAD'S OFFICE, NO ONE WILL BOTHER US THERE...
SHIT
SHIT
IT'S AT THE END OF THE HALLWAY...
CLICK
HEHEHE...
COOL, RIGHT?

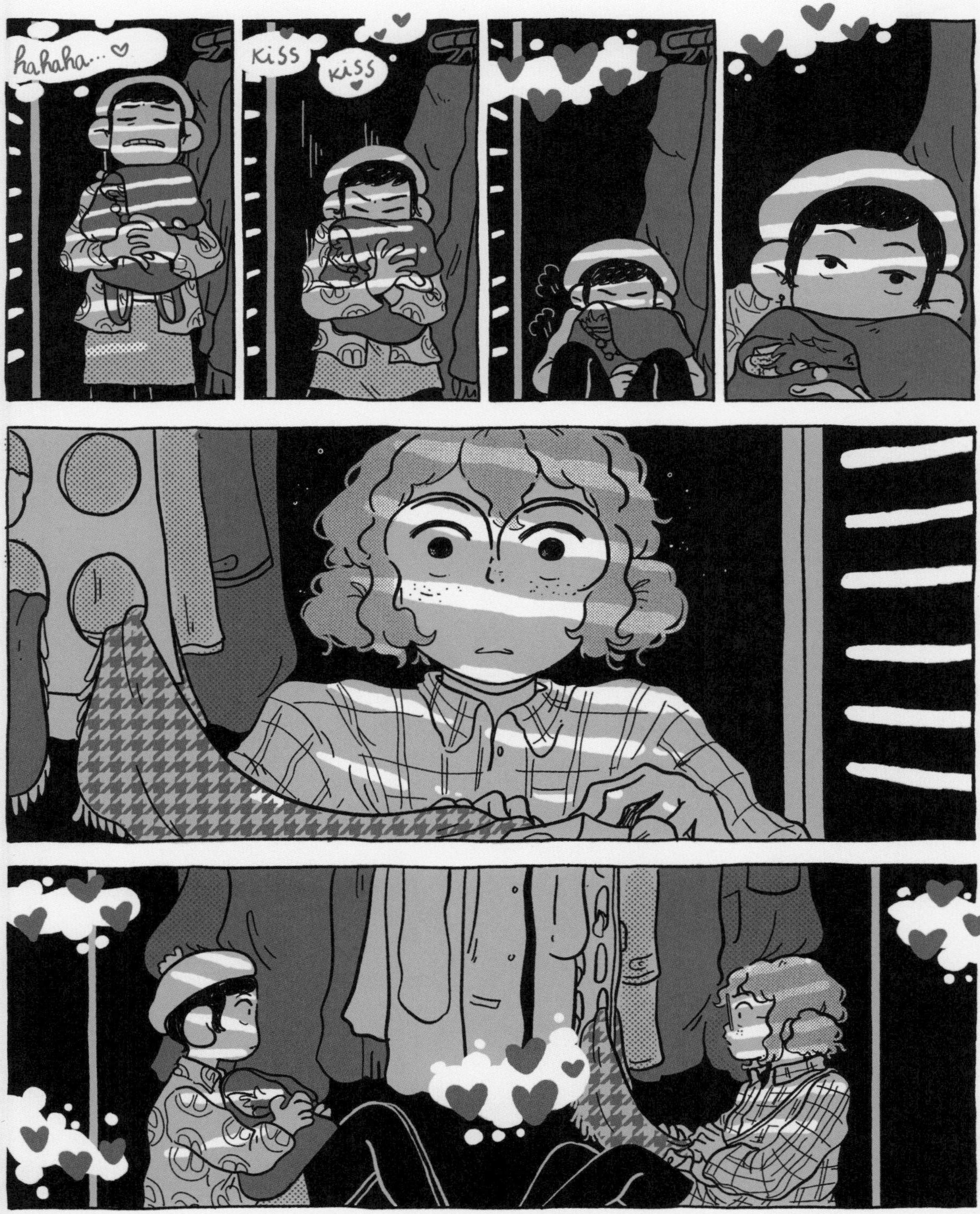
hahaha...♡
KISS
KISS

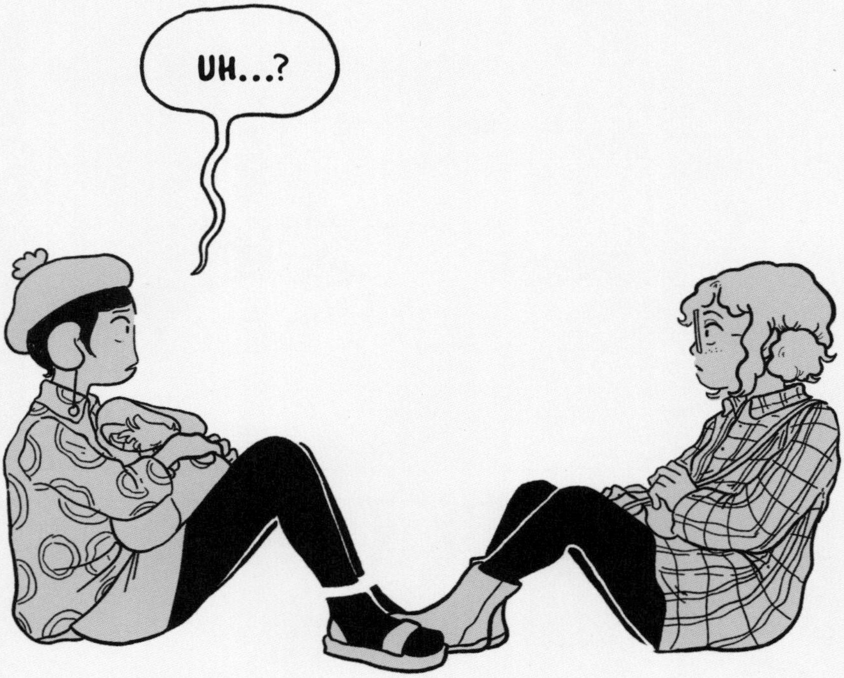
UH...?

2

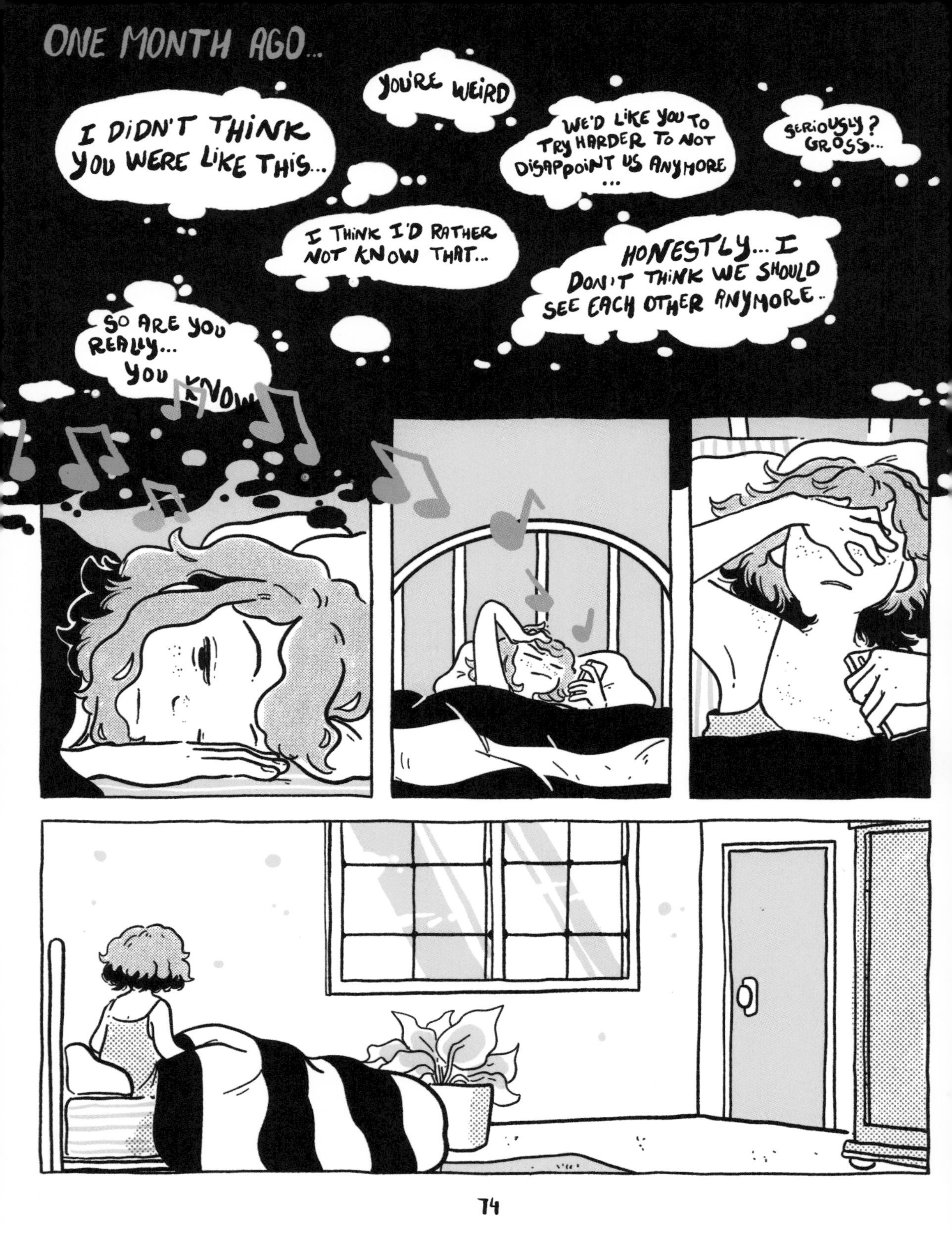
ONE MONTH AGO...
I DIDN'T THINK YOU WERE LIKE THIS...
YOU'RE WEIRD
WE'D LIKE YOU TO TRY HARDER TO NOT DISAPPOINT US ANYMORE ...
SERIOUSLY? GROSS...
I THINK I'D RATHER NOT KNOW THAT...
HONESTLY... I DON'T THINK WE SHOULD SEE EACH OTHER ANYMORE..
SO ARE YOU REALLY... YOU KNOW

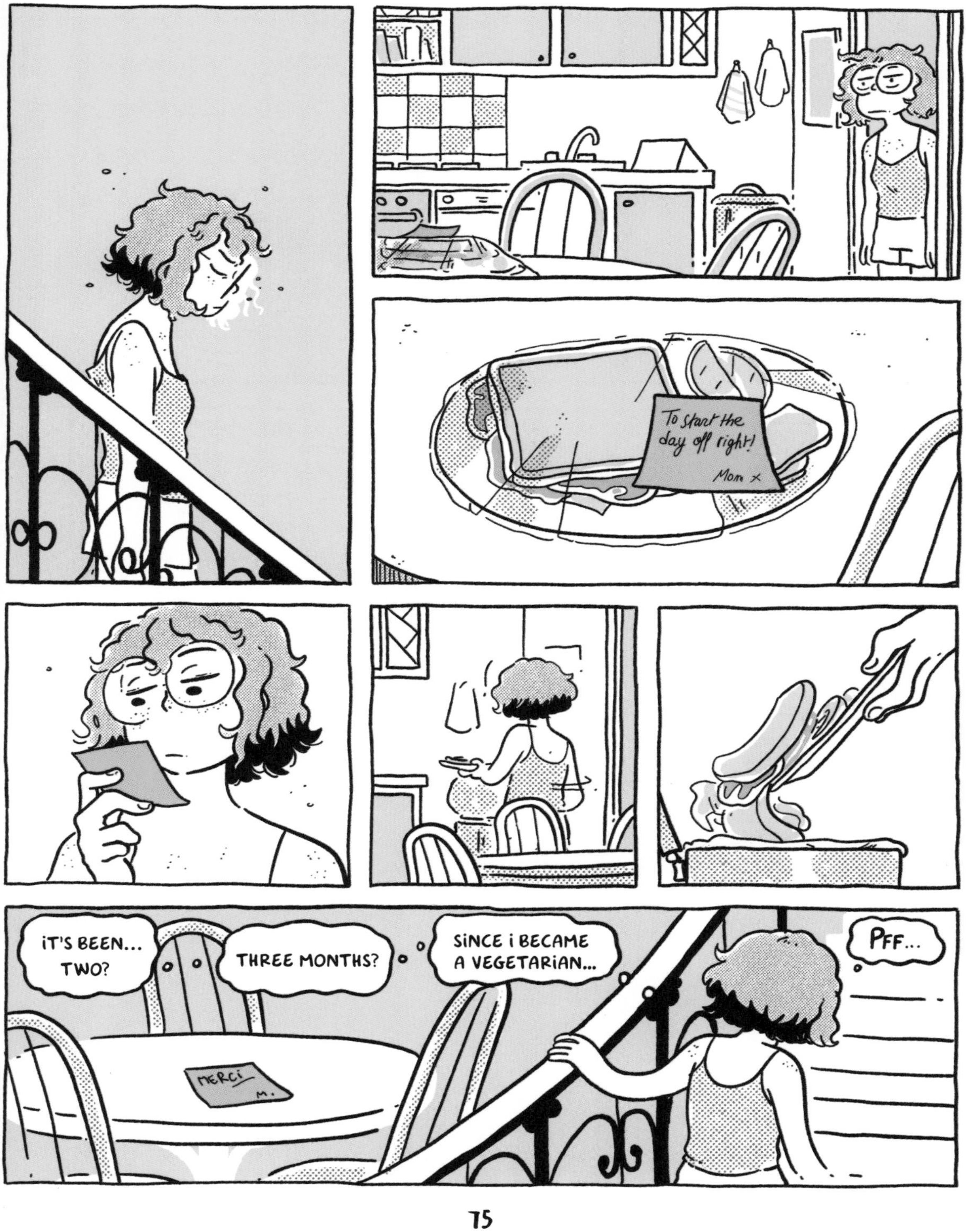
To start the day off right!
Mom x
iT'S BEEN... TWO?
THREE MONTHS?
SiNCE i BECAME A VEGETARiAN...
PFF...
MERCi
M.

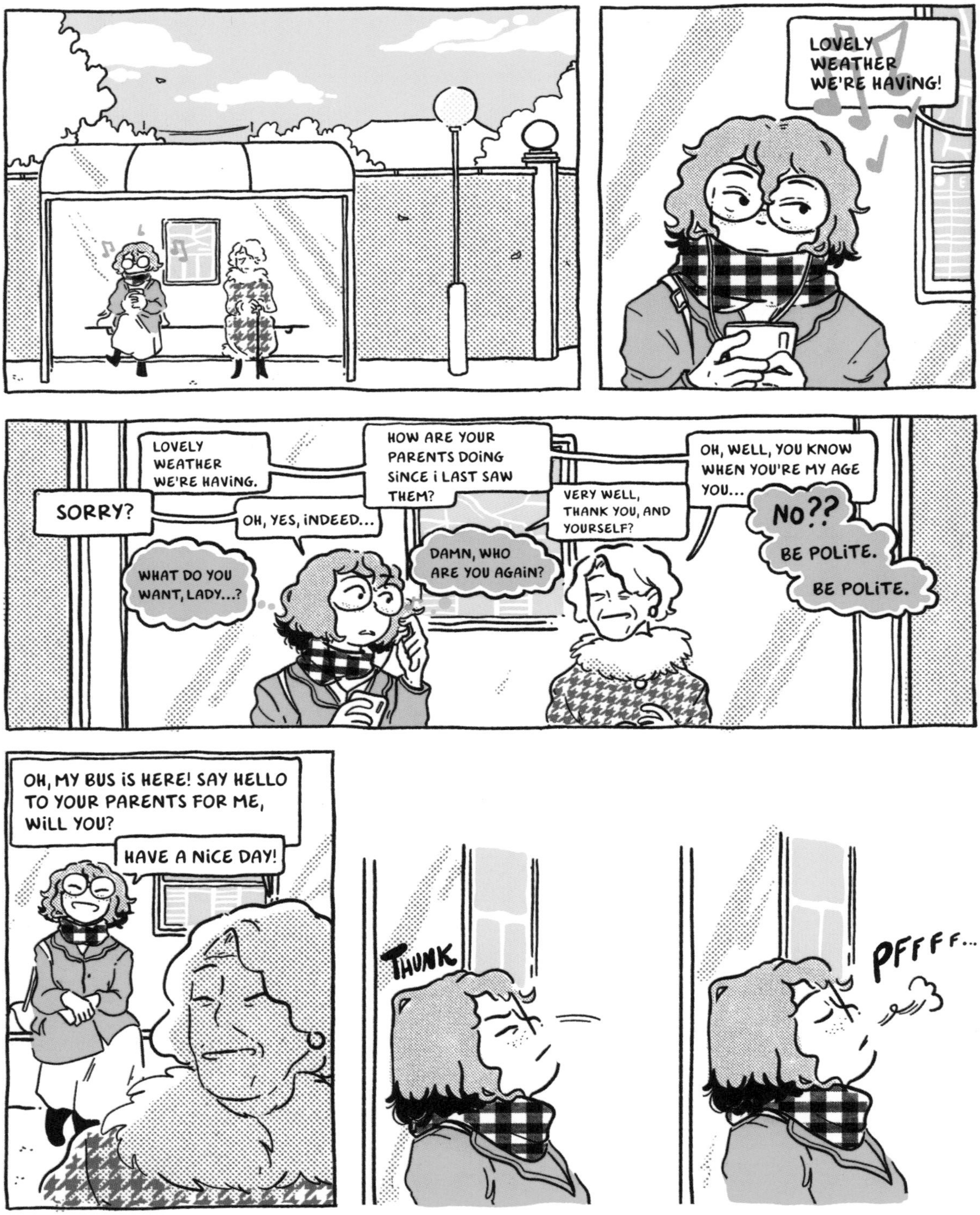
LOVELY WEATHER WE'RE HAVING!
LOVELY WEATHER WE'RE HAVING.
SORRY?
OH, YES, INDEED...
WHAT DO YOU WANT, LADY...?
HOW ARE YOUR PARENTS DOING SINCE I LAST SAW THEM?
DAMN, WHO ARE YOU AGAIN?
VERY WELL, THANK YOU, AND YOURSELF?
OH, WELL, YOU KNOW WHEN YOU'RE MY AGE YOU...
NO??
BE POLITE.
BE POLITE.
OH, MY BUS IS HERE! SAY HELLO TO YOUR PARENTS FOR ME, WILL YOU?
HAVE A NICE DAY!
THUNK
PFFFF...

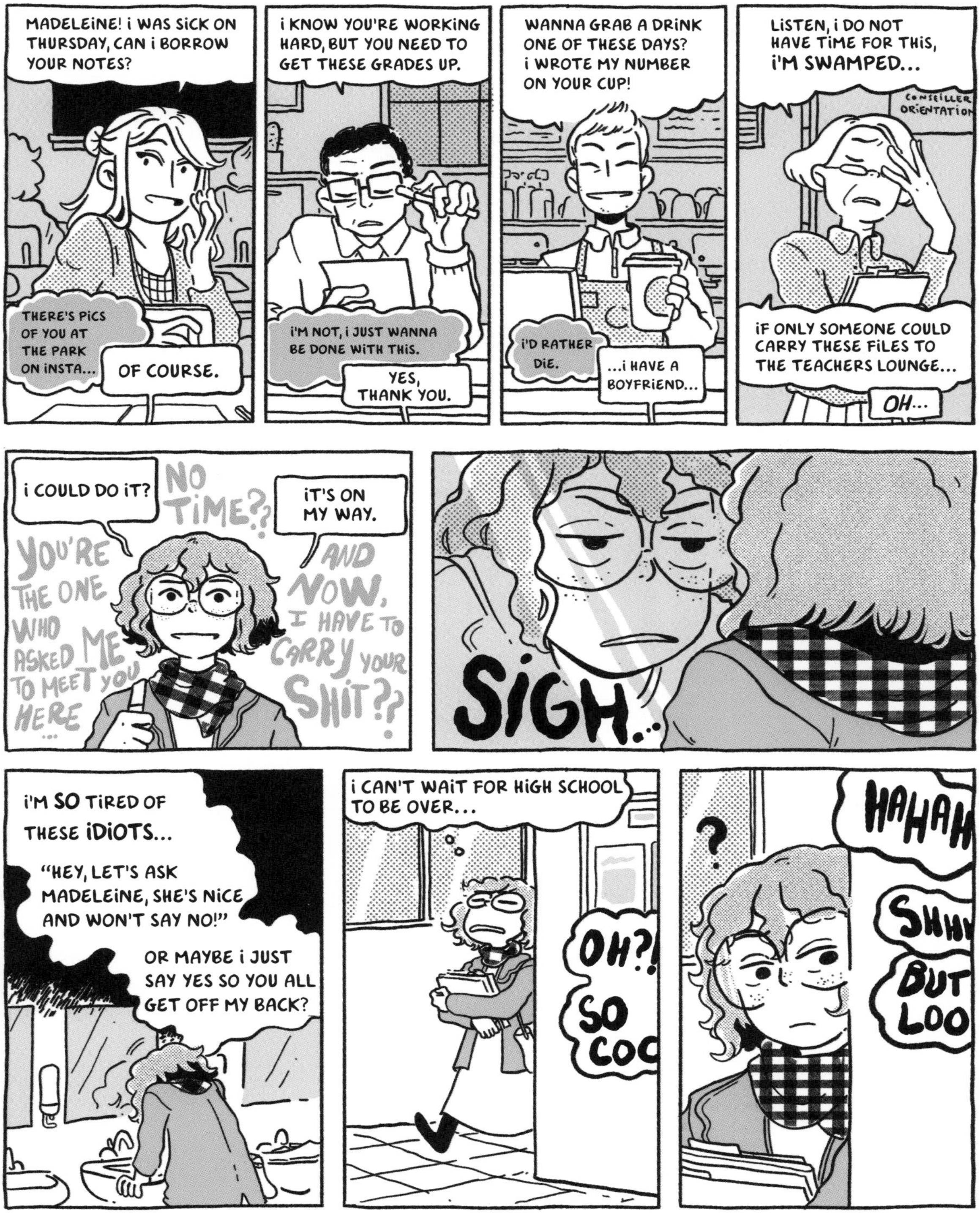

MADELEINE! i WAS SiCK ON THURSDAY, CAN i BORROW YOUR NOTES?
THERE'S PiCS OF YOU AT THE PARK ON iNSTA...
OF COURSE.
i KNOW YOU'RE WORKiNG HARD, BUT YOU NEED TO GET THESE GRADES UP.
i'M NOT, i JUST WANNA BE DONE WiTH THiS.
YES, THANK YOU.
WANNA GRAB A DRiNK ONE OF THESE DAYS? i WROTE MY NUMBER ON YOUR CUP!
i'D RATHER DiE.
...i HAVE A BOYFRiEND...
LiSTEN, i DO NOT HAVE TiME FOR THiS, i'M SWAMPED...
CONSEiLLER ORiENTATiON
iF ONLY SOMEONE COULD CARRY THESE FiLES TO THE TEACHERS LOUNGE...
OH...
i COULD DO iT?
NO TiME??
iT'S ON MY WAY.
YOU'RE THE ONE WHO ASKED ME TO MEET YOU HERE...
AND NOW, I HAVE TO CARRY YOUR SHIT??
SiGH...
i'M SO TiRED OF THESE iDiOTS...
"HEY, LET'S ASK MADELEINE, SHE'S NiCE AND WON'T SAY NO!"
OR MAYBE i JUST SAY YES SO YOU ALL GET OFF MY BACK?
i CAN'T WAiT FOR HiGH SCHOOL TO BE OVER...
OH?!
SO COO
?
HAHAH
SHH
BUT LOO

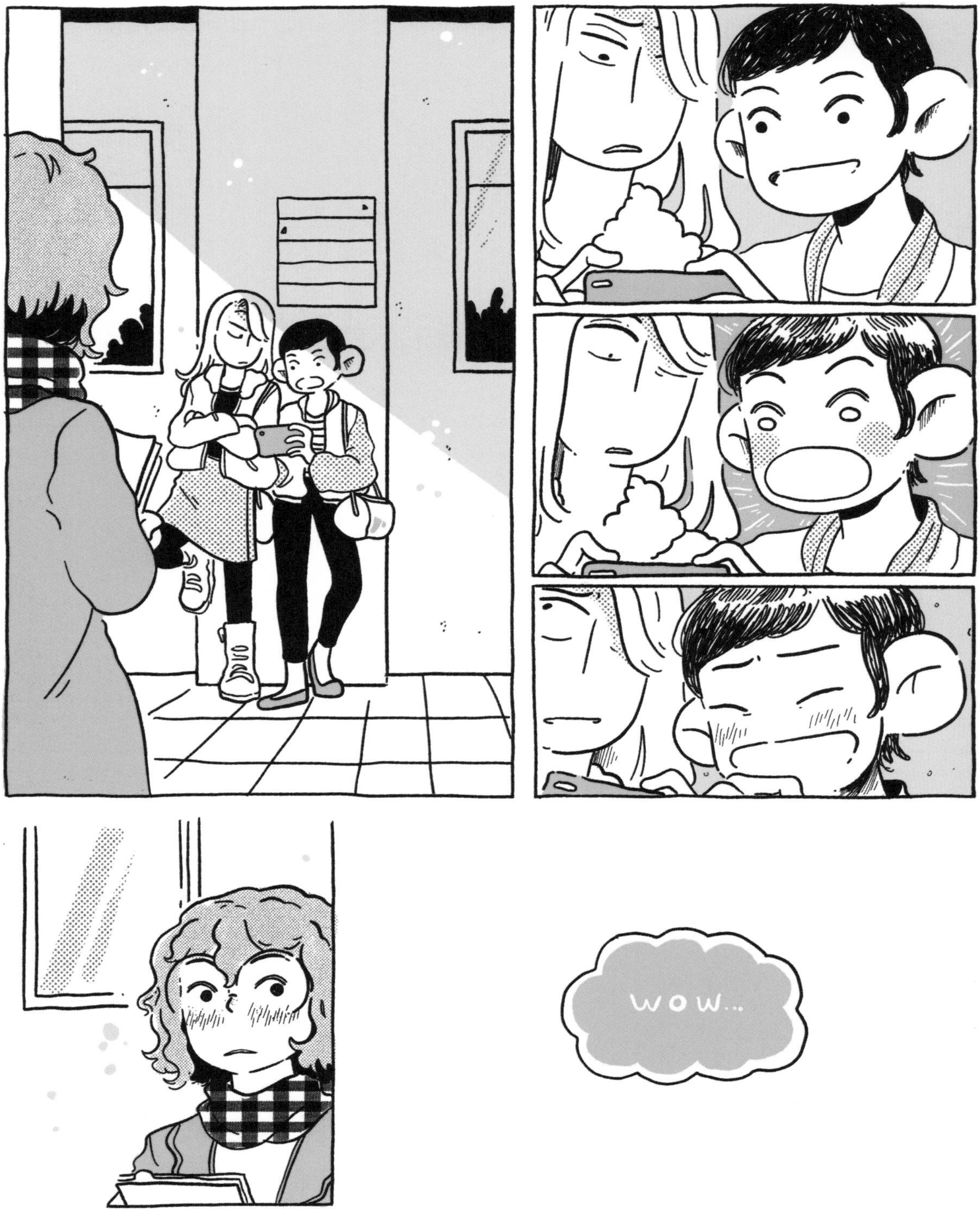
wow...

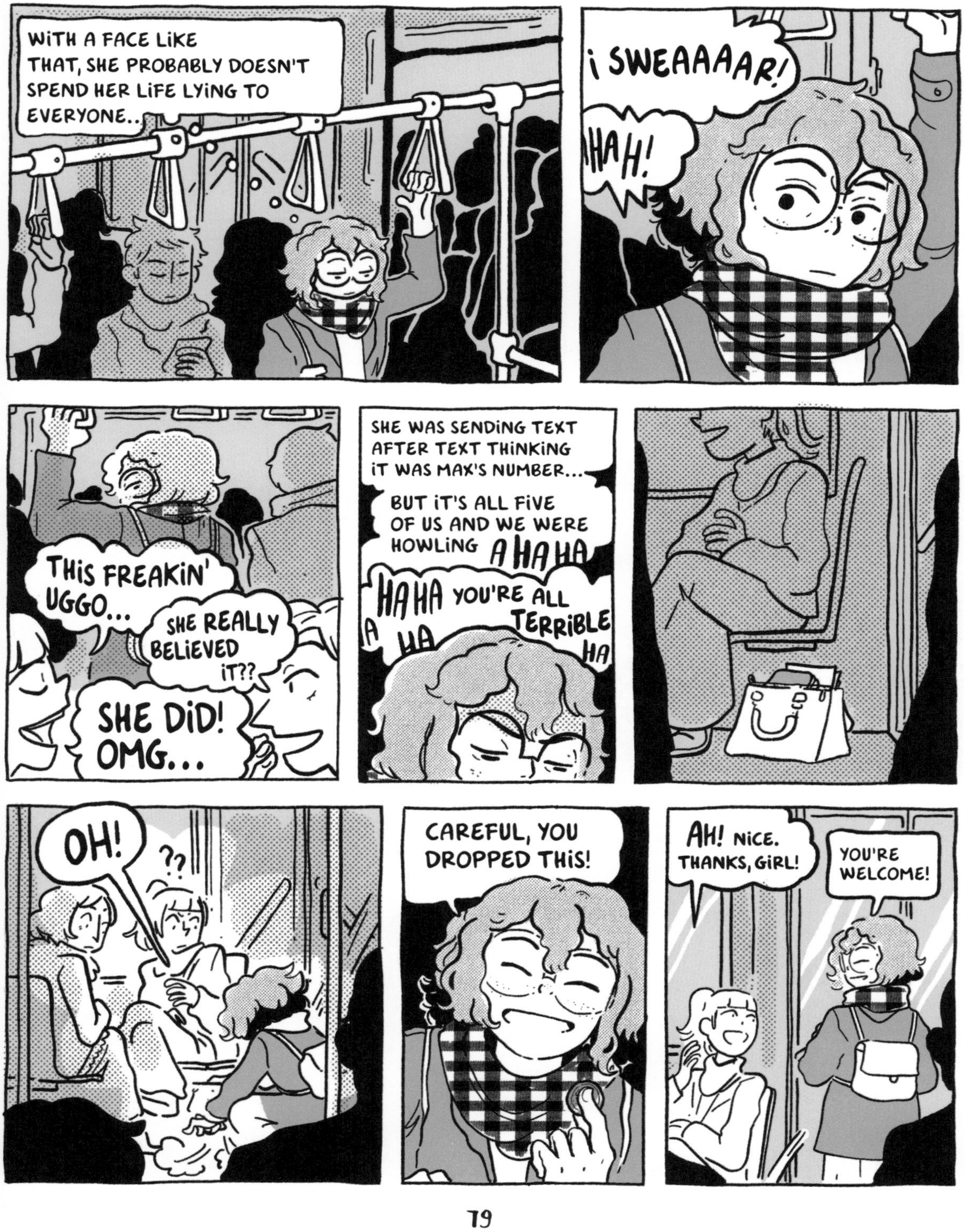
WITH A FACE LIKE THAT, SHE PROBABLY DOESN'T SPEND HER LIFE LYING TO EVERYONE..
¡SWEAAAAR!
HAH!
THIS FREAKIN' UGGO...
SHE REALLY BELIEVED IT??
SHE DID! OMG...
SHE WAS SENDING TEXT AFTER TEXT THINKING IT WAS MAX'S NUMBER...
BUT IT'S ALL FIVE OF US AND WE WERE HOWLING
A HA HA
HA HA
YOU'RE ALL TERRIBLE
HA
HA
HA
OH!
??
CAREFUL, YOU DROPPED THIS!
AH! NICE. THANKS, GIRL!
YOU'RE WELCOME!

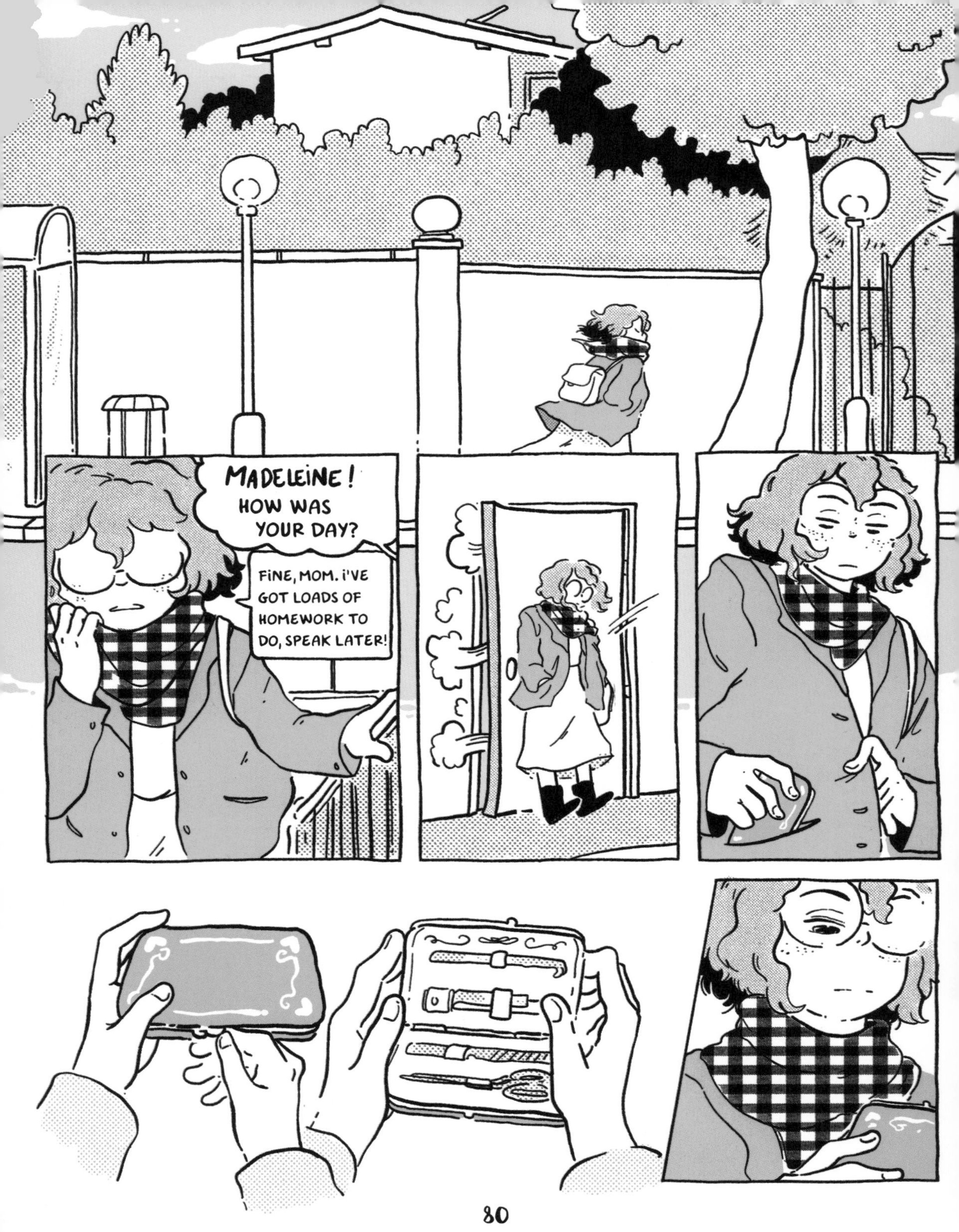
MADELEINE! HOW WAS YOUR DAY?
FiNE, MOM. i'VE GOT LOADS OF HOMEWORK TO DO, SPEAK LATER!

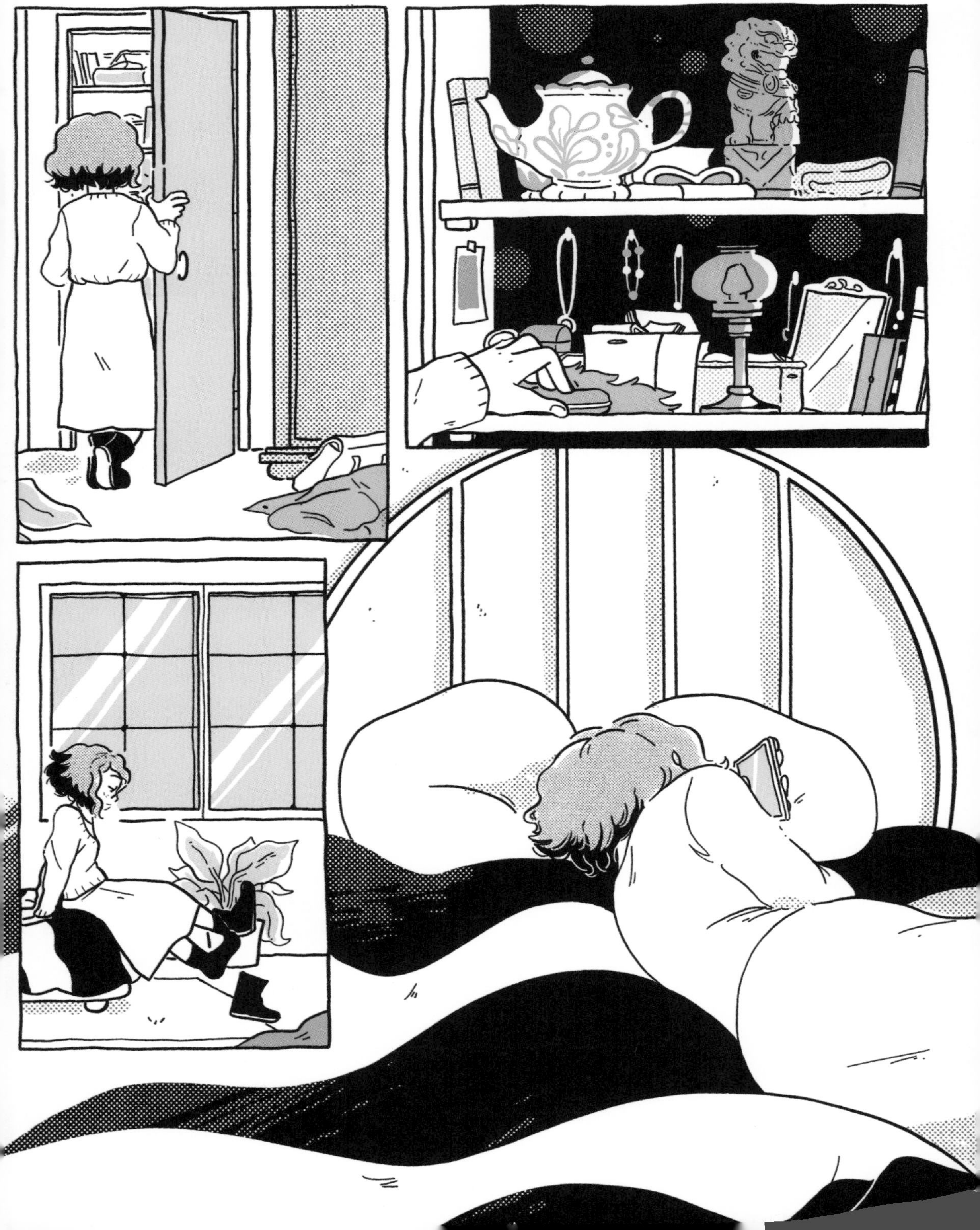

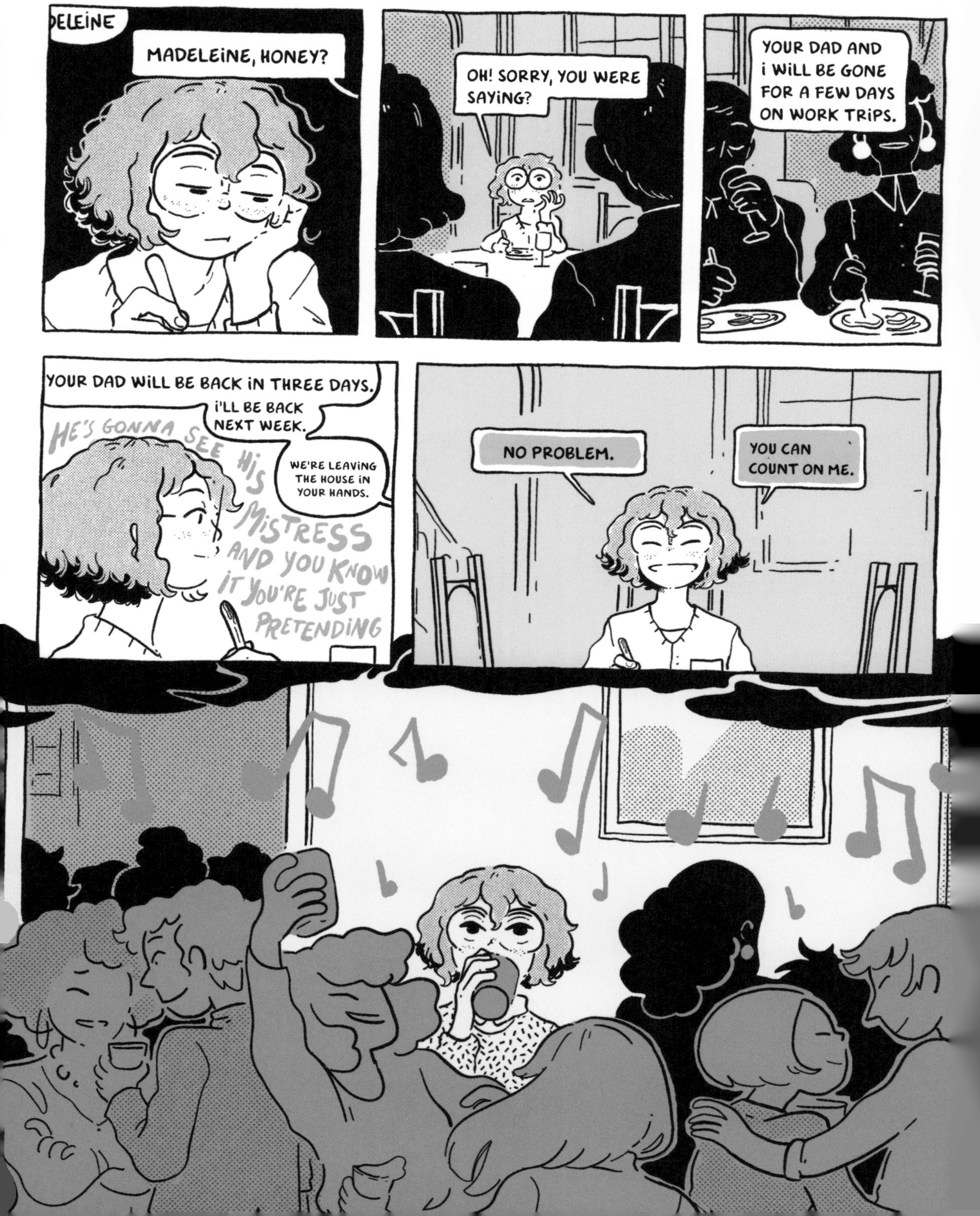
DELEINE
MADELEINE, HONEY?
OH! SORRY, YOU WERE SAYING?
YOUR DAD AND I WILL BE GONE FOR A FEW DAYS ON WORK TRIPS.
YOUR DAD WILL BE BACK IN THREE DAYS.
I'LL BE BACK NEXT WEEK.
WE'RE LEAVING THE HOUSE IN YOUR HANDS.
HE'S GONNA SEE HIS MISTRESS AND YOU KNOW IT YOU'RE JUST PRETENDING
NO PROBLEM.
YOU CAN COUNT ON ME.

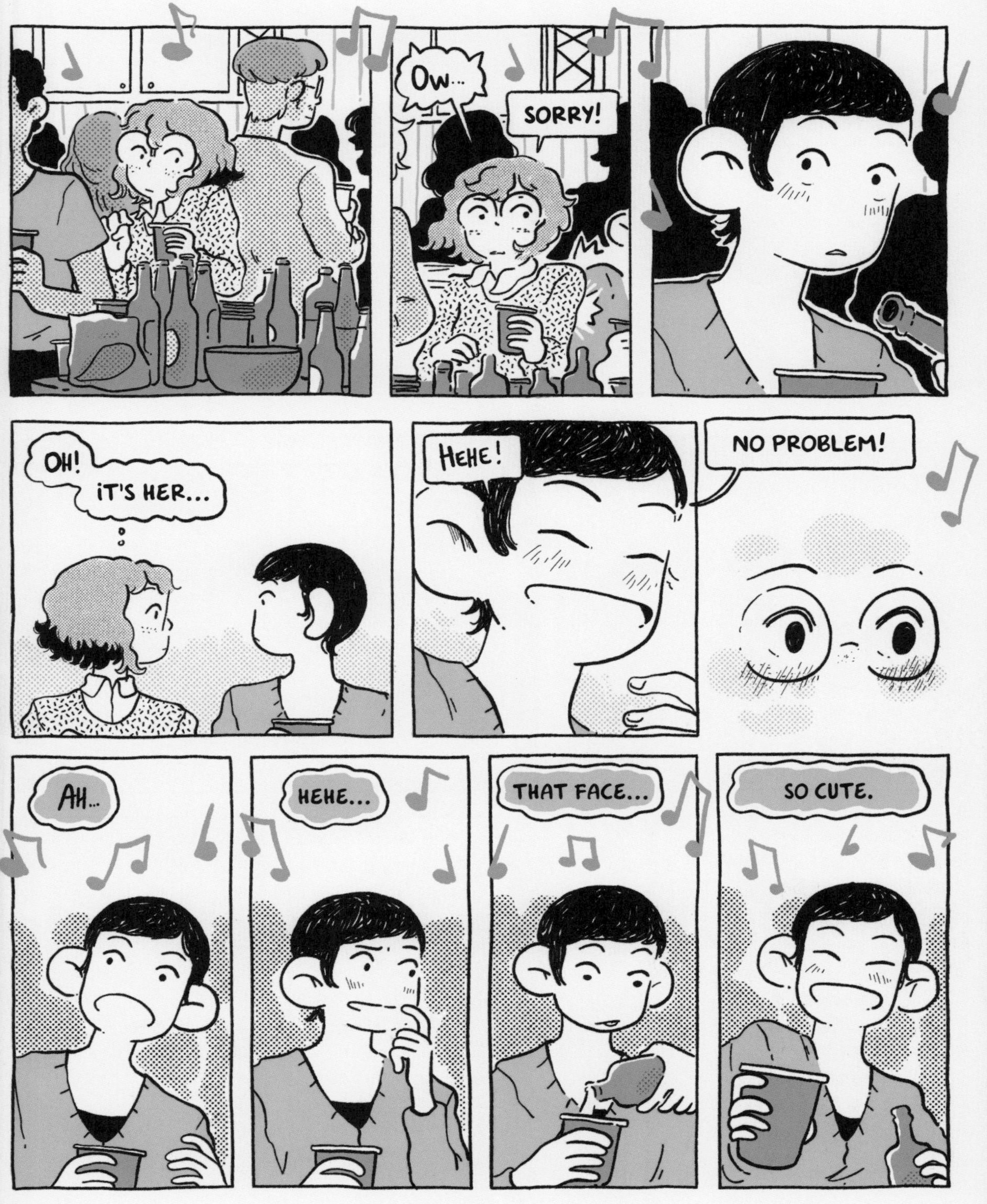

Ow...
SORRY!
OH!
iT'S HER...
HEHE!
NO PROBLEM!
AH...
HEHE...
THAT FACE...
SO CUTE.

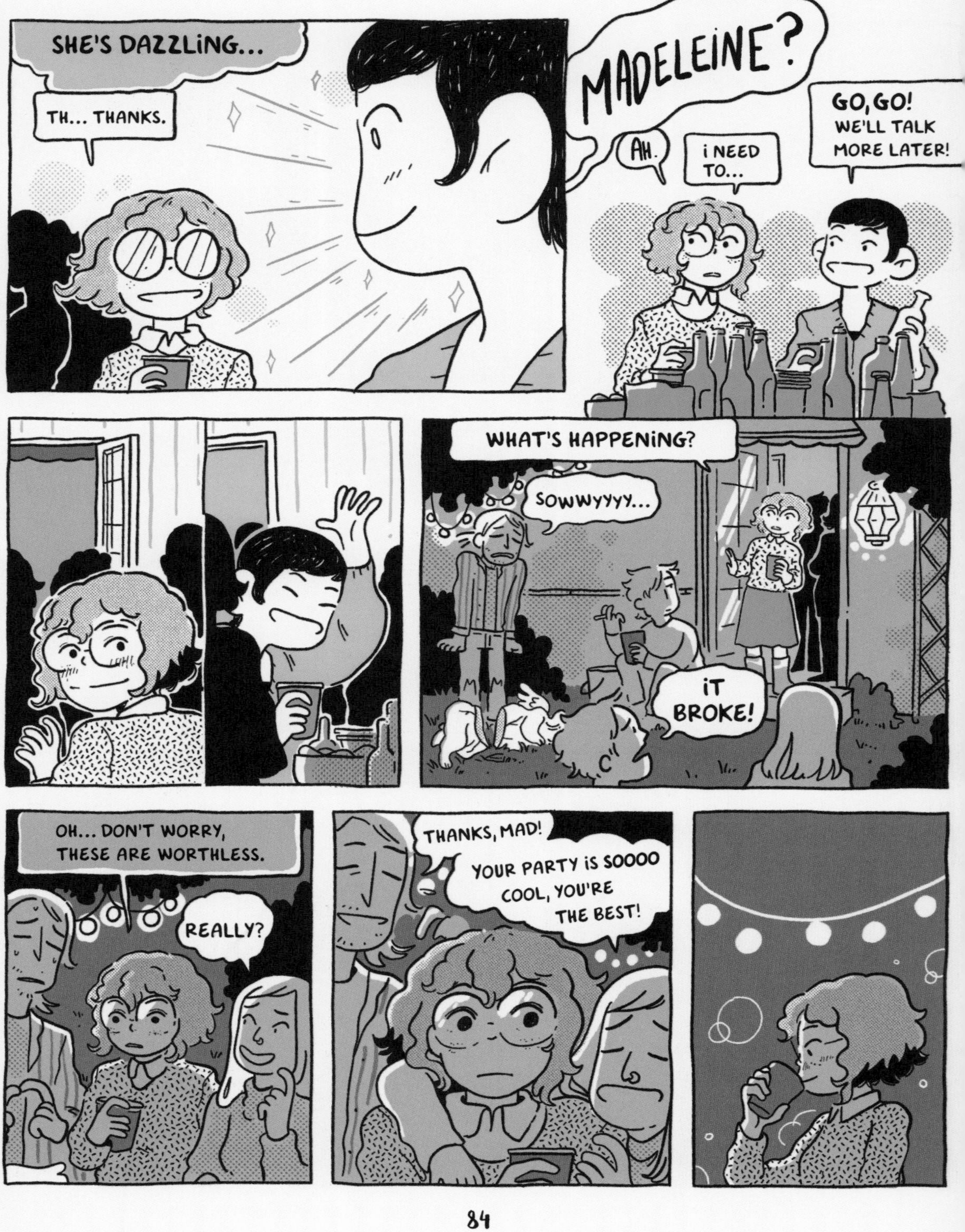
SHE'S DAZZLING...
TH... THANKS.
MADELEINE?
AH.
I NEED TO...
GO, GO! WE'LL TALK MORE LATER!
WHAT'S HAPPENING?
SOWWYYYY...
IT BROKE!
OH... DON'T WORRY, THESE ARE WORTHLESS.
REALLY?
THANKS, MAD!
YOUR PARTY IS SOOOO COOL, YOU'RE THE BEST!

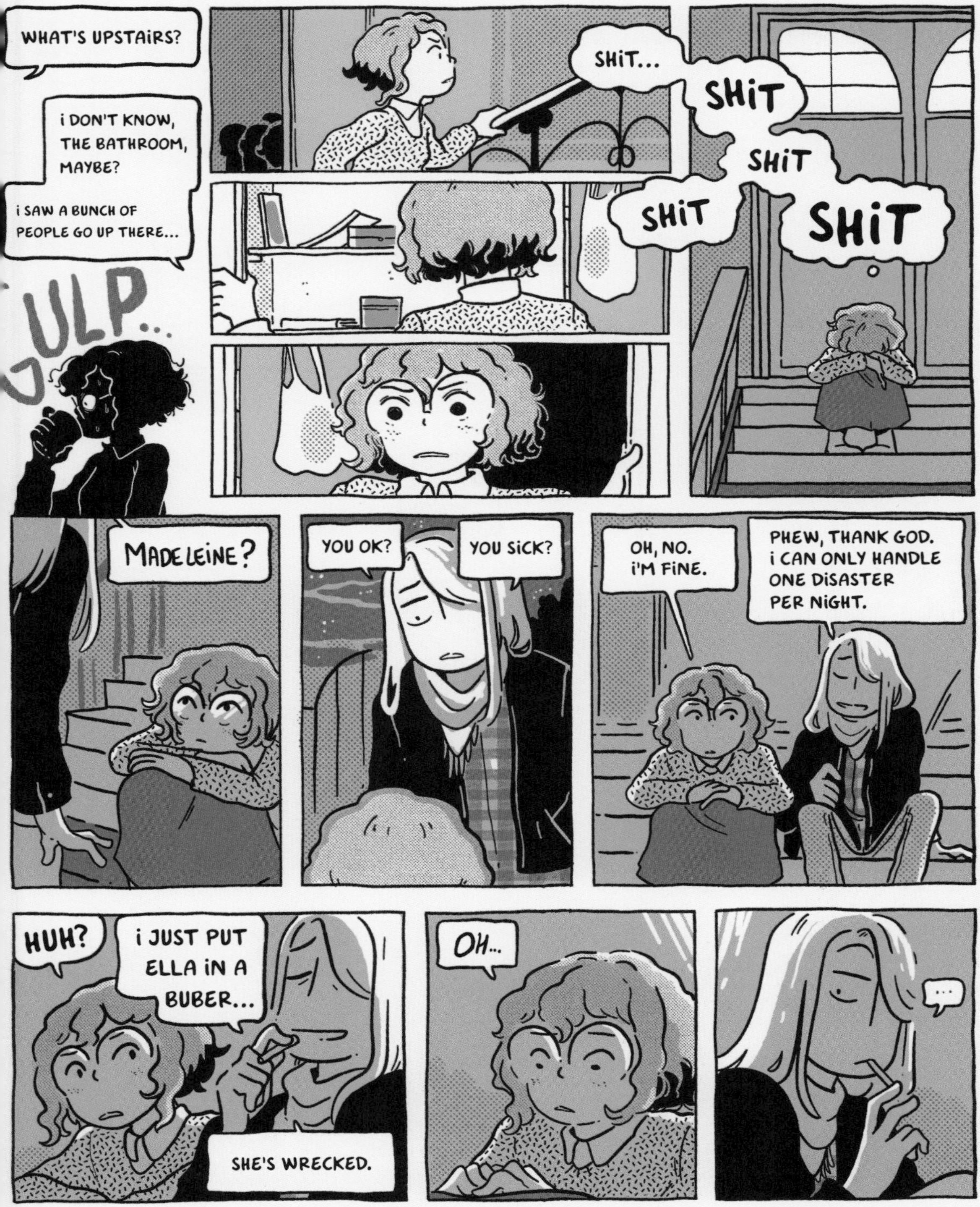
WHAT'S UPSTAIRS?
i DON'T KNOW, THE BATHROOM, MAYBE?
i SAW A BUNCH OF PEOPLE GO UP THERE...
GULP...
SHiT...
SHiT
SHiT
SHiT
SHiT
MADELEINE?
YOU OK?
YOU SiCK?
OH, NO. i'M FiNE.
PHEW, THANK GOD. i CAN ONLY HANDLE ONE DiSASTER PER NiGHT.
HUH?
i JUST PUT ELLA iN A BUBER...
SHE'S WRECKED.
OH...
...

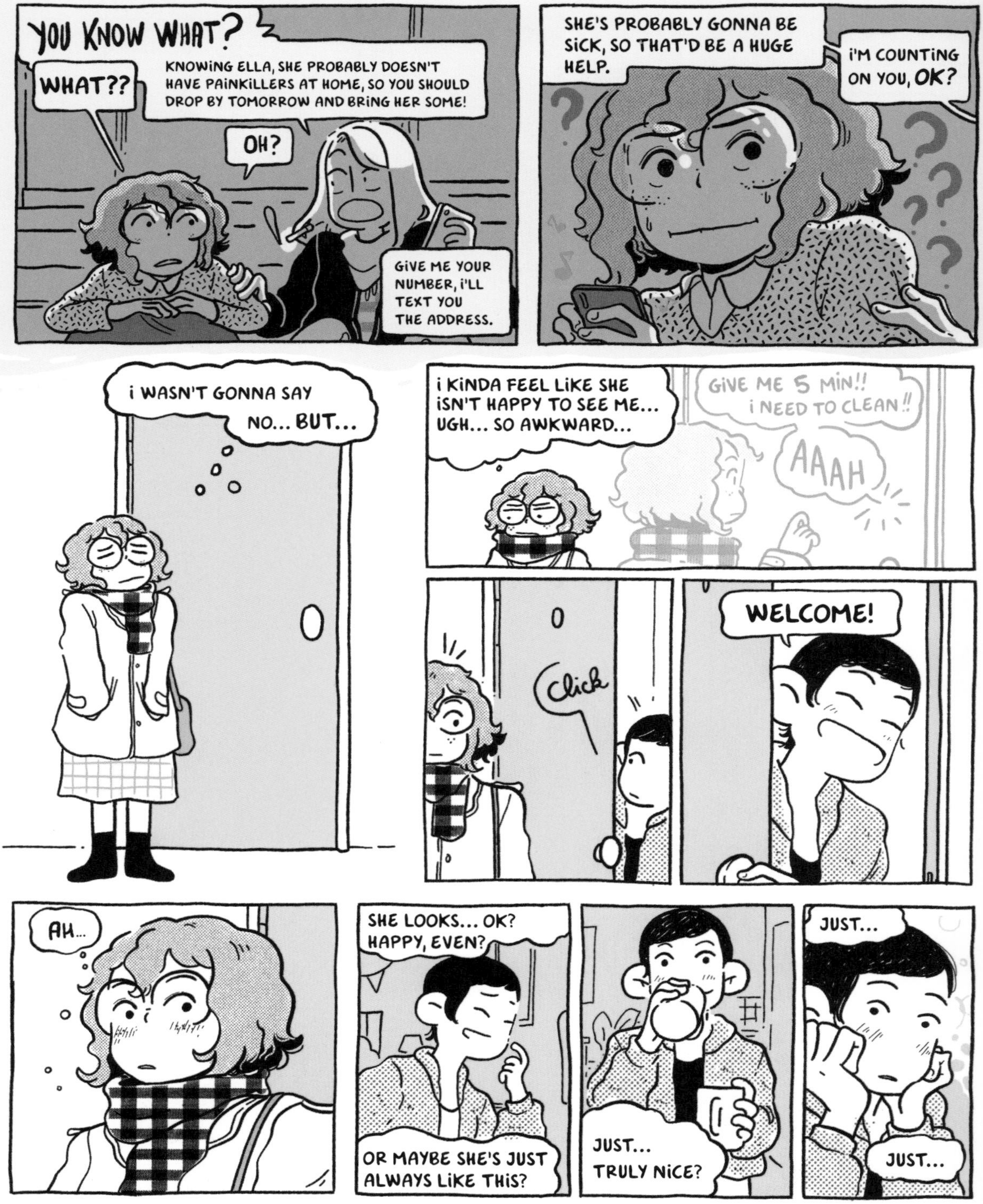
YOU KNOW WHAT?
WHAT??
KNOWING ELLA, SHE PROBABLY DOESN'T HAVE PAINKILLERS AT HOME, SO YOU SHOULD DROP BY TOMORROW AND BRING HER SOME!
OH?
GIVE ME YOUR NUMBER, I'LL TEXT YOU THE ADDRESS.
SHE'S PROBABLY GONNA BE SICK, SO THAT'D BE A HUGE HELP.
I'M COUNTING ON YOU, OK?
I WASN'T GONNA SAY NO... BUT...
I KINDA FEEL LIKE SHE ISN'T HAPPY TO SEE ME... UGH... SO AWKWARD...
GIVE ME 5 MIN!! I NEED TO CLEAN!!
AAAH
Click
WELCOME!
AH...
SHE LOOKS... OK? HAPPY, EVEN?
OR MAYBE SHE'S JUST ALWAYS LIKE THIS?
JUST... TRULY NICE?
JUST...
JUST...

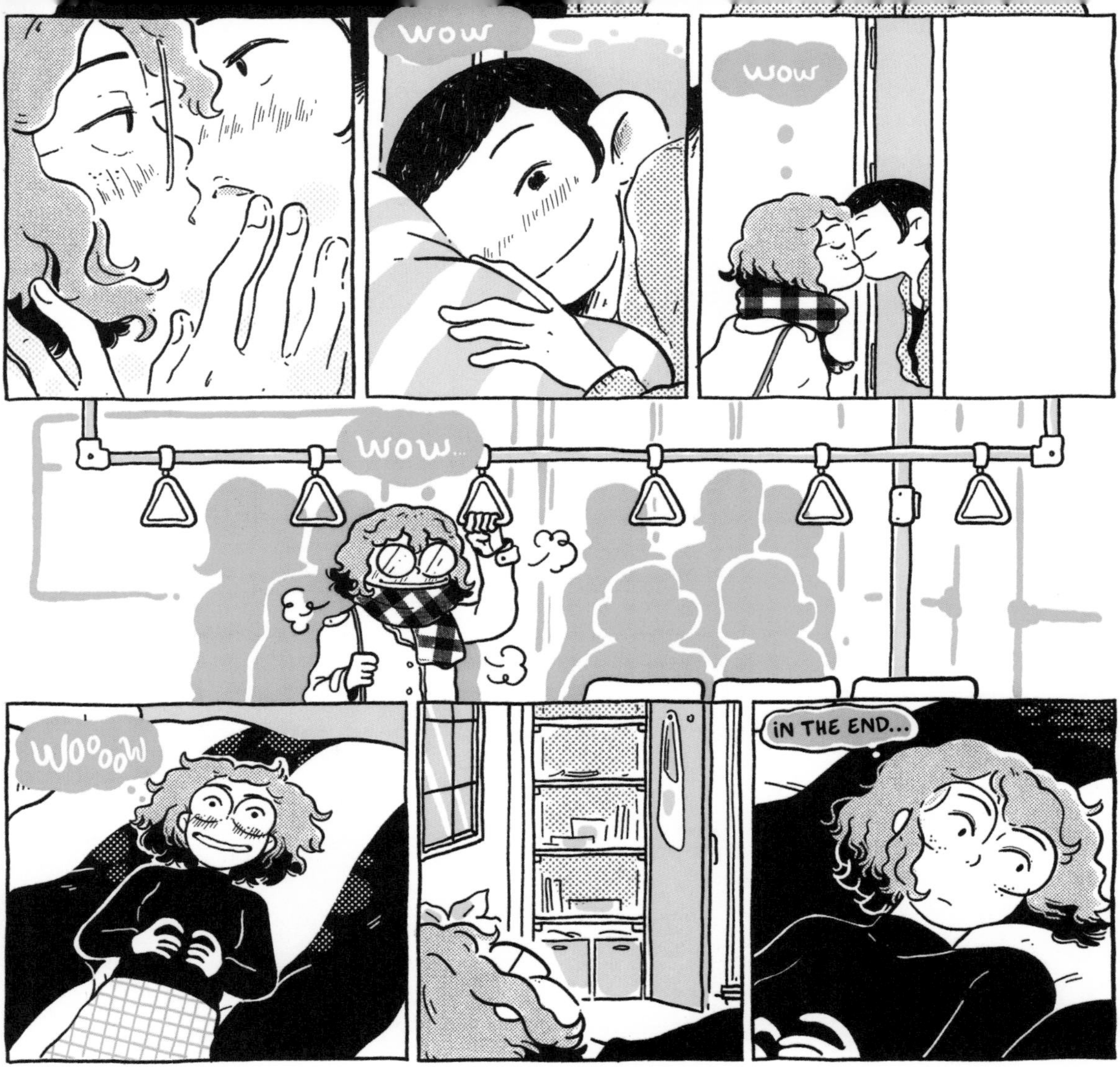
WOW
WOW
WOW...
WOoooW
IN THE END...

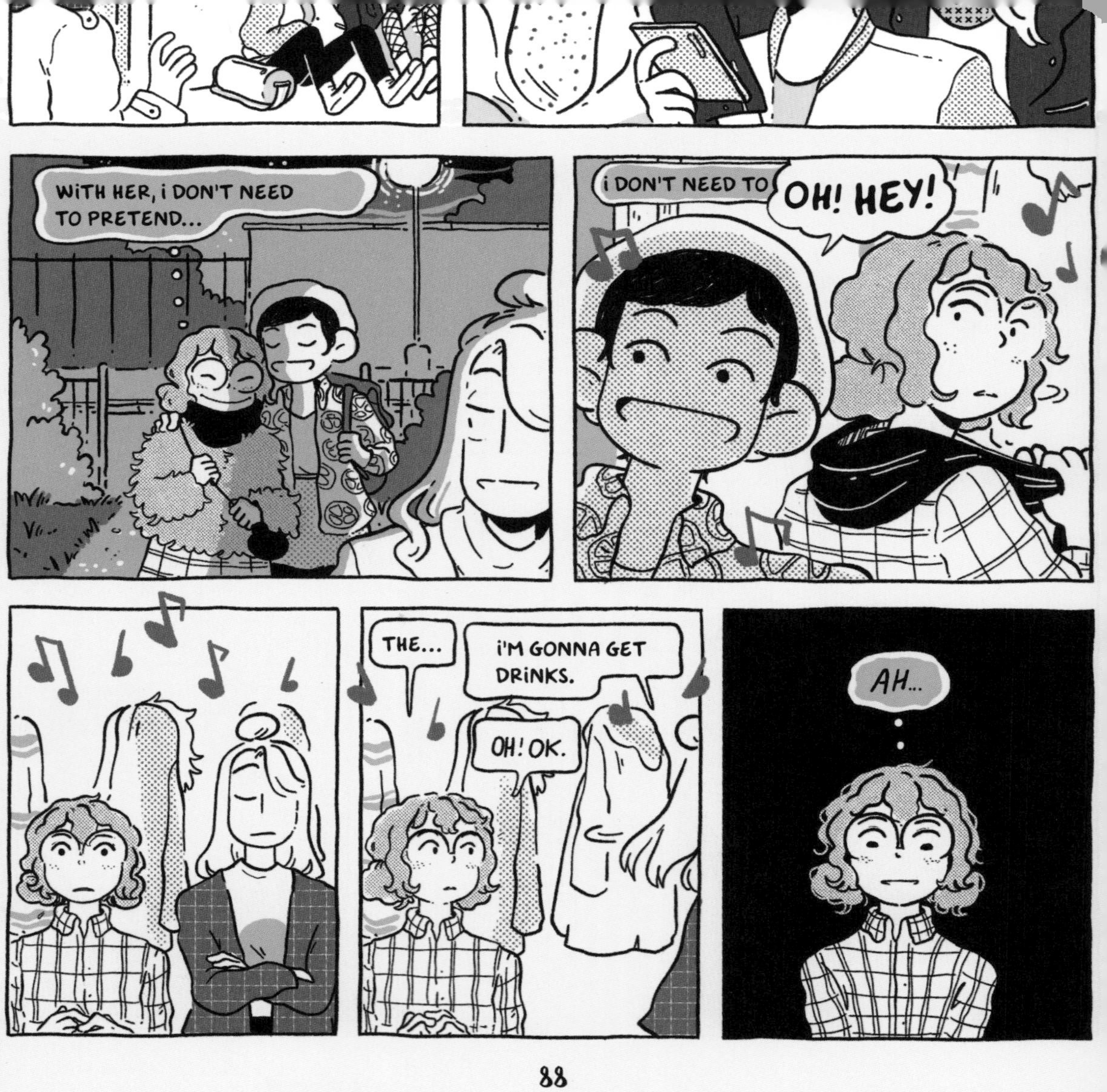
WITH HER, I DON'T NEED TO PRETEND...
I DON'T NEED TO
OH! HEY!
THE...
I'M GONNA GET DRINKS.
OH! OK.
AH...

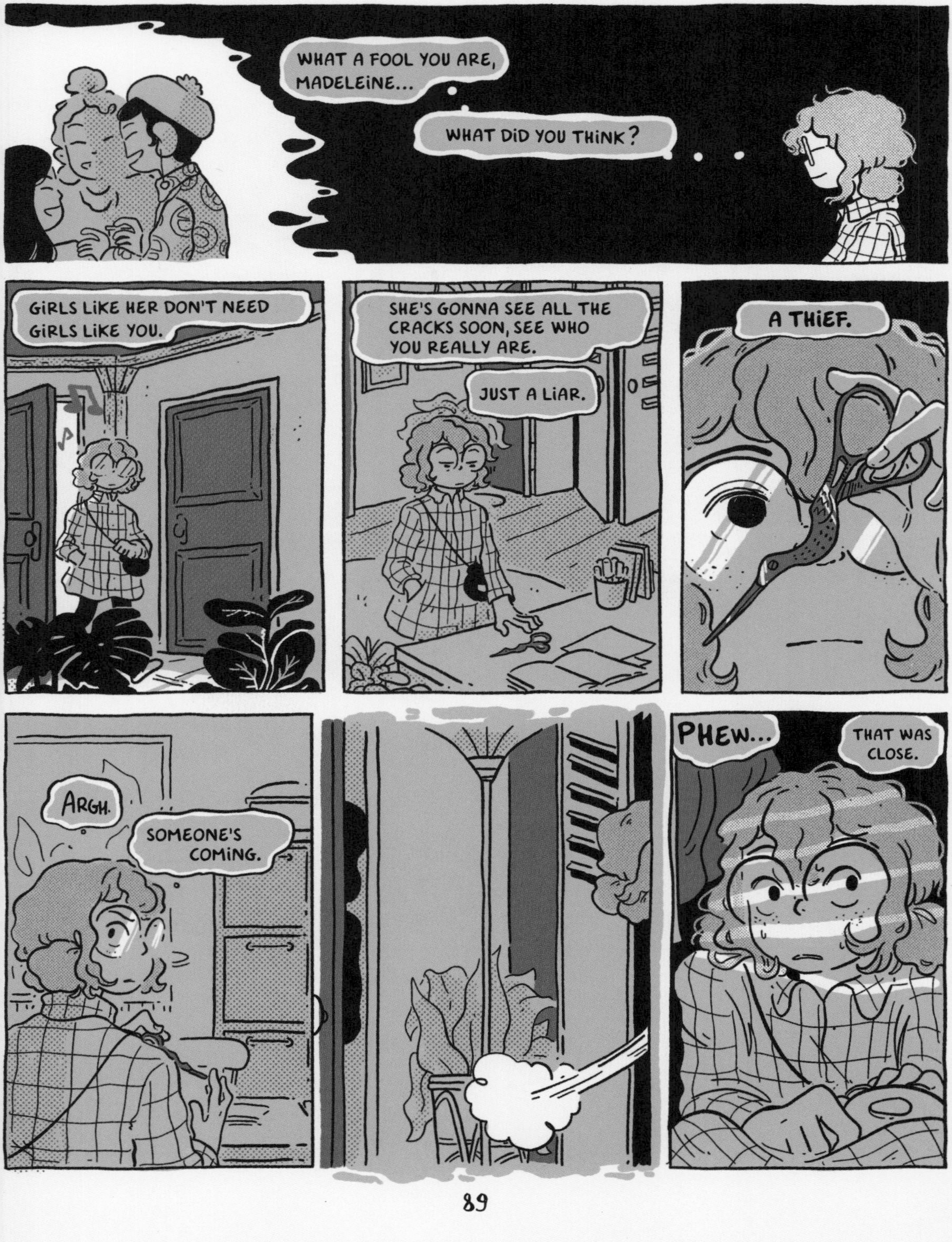
WHAT A FOOL YOU ARE, MADELEINE...
WHAT DID YOU THINK?
GIRLS LIKE HER DON'T NEED GIRLS LIKE YOU.
SHE'S GONNA SEE ALL THE CRACKS SOON, SEE WHO YOU REALLY ARE.
JUST A LIAR.
A THIEF.
ARGH.
SOMEONE'S COMING.
PHEW...
THAT WAS CLOSE.

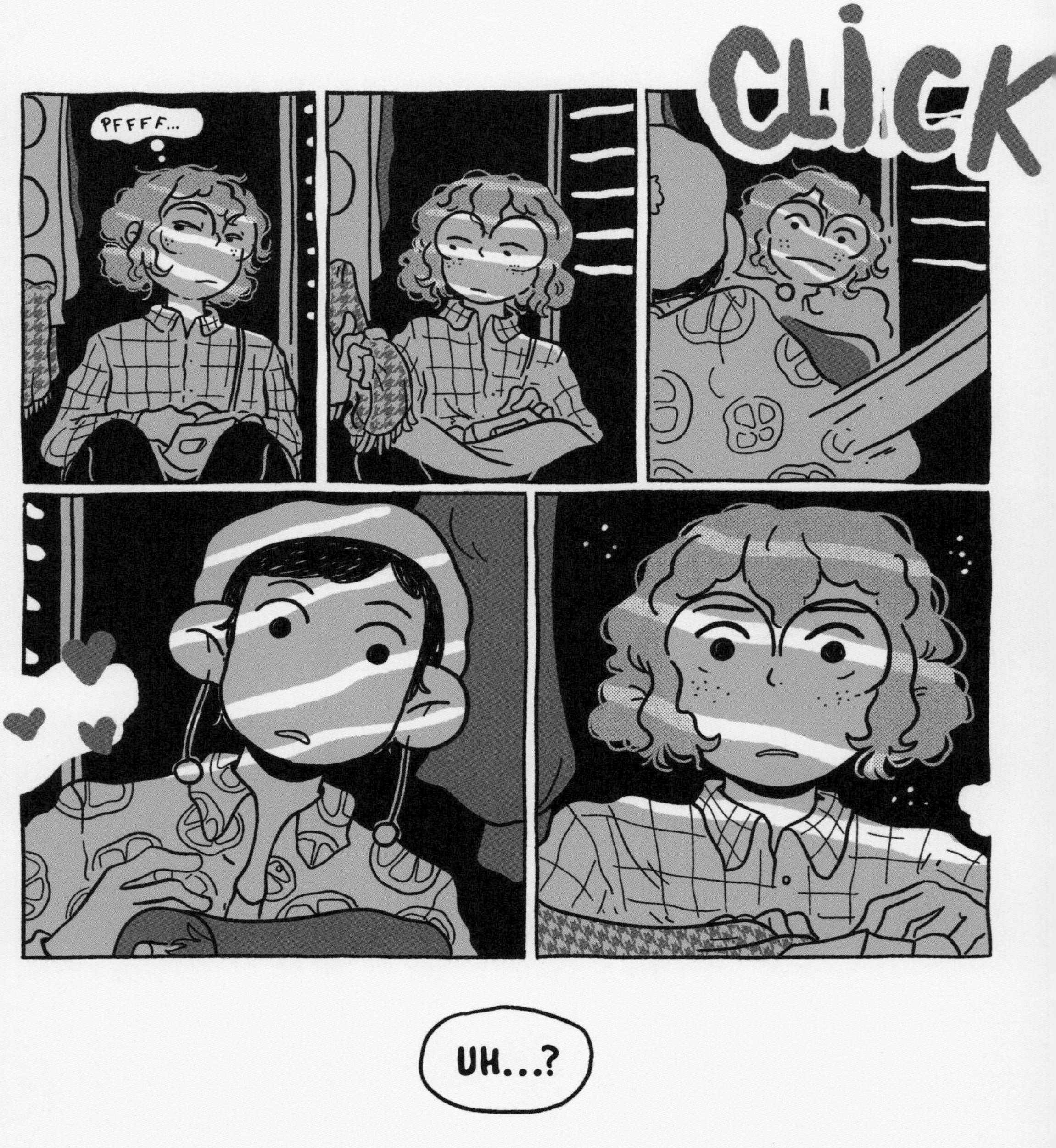
PFFFF...
CLICK
UH...?

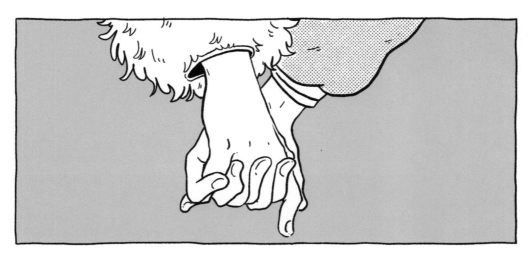

3

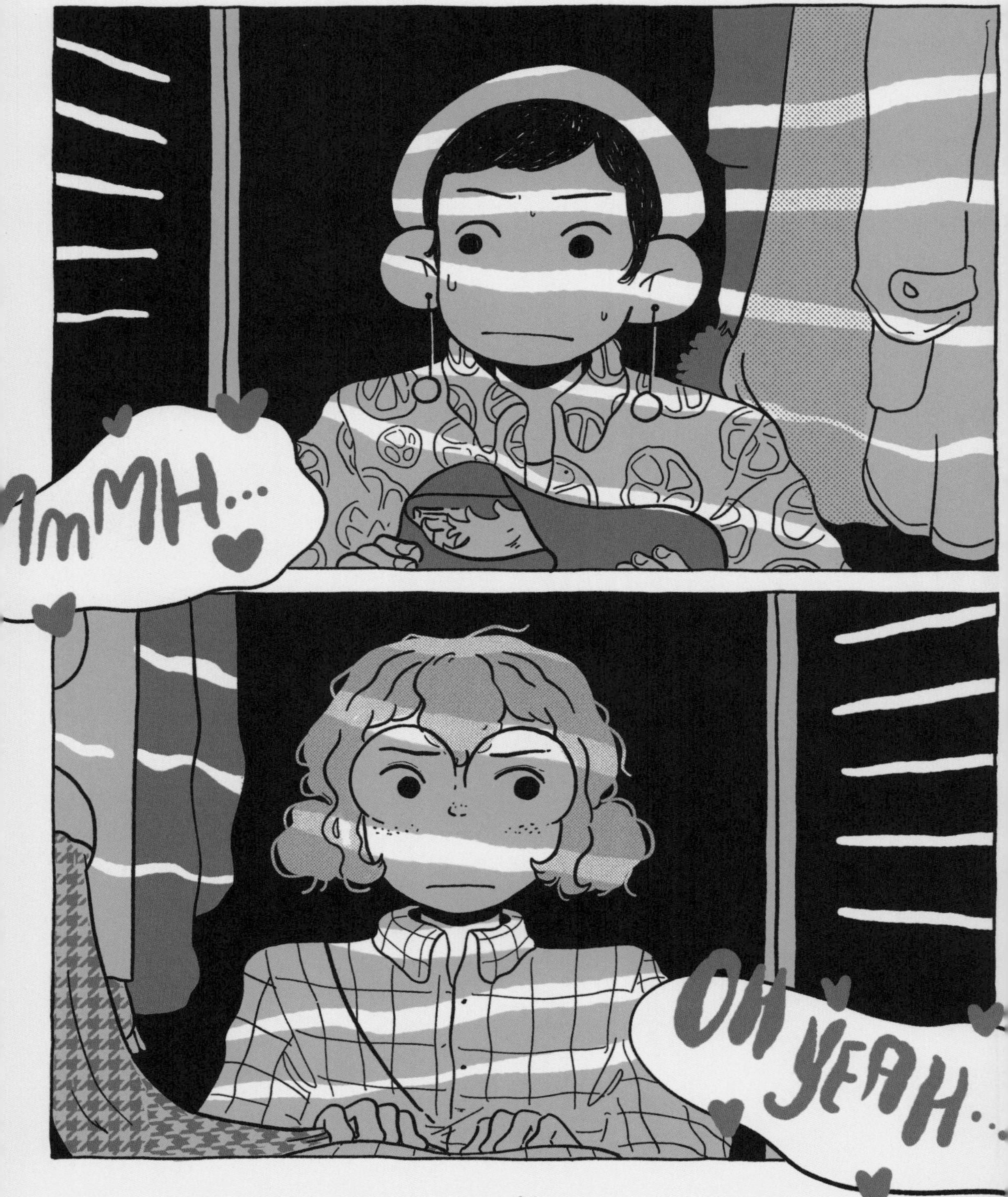
MMMH...
OH YEAH...

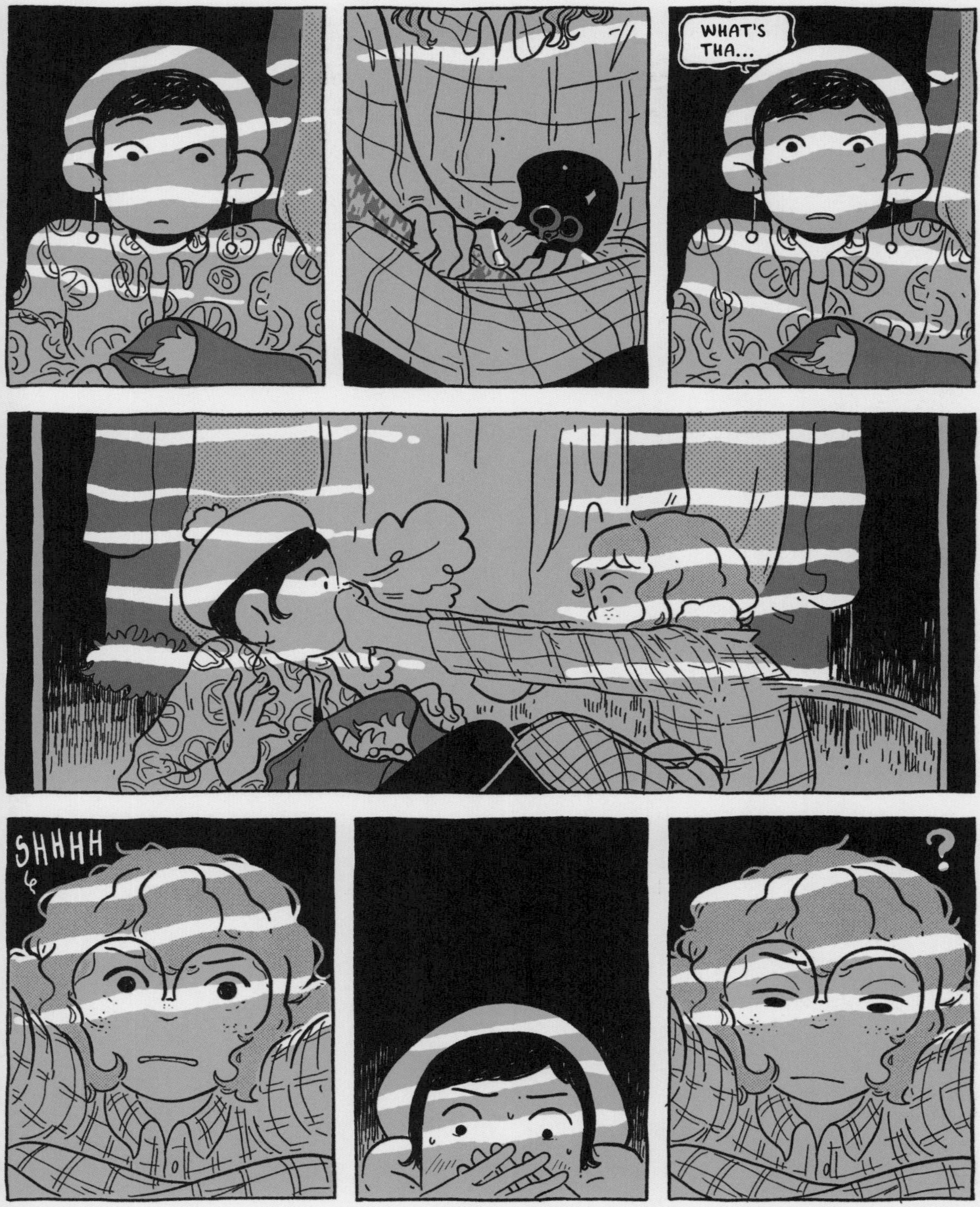
WHAT'S THA...
SHHHH
?

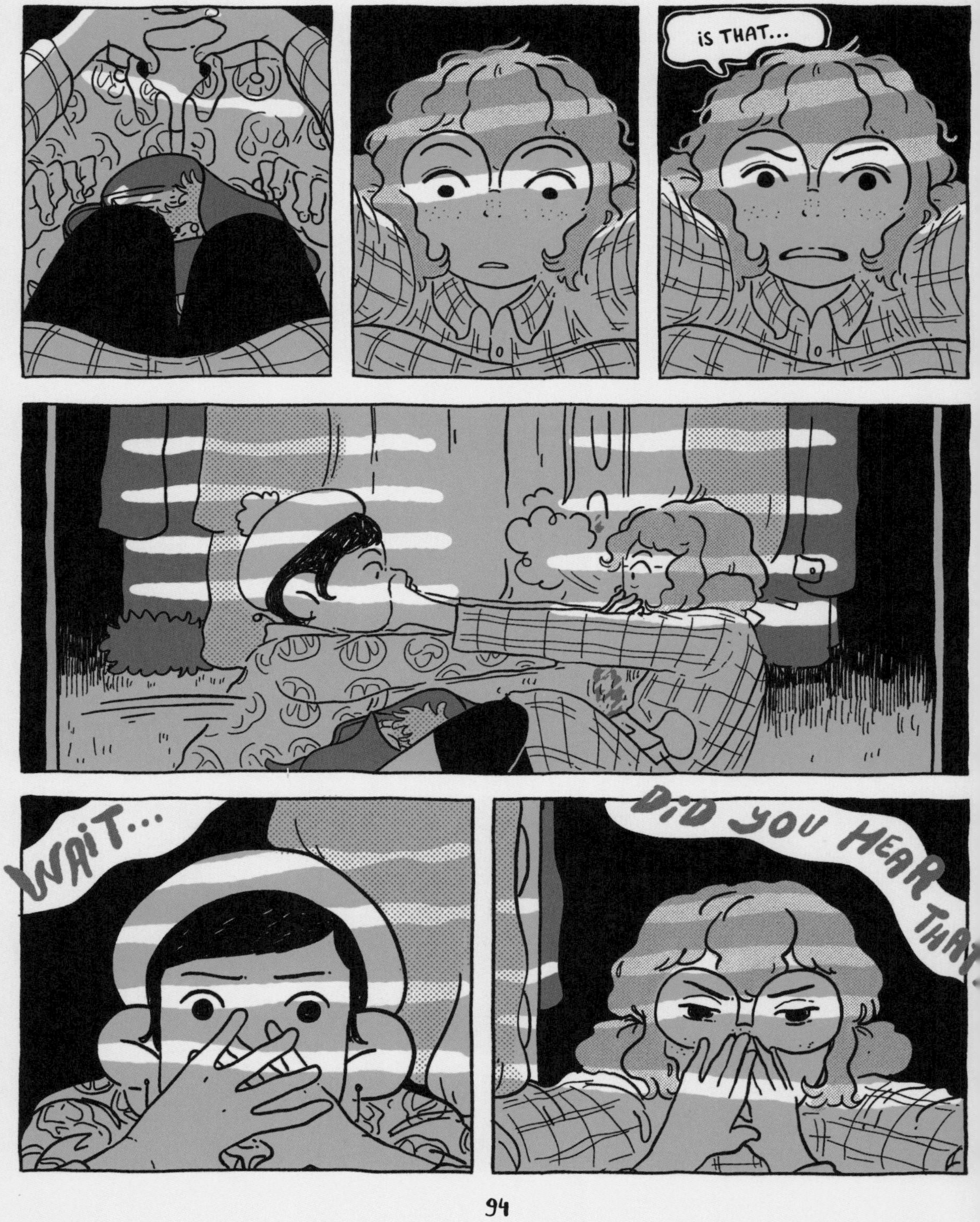
IS THAT...
WAIT...
DID YOU HEAR THAT

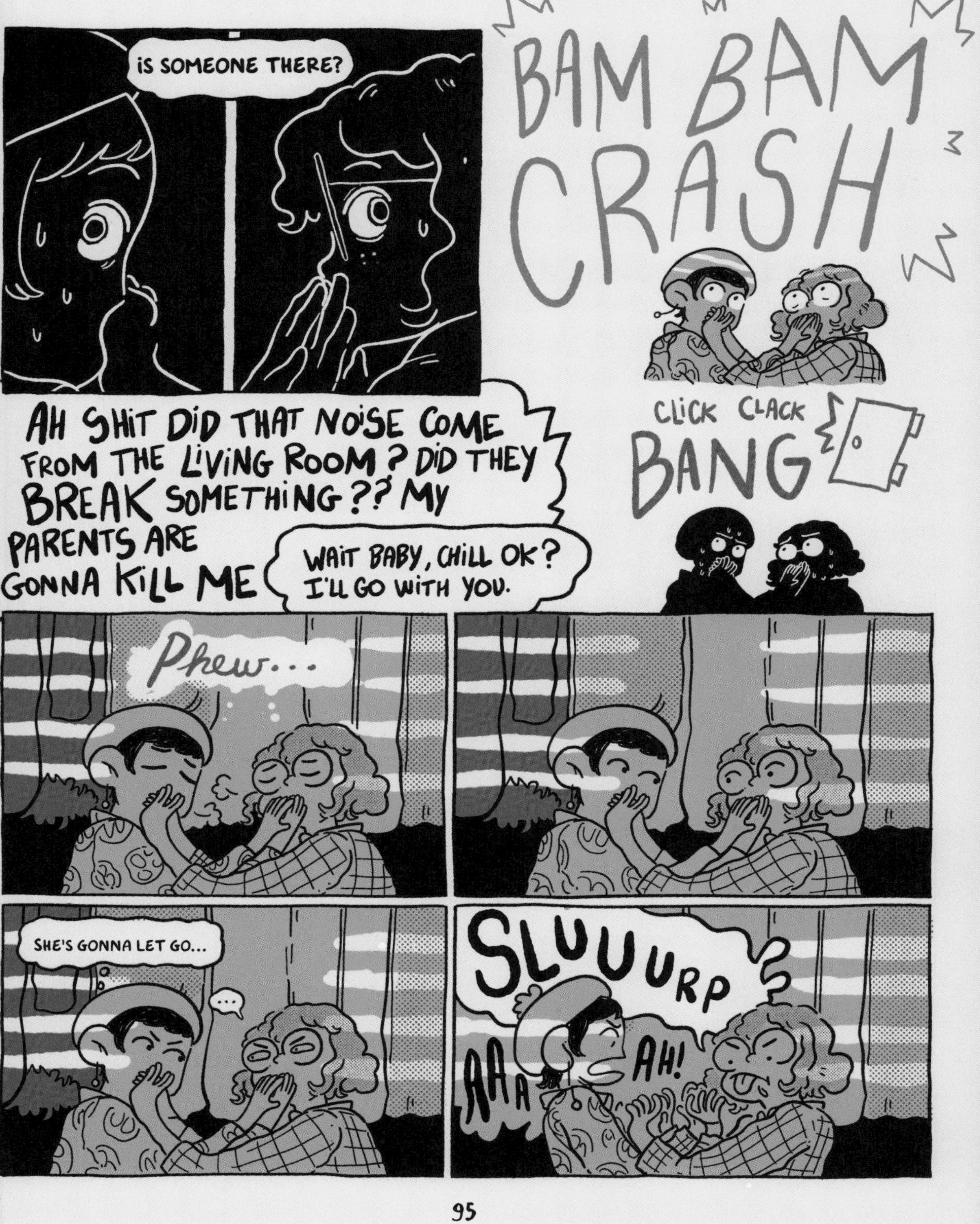
IS SOMEONE THERE?
BAM BAM
CRASH
AH SHIT DID THAT NOISE COME FROM THE LIVING ROOM? DID THEY BREAK SOMETHING?? MY PARENTS ARE GONNA KILL ME
WAIT BABY, CHILL OK? I'LL GO WITH YOU.
CLICK CLACK
BANG
Phew...
SHE'S GONNA LET GO...
...
SLUUUURP
AAA
AH!

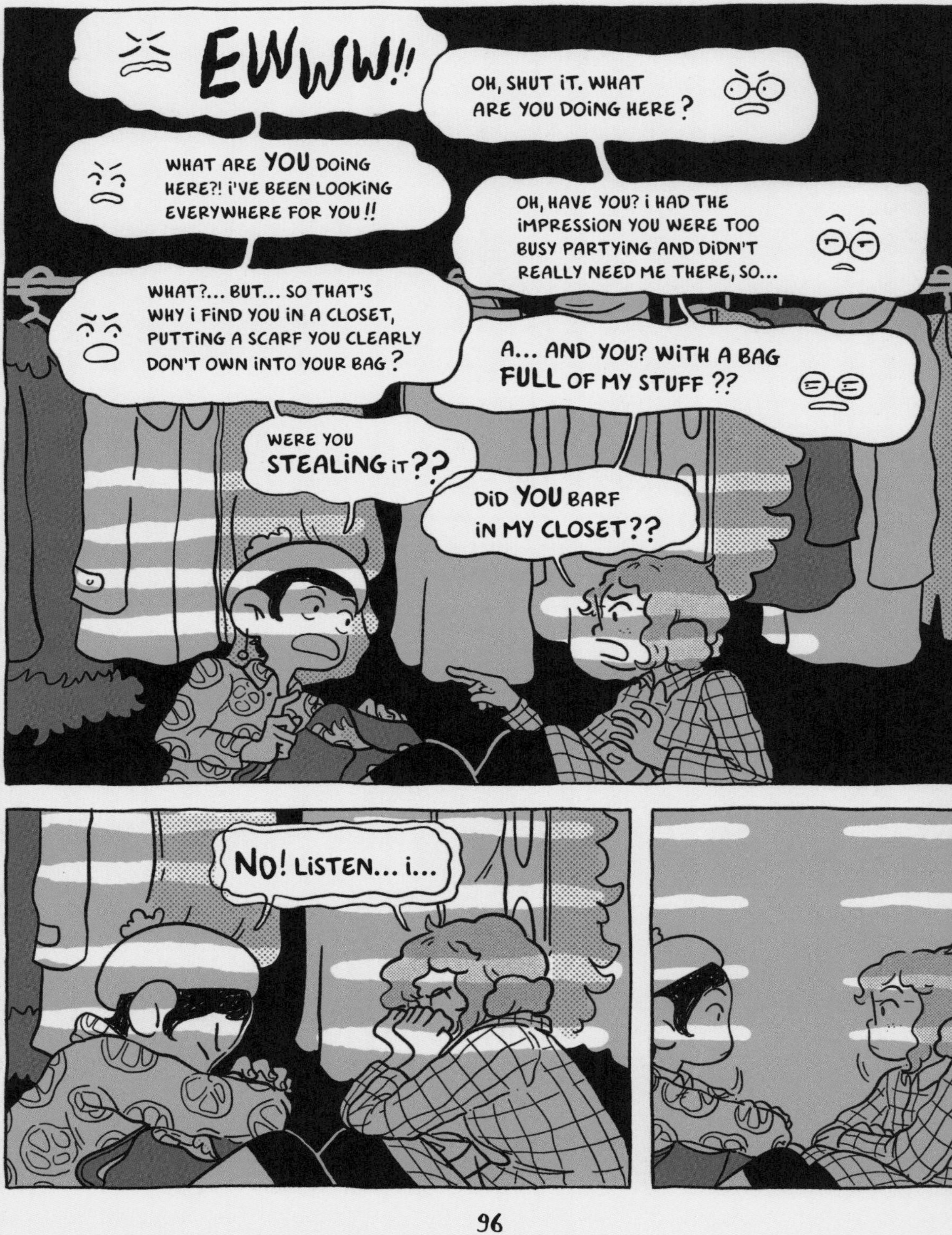
EWWW!!
OH, SHUT IT. WHAT ARE YOU DOING HERE?
WHAT ARE YOU DOING HERE?! I'VE BEEN LOOKING EVERYWHERE FOR YOU!!
OH, HAVE YOU? I HAD THE IMPRESSION YOU WERE TOO BUSY PARTYING AND DIDN'T REALLY NEED ME THERE, SO...
WHAT?... BUT... SO THAT'S WHY I FIND YOU IN A CLOSET, PUTTING A SCARF YOU CLEARLY DON'T OWN INTO YOUR BAG?
A... AND YOU? WITH A BAG FULL OF MY STUFF??
WERE YOU STEALING IT??
DID YOU BARF IN MY CLOSET??
NO! LISTEN... I...

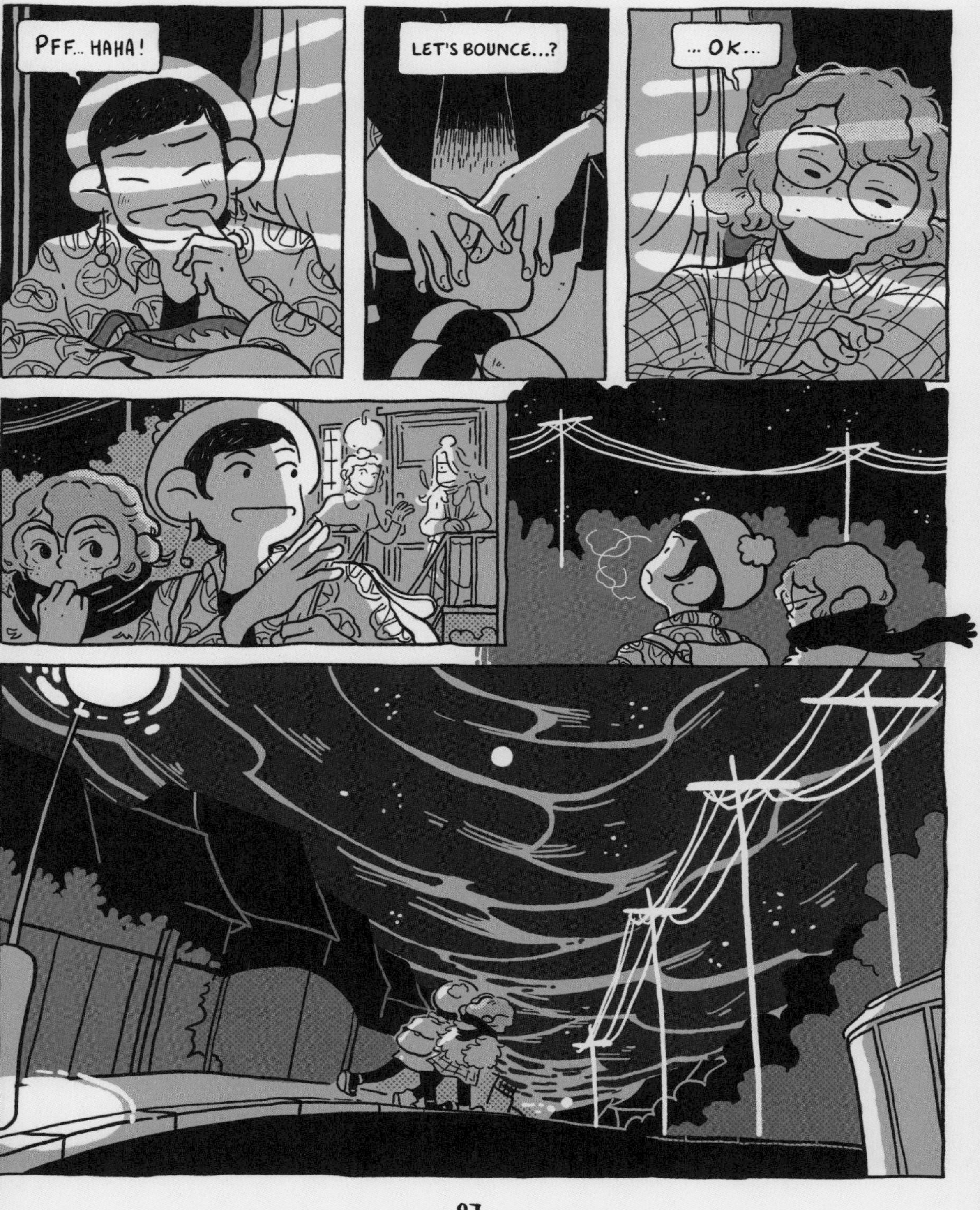
PFF... HAHA!
LET'S BOUNCE...?
... OK...

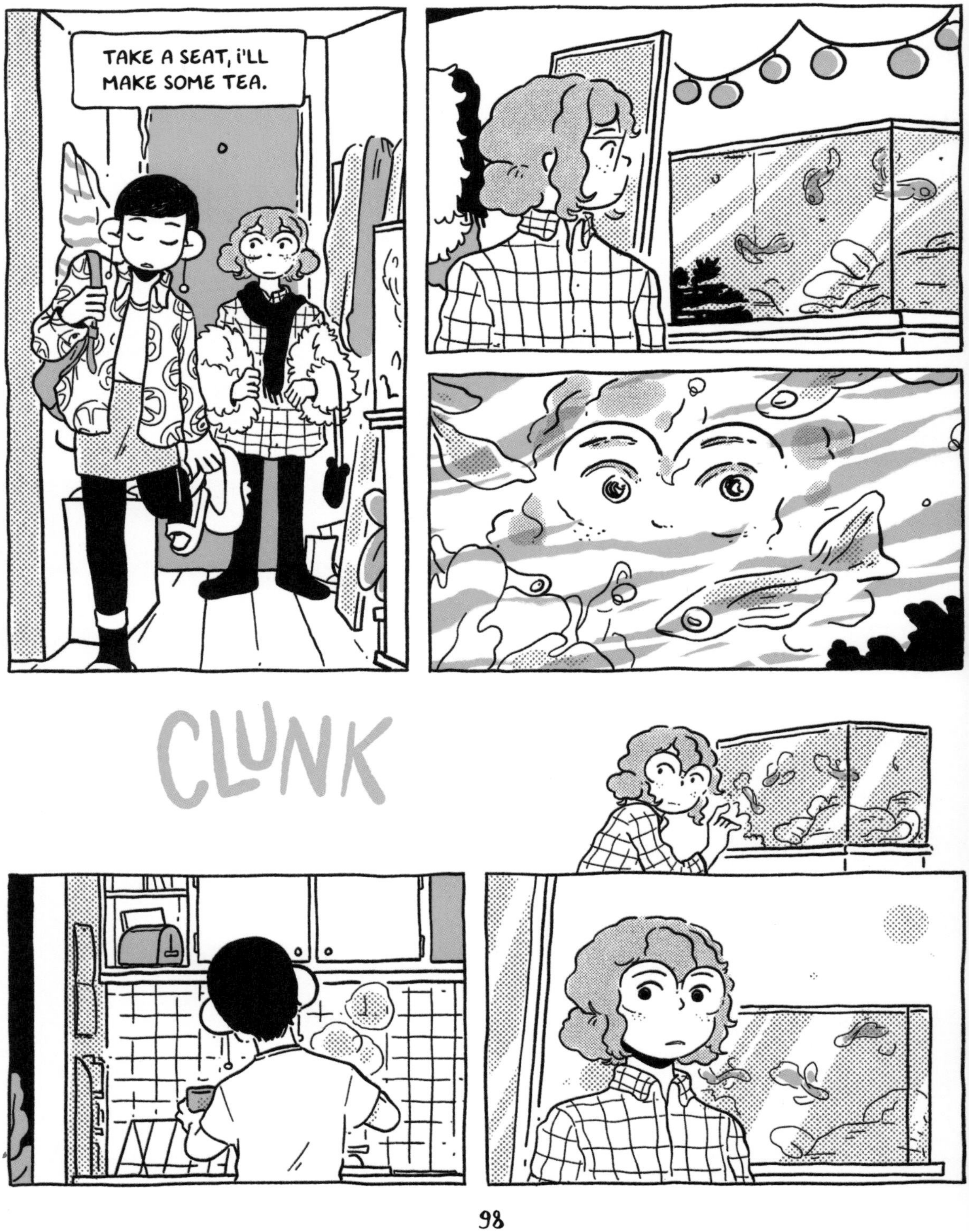
TAKE A SEAT, I'LL MAKE SOME TEA.
CLUNK

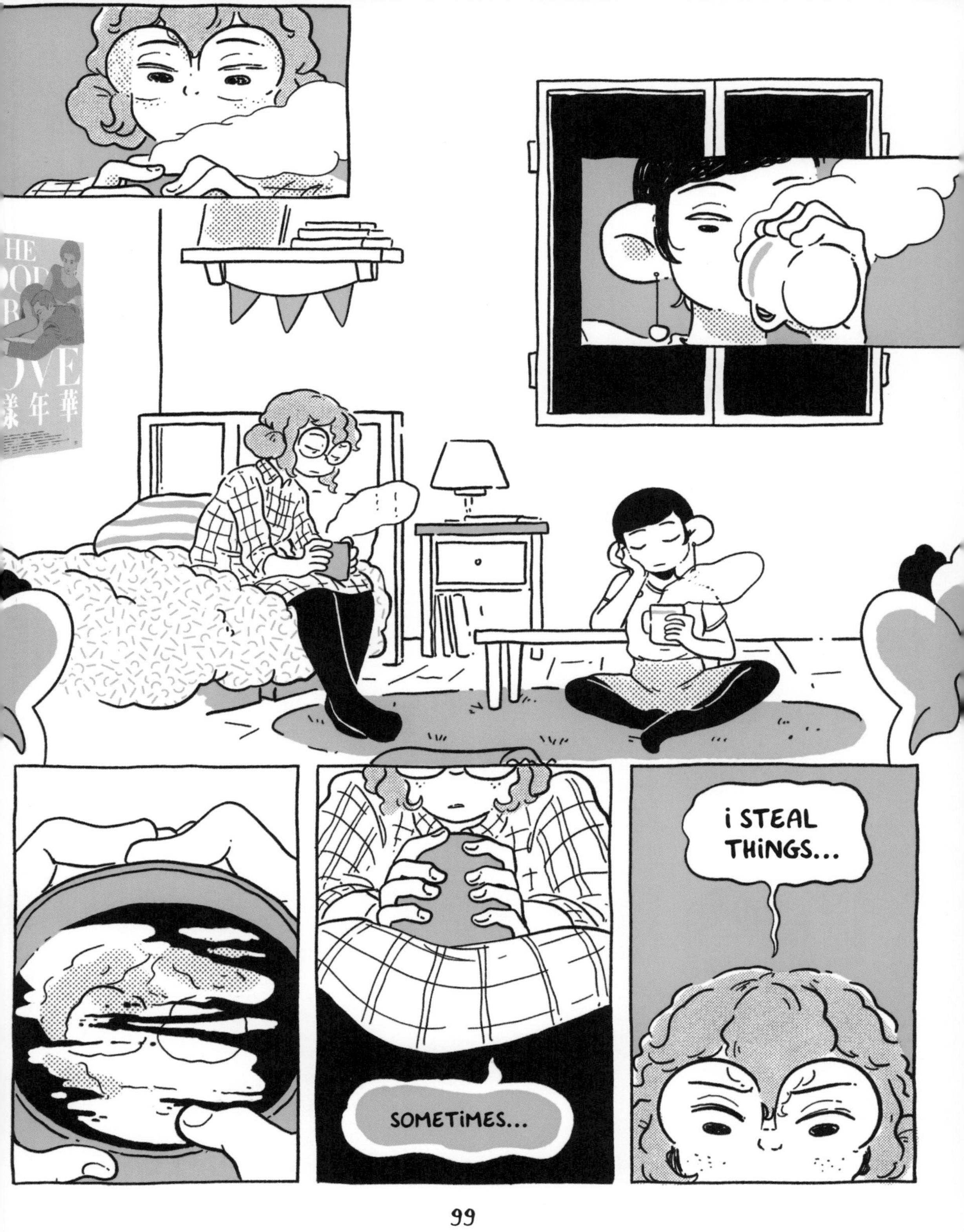
SOMETiMES...
i STEAL THiNGS...

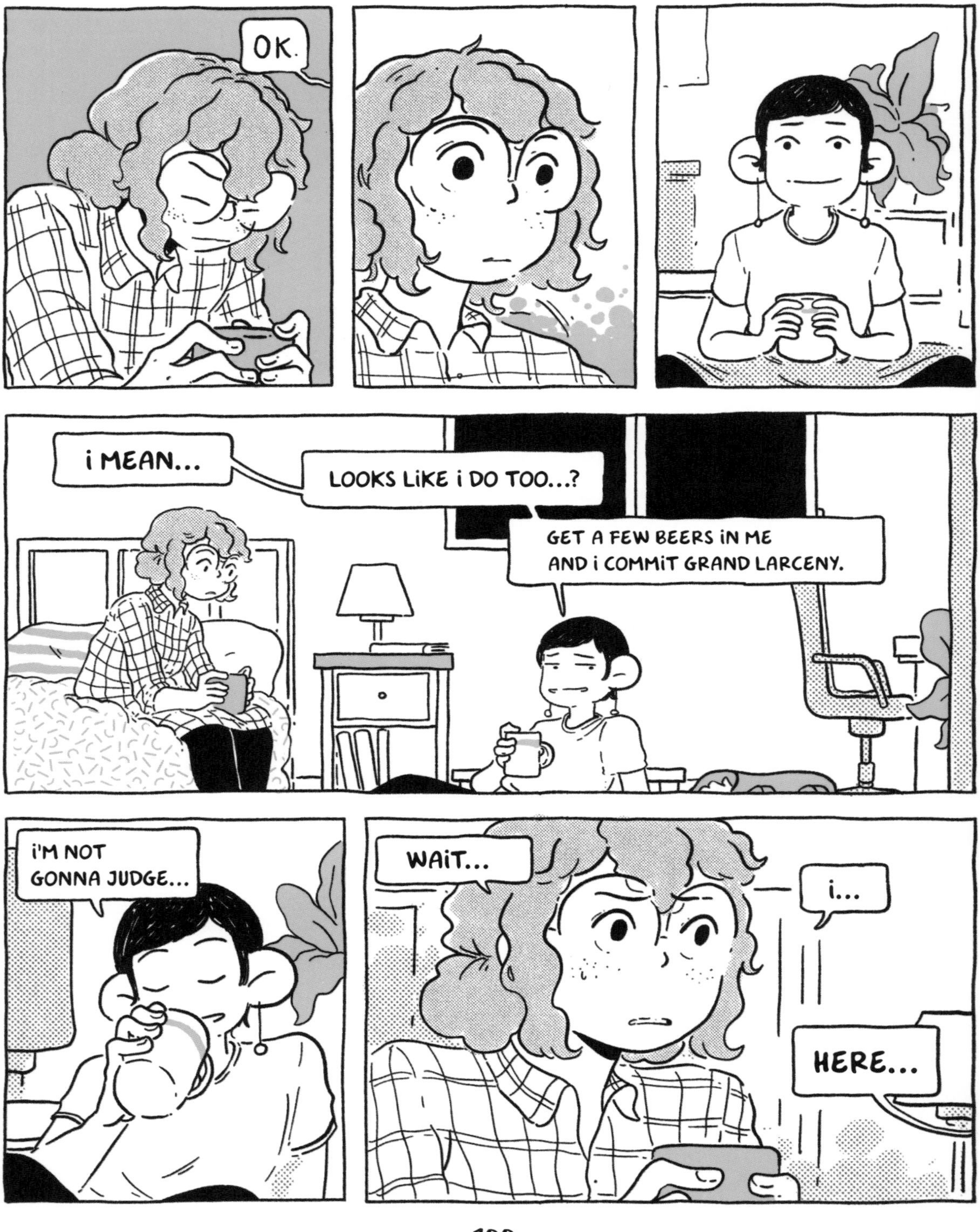
OK.
i MEAN...
LOOKS LiKE i DO TOO...?
GET A FEW BEERS iN ME AND i COMMiT GRAND LARCENY.
i'M NOT GONNA JUDGE...
WAiT...
i...
HERE...

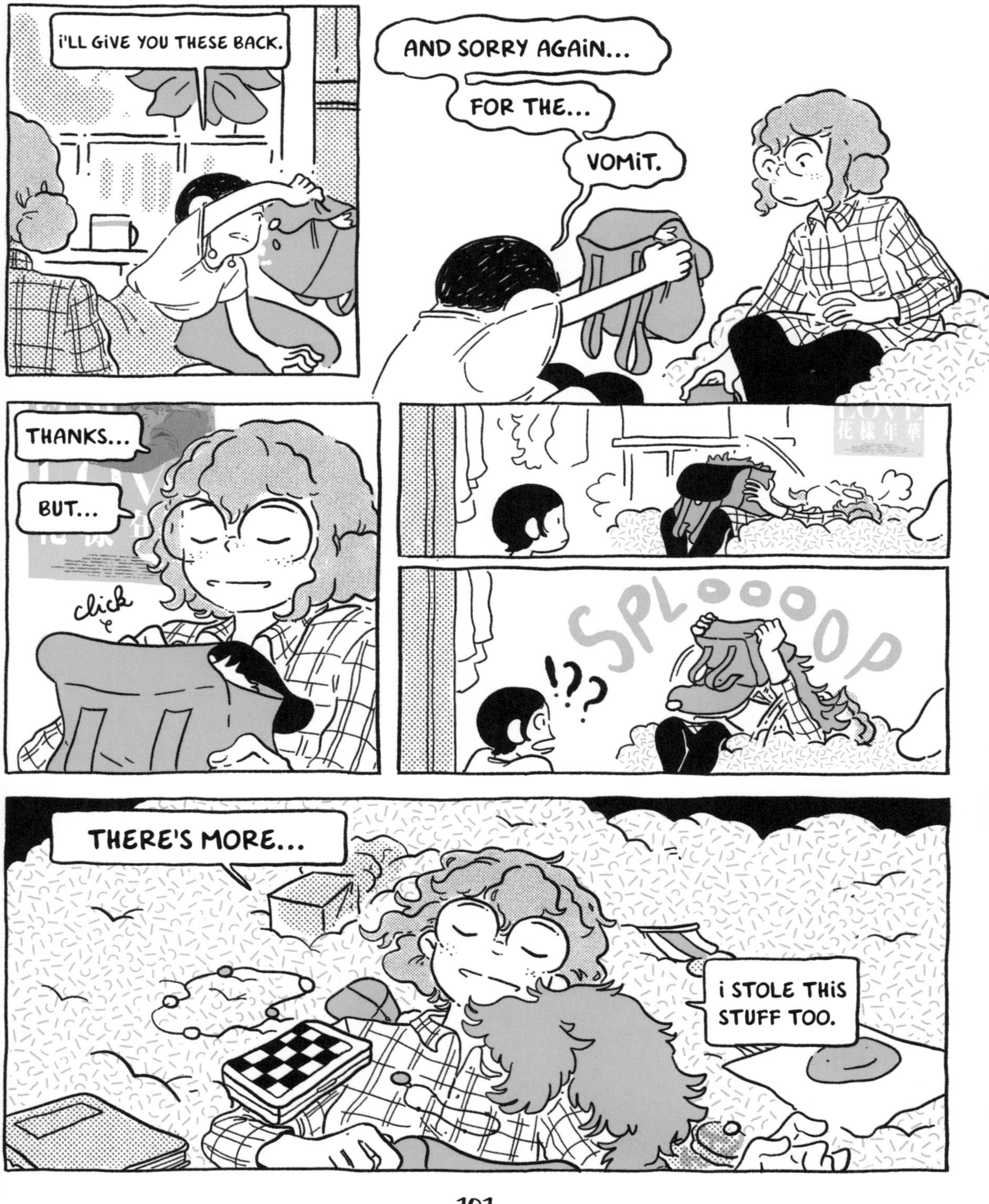
i'LL GiVE YOU THESE BACK.
AND SORRY AGAiN...
FOR THE...
VOMiT.
THANKS...
BUT...
click
LOVE
花樣年華
!??
SPLOOOOOP
THERE'S MORE...
i STOLE THiS STUFF TOO.

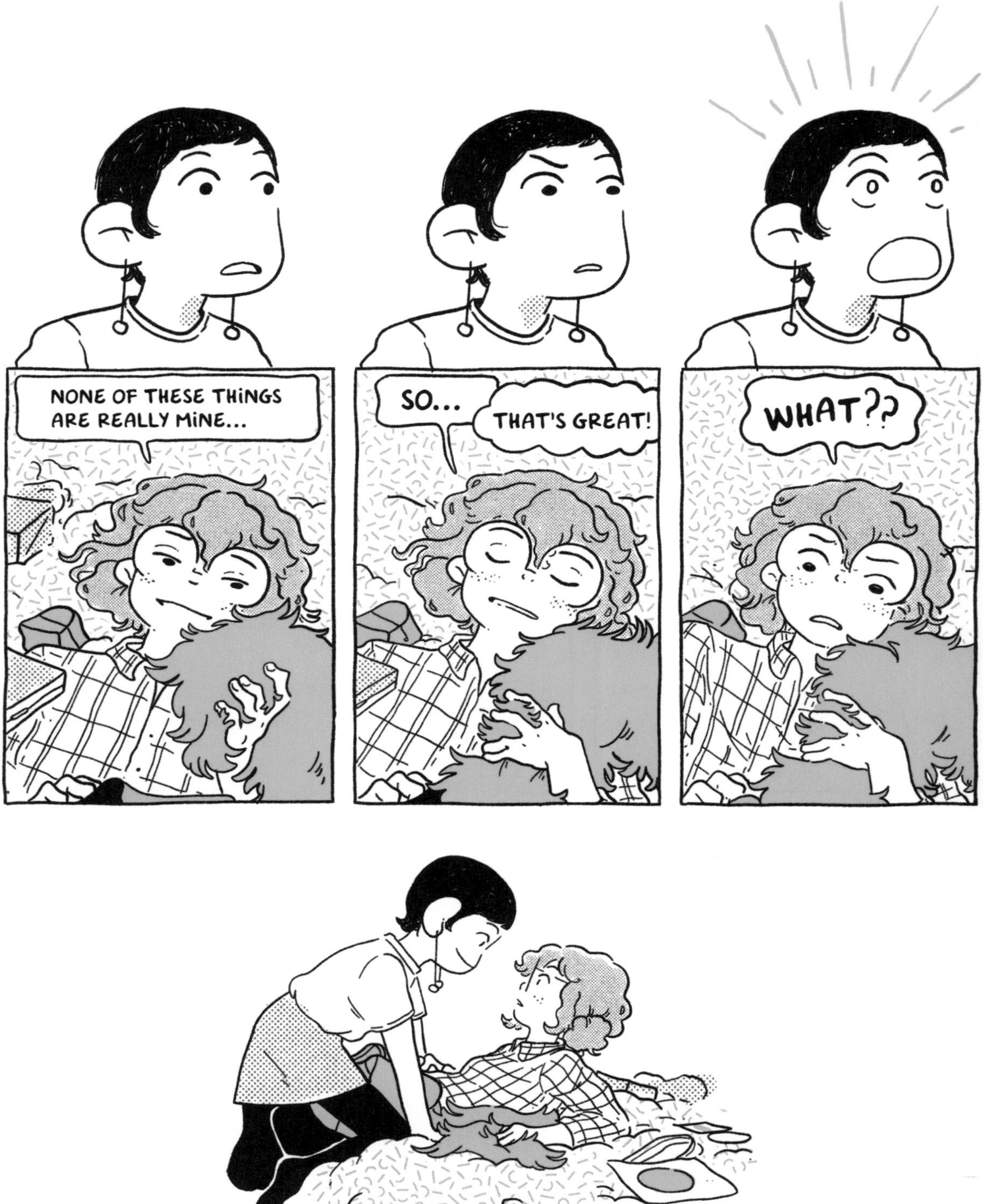
NONE OF THESE THiNGS ARE REALLY MiNE...
SO...
THAT'S GREAT!
WHAT??

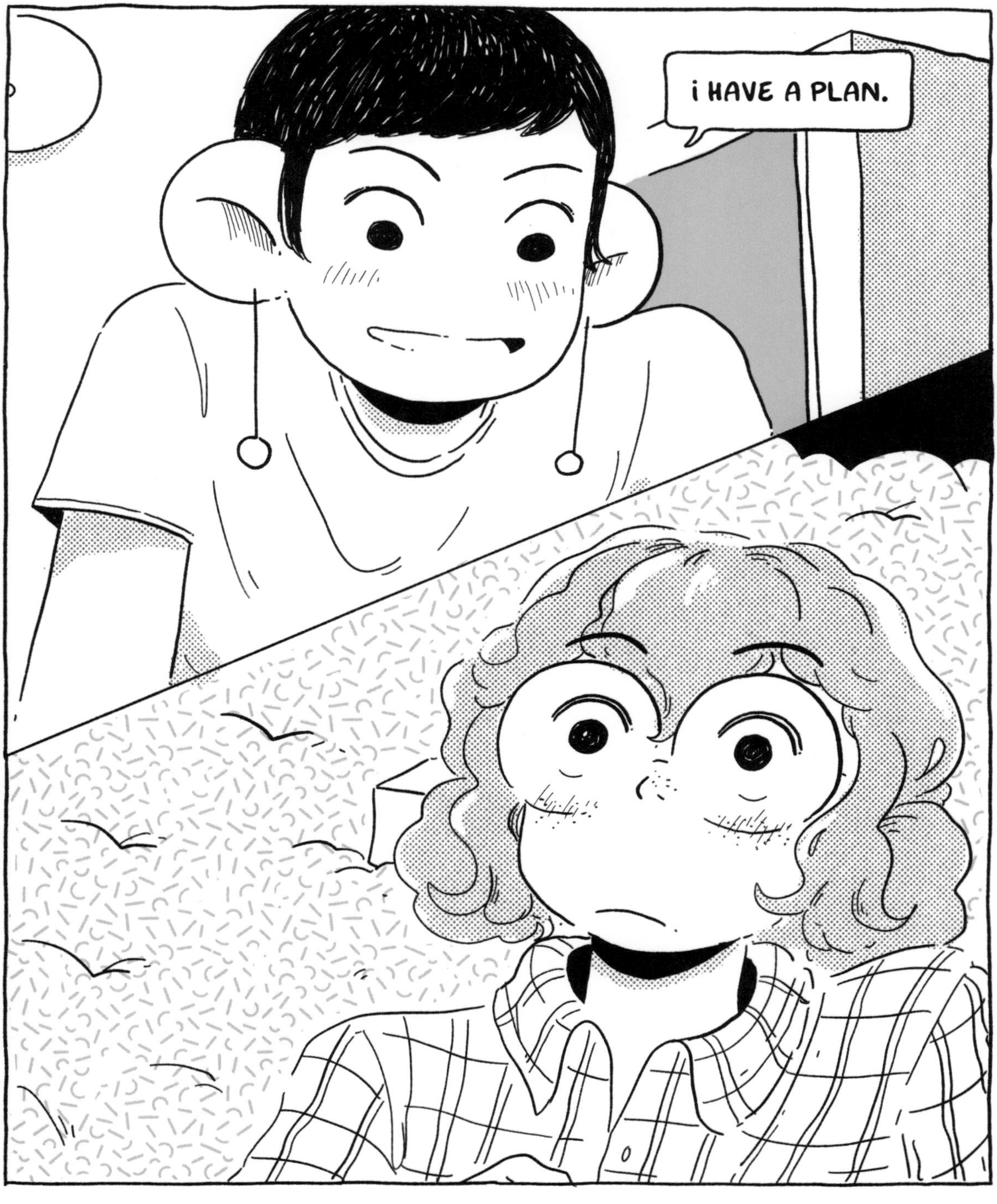
i HAVE A PLAN.

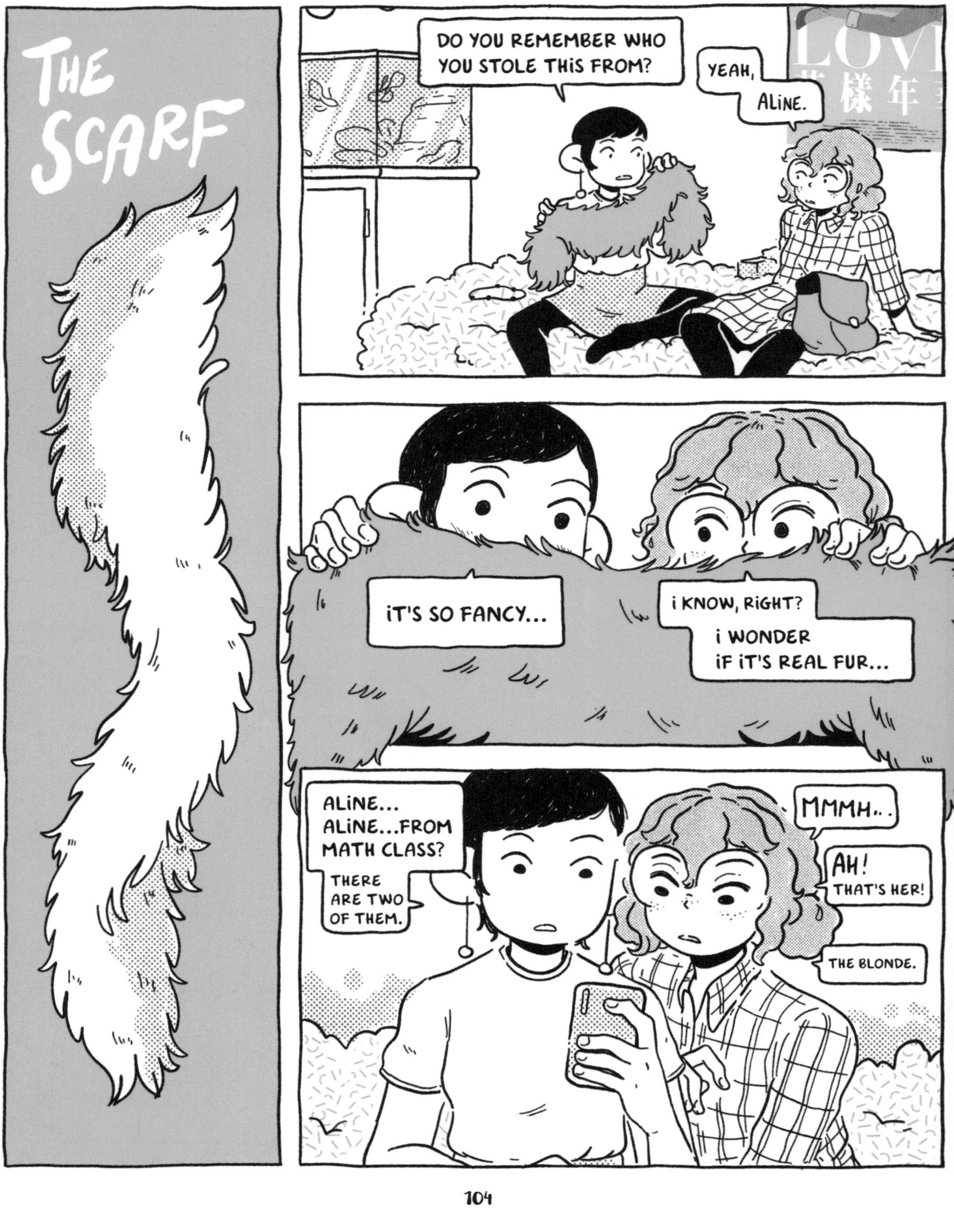
THE SCARF
DO YOU REMEMBER WHO YOU STOLE THIS FROM?
YEAH, ALINE.
IT'S SO FANCY...
I KNOW, RIGHT? I WONDER IF IT'S REAL FUR...
ALINE... ALINE...FROM MATH CLASS?
THERE ARE TWO OF THEM.
MMMH...
AH! THAT'S HER!
THE BLONDE.

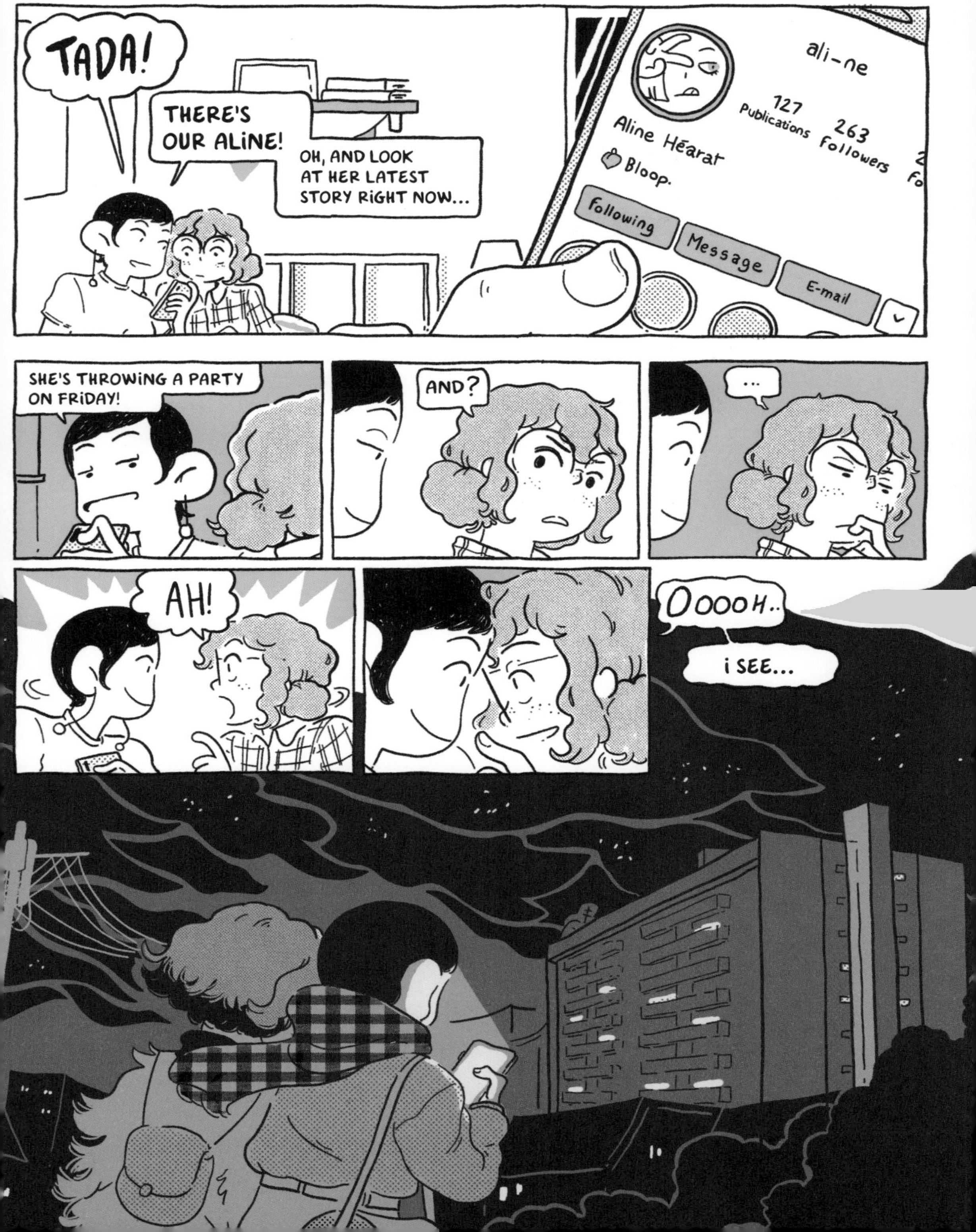
TADA!
THERE'S OUR ALiNE!
OH, AND LOOK AT HER LATEST STORY RiGHT NOW...
ali-ne
127 Publications
263 Followers
Aline Hēarat
Bloop.
Following
Message
E-mail
SHE'S THROWiNG A PARTY ON FRiDAY!
AND?
...
AH!
Ooooh..
i SEE...

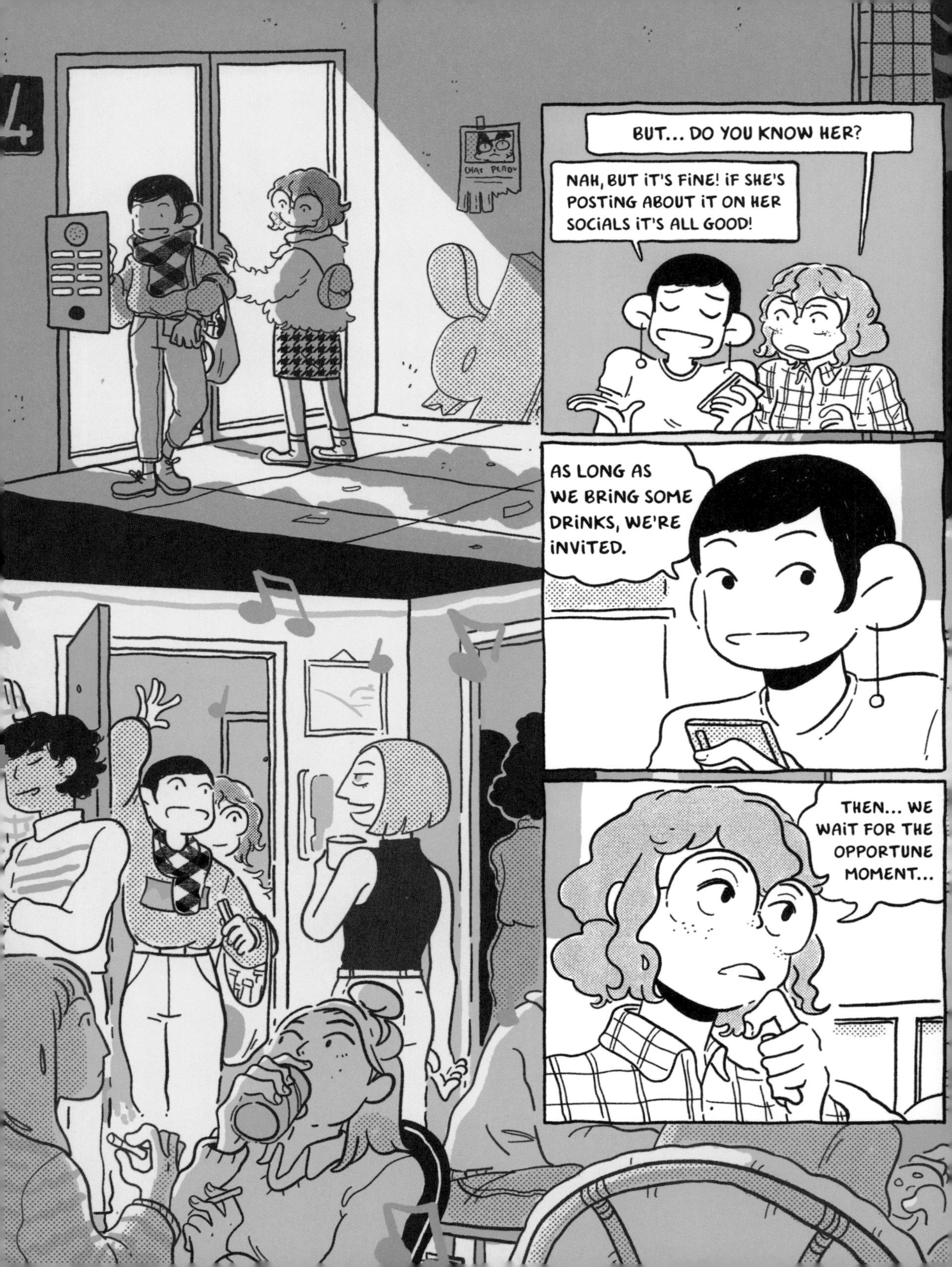
BUT... DO YOU KNOW HER?
NAH, BUT IT'S FINE! IF SHE'S POSTING ABOUT IT ON HER SOCIALS IT'S ALL GOOD!
AS LONG AS WE BRING SOME DRINKS, WE'RE INVITED.
THEN... WE WAIT FOR THE OPPORTUNE MOMENT...

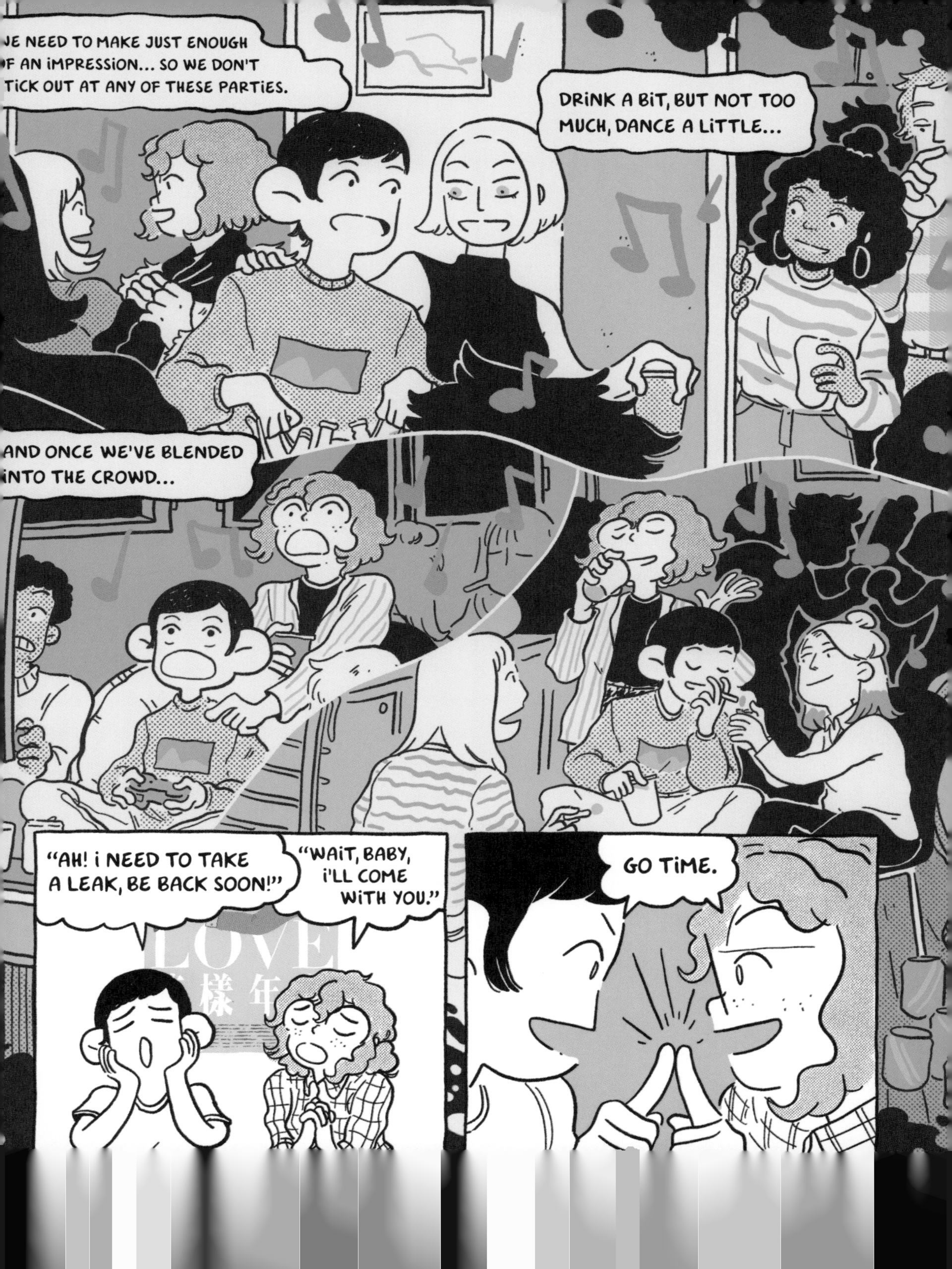

JE NEED TO MAKE JUST ENOUGH
F AN iMPRESSiON... SO WE DON'T
TiCK OUT AT ANY OF THESE PARTiES.
DRiNK A BiT, BUT NOT TOO MUCH, DANCE A LiTTLE...
AND ONCE WE'VE BLENDED iNTO THE CROWD...
"AH! i NEED TO TAKE A LEAK, BE BACK SOON!"
"WAiT, BABY, i'LL COME WiTH YOU."
LOVE
GO TiME.

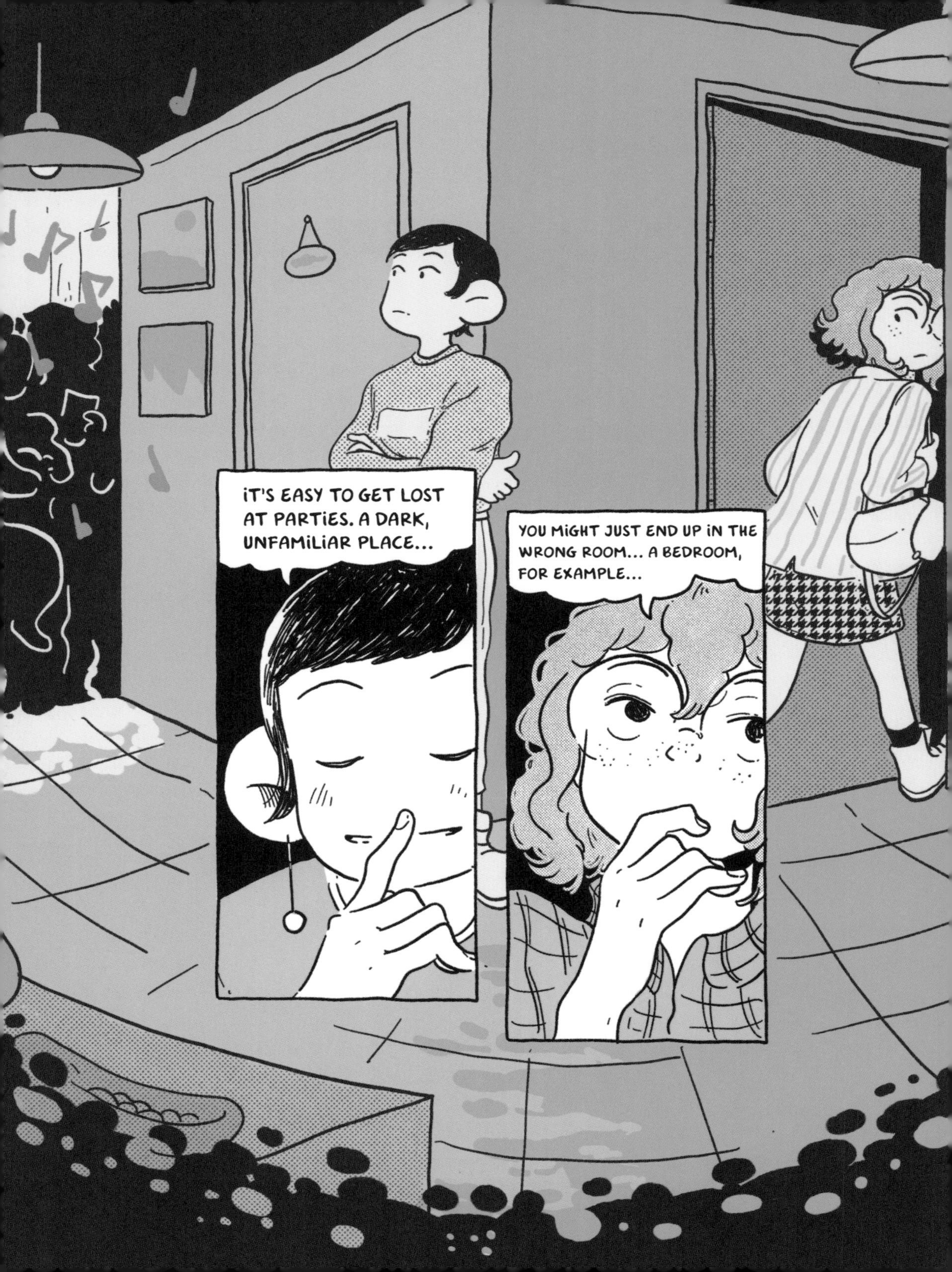
IT'S EASY TO GET LOST AT PARTIES. A DARK, UNFAMILIAR PLACE...
YOU MIGHT JUST END UP IN THE WRONG ROOM... A BEDROOM, FOR EXAMPLE...

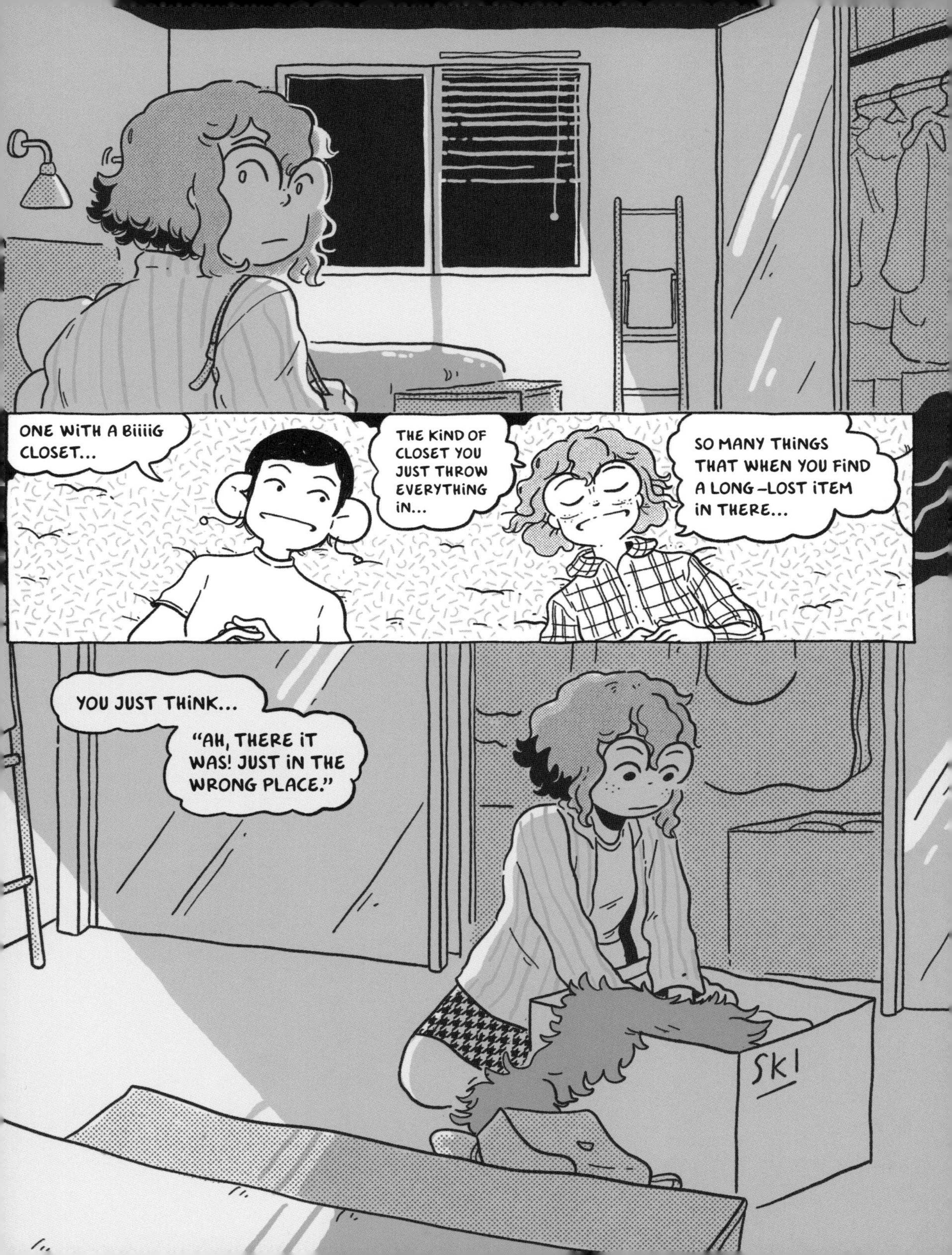
ONE WITH A BIIIIG CLOSET...
THE KIND OF CLOSET YOU JUST THROW EVERYTHING IN...
SO MANY THINGS THAT WHEN YOU FIND A LONG-LOST ITEM IN THERE...
YOU JUST THINK...
"AH, THERE IT WAS! JUST IN THE WRONG PLACE."
SKI

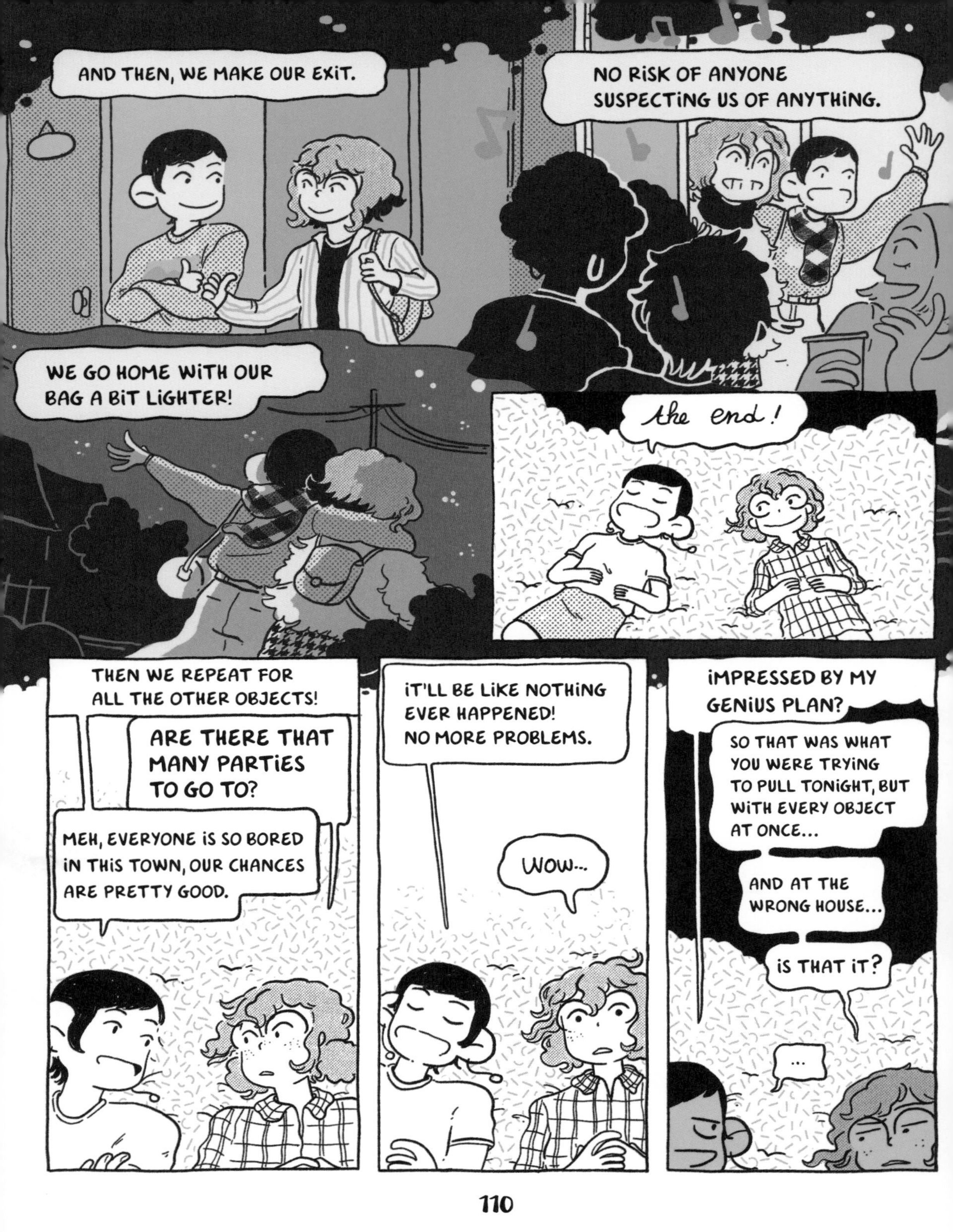
AND THEN, WE MAKE OUR EXIT.
NO RISK OF ANYONE SUSPECTING US OF ANYTHING.
WE GO HOME WITH OUR BAG A BIT LIGHTER!
the end!
THEN WE REPEAT FOR ALL THE OTHER OBJECTS!
ARE THERE THAT MANY PARTIES TO GO TO?
MEH, EVERYONE IS SO BORED IN THIS TOWN, OUR CHANCES ARE PRETTY GOOD.
IT'LL BE LIKE NOTHING EVER HAPPENED! NO MORE PROBLEMS.
WOW...
IMPRESSED BY MY GENIUS PLAN?
SO THAT WAS WHAT YOU WERE TRYING TO PULL TONIGHT, BUT WITH EVERY OBJECT AT ONCE...
AND AT THE WRONG HOUSE...
IS THAT IT?
...

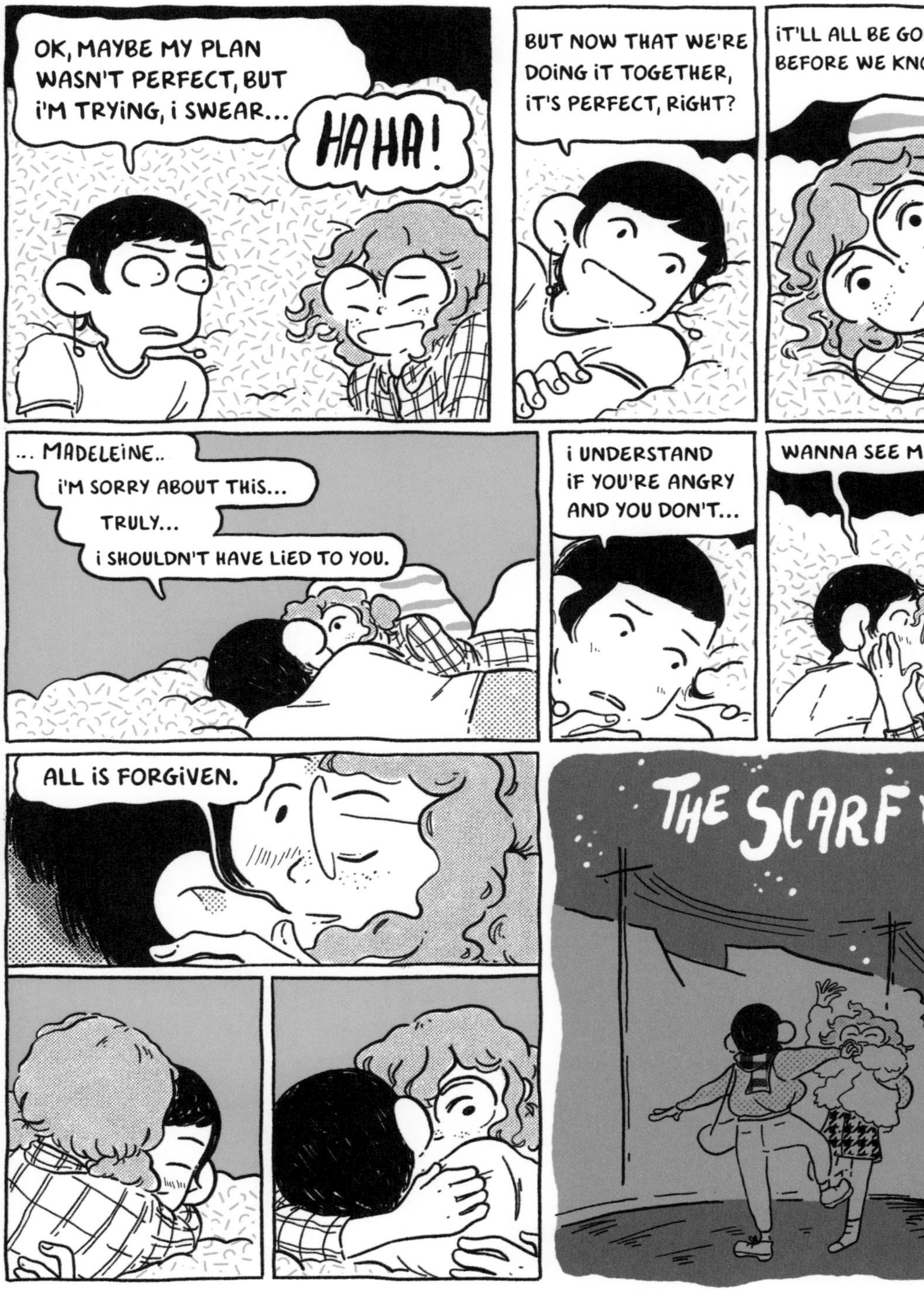
OK, MAYBE MY PLAN WASN'T PERFECT, BUT i'M TRYiNG, i SWEAR...
HAHA!
BUT NOW THAT WE'RE DOiNG iT TOGETHER, iT'S PERFECT, RiGHT?
iT'LL ALL BE GONE BEFORE WE KNOW iT!
... MADELEiNE..
i'M SORRY ABOUT THiS...
TRULY...
i SHOULDN'T HAVE LiED TO YOU.
i UNDERSTAND iF YOU'RE ANGRY AND YOU DON'T...
WANNA SEE ME ANY...
ALL iS FORGiVEN.
THE SCARF

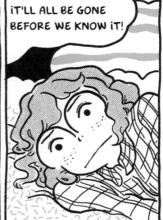

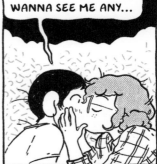

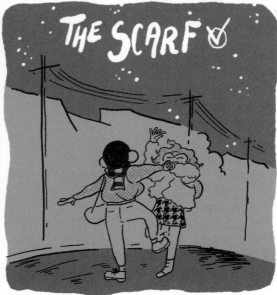

THE NEXT DAY...

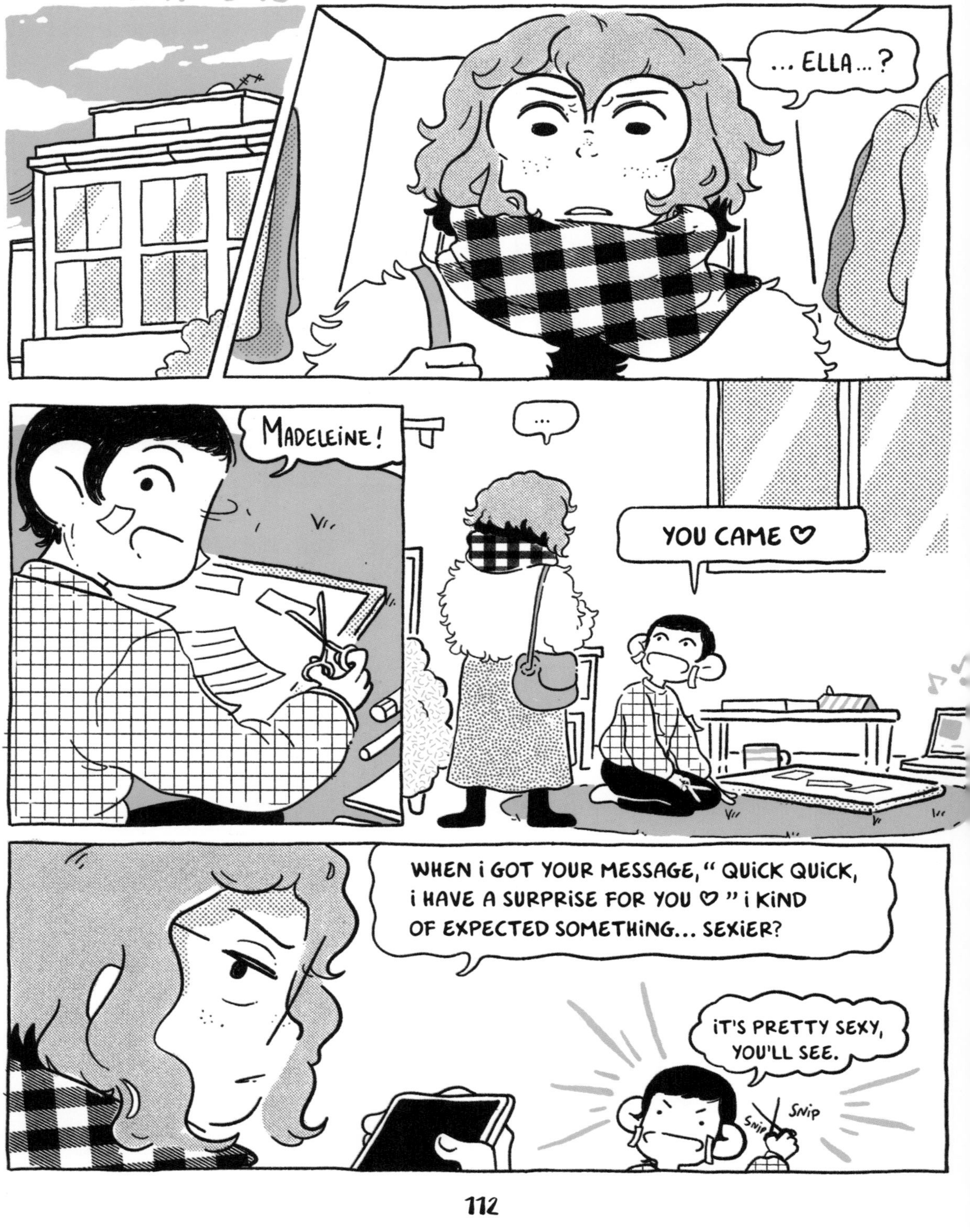
... ELLA ... ?
MADELEINE!
...
YOU CAME ♡
WHEN I GOT YOUR MESSAGE, "QUICK QUICK, I HAVE A SURPRISE FOR YOU ♡" I KIND OF EXPECTED SOMETHING... SEXIER?
IT'S PRETTY SEXY, YOU'LL SEE.
SNIP
SNIP

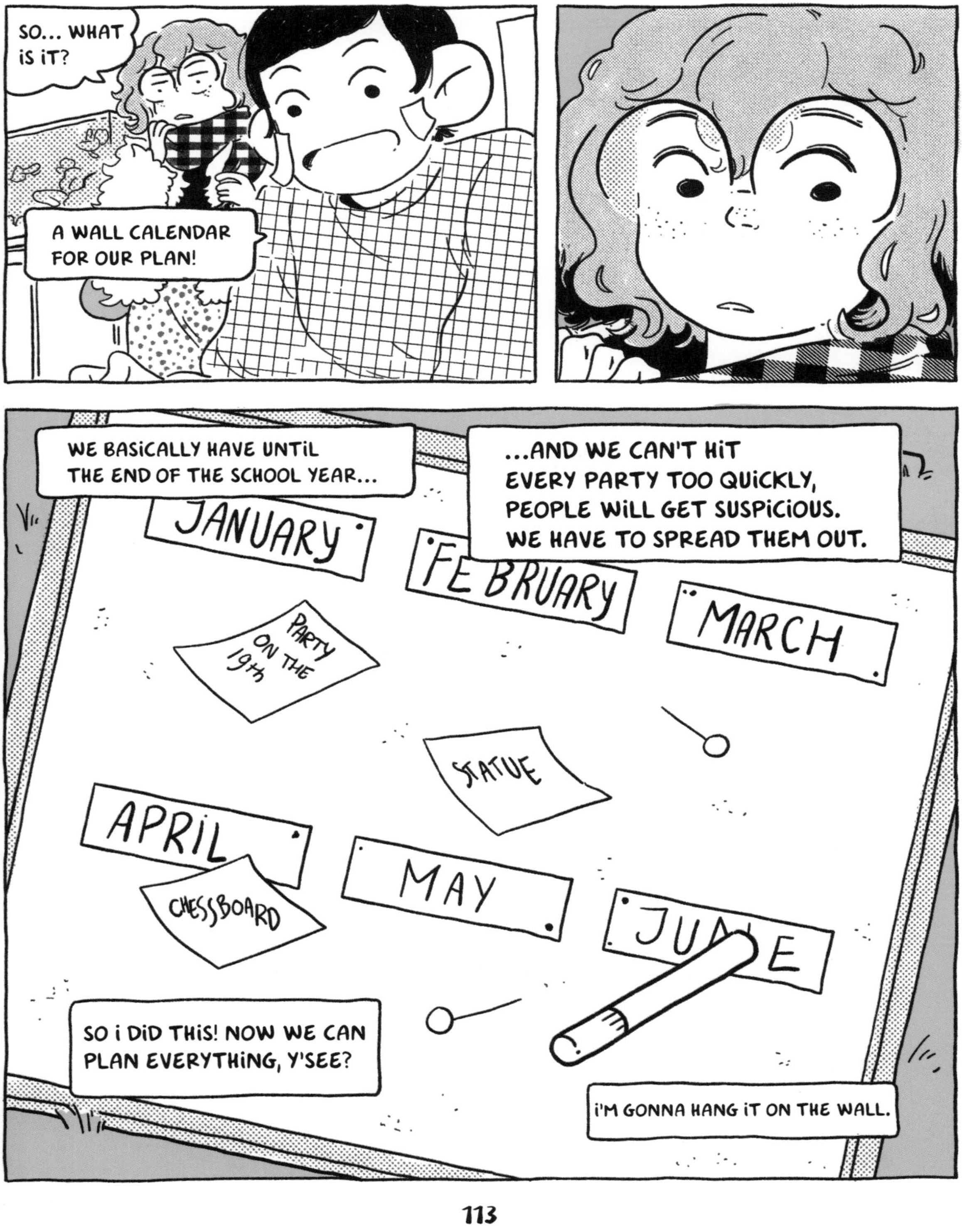

SO... WHAT IS iT?
A WALL CALENDAR FOR OUR PLAN!
WE BASiCALLY HAVE UNTiL THE END OF THE SCHOOL YEAR...
...AND WE CAN'T HiT EVERY PARTY TOO QUiCKLY, PEOPLE WiLL GET SUSPiCiOUS. WE HAVE TO SPREAD THEM OUT.
JANUARY
FEBRUARY
MARCH
PARTY ON THE 19th
STATUE
APRiL
CHESSBOARD
MAY
JUNE
SO i DiD THiS! NOW WE CAN PLAN EVERYTHiNG, Y'SEE?
i'M GONNA HANG iT ON THE WALL.

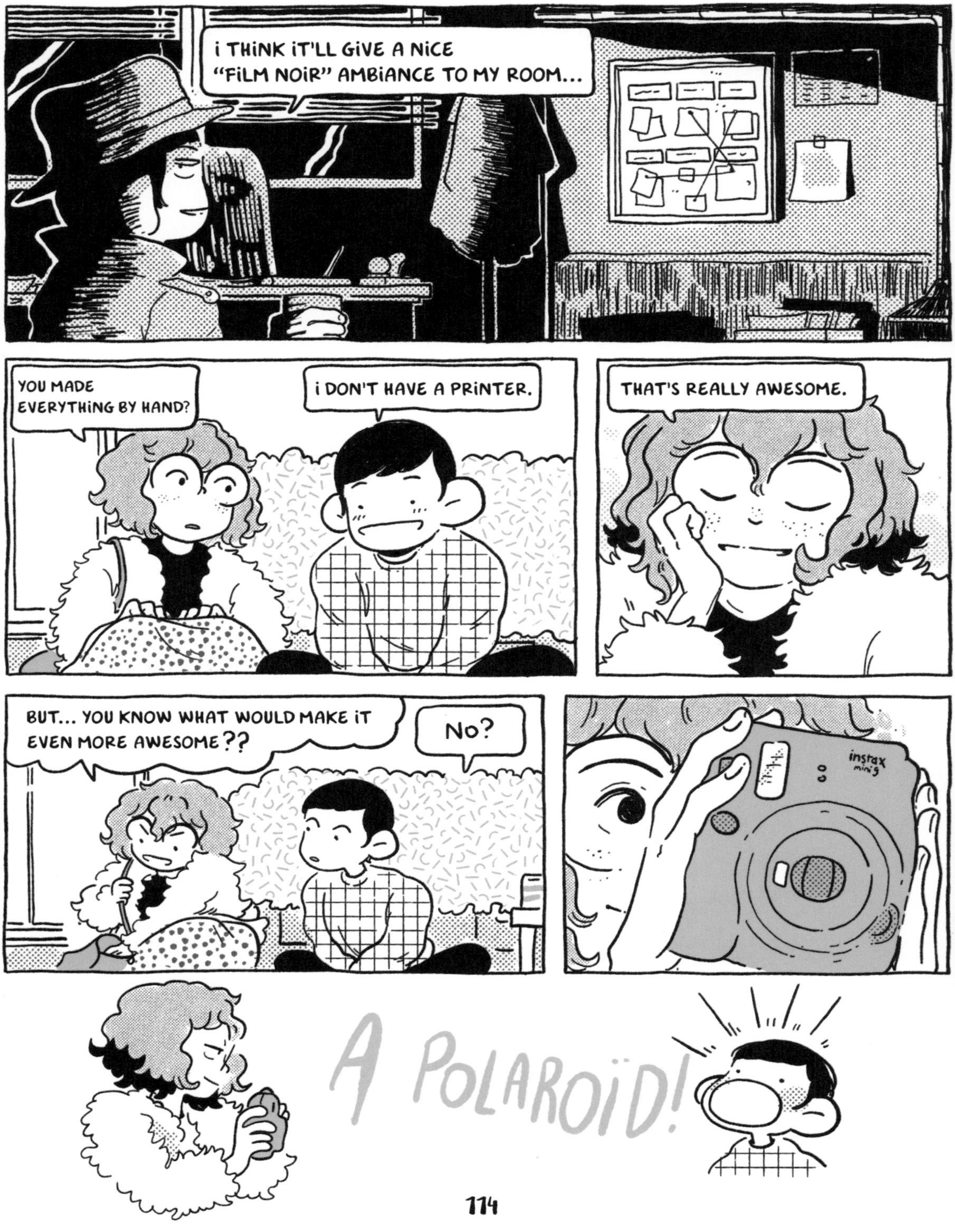
i THiNK iT'LL GiVE A NiCE "FiLM NOiR" AMBiANCE TO MY ROOM...
YOU MADE EVERYTHiNG BY HAND?
i DON'T HAVE A PRiNTER.
THAT'S REALLY AWESOME.
BUT... YOU KNOW WHAT WOULD MAKE iT EVEN MORE AWESOME??
No?
instax mini 9
A POLAROÏD!

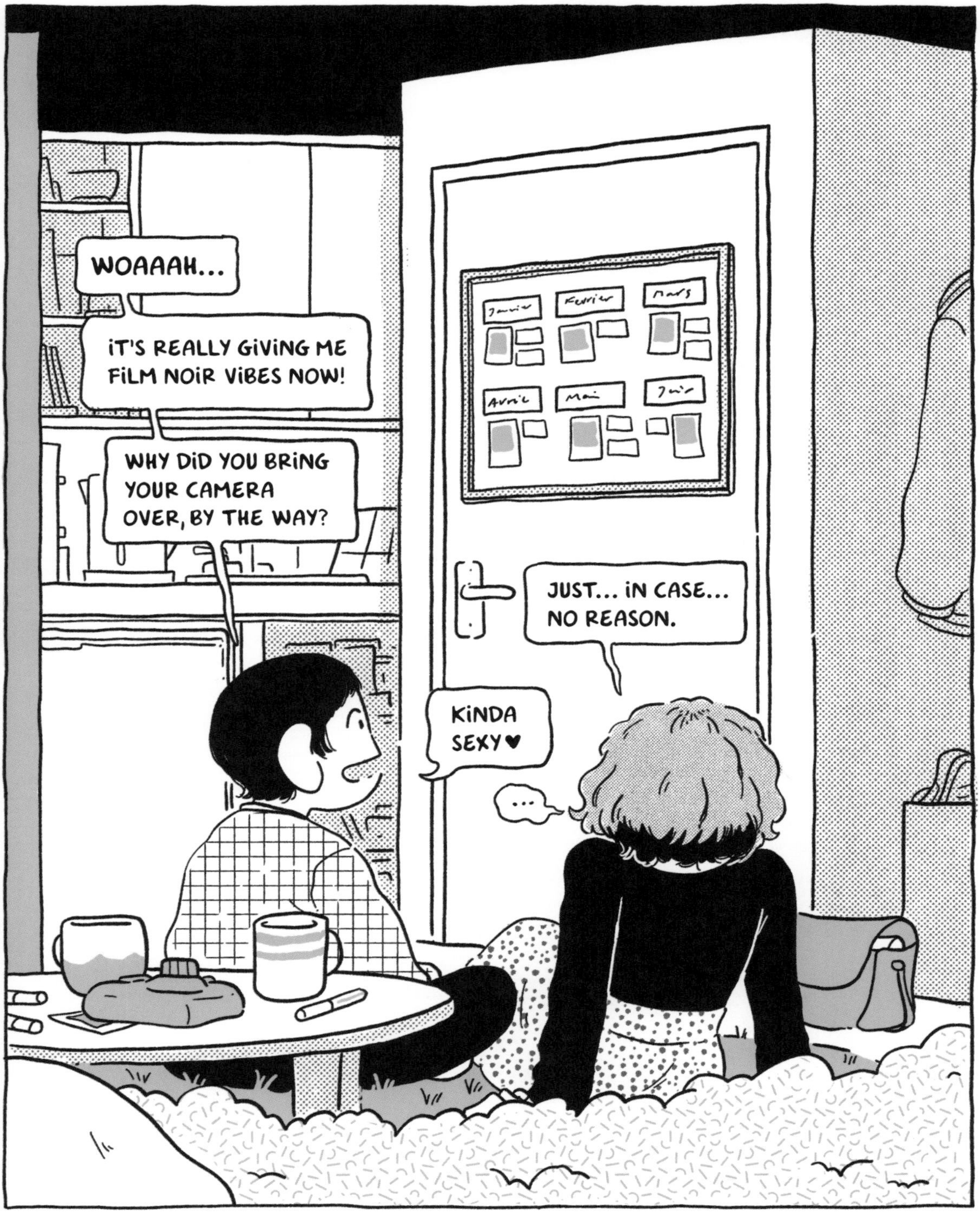
WOAAAH...
IT'S REALLY GIVING ME FILM NOIR VIBES NOW!
WHY DID YOU BRING YOUR CAMERA OVER, BY THE WAY?
JUST... IN CASE... NO REASON.
KINDA SEXY♥
...

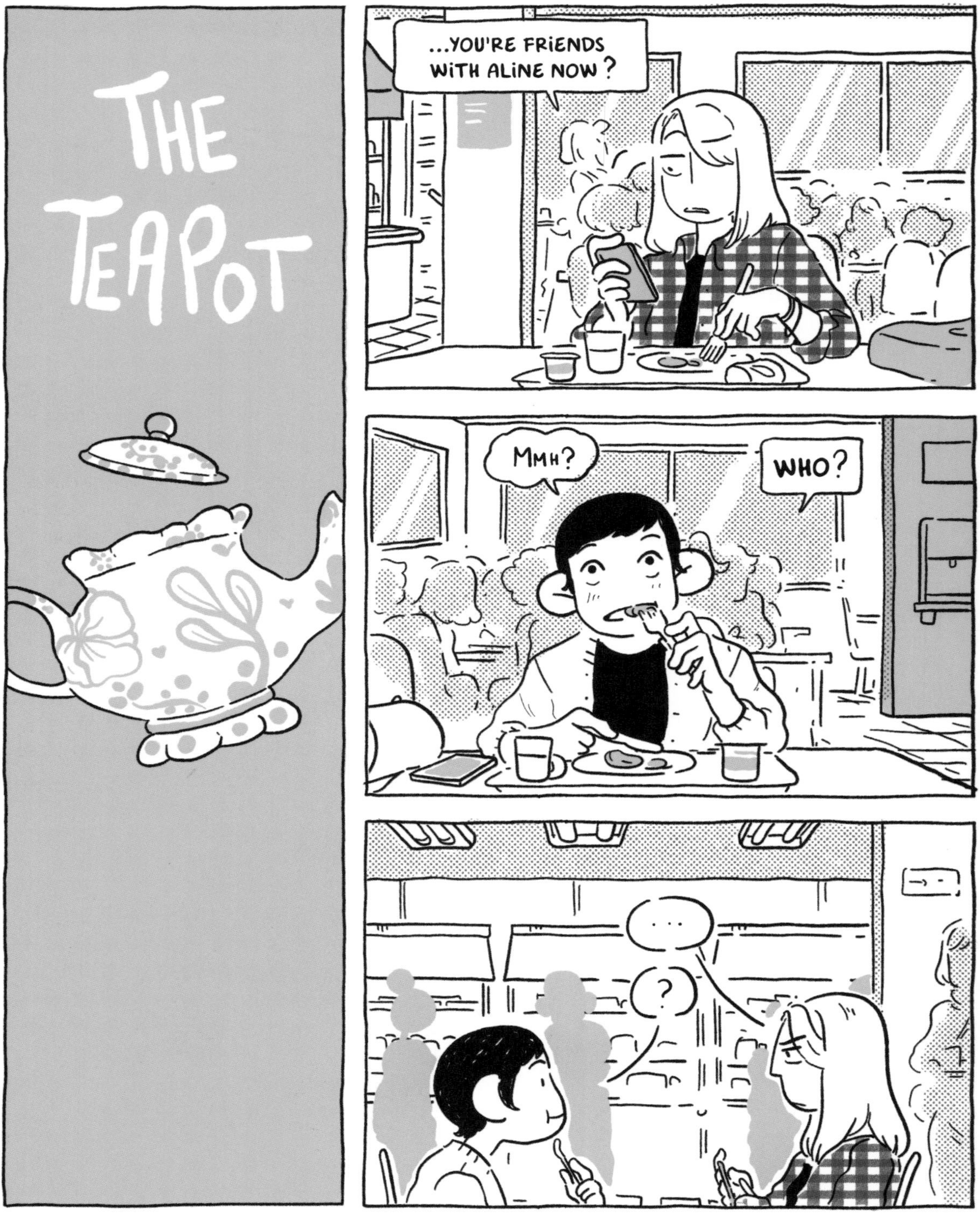
THE TEAPOT
...YOU'RE FRIENDS WITH ALINE NOW?
MMH?
WHO?
...
?

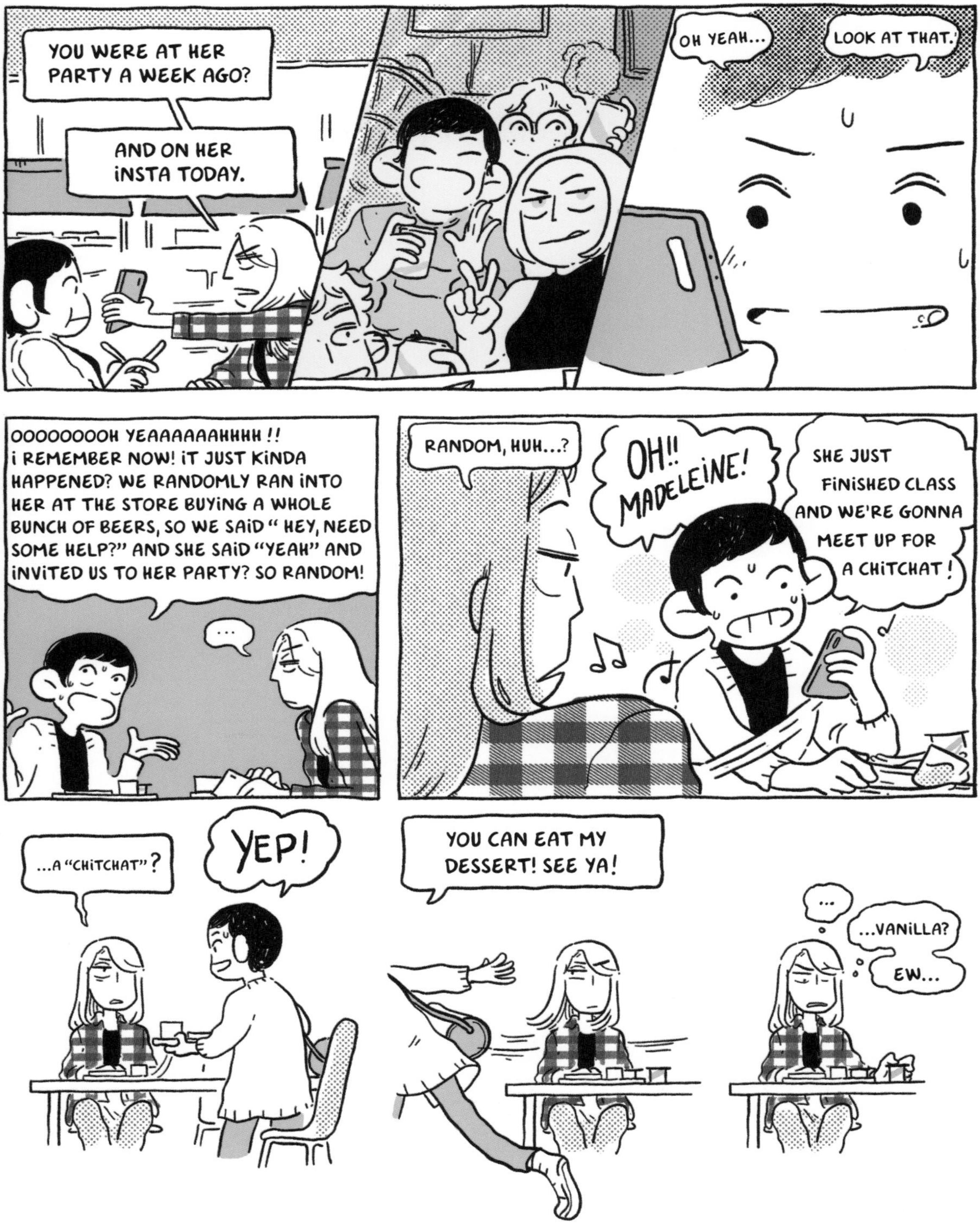
YOU WERE AT HER PARTY A WEEK AGO?
AND ON HER iNSTA TODAY.
OH YEAH...
LOOK AT THAT.
OOOOOOOOH YEAAAAAAHHHH!! i REMEMBER NOW! iT JUST KiNDA HAPPENED? WE RANDOMLY RAN iNTO HER AT THE STORE BUYiNG A WHOLE BUNCH OF BEERS, SO WE SAiD "HEY, NEED SOME HELP?" AND SHE SAiD "YEAH" AND iNVITED US TO HER PARTY? SO RANDOM!
...
RANDOM, HUH...?
OH!! MADELEINE!
SHE JUST FiNiSHED CLASS AND WE'RE GONNA MEET UP FOR A CHiTCHAT!
...A "CHiTCHAT"?
YEP!
YOU CAN EAT MY DESSERT! SEE YA!
...
...VANiLLA?
EW...

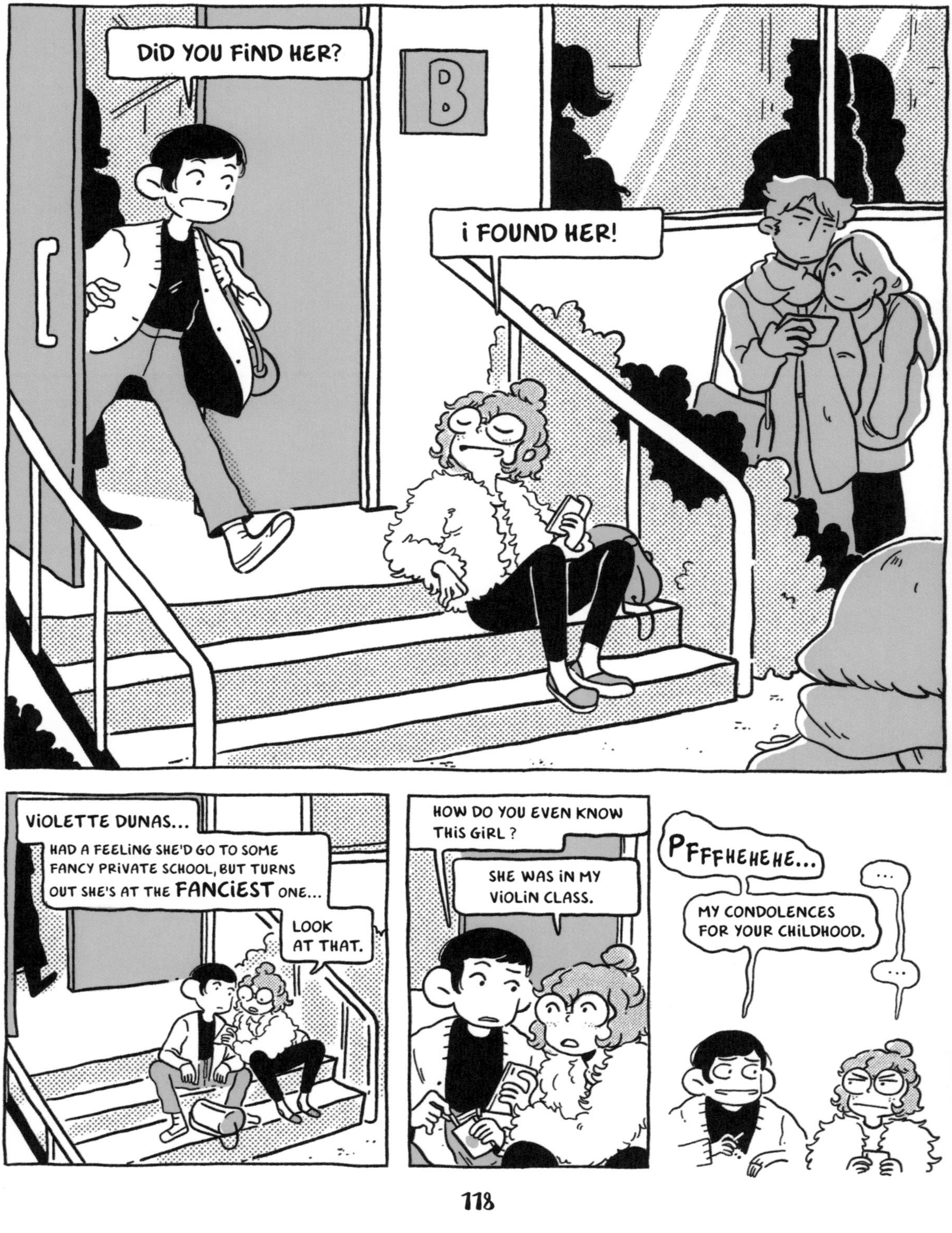
DiD YOU FiND HER?
B
i FOUND HER!
ViOLETTE DUNAS...
HAD A FEELiNG SHE'D GO TO SOME FANCY PRIVATE SCHOOL, BUT TURNS OUT SHE'S AT THE FANCiEST ONE...
LOOK AT THAT.
HOW DO YOU EVEN KNOW THiS GiRL ?
SHE WAS iN MY ViOLiN CLASS.
PFFFHEHEHE...
MY CONDOLENCES FOR YOUR CHiLDHOOD.
...
...

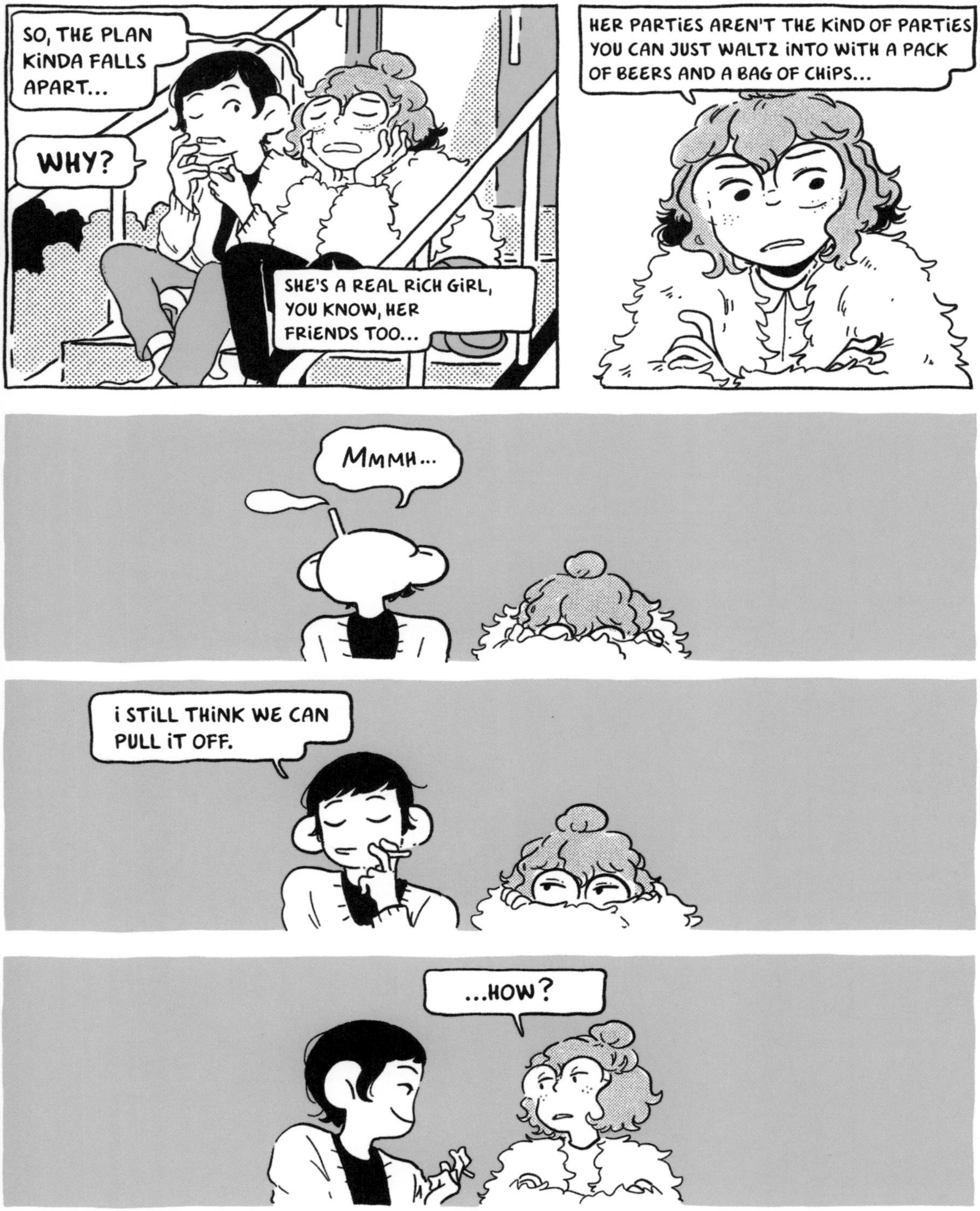
SO, THE PLAN KiNDA FALLS APART...
WHY?
SHE'S A REAL RiCH GiRL, YOU KNOW, HER FRiENDS TOO...
HER PARTiES AREN'T THE KiND OF PARTiES YOU CAN JUST WALTZ iNTO WiTH A PACK OF BEERS AND A BAG OF CHiPS...
MMMH...
i STiLL THiNK WE CAN PULL iT OFF.
...HOW?

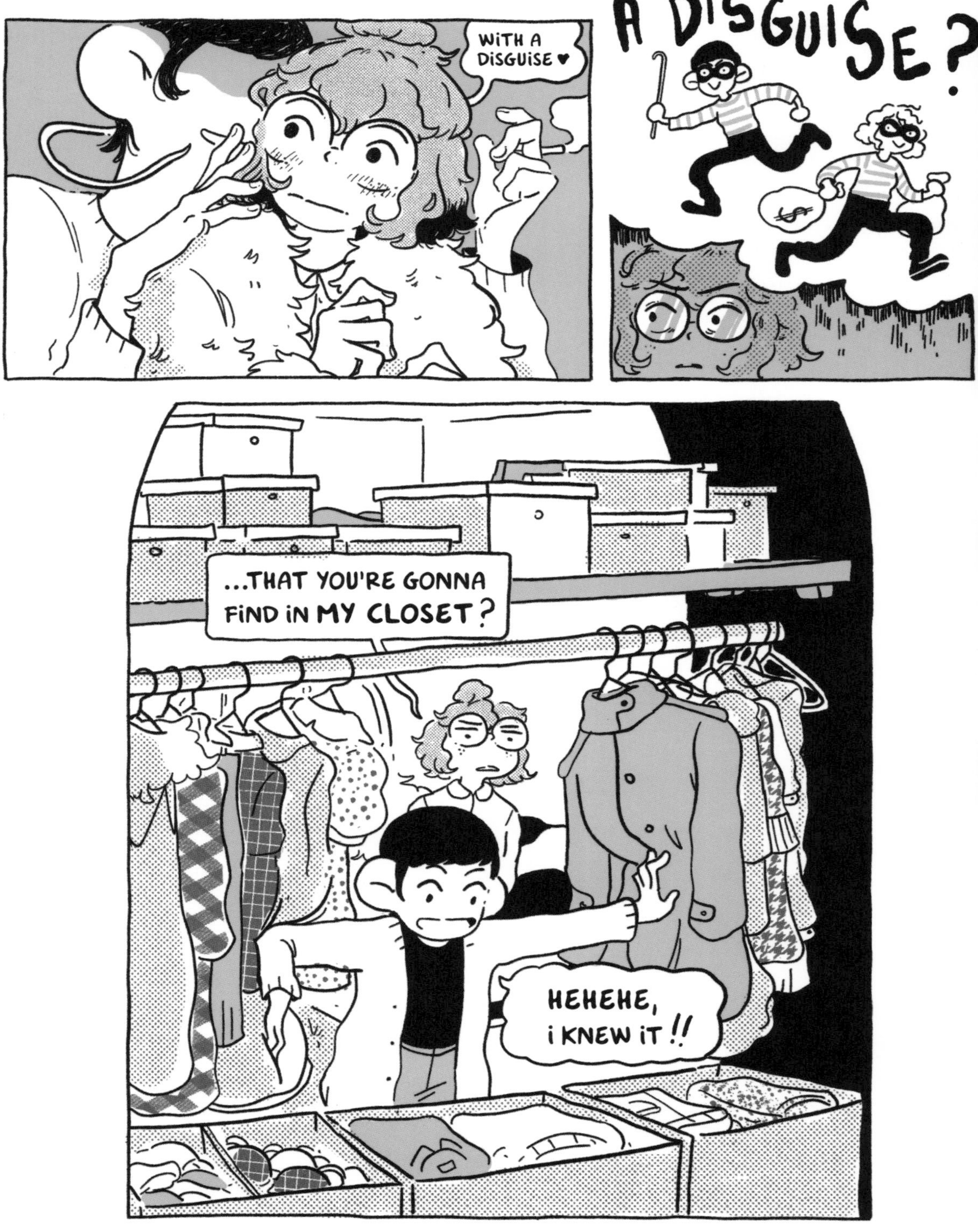
WiTH A DiSGUiSE ♥
A DiSGUiSE?
...THAT YOU'RE GONNA FiND iN MY CLOSET?
HEHEHE, i KNEW iT!!

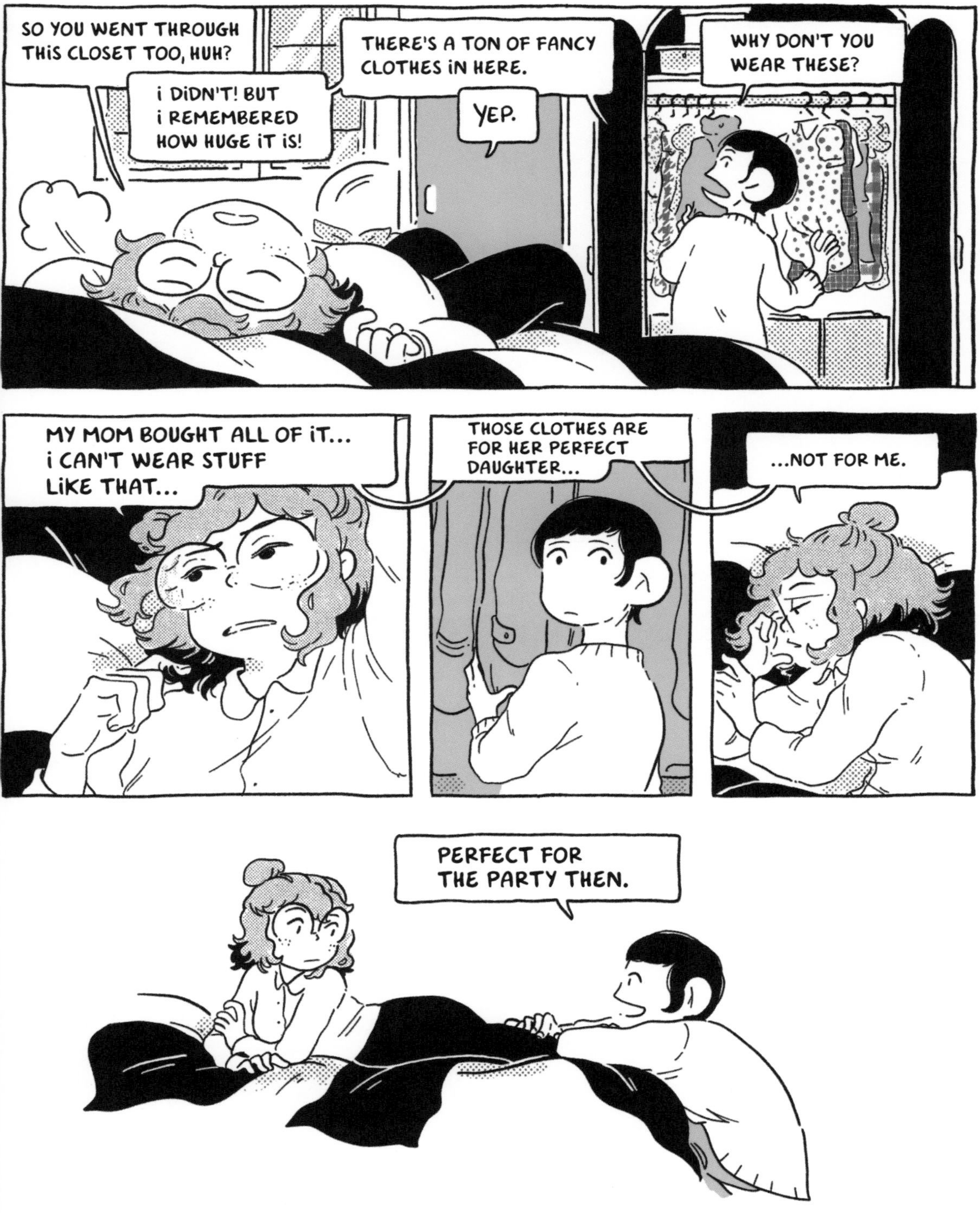
SO YOU WENT THROUGH THIS CLOSET TOO, HUH?
I DIDN'T! BUT I REMEMBERED HOW HUGE IT IS!
THERE'S A TON OF FANCY CLOTHES IN HERE.
YEP.
WHY DON'T YOU WEAR THESE?
MY MOM BOUGHT ALL OF IT... I CAN'T WEAR STUFF LIKE THAT...
THOSE CLOTHES ARE FOR HER PERFECT DAUGHTER...
...NOT FOR ME.
PERFECT FOR THE PARTY THEN.

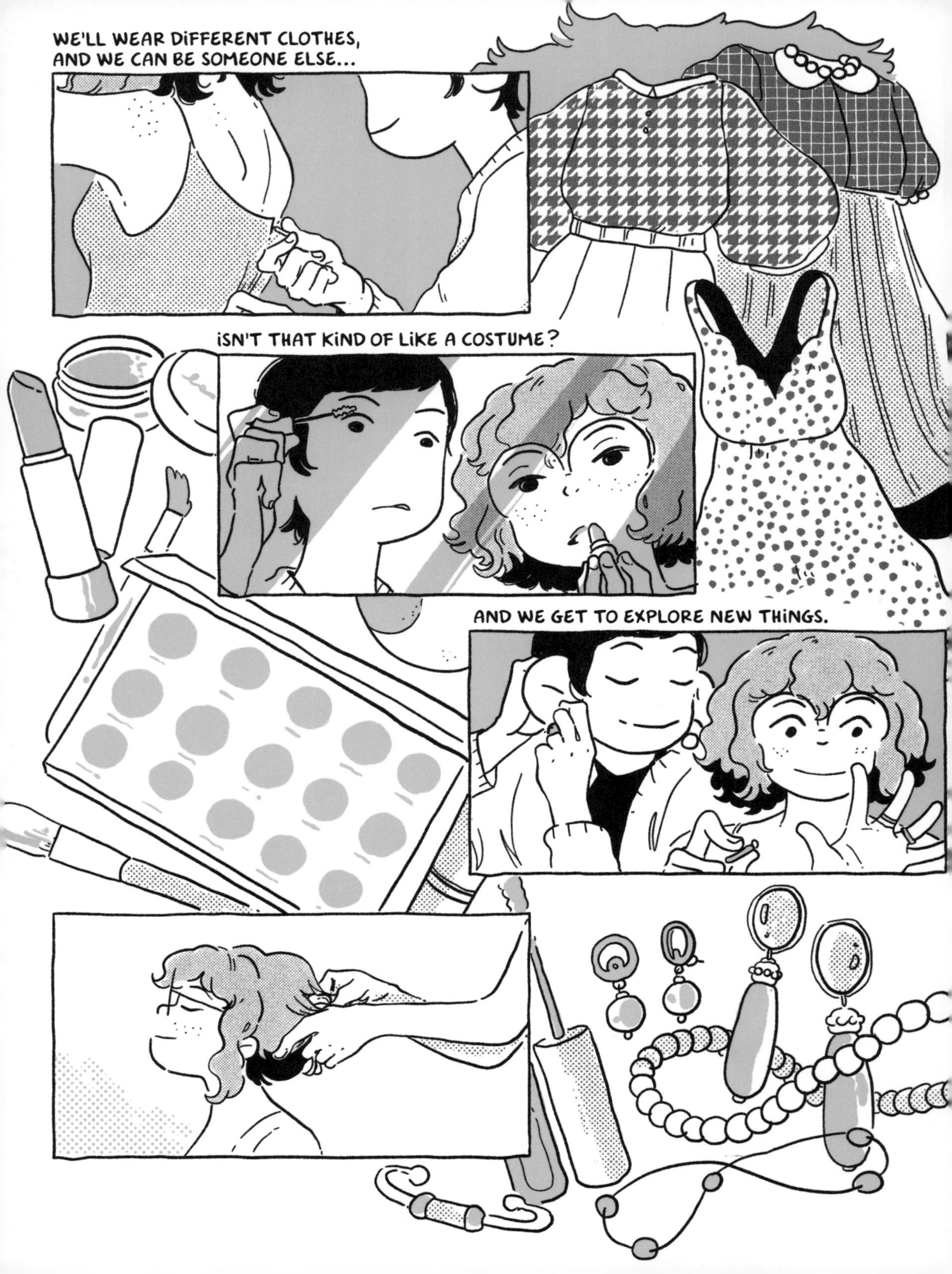
WE'LL WEAR DIFFERENT CLOTHES, AND WE CAN BE SOMEONE ELSE...
ISN'T THAT KIND OF LIKE A COSTUME?
AND WE GET TO EXPLORE NEW THINGS.

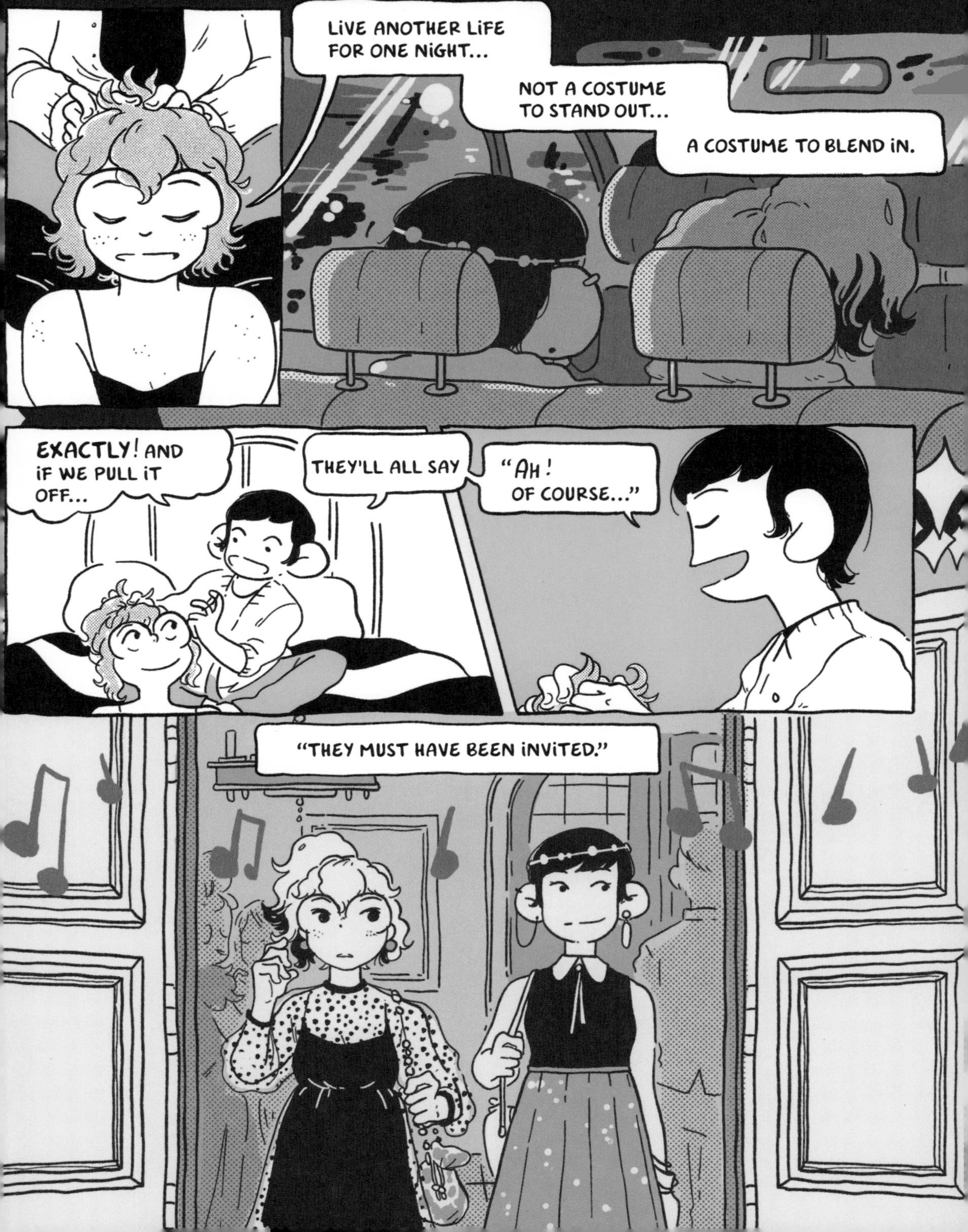
LIVE ANOTHER LIFE FOR ONE NIGHT...
NOT A COSTUME TO STAND OUT...
A COSTUME TO BLEND IN.
EXACTLY! AND IF WE PULL IT OFF...
THEY'LL ALL SAY
"AH! OF COURSE..."
"THEY MUST HAVE BEEN INVITED."

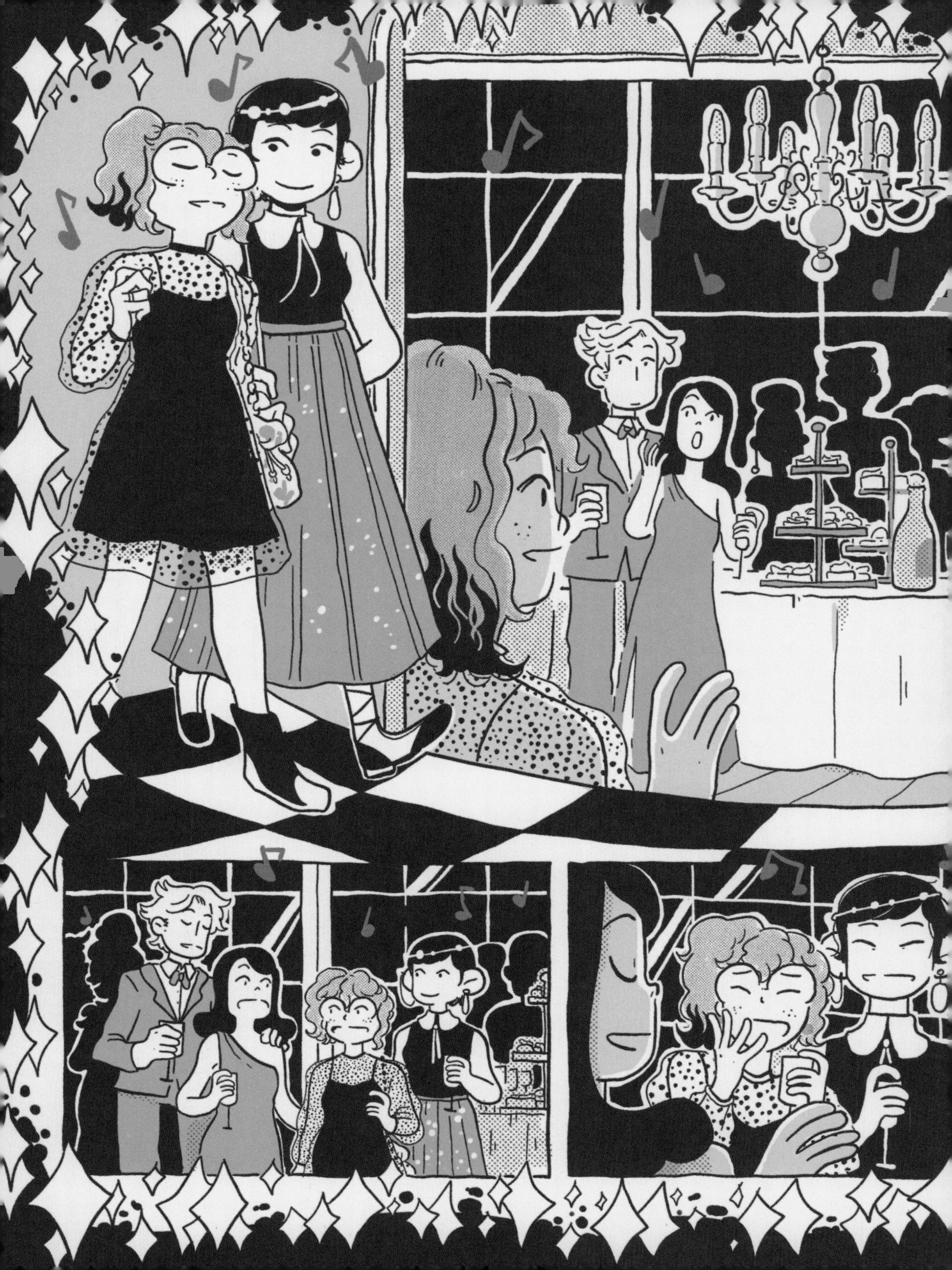

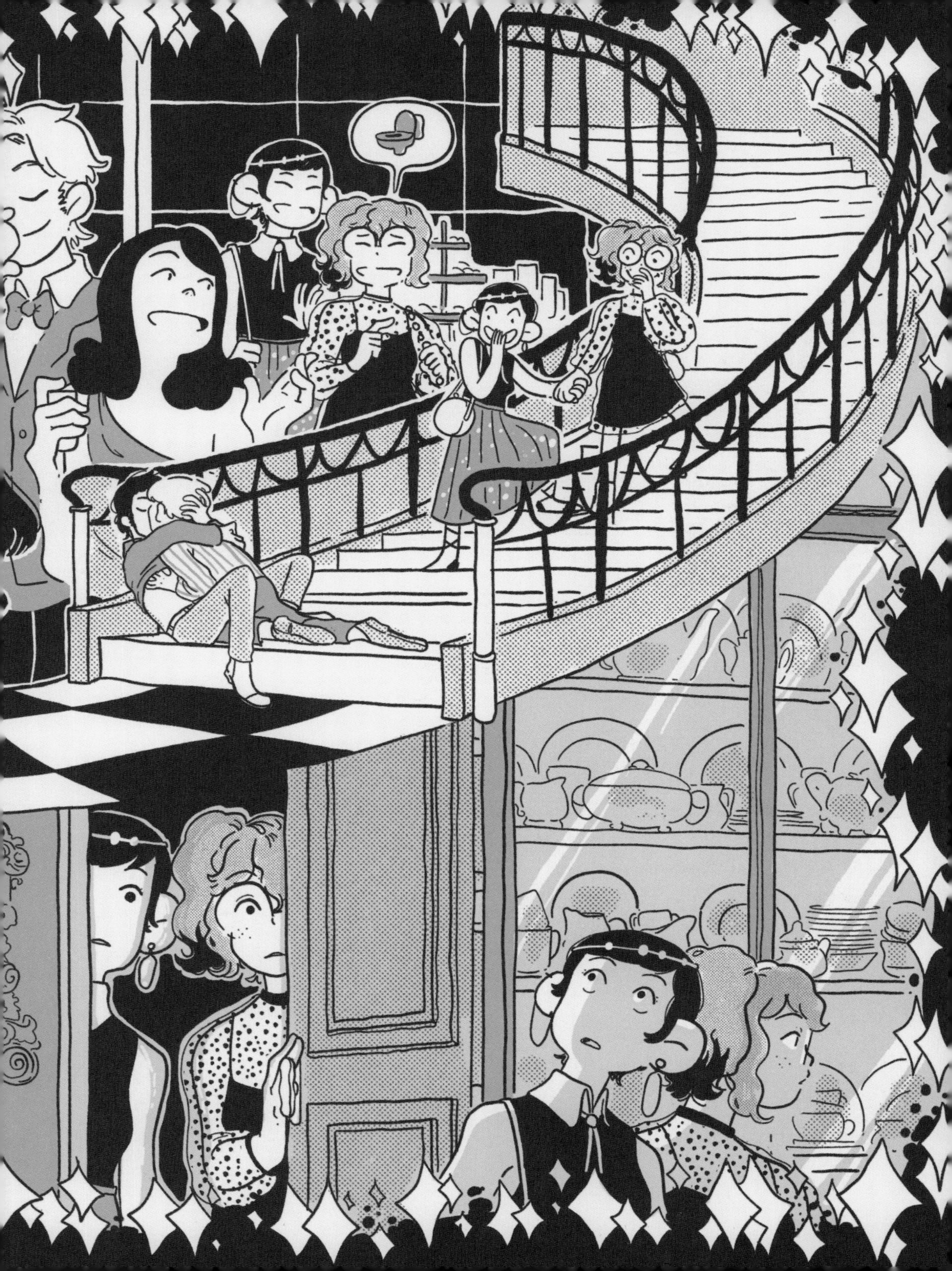

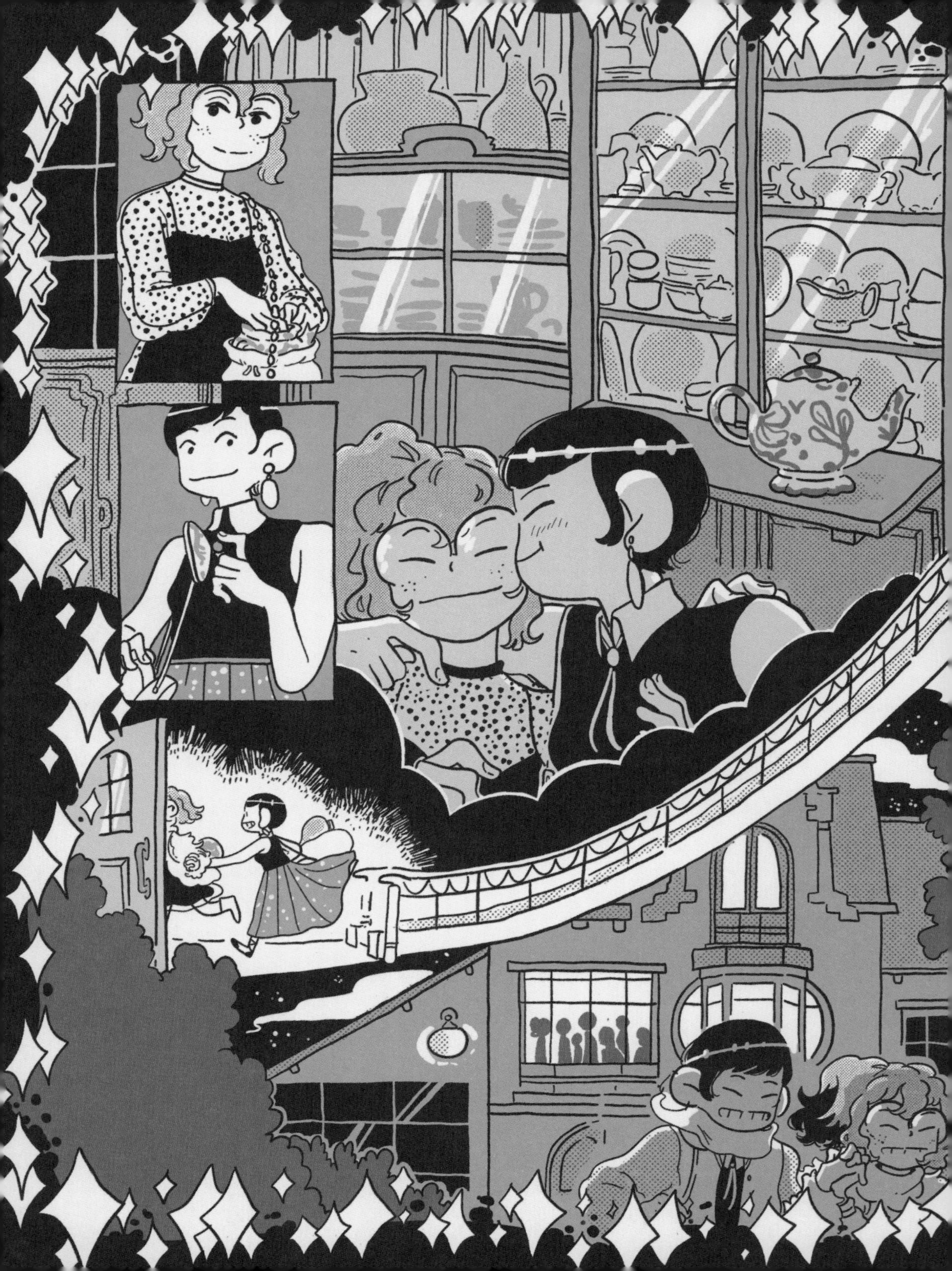

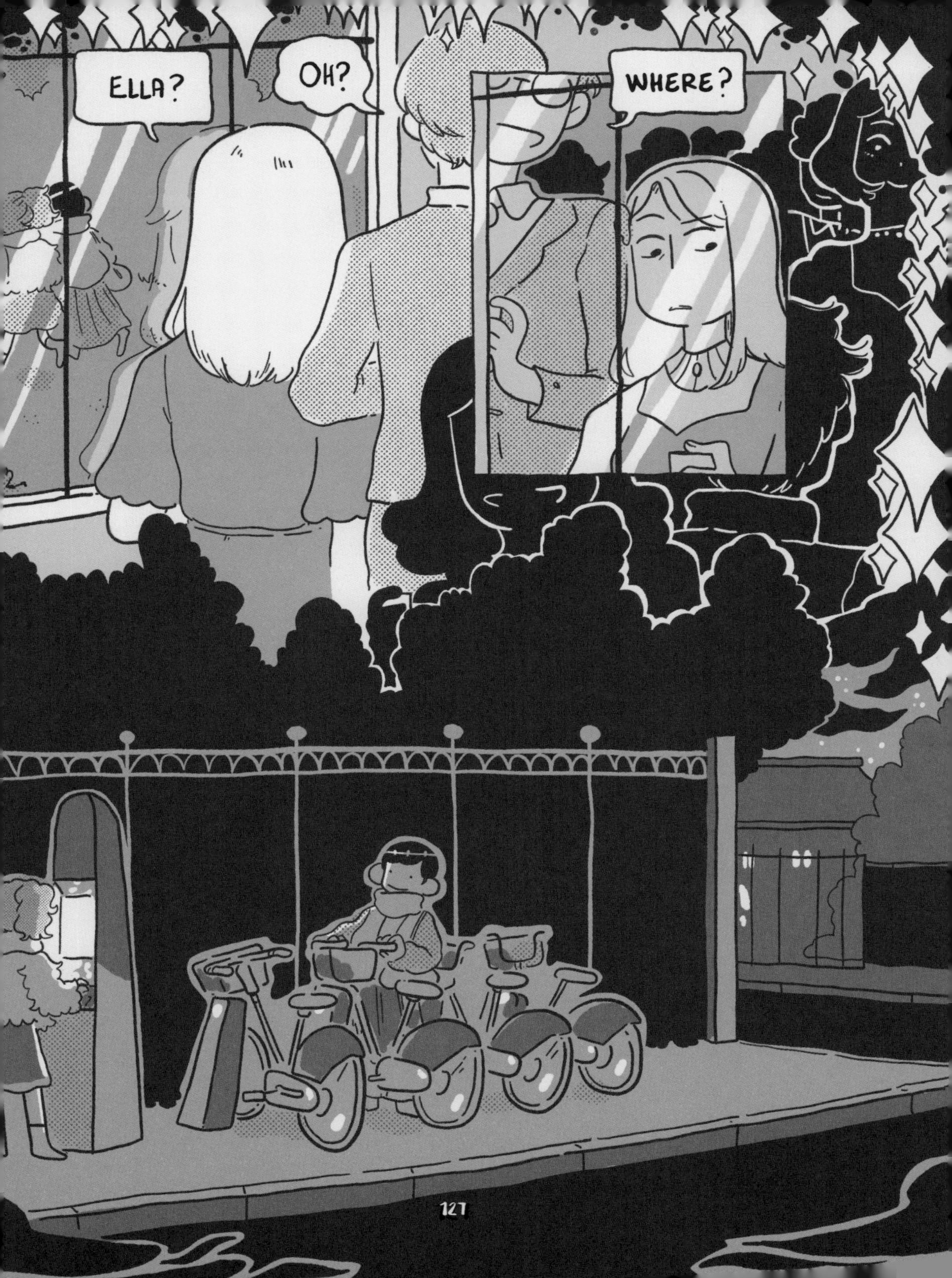
ELLA?
OH?
WHERE?

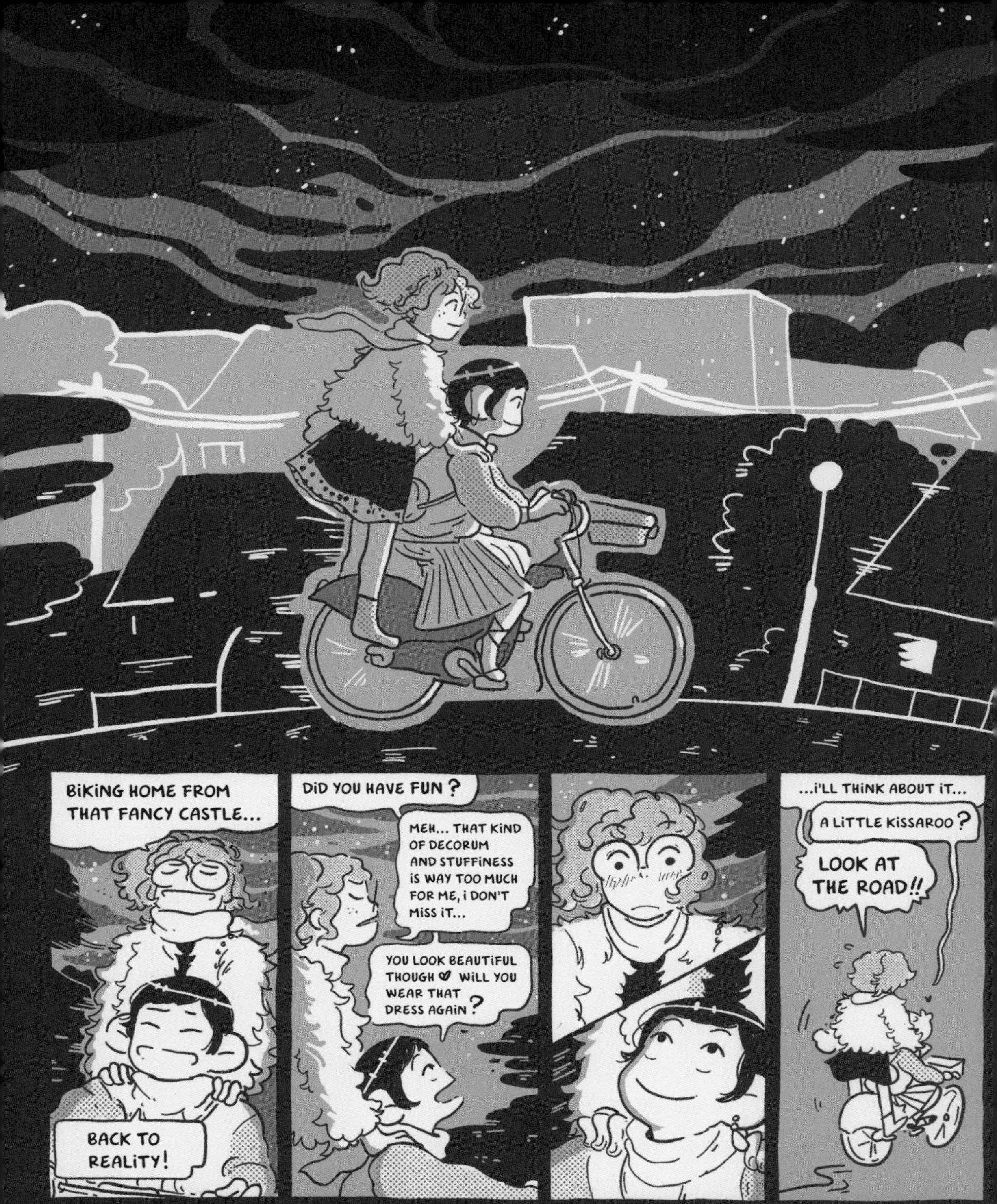

BiKiNG HOME FROM THAT FANCY CASTLE...
BACK TO REALiTY!
DiD YOU HAVE FUN?
MEH... THAT KiND OF DECORUM AND STUFFiNESS iS WAY TOO MUCH FOR ME, i DON'T MiSS iT...
YOU LOOK BEAUTiFUL THOUGH ♥ WiLL YOU WEAR THAT DRESS AGAiN?
...i'LL THiNK ABOUT iT...
A LiTTLE KiSSAROO?
LOOK AT THE ROAD!!

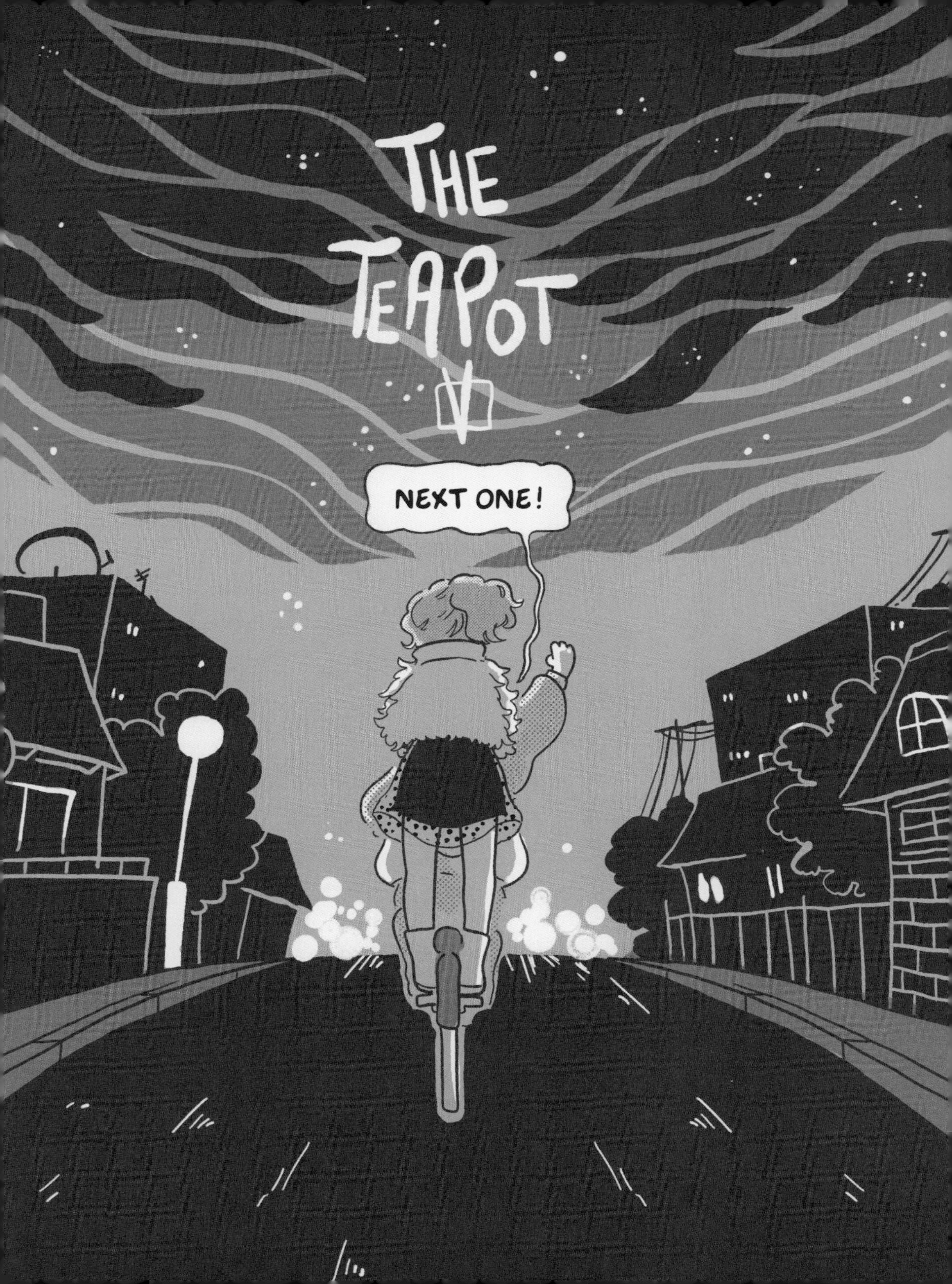
THE TEAPOT
V
NEXT ONE!

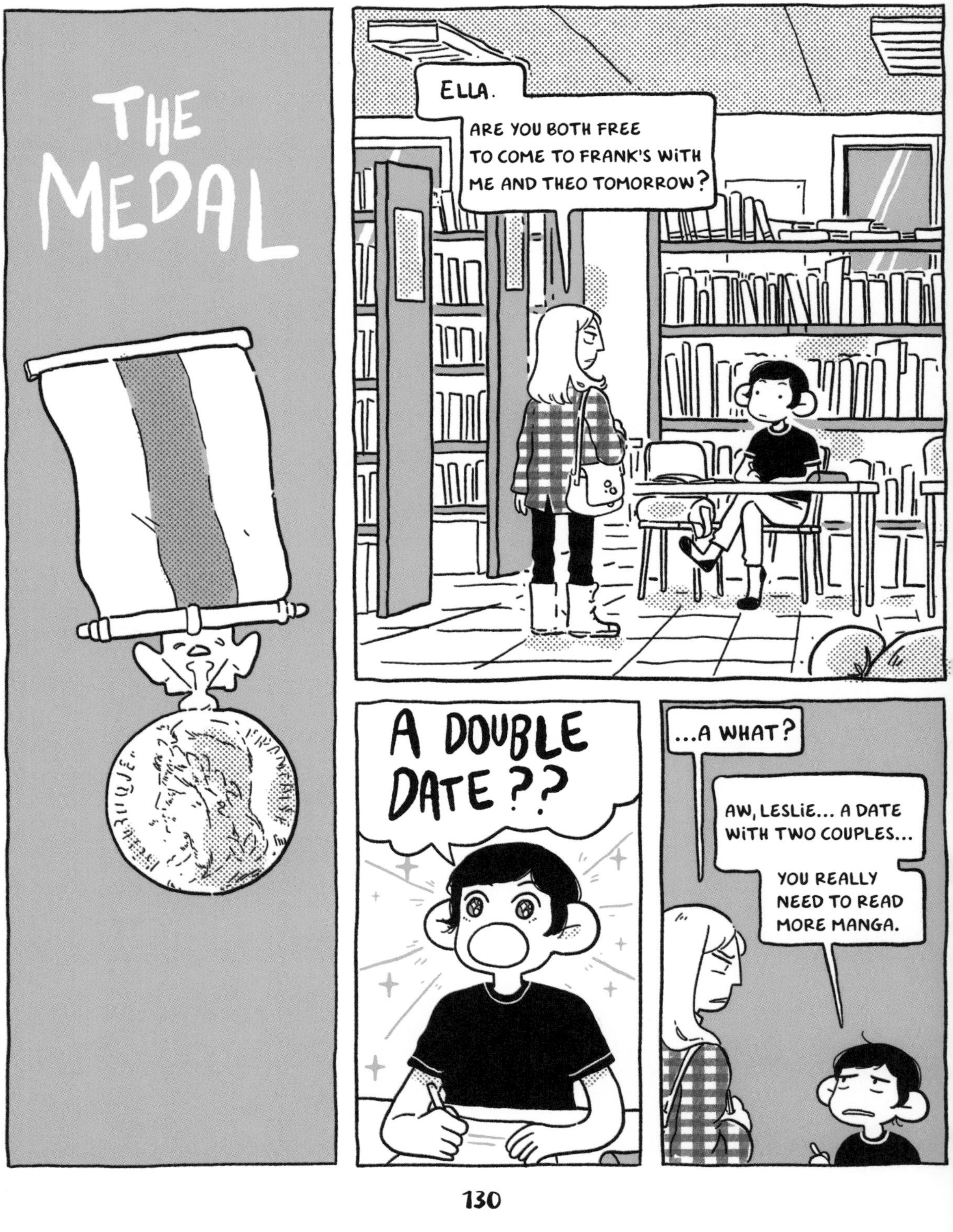
THE MEDAL
ELLA.
ARE YOU BOTH FREE TO COME TO FRANK'S WITH ME AND THEO TOMORROW?
A DOUBLE DATE??
...A WHAT?
AW, LESLIE... A DATE WITH TWO COUPLES...
YOU REALLY NEED TO READ MORE MANGA.

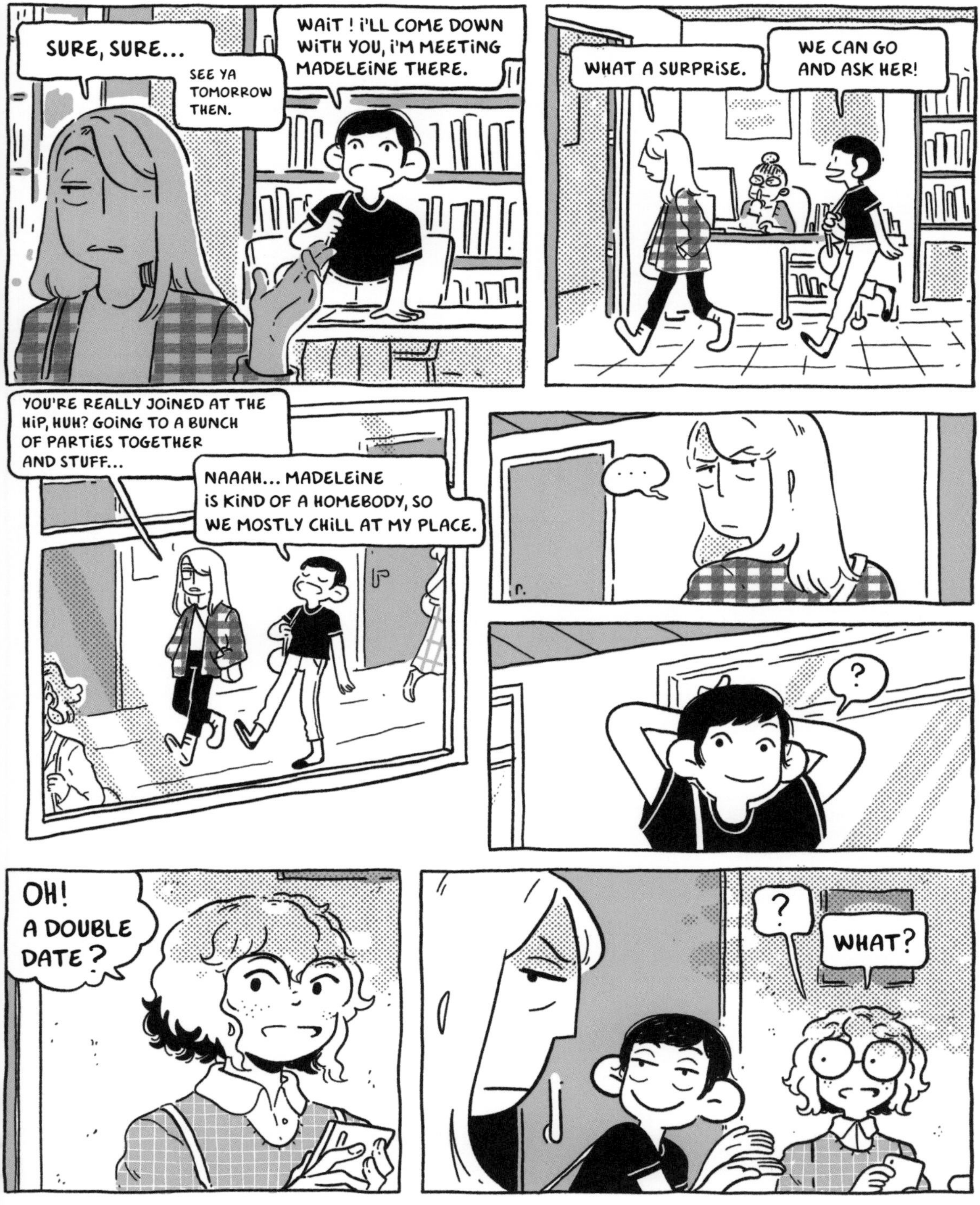
SURE, SURE...
SEE YA TOMORROW THEN.
WAIT! I'LL COME DOWN WITH YOU, I'M MEETING MADELEINE THERE.
WHAT A SURPRISE.
WE CAN GO AND ASK HER!
YOU'RE REALLY JOINED AT THE HIP, HUH? GOING TO A BUNCH OF PARTIES TOGETHER AND STUFF...
NAAAH... MADELEINE IS KIND OF A HOMEBODY, SO WE MOSTLY CHILL AT MY PLACE.
...
?
OH! A DOUBLE DATE?
?
WHAT?

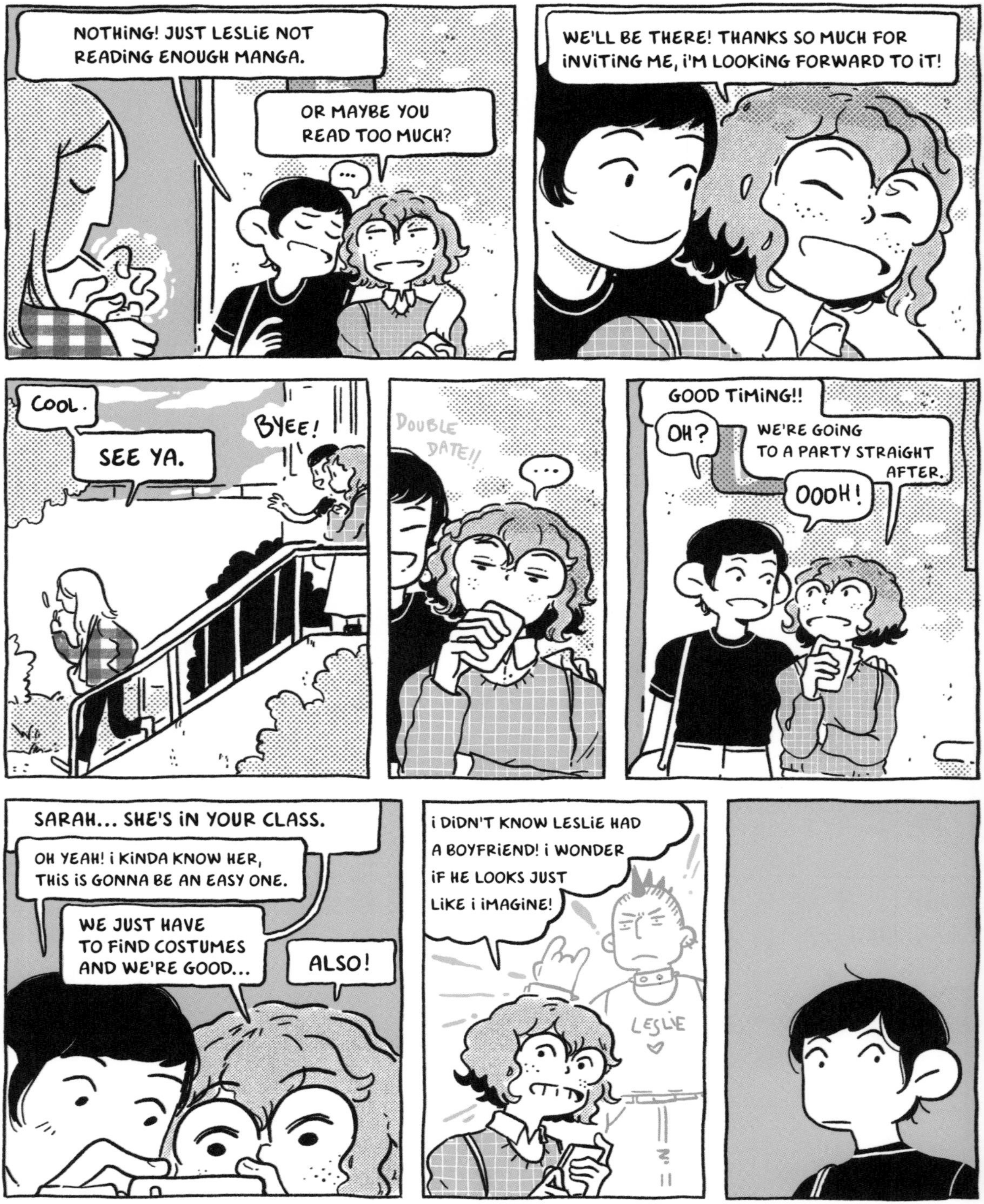
NOTHING! JUST LESLIE NOT READING ENOUGH MANGA.
OR MAYBE YOU READ TOO MUCH?
...
WE'LL BE THERE! THANKS SO MUCH FOR INVITING ME, I'M LOOKING FORWARD TO IT!
COOL.
SEE YA.
BYEE!
DOUBLE DATE!!
...
GOOD TIMING!!
OH?
WE'RE GOING TO A PARTY STRAIGHT AFTER.
OOOH!
SARAH... SHE'S IN YOUR CLASS.
OH YEAH! I KINDA KNOW HER, THIS IS GONNA BE AN EASY ONE.
WE JUST HAVE TO FIND COSTUMES AND WE'RE GOOD...
ALSO!
I DIDN'T KNOW LESLIE HAD A BOYFRIEND! I WONDER IF HE LOOKS JUST LIKE I IMAGINE!
LESLIE

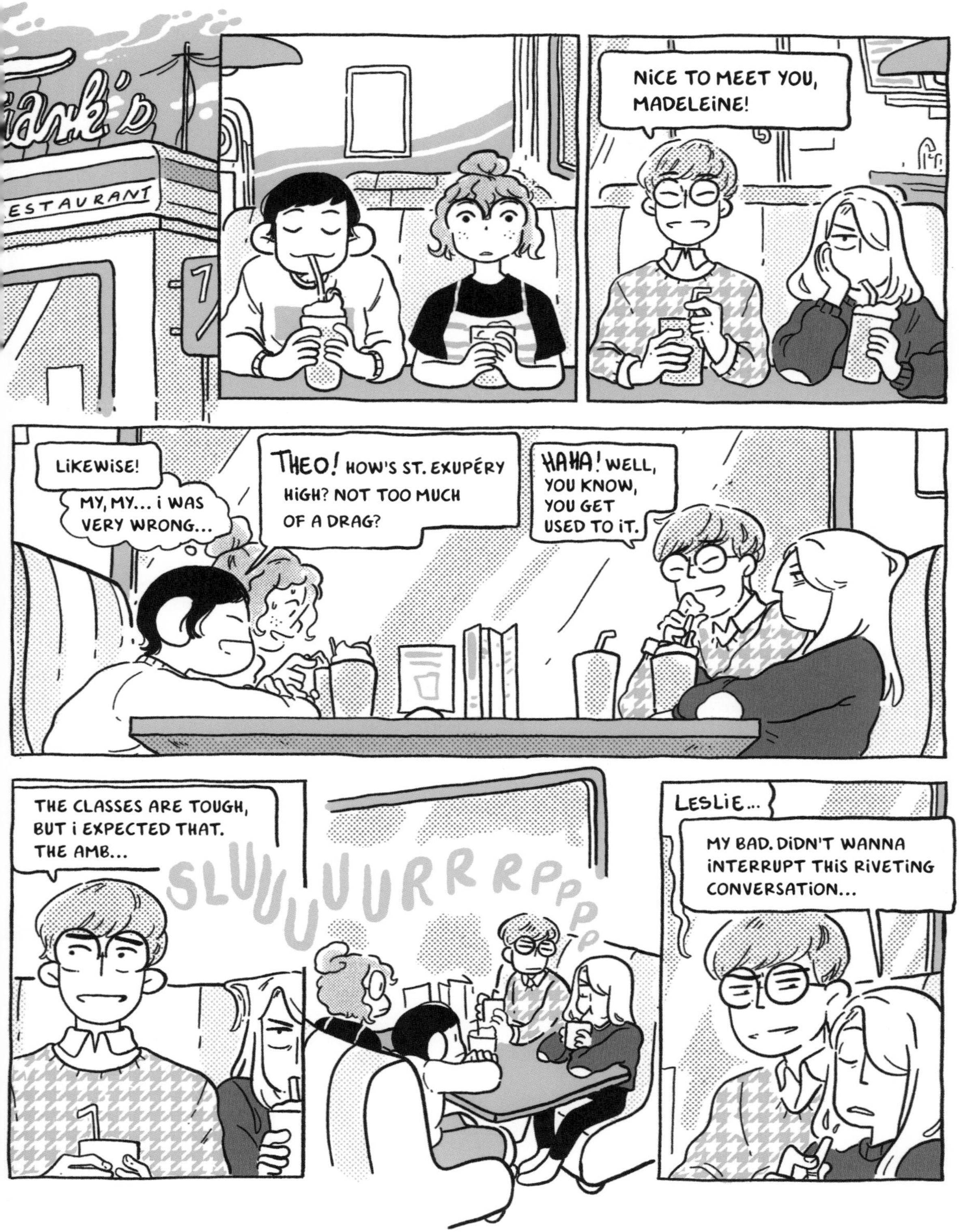

RESTAURANT
NICE TO MEET YOU, MADELEINE!
LIKEWISE!
MY, MY... I WAS VERY WRONG...
THEO! HOW'S ST. EXUPÉRY HIGH? NOT TOO MUCH OF A DRAG?
HAHA! WELL, YOU KNOW, YOU GET USED TO IT.
THE CLASSES ARE TOUGH, BUT I EXPECTED THAT. THE AMB...
SLUUUUUURRRRPPPPP
LESLIE...
MY BAD. DIDN'T WANNA INTERRUPT THIS RIVETING CONVERSATION...

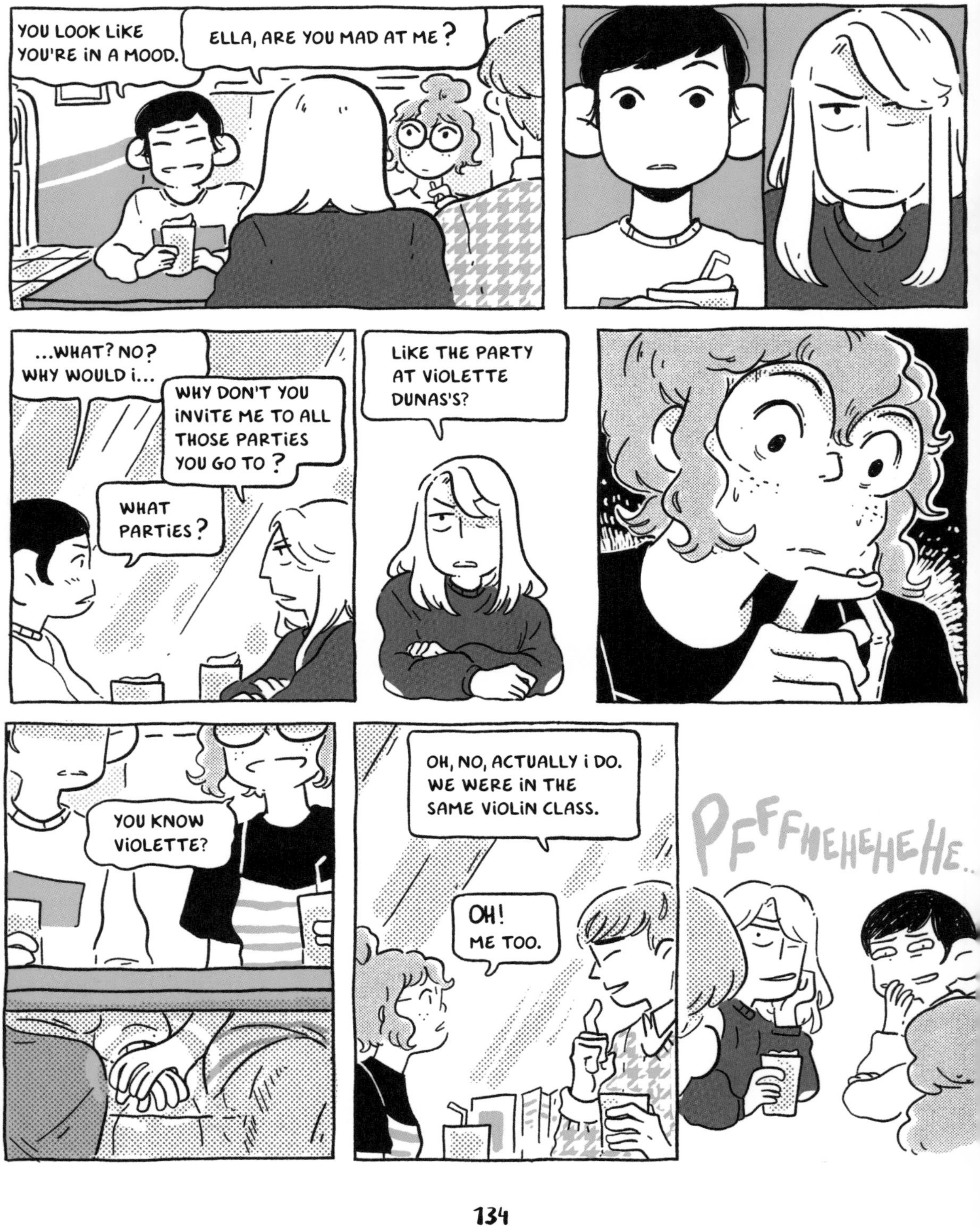
YOU LOOK LIKE YOU'RE IN A MOOD.
ELLA, ARE YOU MAD AT ME?
...WHAT? NO? WHY WOULD I...
WHY DON'T YOU INVITE ME TO ALL THOSE PARTIES YOU GO TO?
WHAT PARTIES?
LIKE THE PARTY AT VIOLETTE DUNAS'S?
YOU KNOW VIOLETTE?
OH, NO, ACTUALLY I DO. WE WERE IN THE SAME VIOLIN CLASS.
OH! ME TOO.
PFFFHEHEHEHEHE...

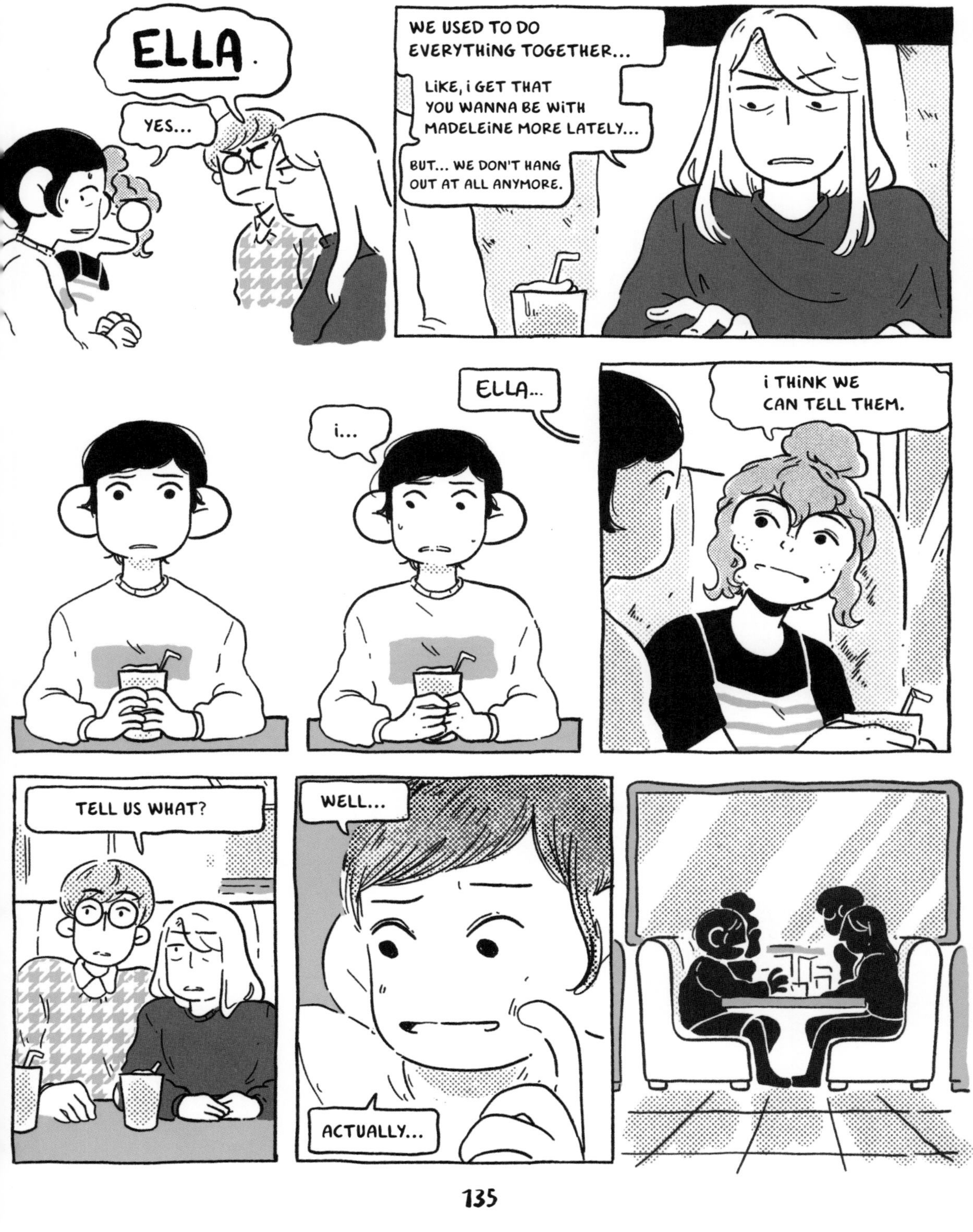
ELLA.
YES...
WE USED TO DO EVERYTHING TOGETHER...
LIKE, I GET THAT YOU WANNA BE WITH MADELEINE MORE LATELY...
BUT... WE DON'T HANG OUT AT ALL ANYMORE.
ELLA...
I...
I THINK WE CAN TELL THEM.
TELL US WHAT?
WELL...
ACTUALLY...

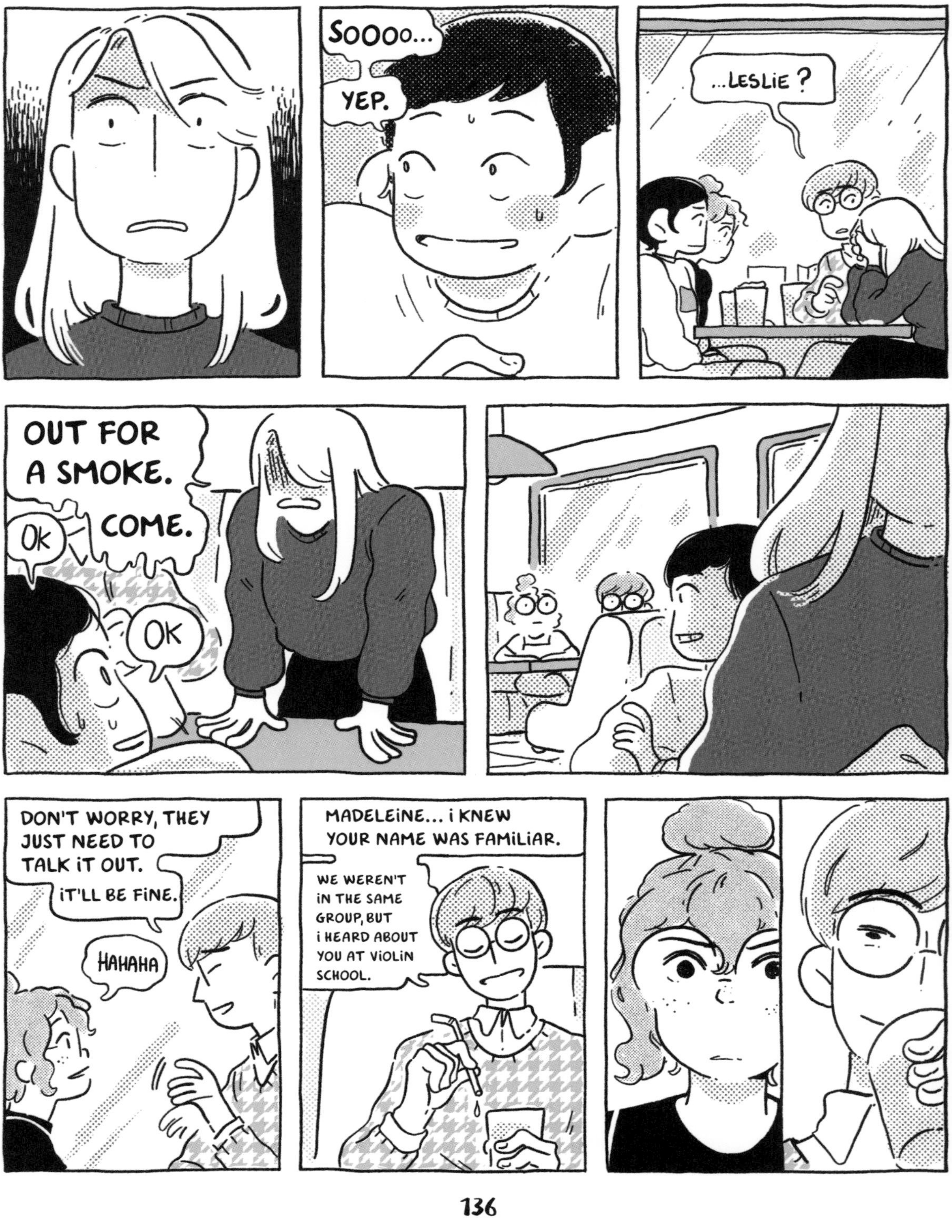
SOOOo...
YEP.
...LESLIE ?
OUT FOR A SMOKE.
COME.
OK
OK
DON'T WORRY, THEY JUST NEED TO TALK IT OUT.
IT'LL BE FINE.
HAHAHA
MADELEINE... I KNEW YOUR NAME WAS FAMILIAR.
WE WEREN'T IN THE SAME GROUP, BUT I HEARD ABOUT YOU AT VIOLIN SCHOOL.

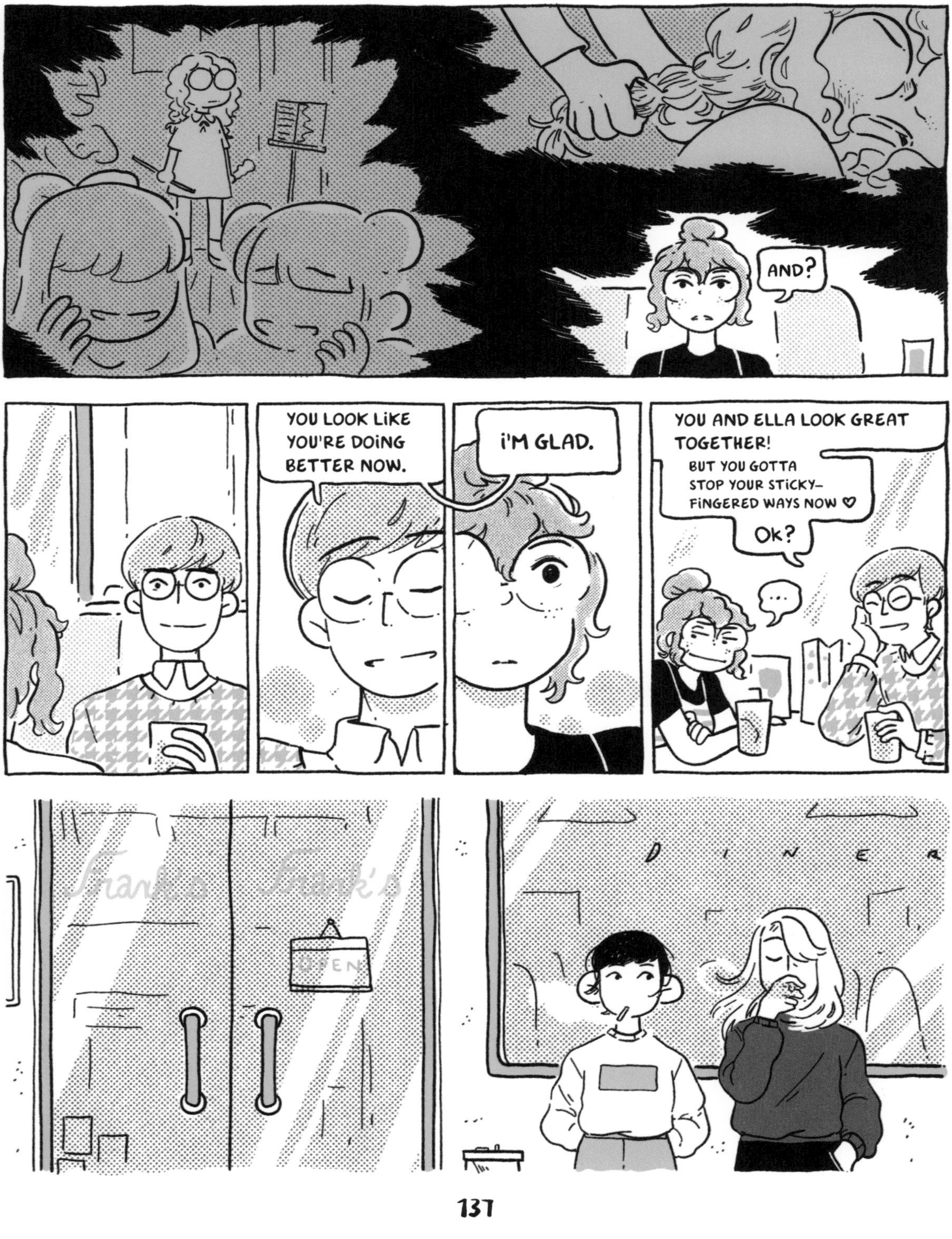

AND?
YOU LOOK LIKE YOU'RE DOING BETTER NOW.
I'M GLAD.
YOU AND ELLA LOOK GREAT TOGETHER!
BUT YOU GOTTA STOP YOUR STICKY-FINGERED WAYS NOW ♡
OK?
...
Frank's Frank's
OPEN
DINER

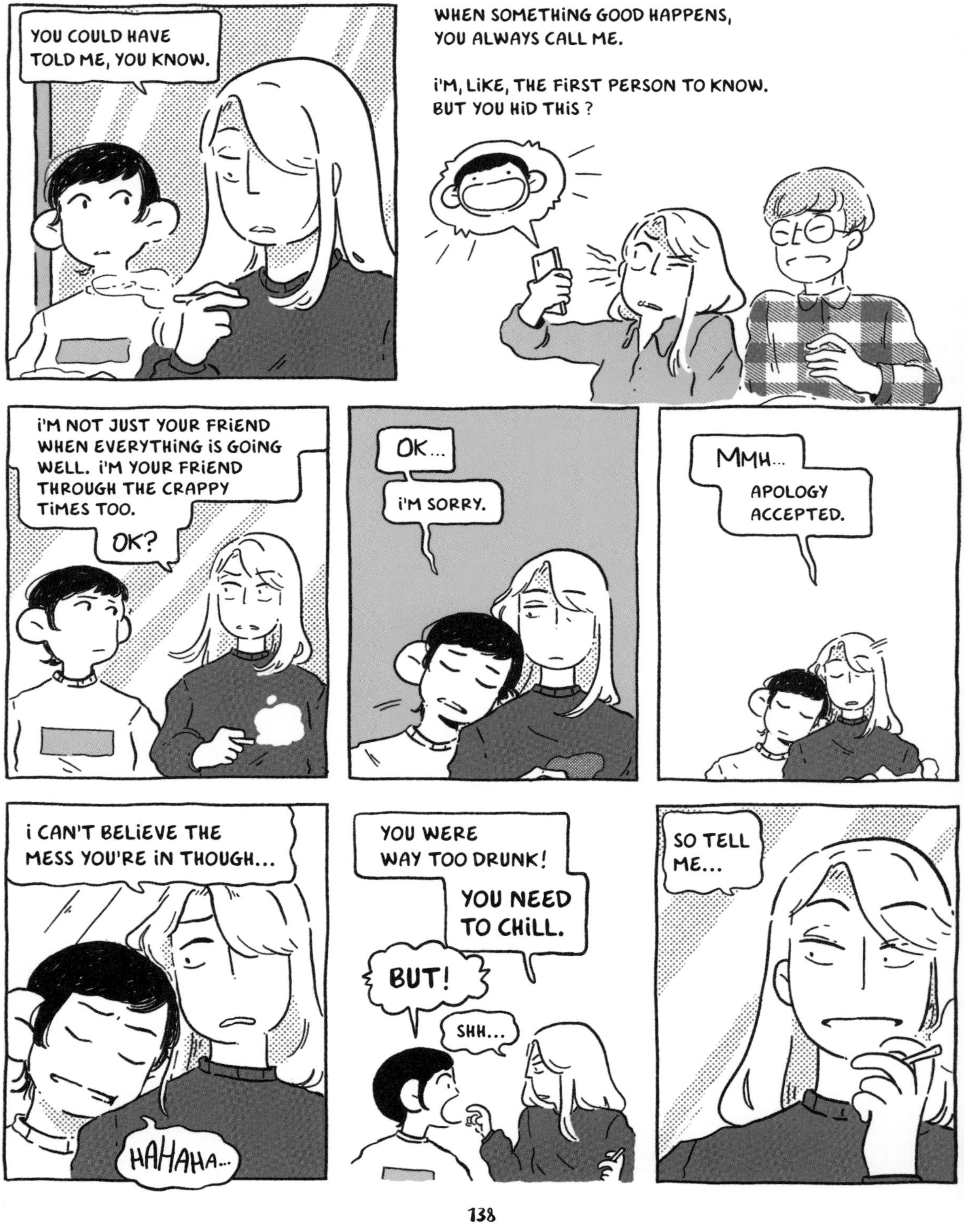
YOU COULD HAVE TOLD ME, YOU KNOW.
WHEN SOMETHING GOOD HAPPENS, YOU ALWAYS CALL ME.
I'M, LIKE, THE FIRST PERSON TO KNOW. BUT YOU HID THIS ?
I'M NOT JUST YOUR FRIEND WHEN EVERYTHING IS GOING WELL. I'M YOUR FRIEND THROUGH THE CRAPPY TIMES TOO.
OK?
OK...
I'M SORRY.
MMH...
APOLOGY ACCEPTED.
I CAN'T BELIEVE THE MESS YOU'RE IN THOUGH...
HAHAHA...
YOU WERE WAY TOO DRUNK!
YOU NEED TO CHILL.
BUT!
SHH...
SO TELL ME...

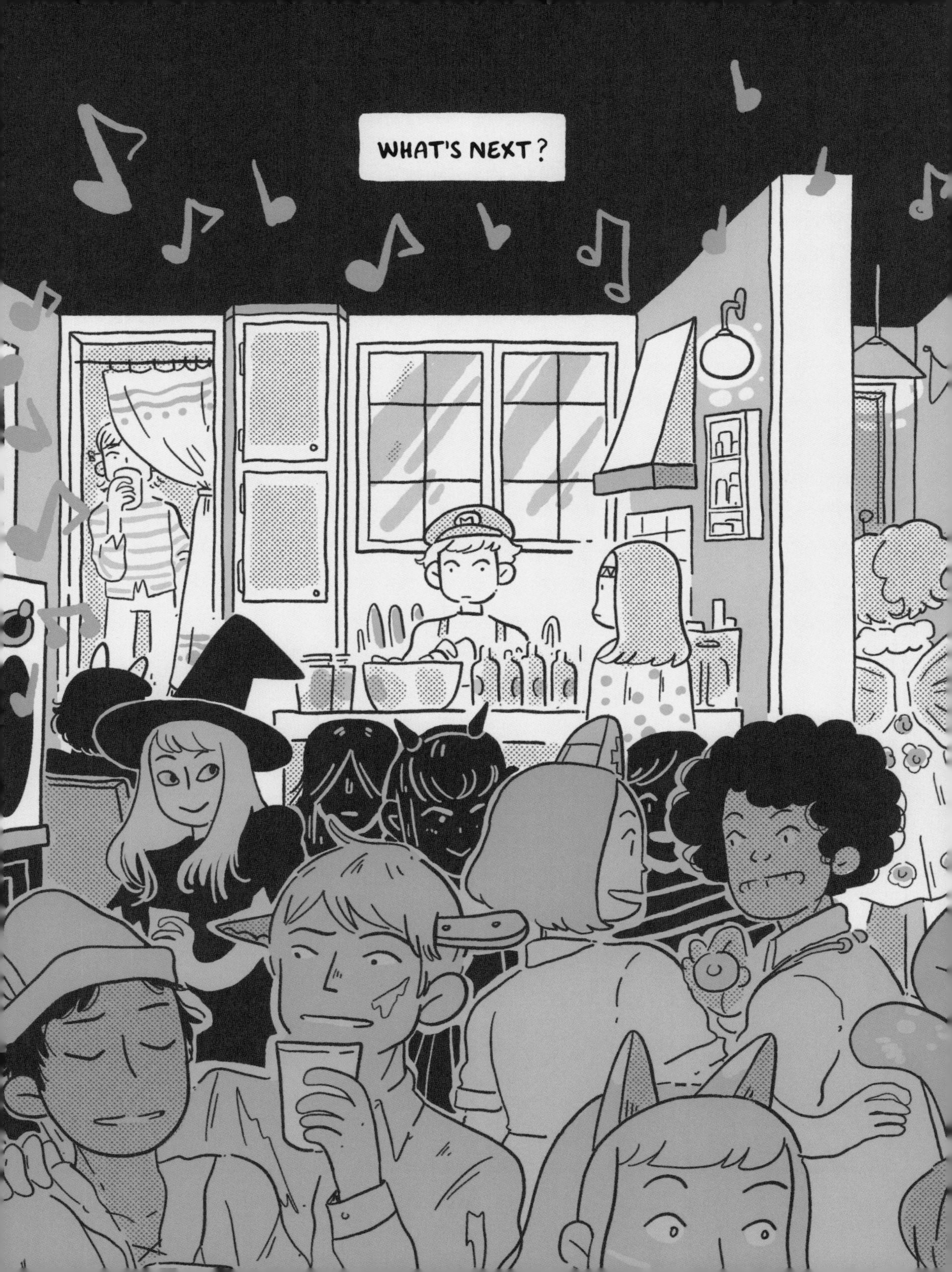
WHAT'S NEXT?

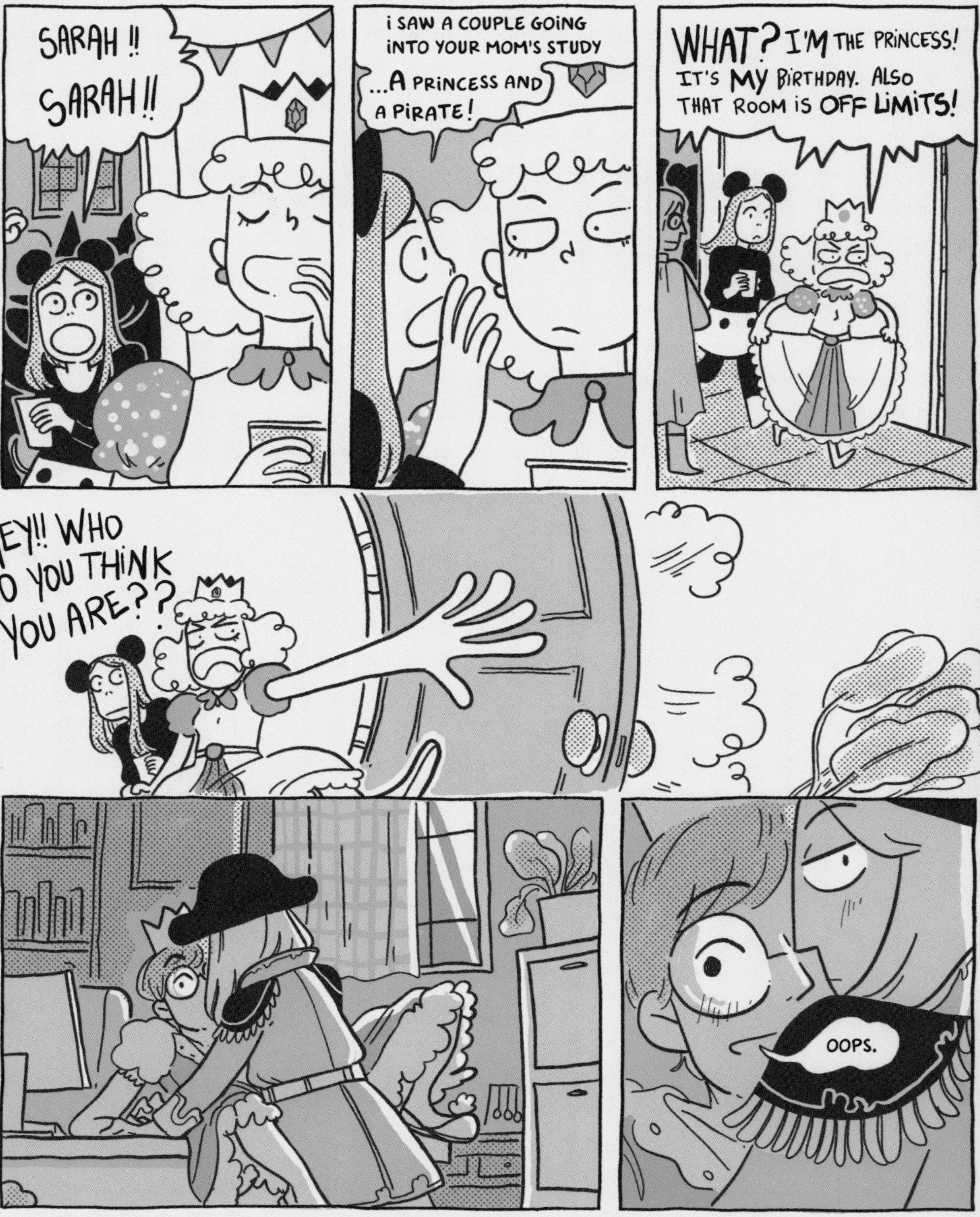
SARAH !!
SARAH !!
i SAW A COUPLE GOiNG iNTO YOUR MOM'S STUDY
...A PRiNCESS AND A PiRATE!
WHAT? I'M THE PRiNCESS! IT'S MY BiRTHDAY. ALSO THAT ROOM iS OFF LiMiTS!
HEY!! WHO DO YOU THiNK YOU ARE??
OOPS.

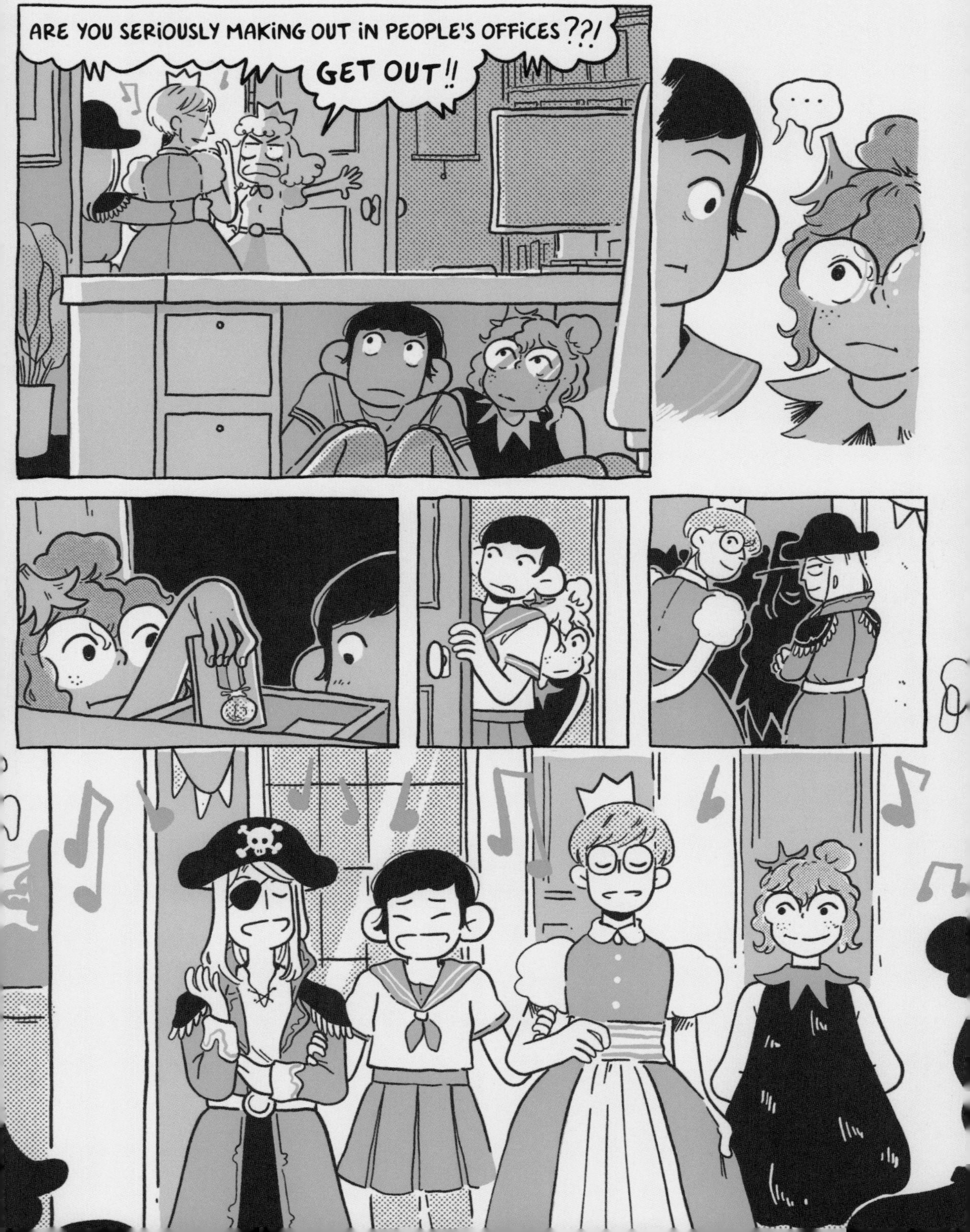

ARE YOU SERIOUSLY MAKING OUT IN PEOPLE'S OFFICES ??!
GET OUT!!
...

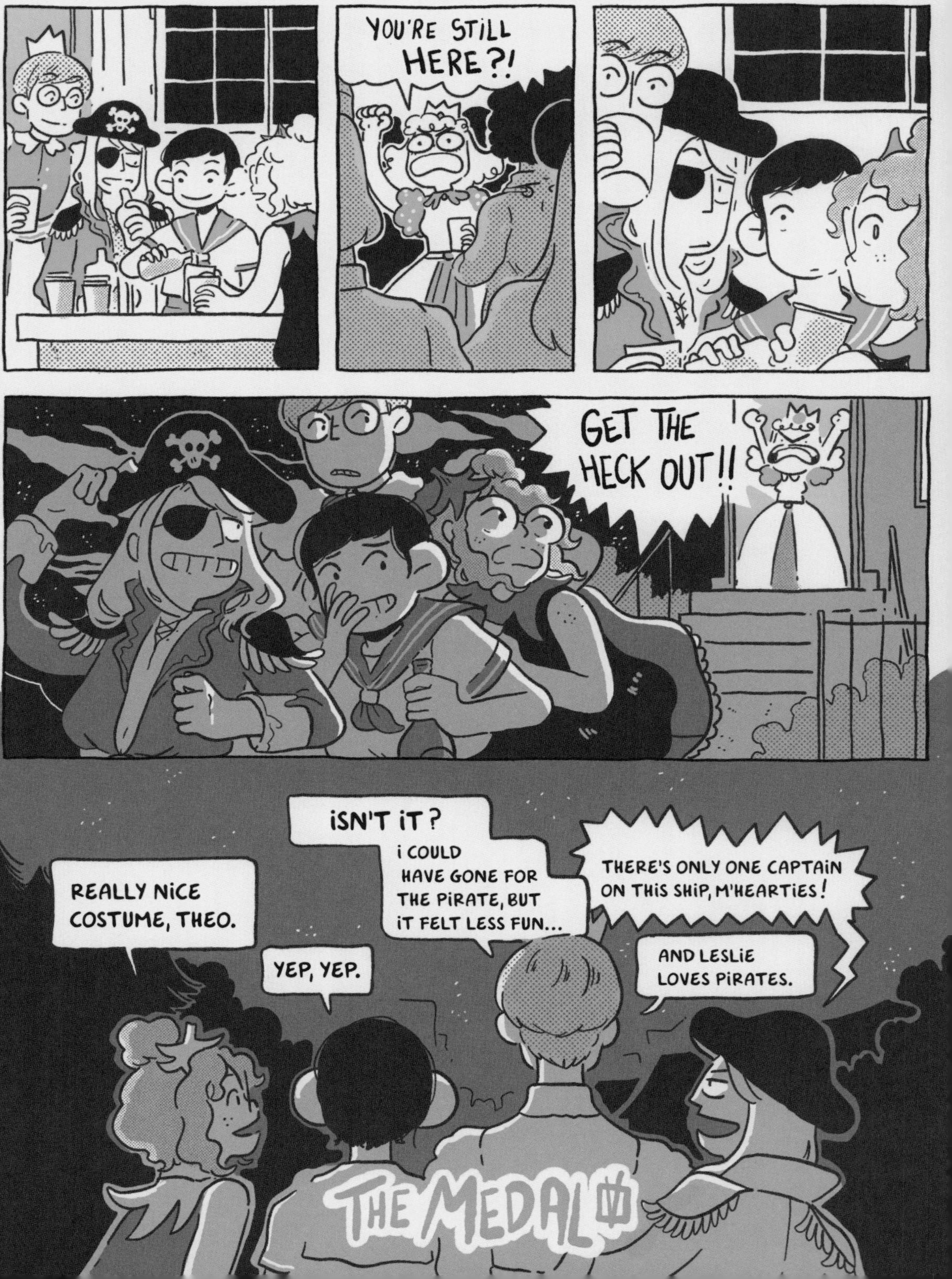
YOU'RE STILL HERE?!
GET THE HECK OUT!!
REALLY NICE COSTUME, THEO.
YEP, YEP.
ISN'T IT?
I COULD HAVE GONE FOR THE PIRATE, BUT IT FELT LESS FUN...
THERE'S ONLY ONE CAPTAIN ON THIS SHIP, M'HEARTIES!
AND LESLIE LOVES PIRATES.
THE MEDAL

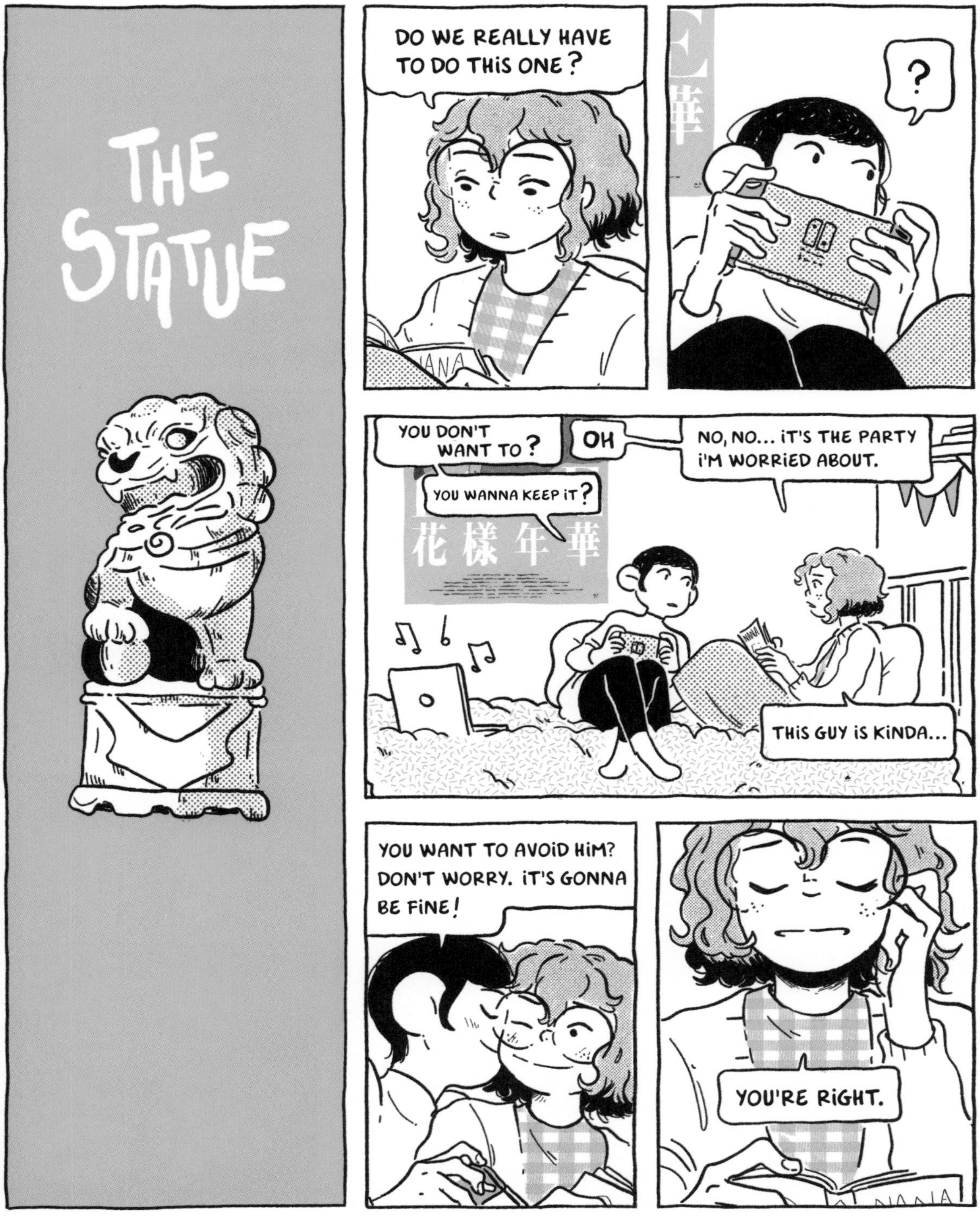
THE STATUE
DO WE REALLY HAVE TO DO THIS ONE?
?
NANA
華
YOU DON'T WANT TO?
OH
NO, NO... IT'S THE PARTY I'M WORRIED ABOUT.
YOU WANNA KEEP IT?
花様年華
THIS GUY IS KINDA...
YOU WANT TO AVOID HIM? DON'T WORRY. IT'S GONNA BE FINE!
YOU'RE RIGHT.
NANA

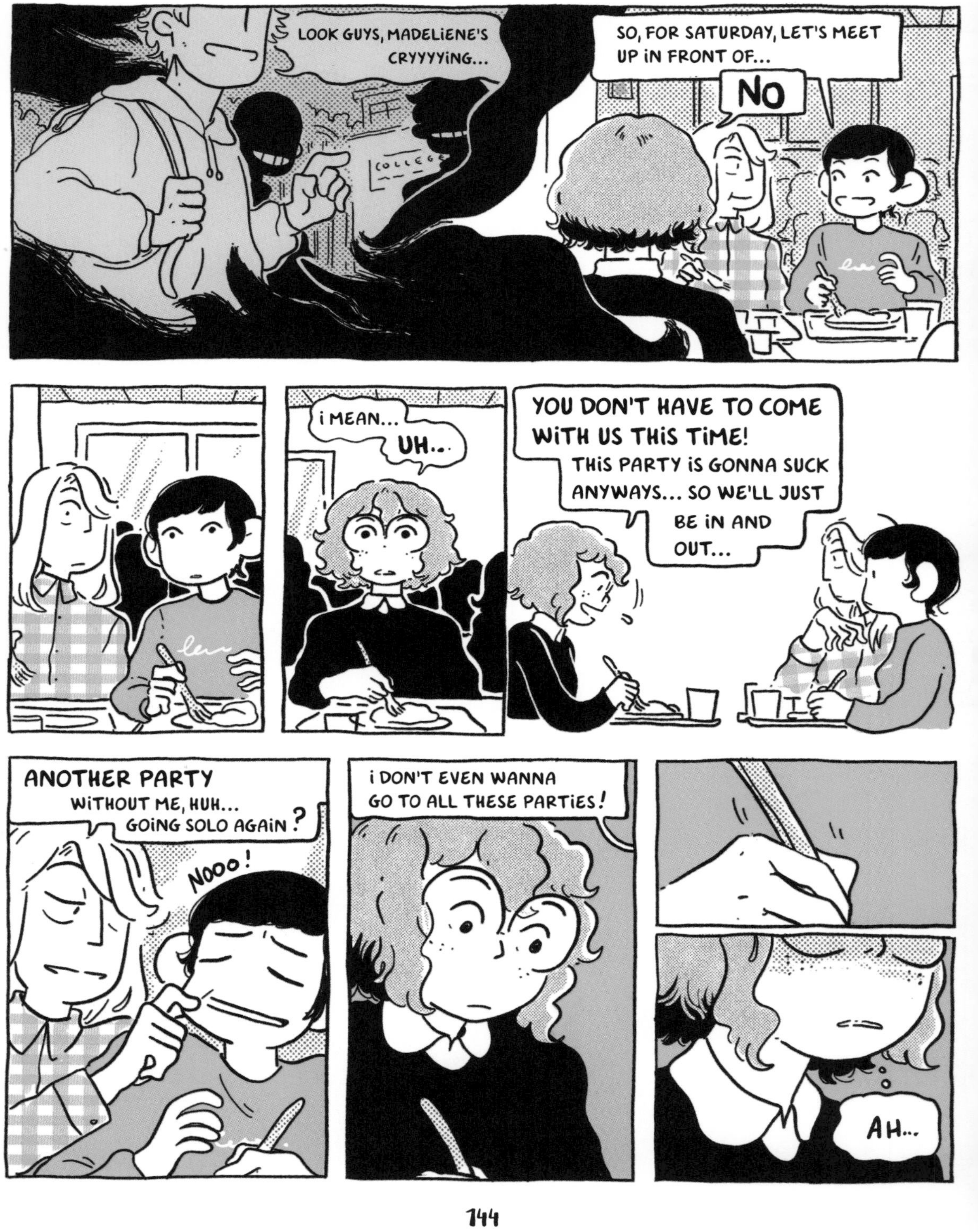
LOOK GUYS, MADELIENE'S CRYYYYING...
SO, FOR SATURDAY, LET'S MEET UP IN FRONT OF...
NO
I MEAN...
UH...
YOU DON'T HAVE TO COME WITH US THIS TIME!
THIS PARTY IS GONNA SUCK ANYWAYS... SO WE'LL JUST BE IN AND OUT...
ANOTHER PARTY WITHOUT ME, HUH... GOING SOLO AGAIN?
NOOO!
I DON'T EVEN WANNA GO TO ALL THESE PARTIES!
AH...

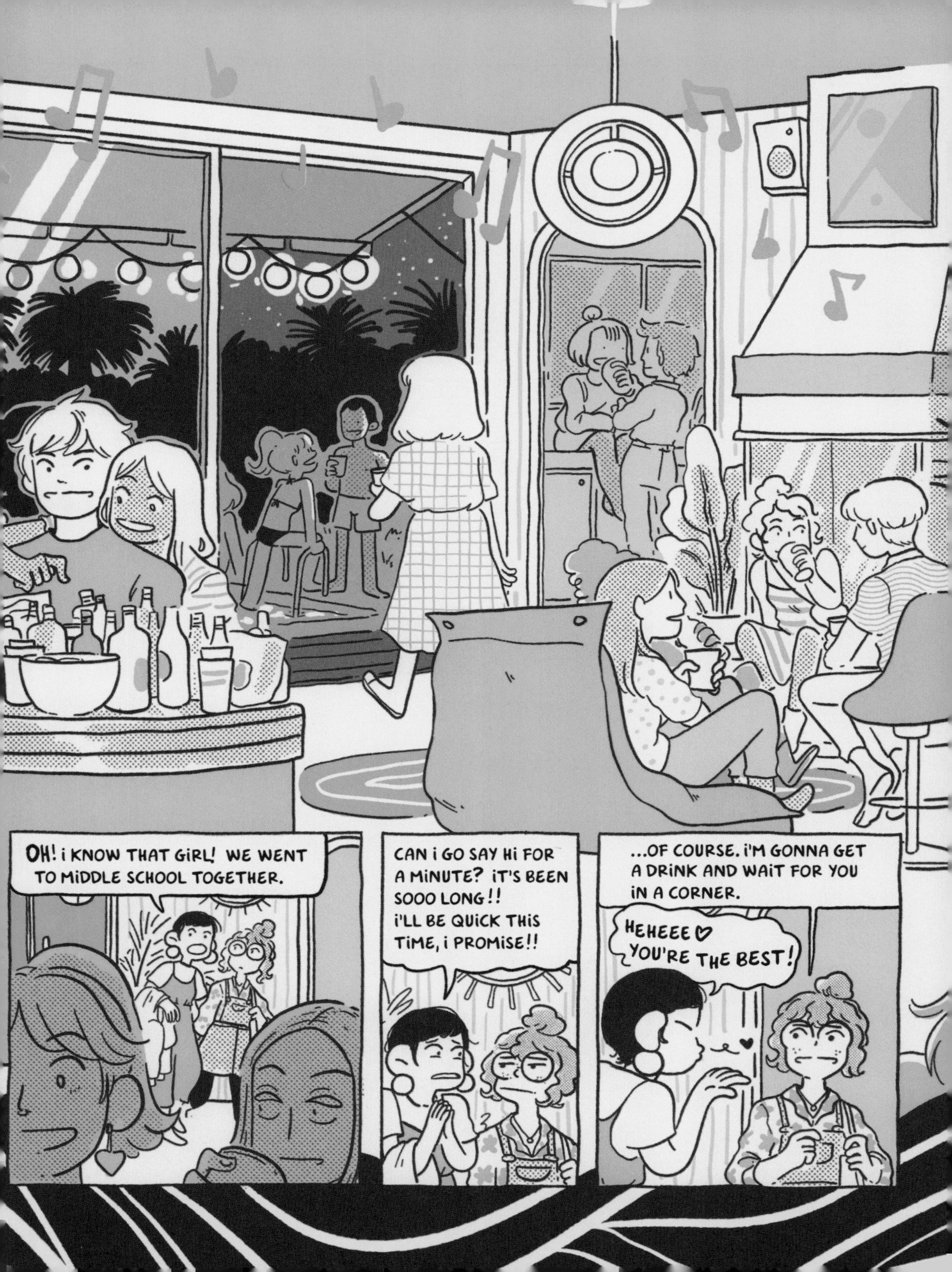
OH! i KNOW THAT GiRL! WE WENT TO MiDDLE SCHOOL TOGETHER.
CAN i GO SAY Hi FOR A MiNUTE? iT'S BEEN SOOO LONG!! i'LL BE QUICK THIS TiME, i PROMiSE!!
...OF COURSE. i'M GONNA GET A DRiNK AND WAIT FOR YOU iN A CORNER.
HEHEEE ♡ YOU'RE THE BEST!

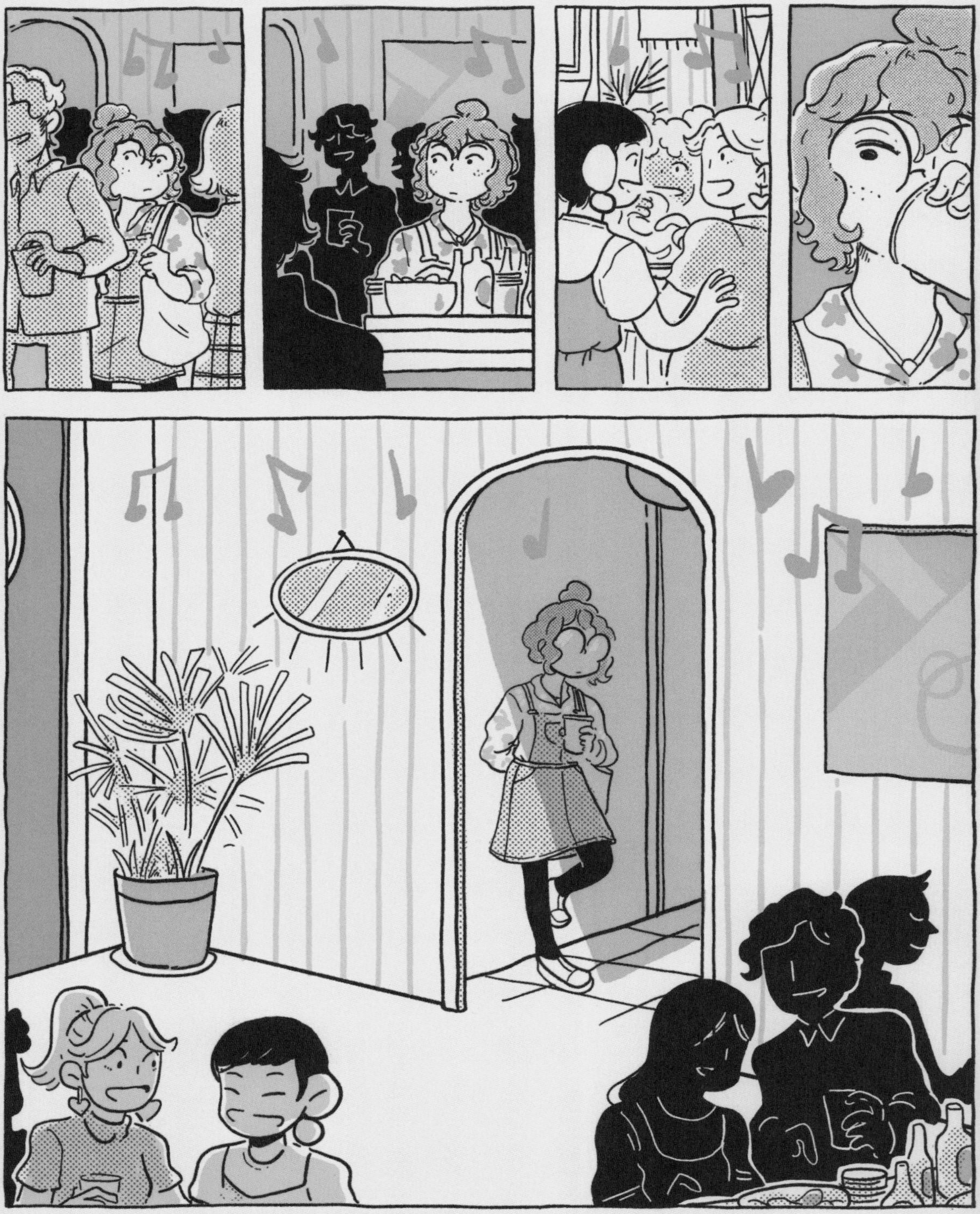

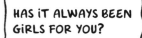
HAS IT ALWAYS BEEN GIRLS FOR YOU?

··· NO.

OH!

WANNA HEAR ABOUT MY HOT AND STEAMY PAST?

NO NEED FOR DETAILS, THANK YOU...

MY FIRST LOVE WAS MARCEL. HE HAD A RED PLASTIC SHOVEL AND LONG BLOND HAIR.

MY HEART SHATTERED.

SO YOU ONLY LIKED HIM FOR HIS BODY... HOW SCANDALOUS!

HE LET ME BRAID THEM EVERY RECESS, IT WAS ✦REAL✦ LOVE

AND ONE DAY... HE HAD A BUZZCUT!!

147

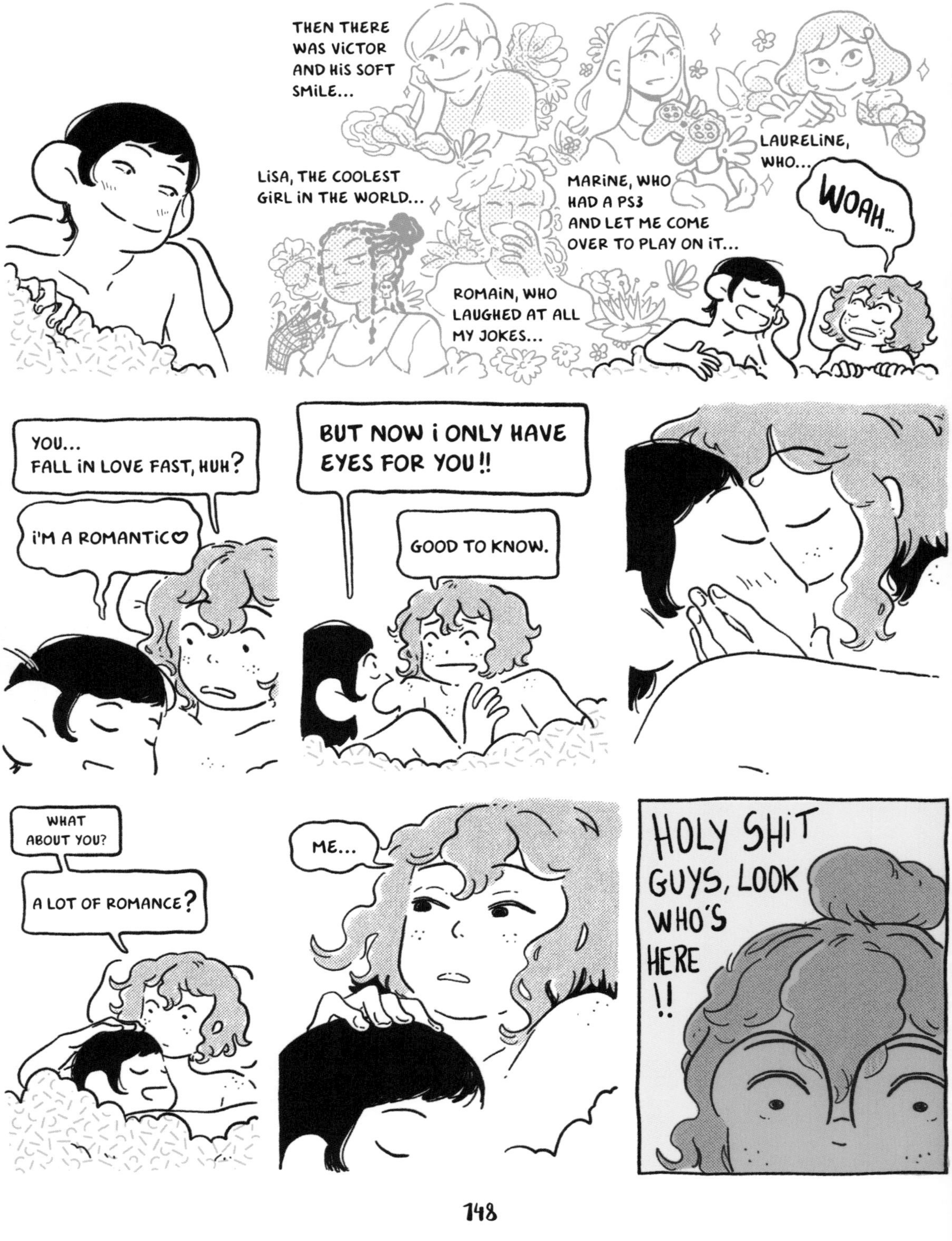
THEN THERE WAS ViCTOR AND HiS SOFT SMiLE...
LiSA, THE COOLEST GiRL iN THE WORLD...
ROMAiN, WHO LAUGHED AT ALL MY JOKES...
MARiNE, WHO HAD A PS3 AND LET ME COME OVER TO PLAY ON iT...
LAURELiNE, WHO...
WOAH...
YOU... FALL iN LOVE FAST, HUH?
i'M A ROMANTiC♡
BUT NOW i ONLY HAVE EYES FOR YOU!!
GOOD TO KNOW.
WHAT ABOUT YOU?
A LOT OF ROMANCE?
ME...
HOLY SHiT GUYS, LOOK WHO'S HERE !!

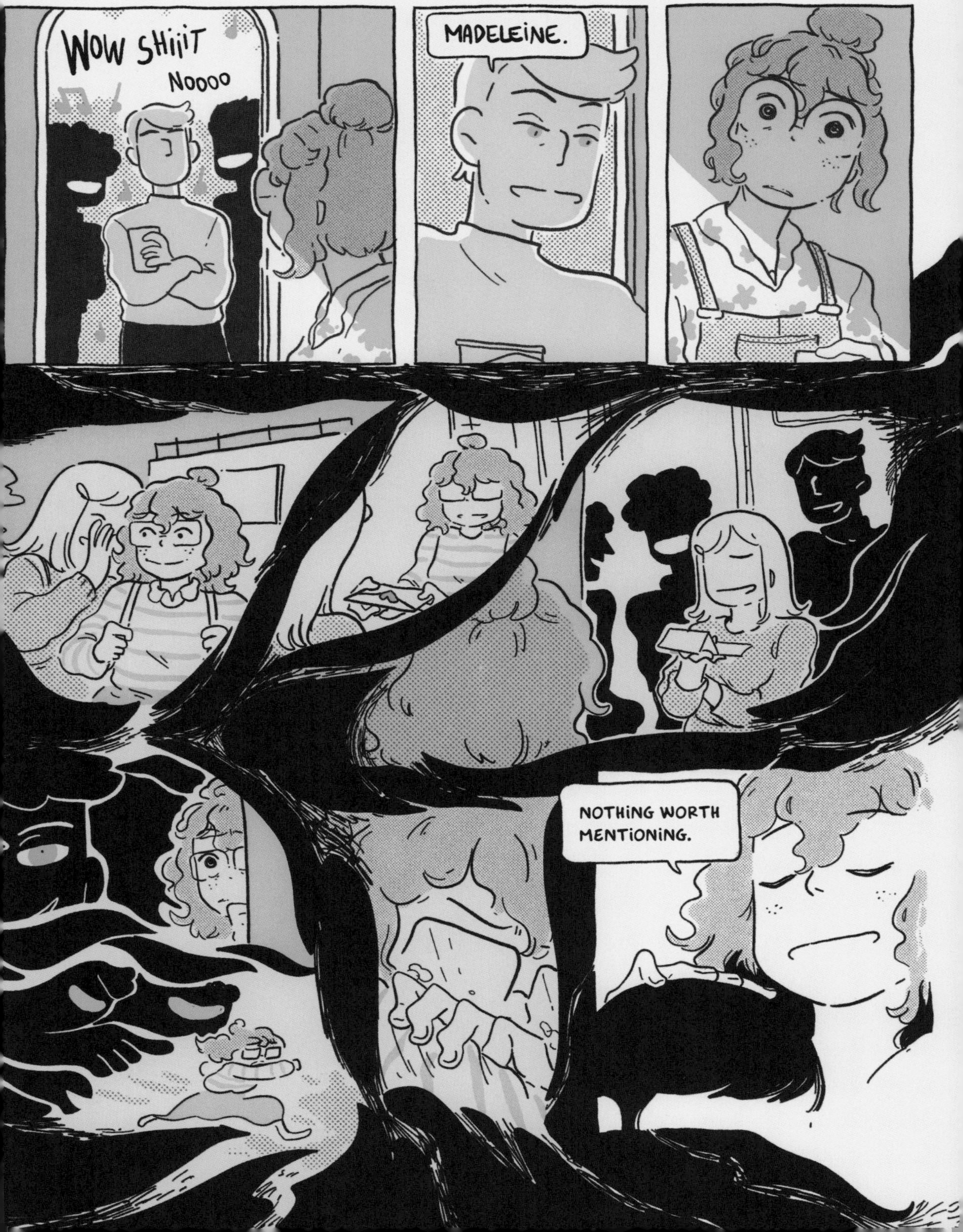
WOW SHIiiT
NOOOO
MADELEINE.
NOTHING WORTH MENTIONING.

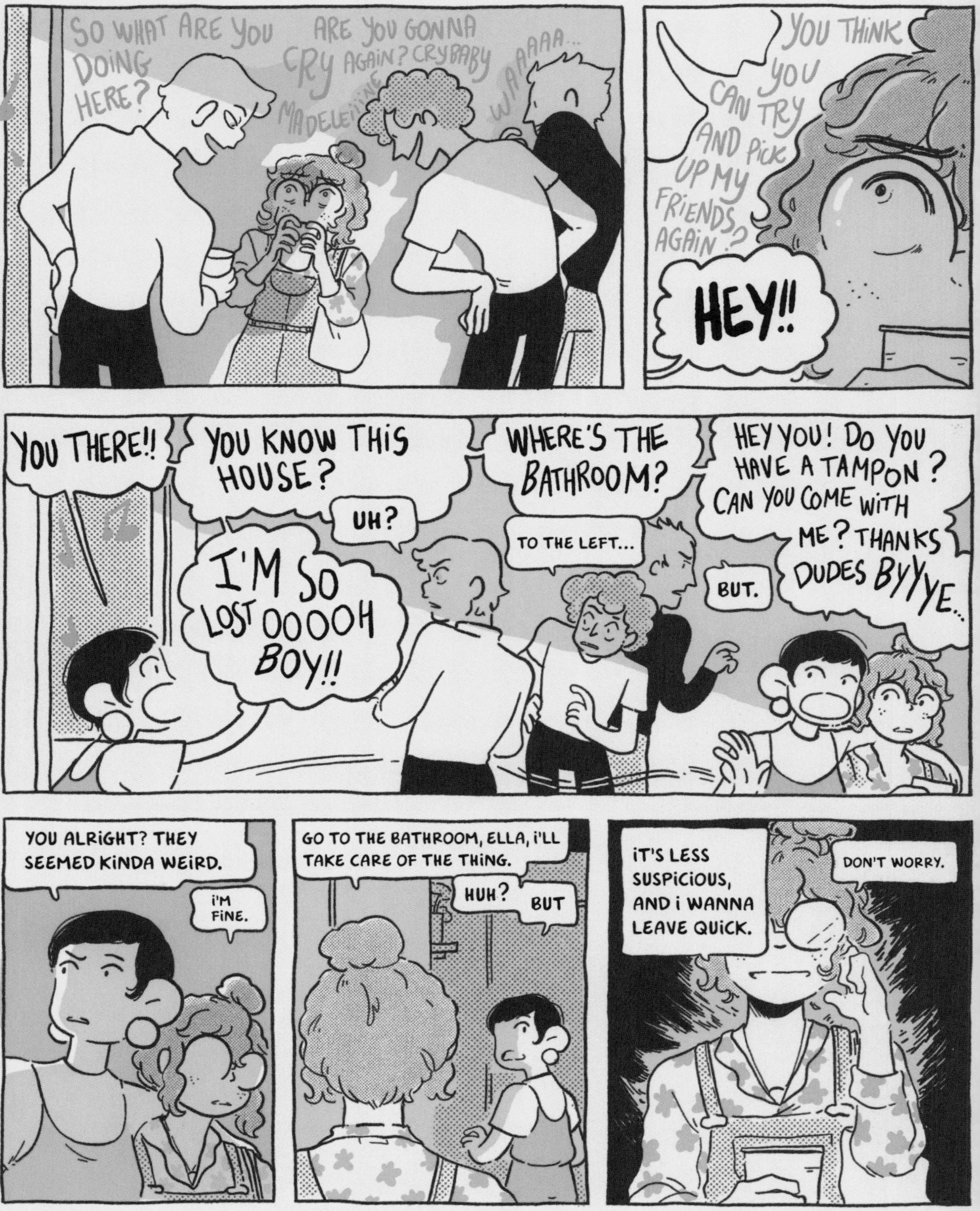
SO WHAT ARE YOU DOING HERE?
ARE YOU GONNA CRY AGAIN? CRYBABY
MADELEIIIINE
WAAAAAA...
YOU THINK YOU CAN TRY AND PICK UP MY FRIENDS AGAIN?
HEY!!
YOU THERE!!
YOU KNOW THIS HOUSE?
UH?
I'M SO LOST OOOOH BOY!!
WHERE'S THE BATHROOM?
TO THE LEFT...
HEY YOU! DO YOU HAVE A TAMPON? CAN YOU COME WITH ME? THANKS DUDES BYYYE...
BUT.
YOU ALRIGHT? THEY SEEMED KINDA WEIRD.
I'M FINE.
GO TO THE BATHROOM, ELLA, I'LL TAKE CARE OF THE THING.
HUH?
BUT
IT'S LESS SUSPICIOUS, AND I WANNA LEAVE QUICK.
DON'T WORRY.

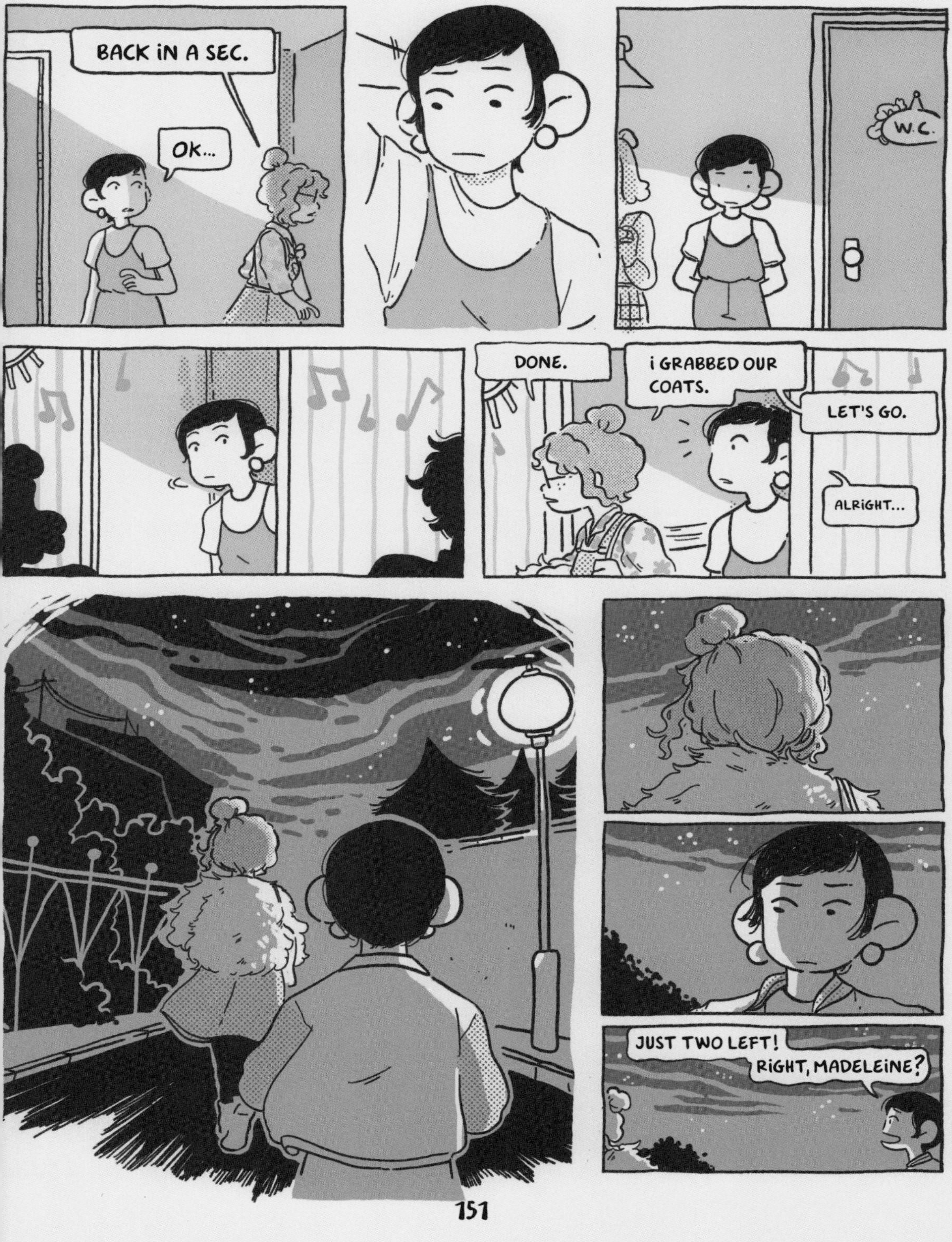

BACK IN A SEC.
OK...
W.C.
DONE.
I GRABBED OUR COATS.
LET'S GO.
ALRIGHT...
JUST TWO LEFT!
RIGHT, MADELEINE?

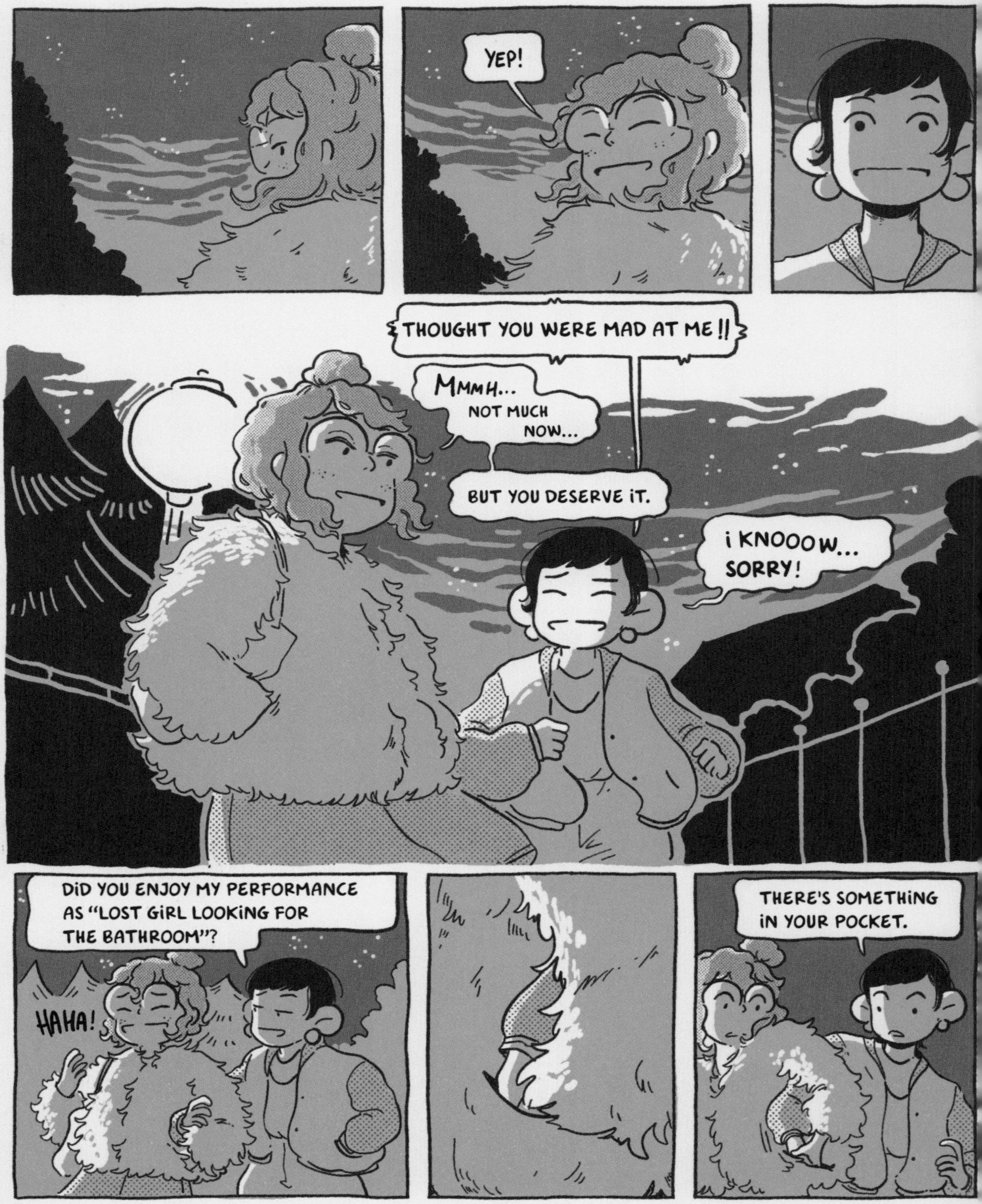
YEP!
THOUGHT YOU WERE MAD AT ME!!
MMMH... NOT MUCH NOW...
BUT YOU DESERVE iT.
i KNOOOW... SORRY!
DiD YOU ENJOY MY PERFORMANCE AS "LOST GiRL LOOKiNG FOR THE BATHROOM"?
HAHA!
THERE'S SOMETHiNG iN YOUR POCKET.

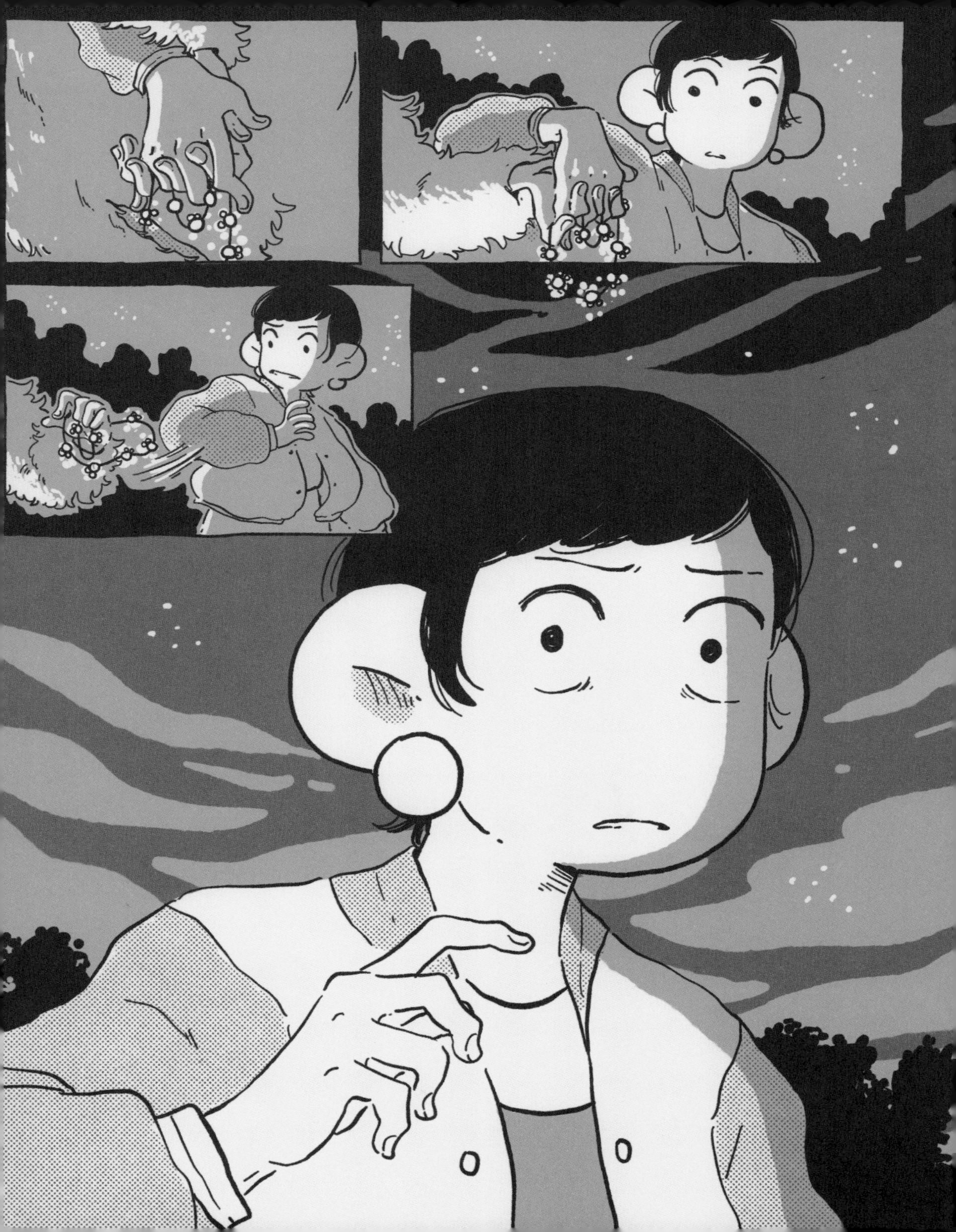

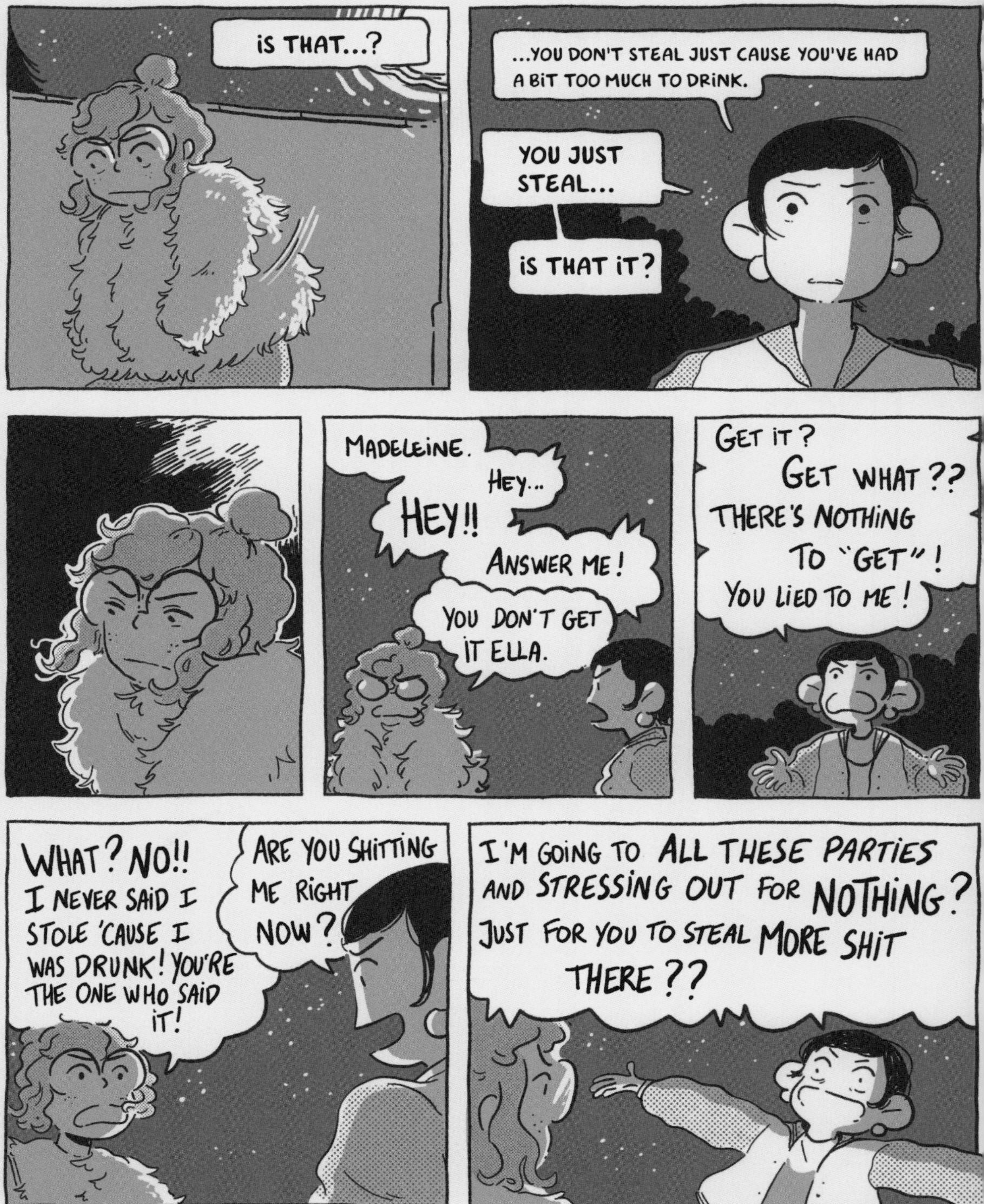
IS THAT...?
...YOU DON'T STEAL JUST CAUSE YOU'VE HAD A BIT TOO MUCH TO DRINK.
YOU JUST STEAL...
IS THAT IT?
MADELEINE.
Hey...
HEY!!
ANSWER ME!
YOU DON'T GET IT ELLA.
GET IT?
GET WHAT?? THERE'S NOTHING TO "GET"! YOU LIED TO ME!
WHAT? NO!! I NEVER SAID I STOLE 'CAUSE I WAS DRUNK! YOU'RE THE ONE WHO SAID IT!
ARE YOU SHITTING ME RIGHT NOW?
I'M GOING TO ALL THESE PARTIES AND STRESSING OUT FOR NOTHING? JUST FOR YOU TO STEAL MORE SHIT THERE??

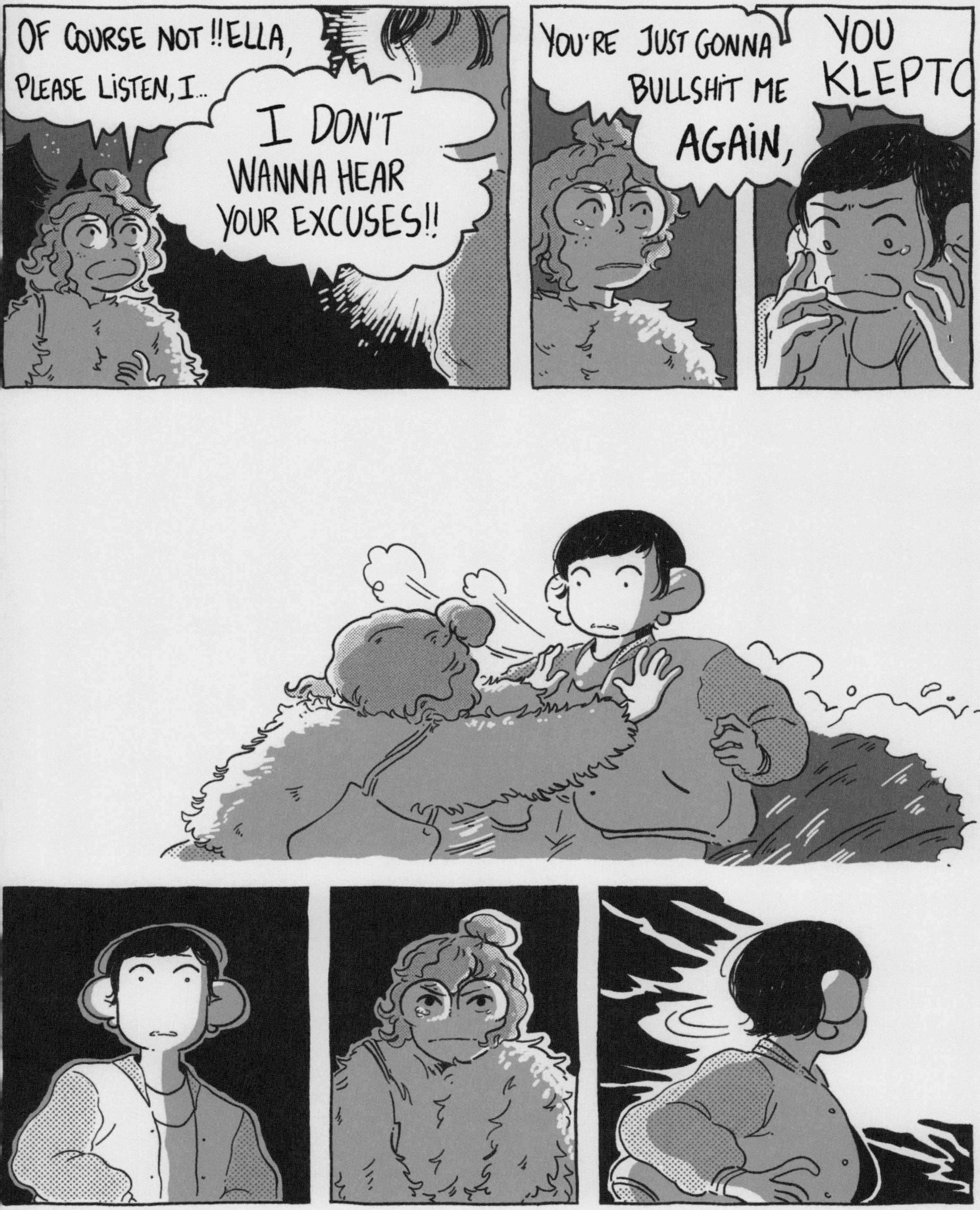
OF COURSE NOT!! ELLA, PLEASE LISTEN, I...
I DON'T WANNA HEAR YOUR EXCUSES!!
YOU'RE JUST GONNA BULLSHIT ME AGAIN,
YOU KLEPTO

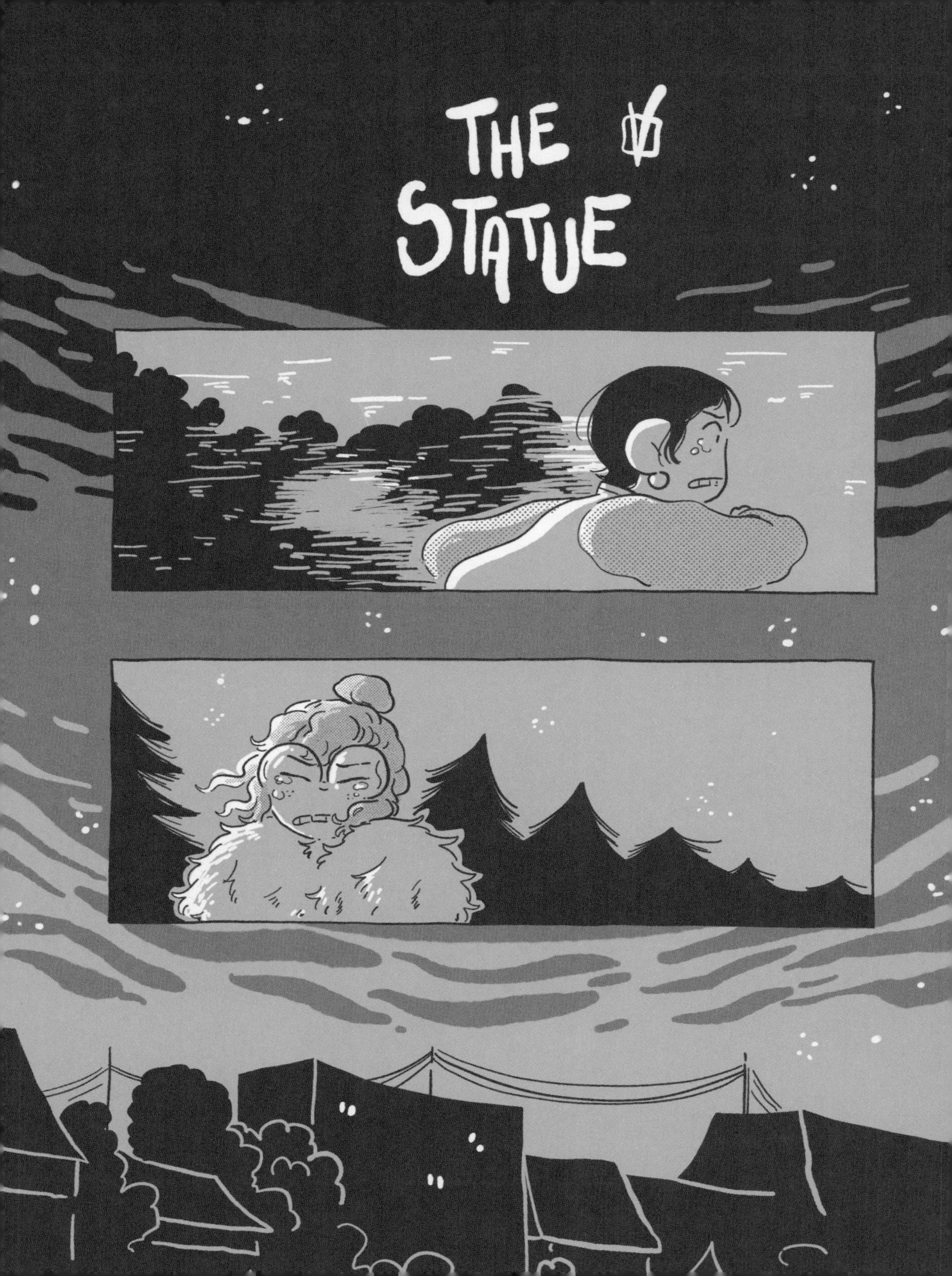
THE STATUE

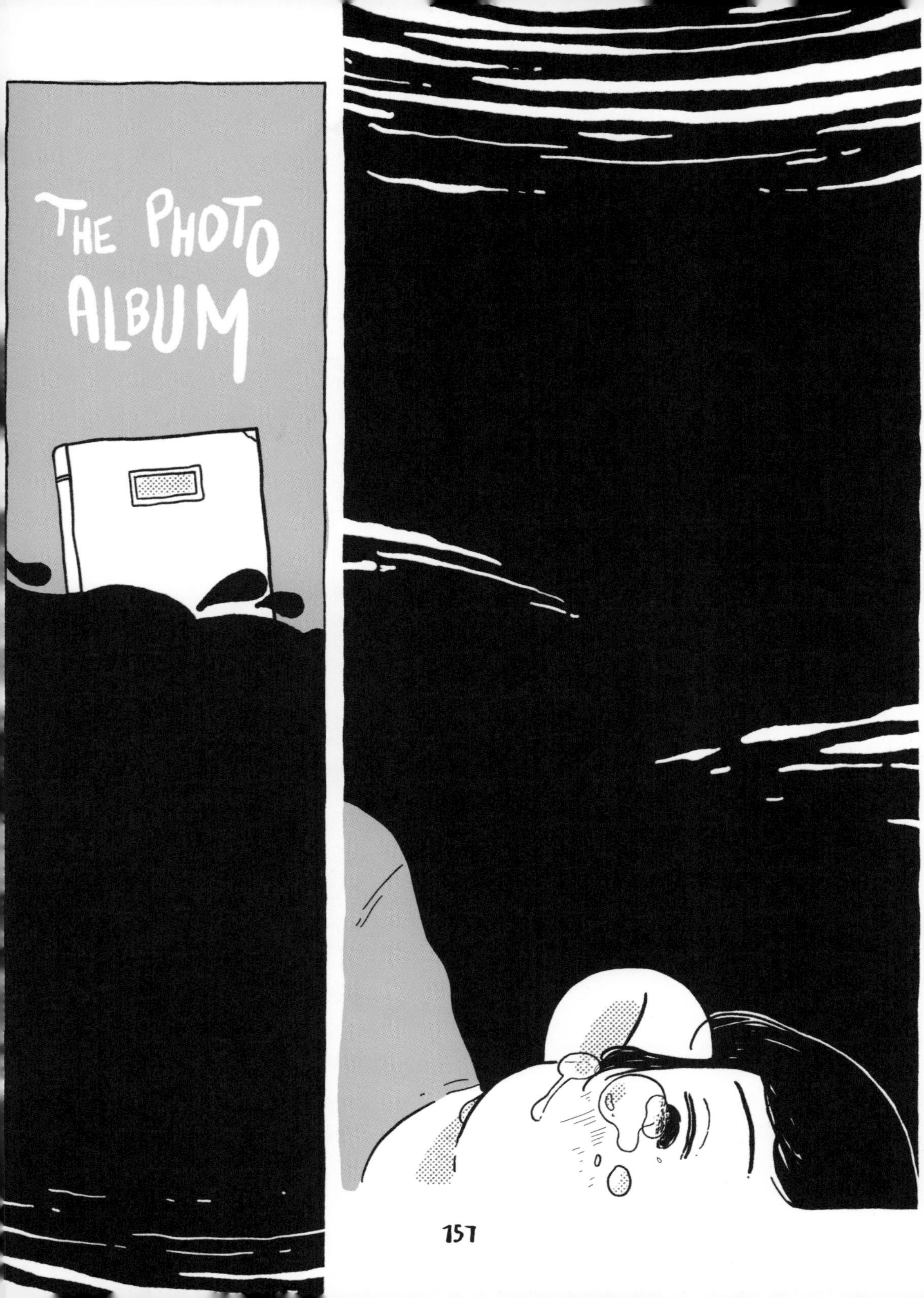
THE PHOTO ALBUM

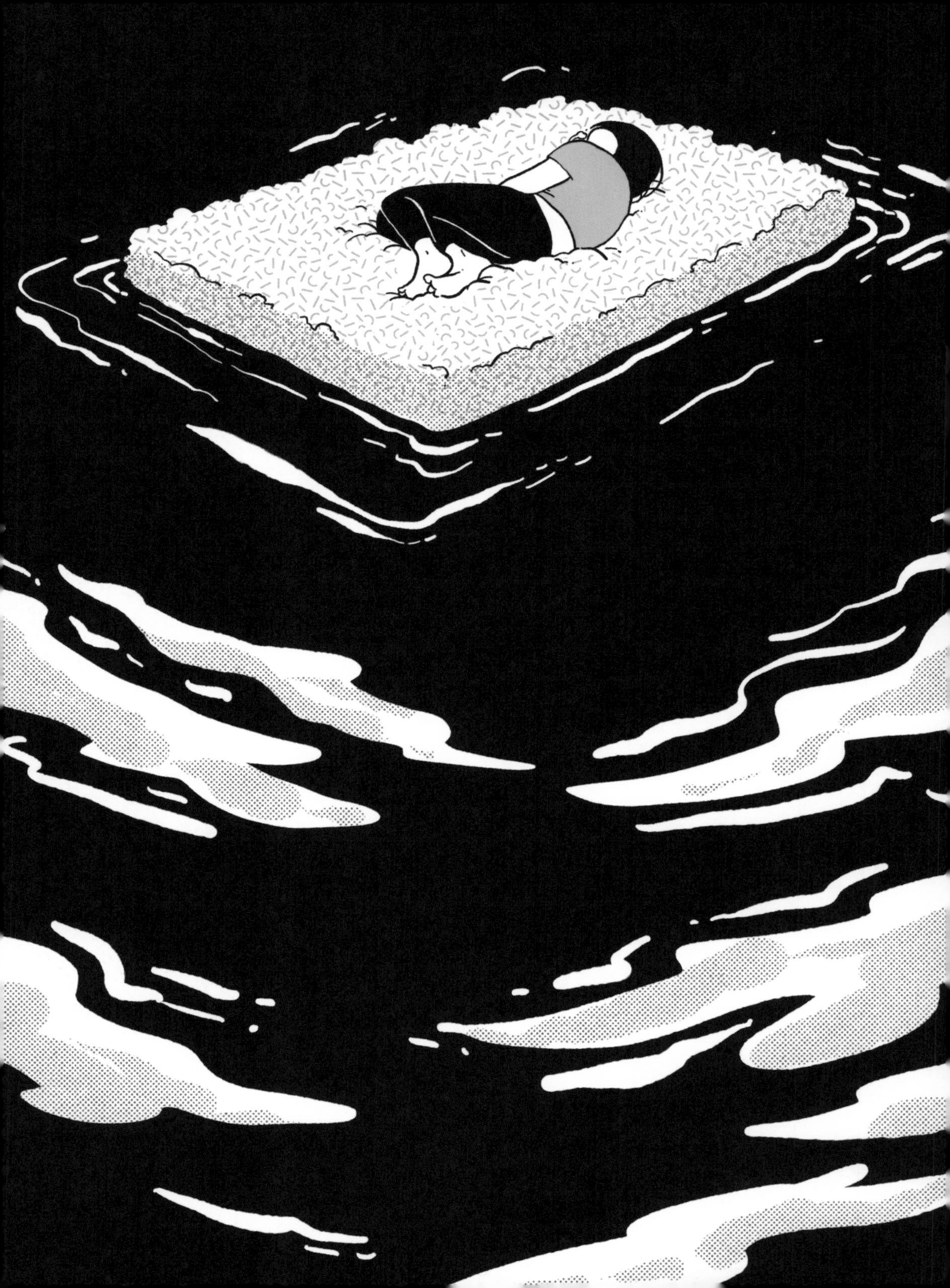

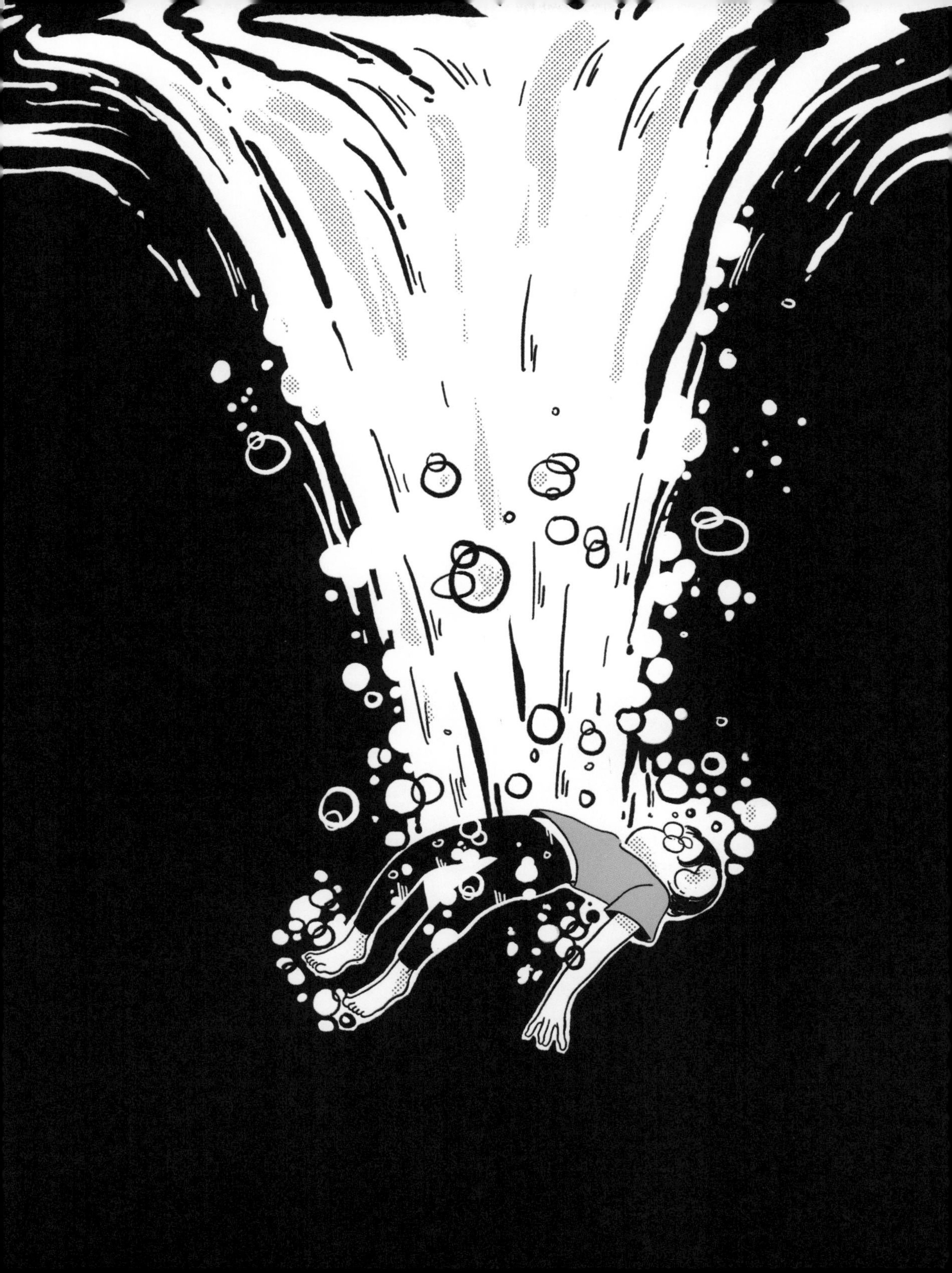

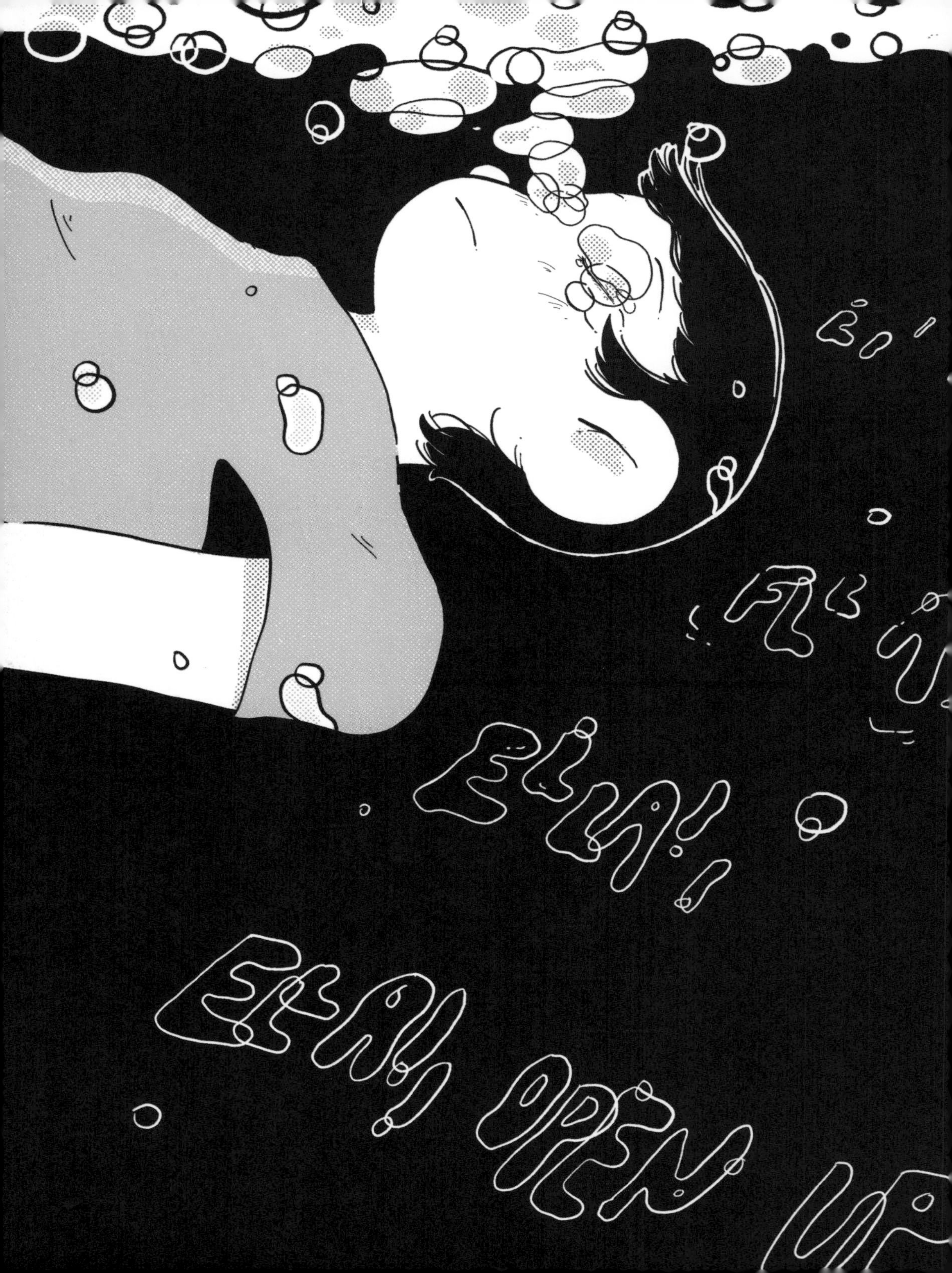
ELLA!
ELLA, OPEN UP

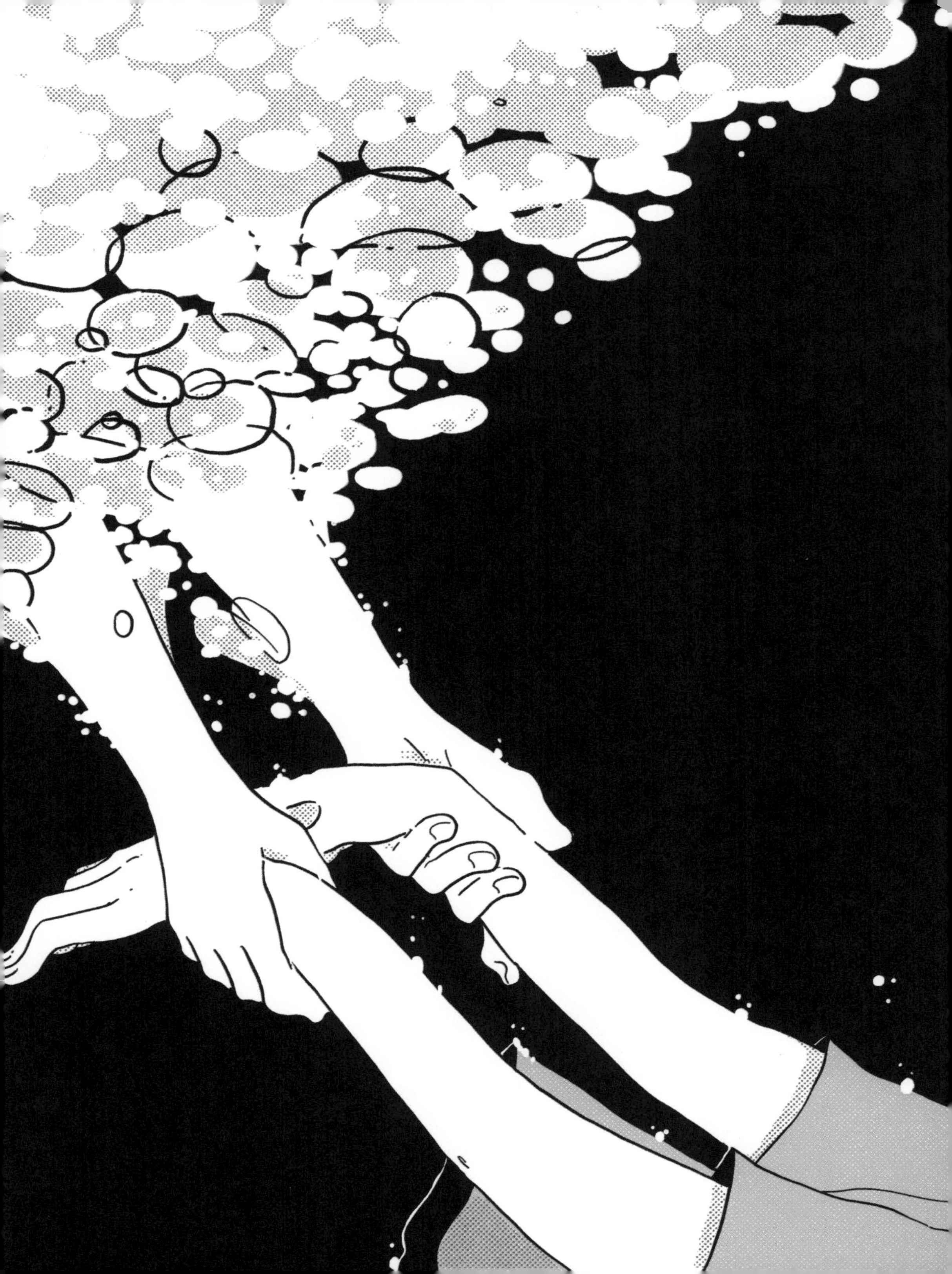

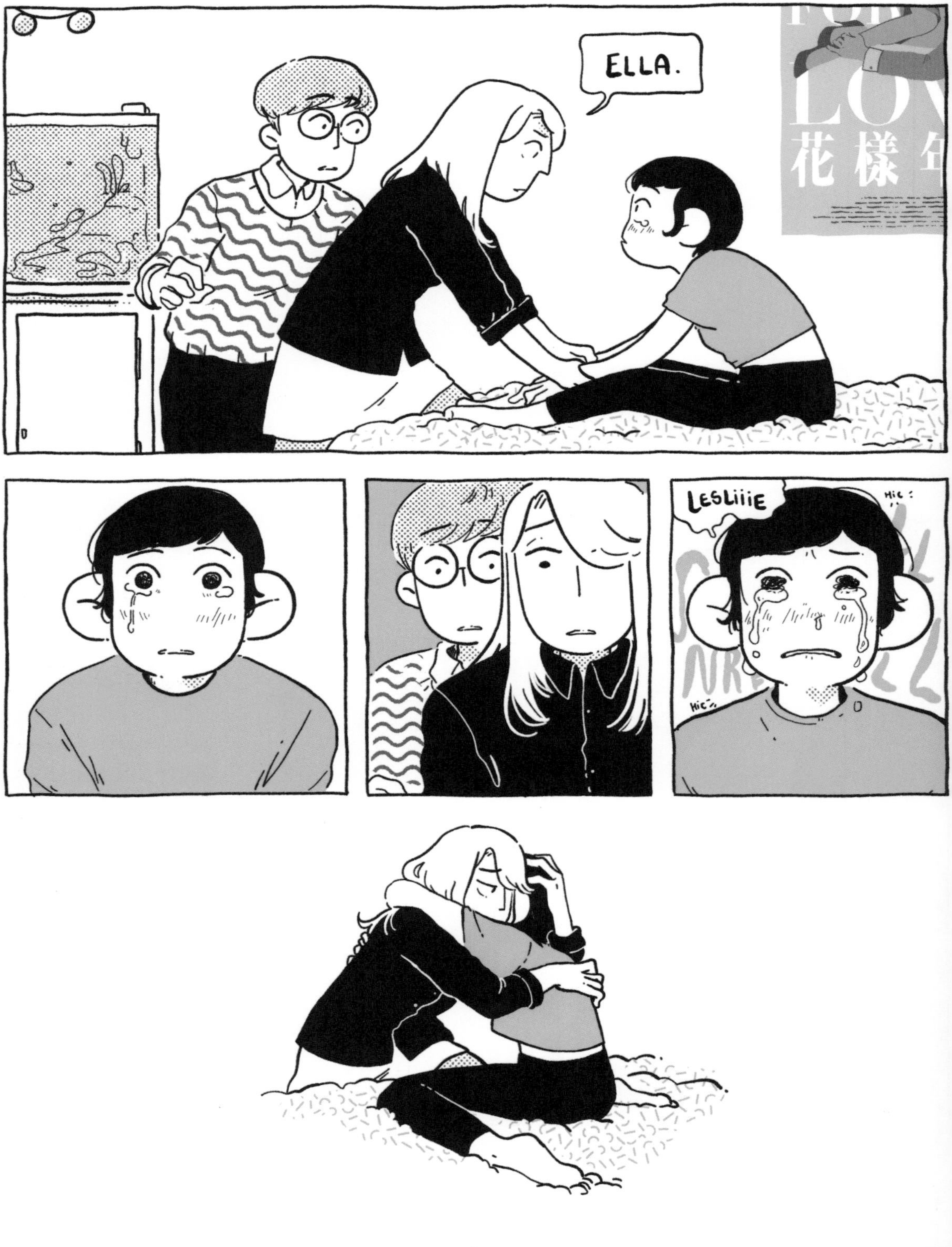
ELLA.
LESLIIIE
HIC
HIC

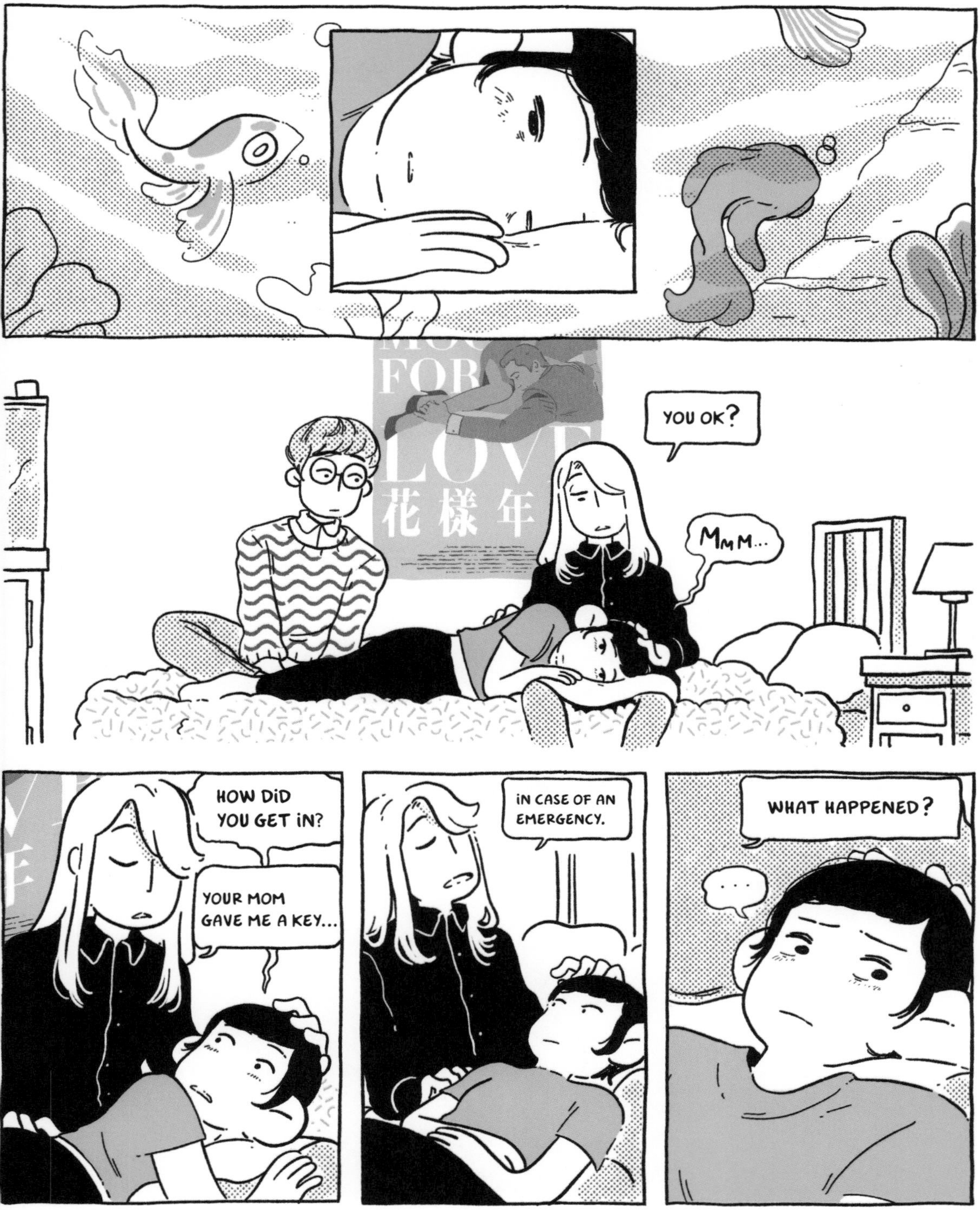
YOU OK?
MMM...
HOW DID YOU GET IN?
YOUR MOM GAVE ME A KEY...
IN CASE OF AN EMERGENCY.
WHAT HAPPENED?
...

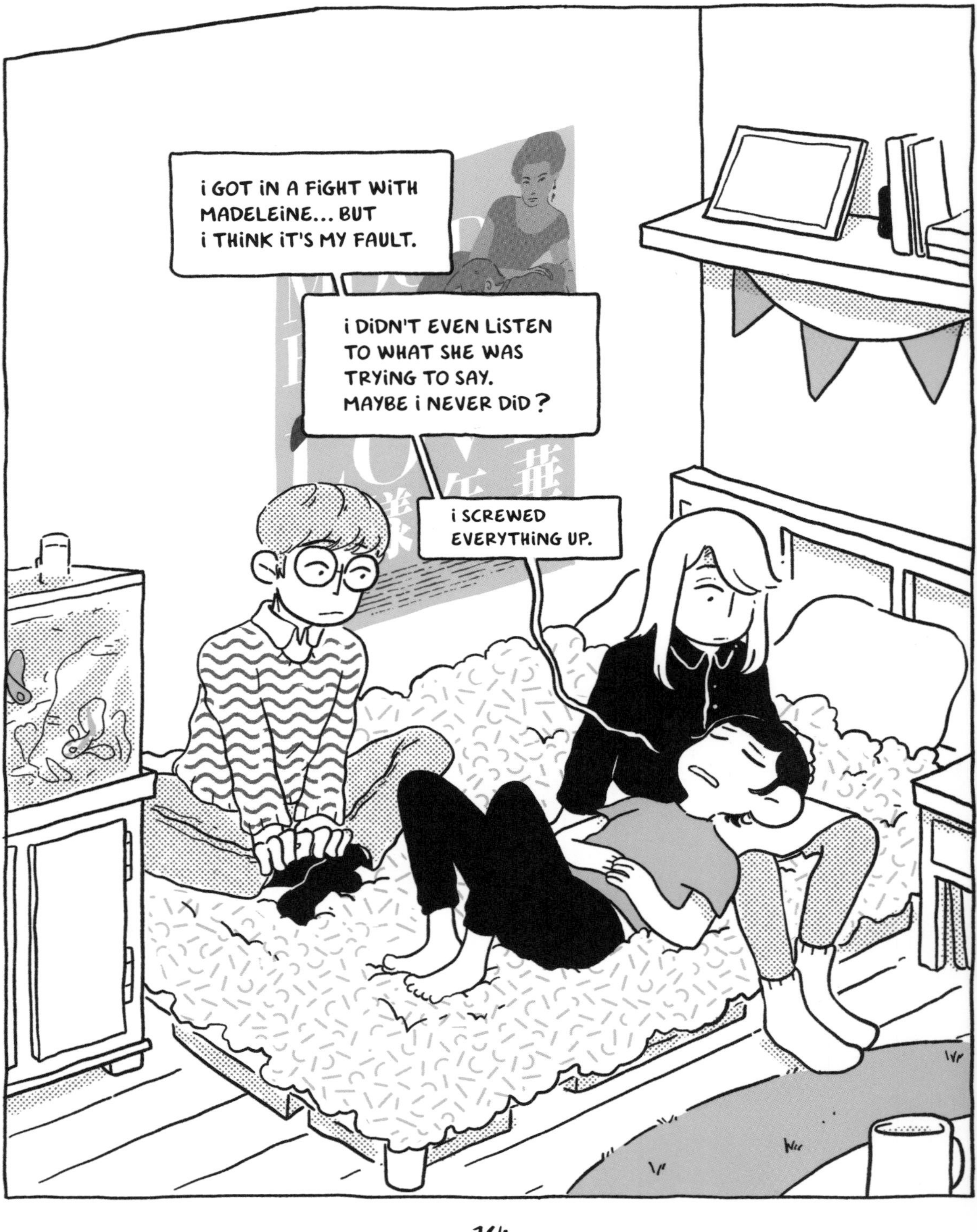
I GOT IN A FIGHT WITH MADELEINE... BUT I THINK IT'S MY FAULT.
I DIDN'T EVEN LISTEN TO WHAT SHE WAS TRYING TO SAY. MAYBE I NEVER DID?
I SCREWED EVERYTHING UP.

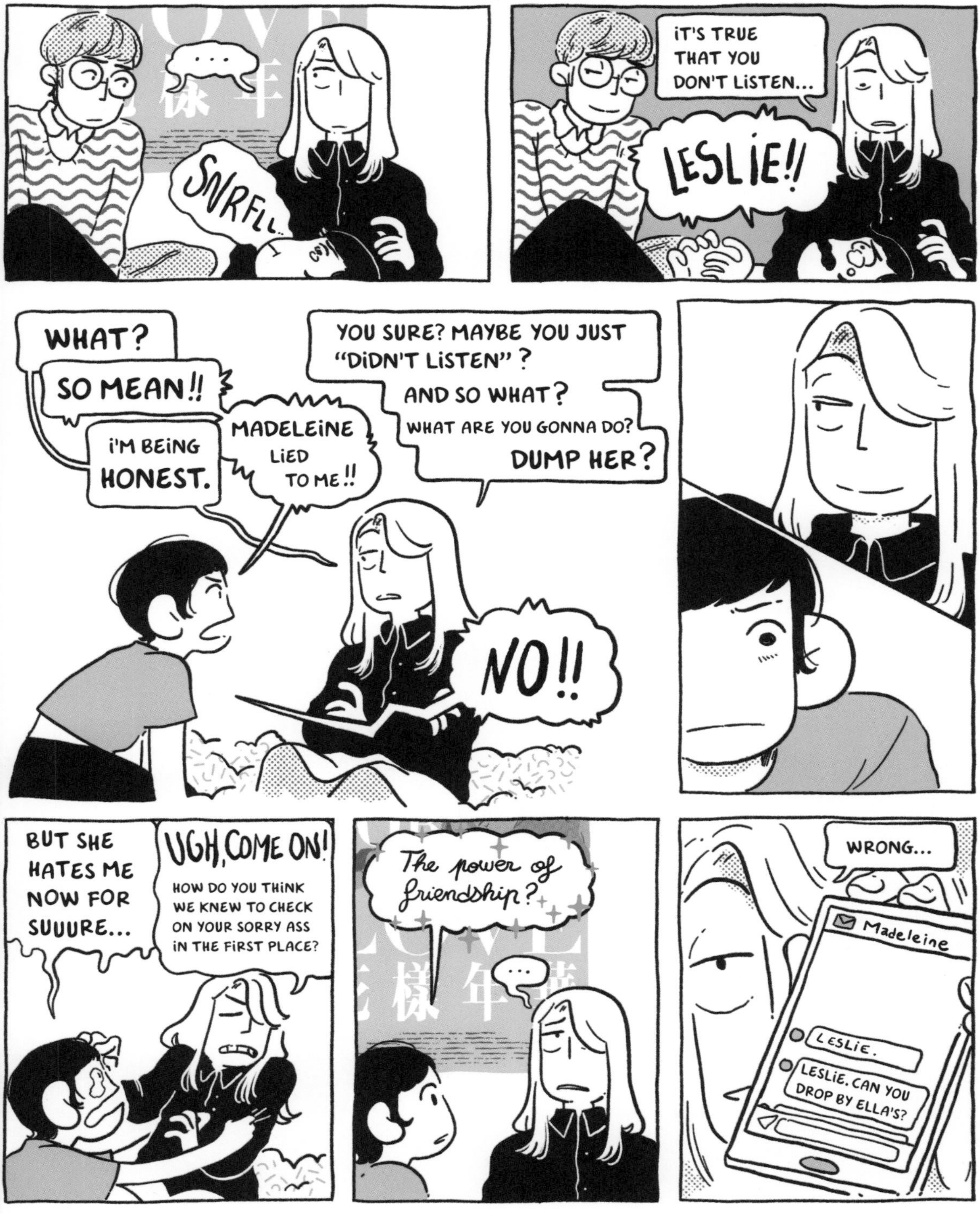
...
SNRFL...
IT'S TRUE THAT YOU DON'T LISTEN...
LESLIE!!
WHAT?
SO MEAN!!
I'M BEING HONEST.
MADELEINE LIED TO ME!!
YOU SURE? MAYBE YOU JUST "DIDN'T LISTEN"?
AND SO WHAT?
WHAT ARE YOU GONNA DO?
DUMP HER?
NO!!
BUT SHE HATES ME NOW FOR SUUURE...
UGH, COME ON!
HOW DO YOU THINK WE KNEW TO CHECK ON YOUR SORRY ASS IN THE FIRST PLACE?
The power of friendship?
...
WRONG...
Madeleine
LESLIE.
LESLIE. CAN YOU DROP BY ELLA'S?

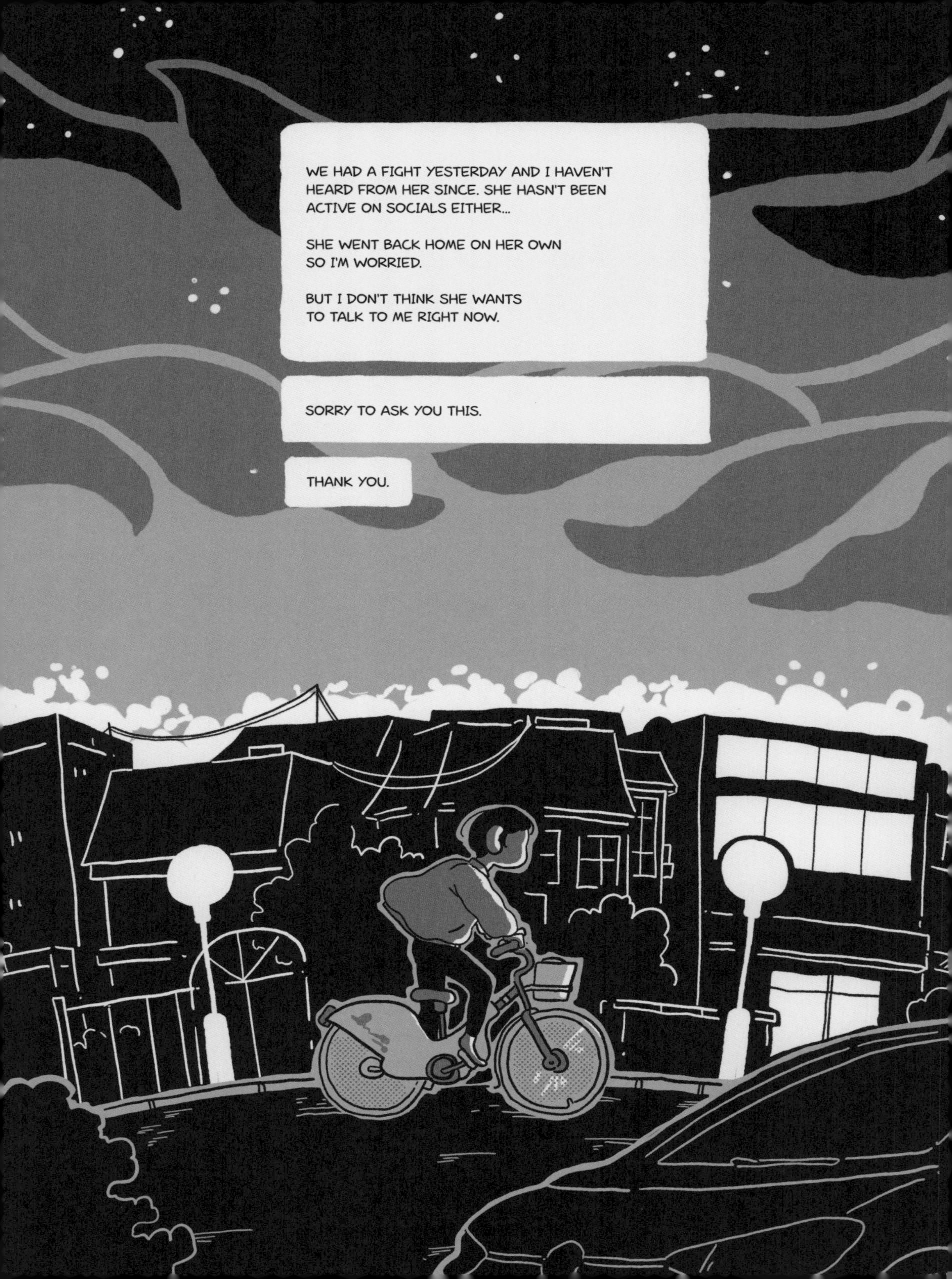
WE HAD A FIGHT YESTERDAY AND I HAVEN'T HEARD FROM HER SINCE. SHE HASN'T BEEN ACTIVE ON SOCIALS EITHER...
SHE WENT BACK HOME ON HER OWN SO I'M WORRIED.
BUT I DON'T THINK SHE WANTS TO TALK TO ME RIGHT NOW.
SORRY TO ASK YOU THIS.
THANK YOU.

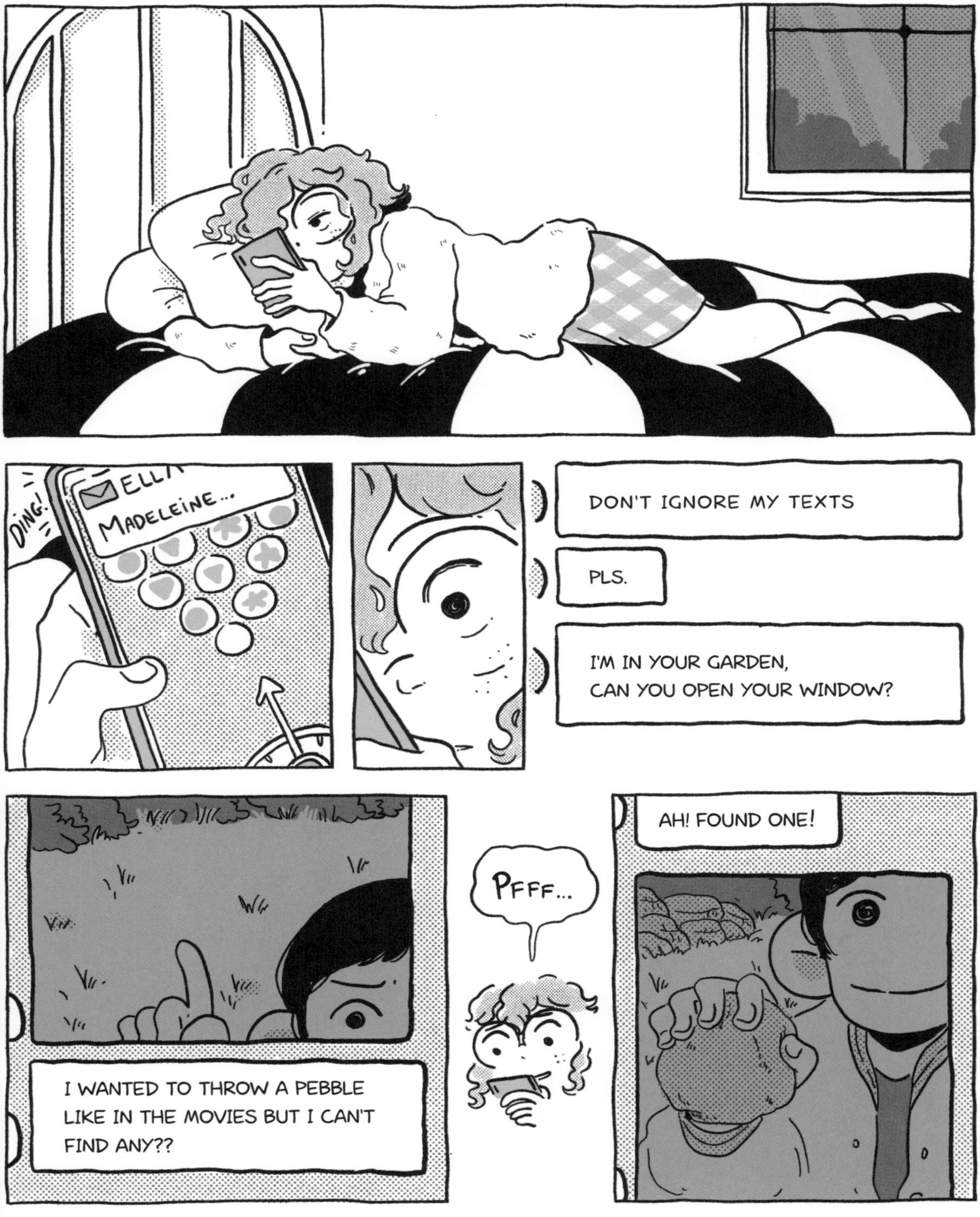
DING!
MADELEINE...
DON'T IGNORE MY TEXTS
PLS.
I'M IN YOUR GARDEN,
CAN YOU OPEN YOUR WINDOW?
I WANTED TO THROW A PEBBLE LIKE IN THE MOVIES BUT I CAN'T FIND ANY??
PFFF...
AH! FOUND ONE!

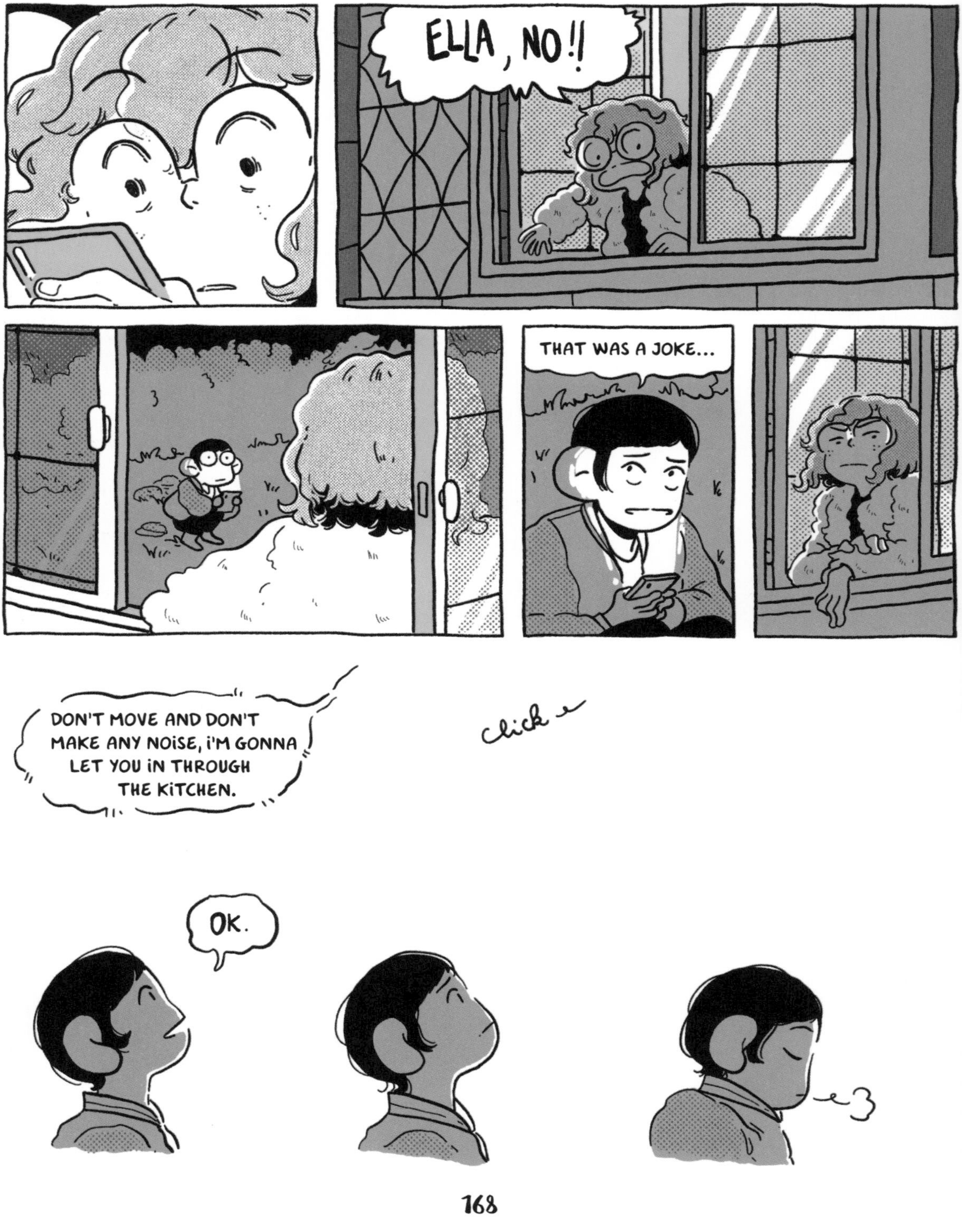
ELLA, NO!!
THAT WAS A JOKE...
DON'T MOVE AND DON'T MAKE ANY NOISE, I'M GONNA LET YOU IN THROUGH THE KITCHEN.
Click
OK.

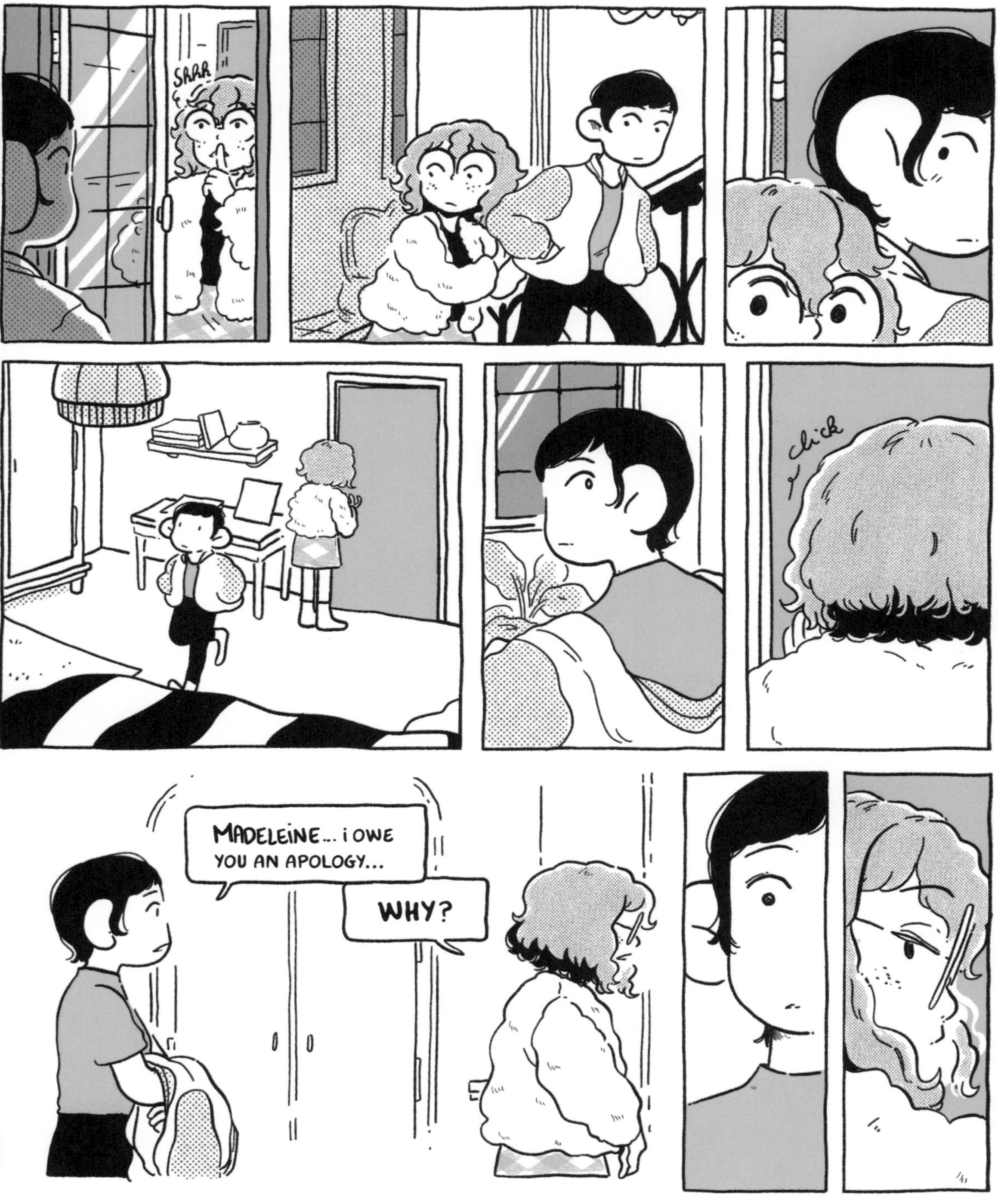
SHHH
click
MADELEINE... I OWE YOU AN APOLOGY...
WHY?

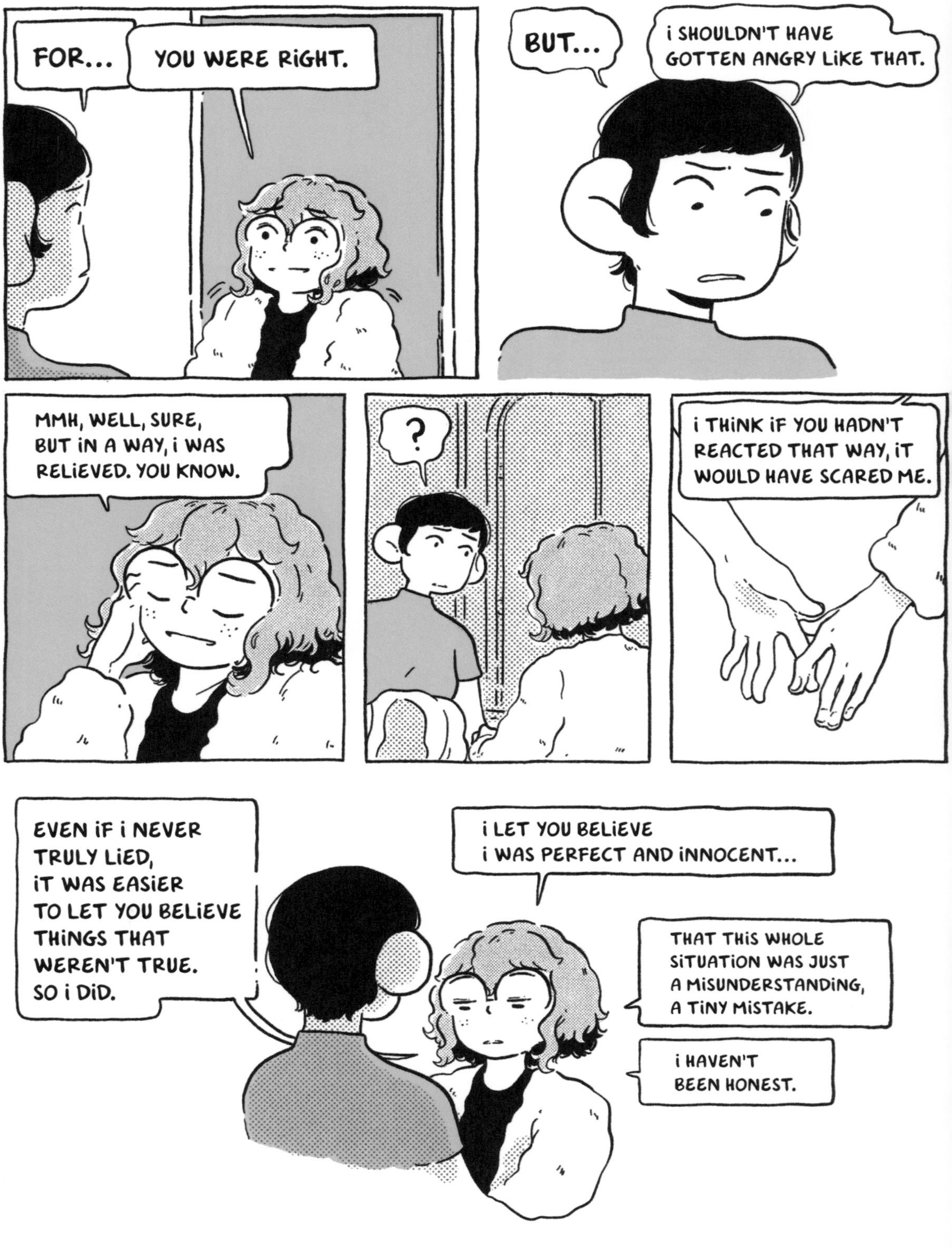
FOR...
YOU WERE RIGHT.
BUT...
i SHOULDN'T HAVE GOTTEN ANGRY LiKE THAT.
MMH, WELL, SURE, BUT iN A WAY, i WAS RELiEVED. YOU KNOW.
?
i THiNK iF YOU HADN'T REACTED THAT WAY, iT WOULD HAVE SCARED ME.
EVEN iF i NEVER TRULY LiED, iT WAS EASiER TO LET YOU BELiEVE THiNGS THAT WEREN'T TRUE. SO i DiD.
i LET YOU BELiEVE i WAS PERFECT AND iNNOCENT...
THAT THiS WHOLE SiTUATiON WAS JUST A MiSUNDERSTANDiNG, A TiNY MiSTAKE.
i HAVEN'T BEEN HONEST.

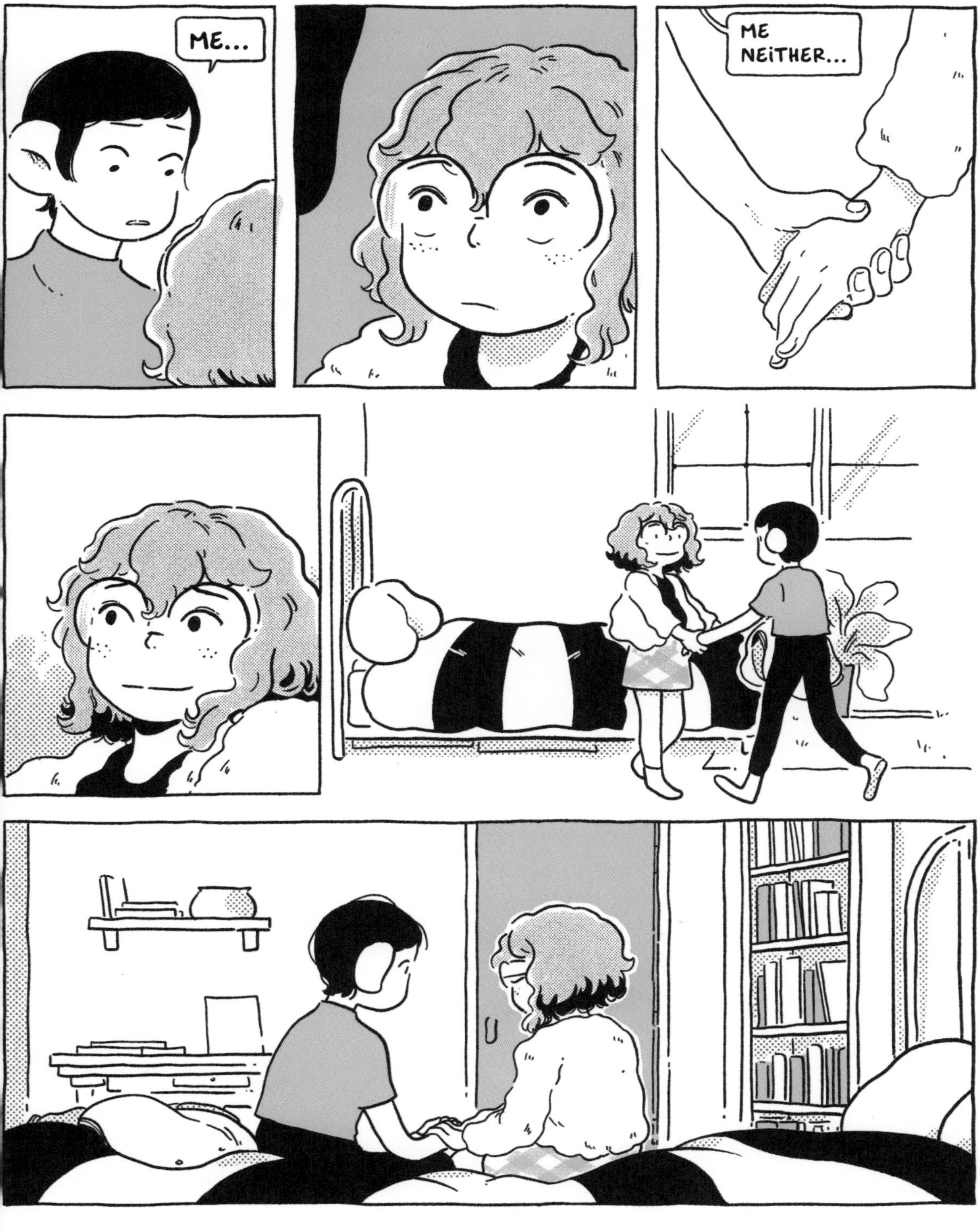
ME...
ME NEITHER...

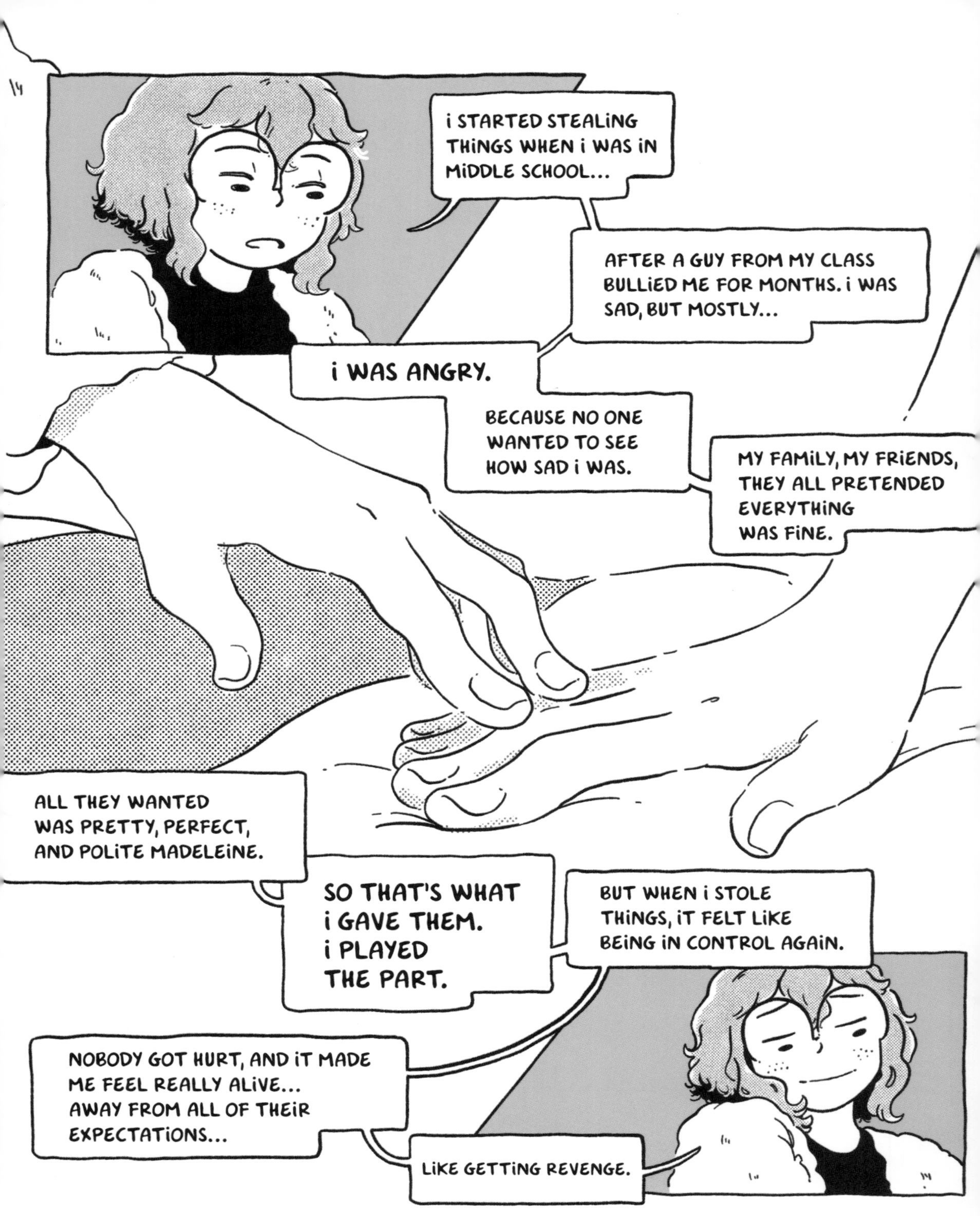
i STARTED STEALiNG THiNGS WHEN i WAS iN MiDDLE SCHOOL...
AFTER A GUY FROM MY CLASS BULLiED ME FOR MONTHS. i WAS SAD, BUT MOSTLY...
i WAS ANGRY.
BECAUSE NO ONE WANTED TO SEE HOW SAD i WAS.
MY FAMiLY, MY FRiENDS, THEY ALL PRETENDED EVERYTHiNG WAS FiNE.
ALL THEY WANTED WAS PRETTY, PERFECT, AND POLiTE MADELEiNE.
SO THAT'S WHAT i GAVE THEM. i PLAYED THE PART.
BUT WHEN i STOLE THiNGS, iT FELT LiKE BEiNG iN CONTROL AGAiN.
NOBODY GOT HURT, AND iT MADE ME FEEL REALLY ALiVE... AWAY FROM ALL OF THEiR EXPECTATiONS...
LiKE GETTiNG REVENGE.

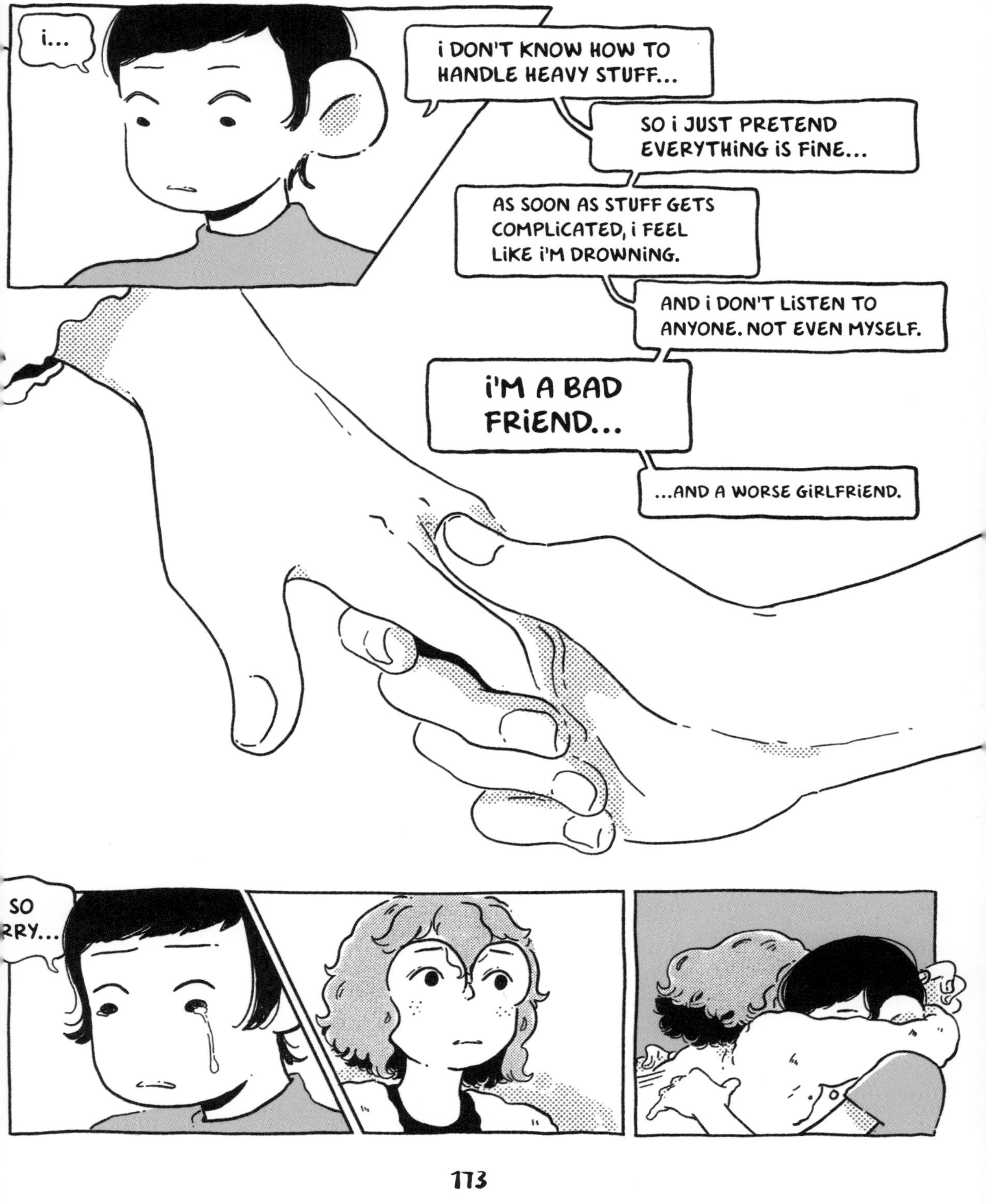
i...
i DON'T KNOW HOW TO HANDLE HEAVY STUFF...
SO i JUST PRETEND EVERYTHiNG iS FiNE...
AS SOON AS STUFF GETS COMPLiCATED, i FEEL LiKE i'M DROWNiNG.
AND i DON'T LiSTEN TO ANYONE. NOT EVEN MYSELF.
i'M A BAD FRiEND...
...AND A WORSE GiRLFRiEND.
SO
RRY...

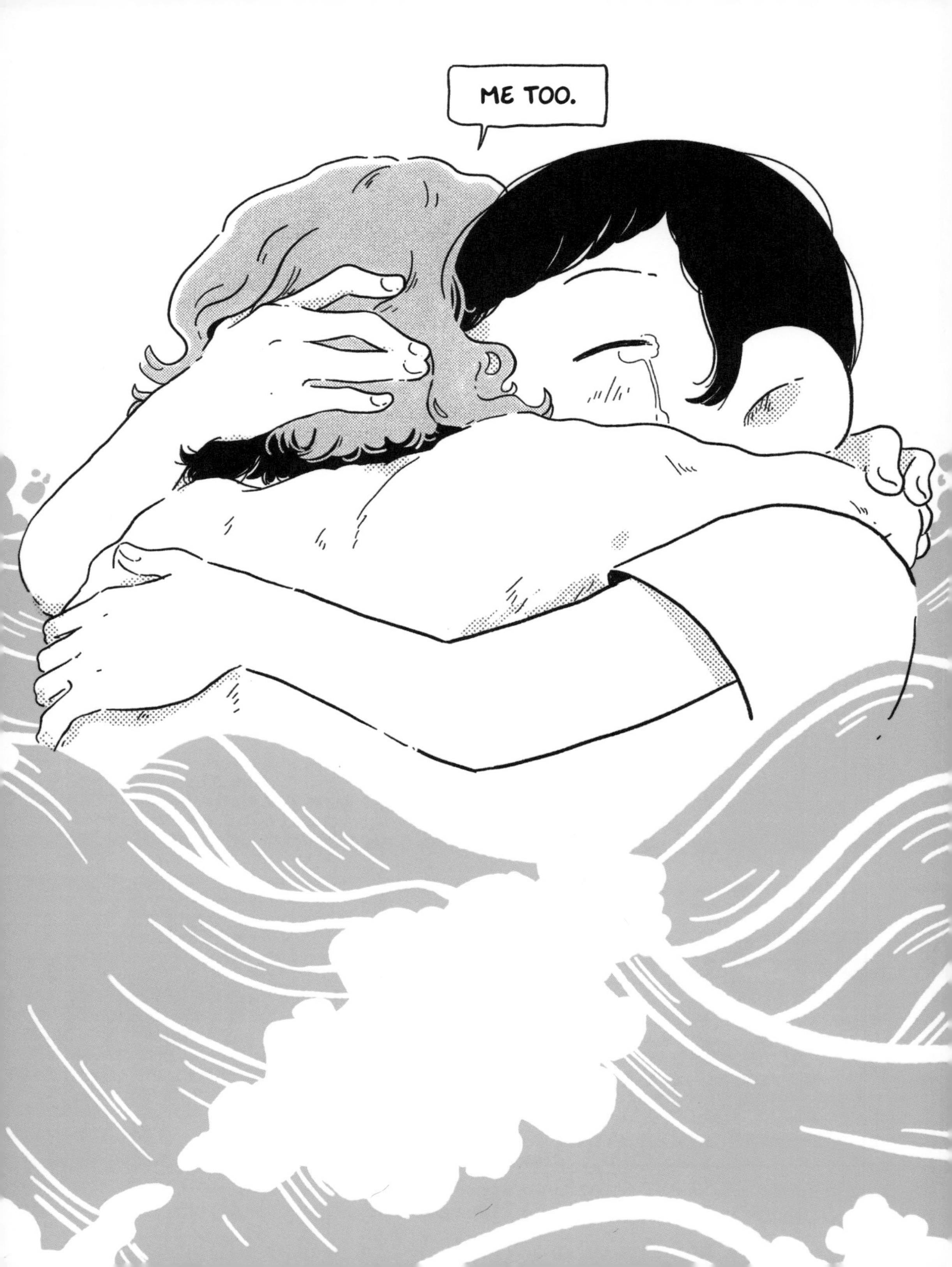
ME TOO.

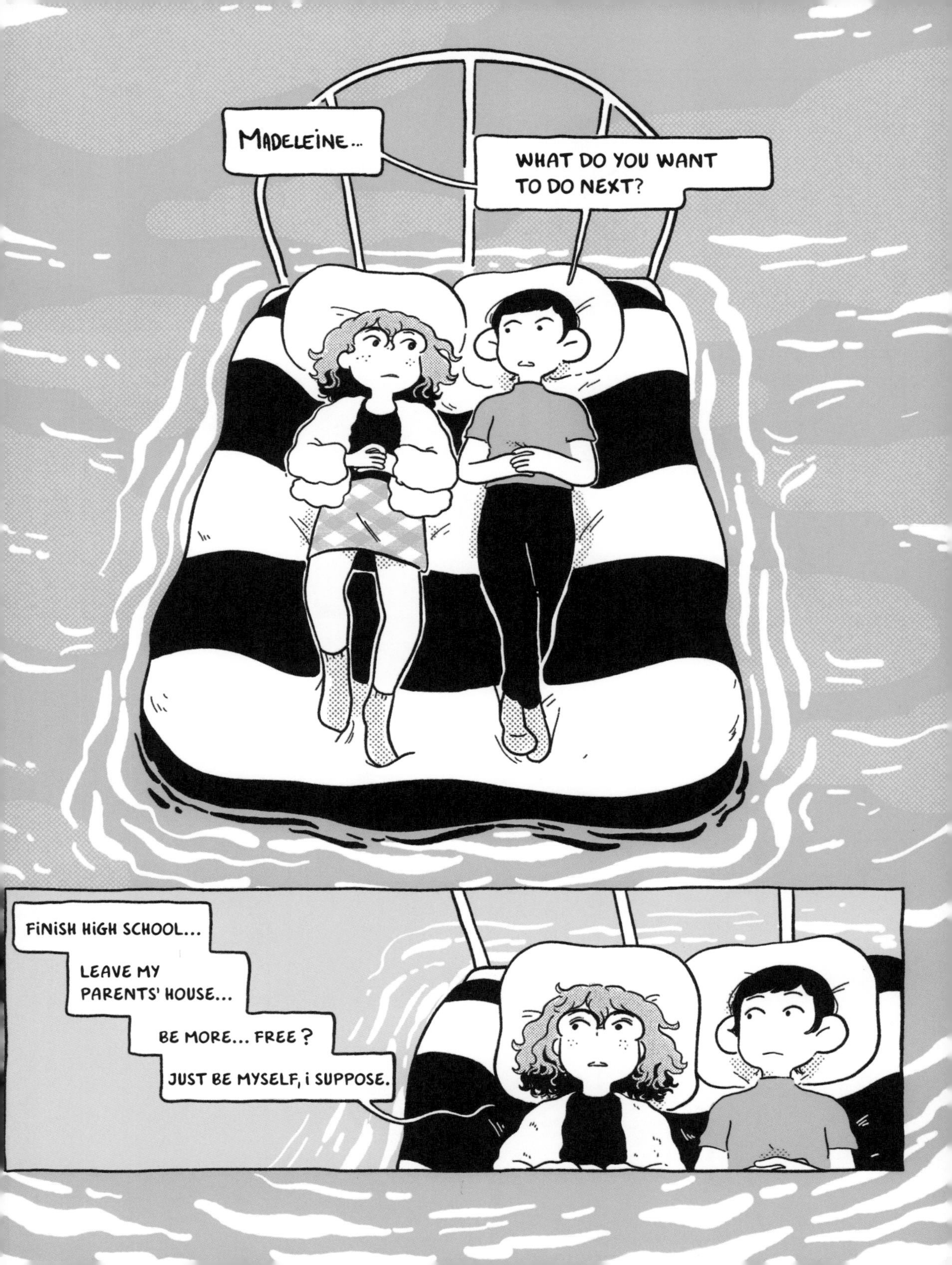
MADELEINE...
WHAT DO YOU WANT TO DO NEXT?
FINISH HIGH SCHOOL...
LEAVE MY PARENTS' HOUSE...
BE MORE... FREE?
JUST BE MYSELF, I SUPPOSE.

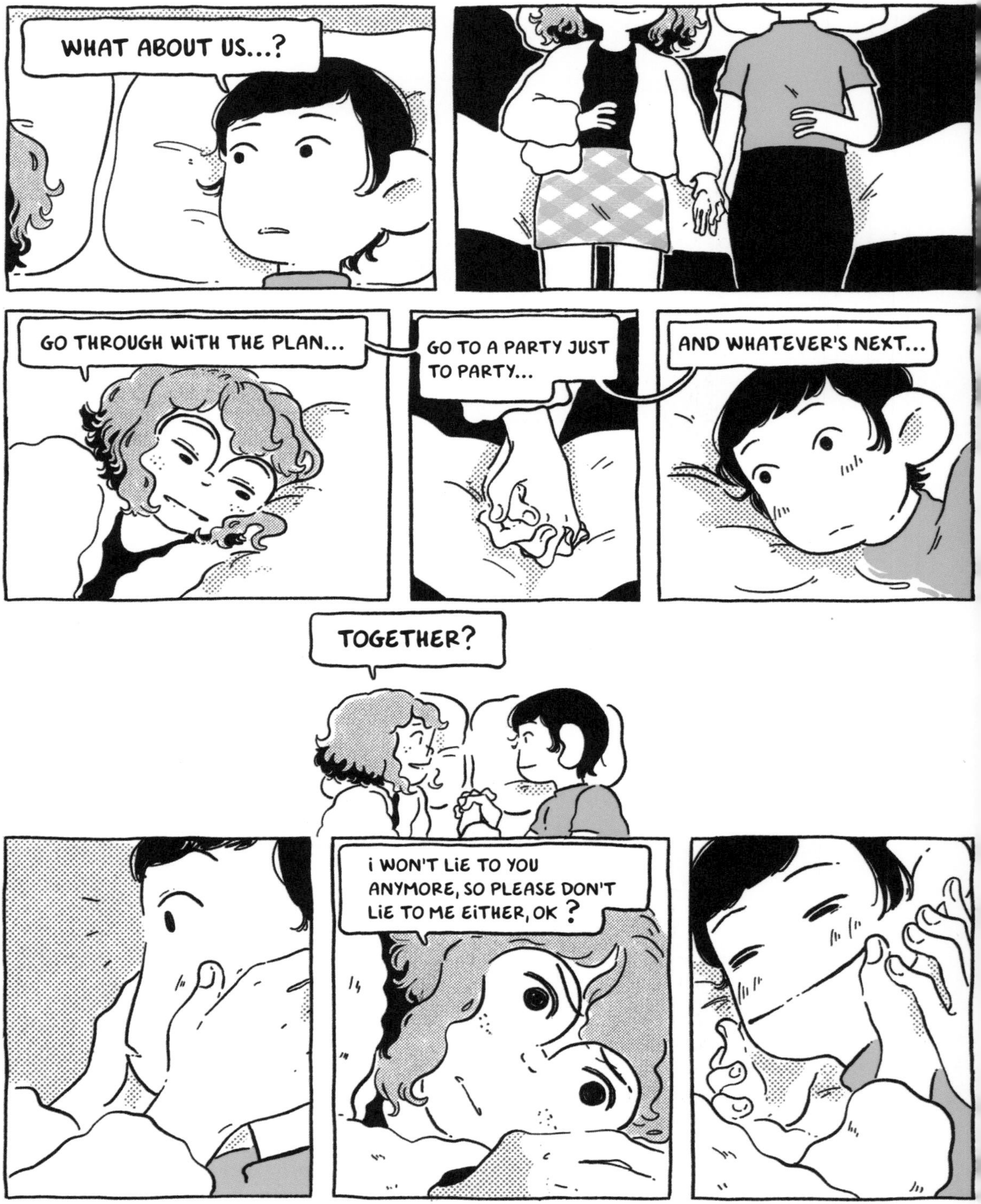
WHAT ABOUT US...?
GO THROUGH WITH THE PLAN...
GO TO A PARTY JUST TO PARTY...
AND WHATEVER'S NEXT...
TOGETHER?
I WON'T LIE TO YOU ANYMORE, SO PLEASE DON'T LIE TO ME EITHER, OK?

YOU WANNA GO TO MY PLACE?

i ALREADY TOLD MY PARENTS i WAS STAYING HOME TONIGHT BECAUSE MY PLANS FELL THROUGH.

OOOH...

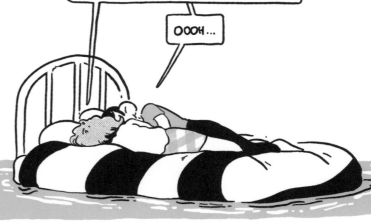

THAT'S RIGHT, WE WERE SUPPOSED TO GO TO A PARTY AGAIN TONIGHT... BACK TO BACK PARTIES?

WHY DID WE PLAN THAT?

AH!! ELISE iS MOVING!!

SHE JUST POSTED ABOUT IT.

SHE'S THE PHOTO ALBUM'S OWNER!

SHE'S THROWING A PARTY RIGHT BEFORE SHE MOVES. iT'S OUR LAST CHANCE.

THAT'S GONNA BE TWO IN A ROW...

MEH, WE'LL MANAGE.

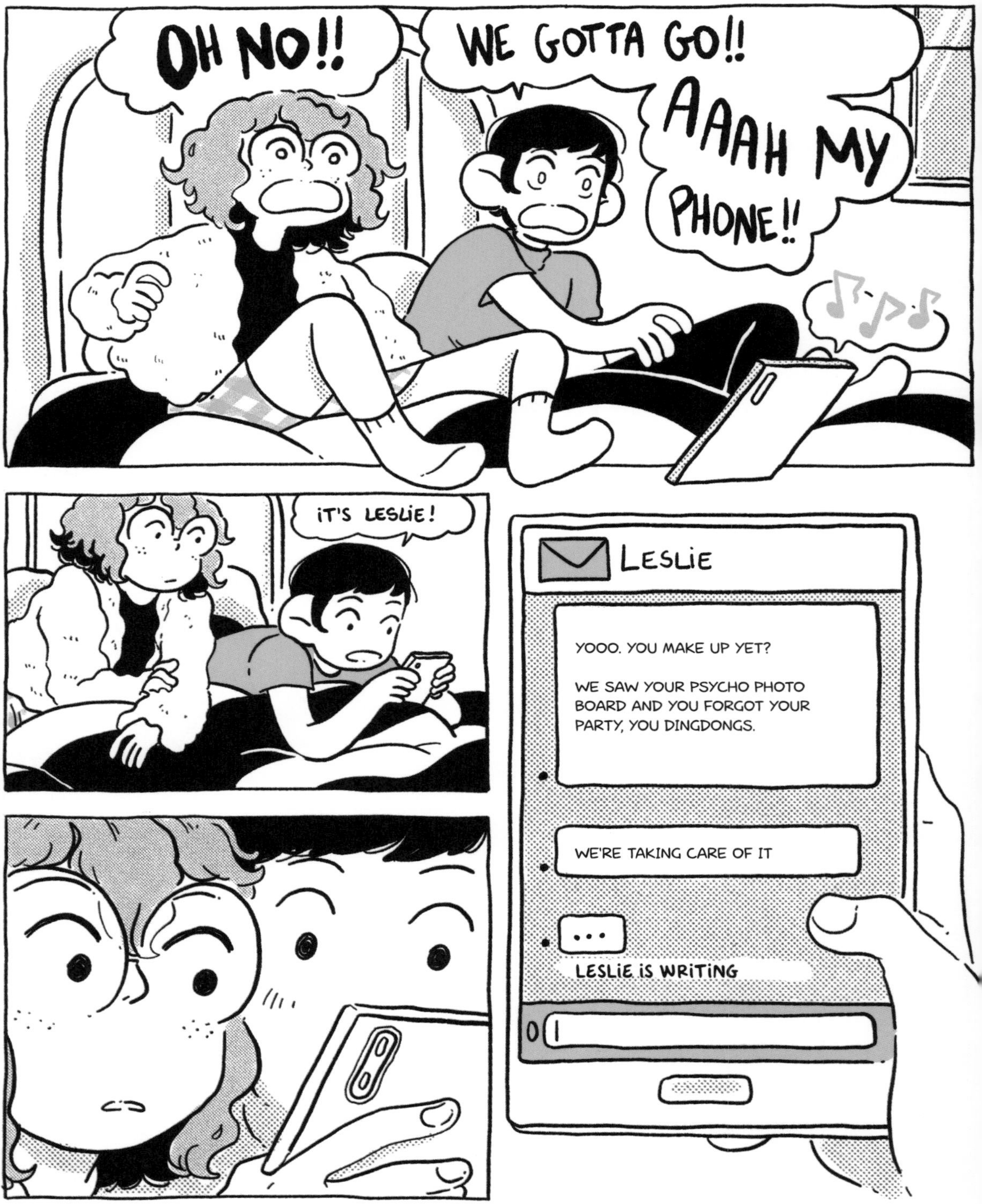
OH NO!!
WE GOTTA GO!!
AAAH MY PHONE!!
IT'S LESLIE!
LESLIE
YOOO. YOU MAKE UP YET?
WE SAW YOUR PSYCHO PHOTO BOARD AND YOU FORGOT YOUR PARTY, YOU DINGDONGS.
WE'RE TAKING CARE OF IT
...
LESLIE IS WRITING

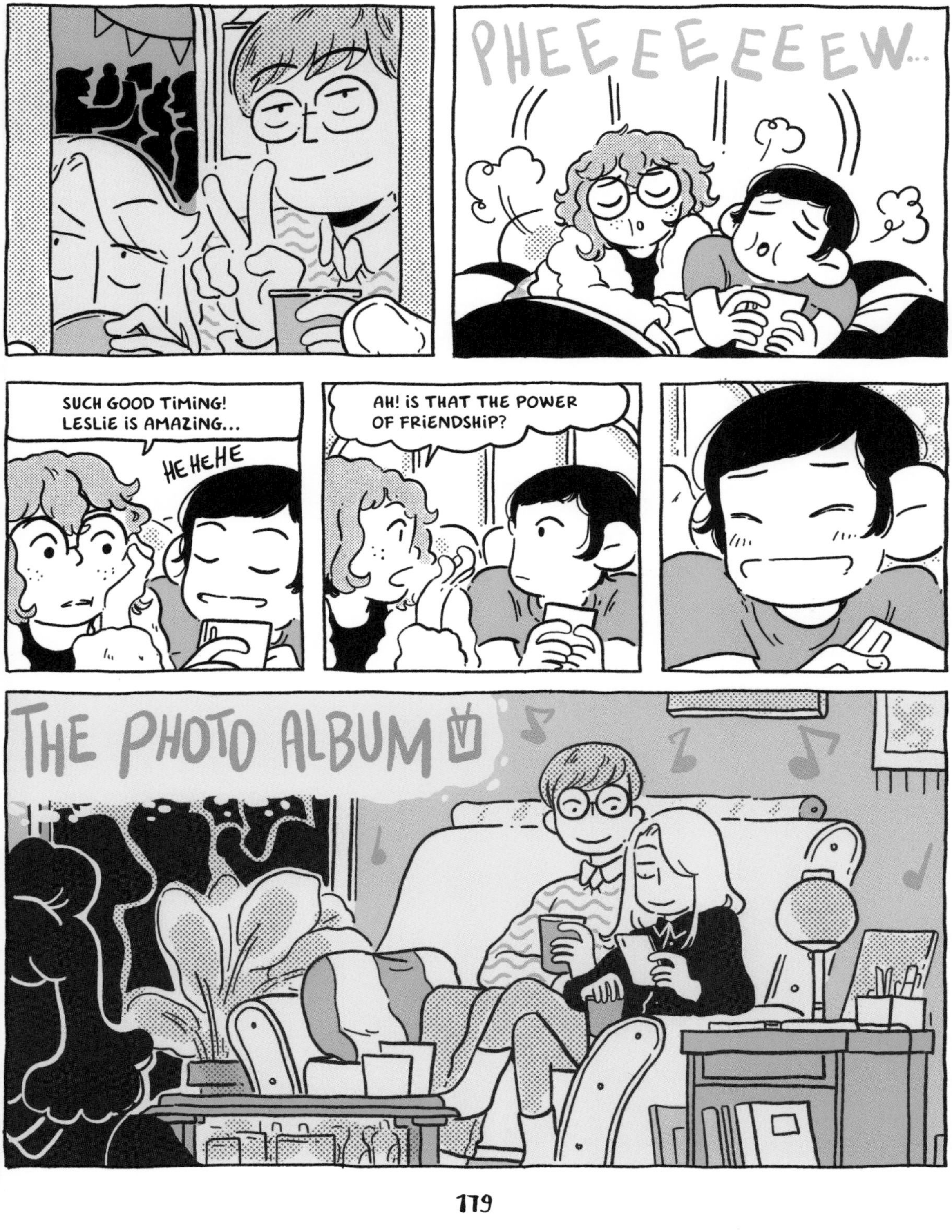
PHEEEEEEEW...
SUCH GOOD TIMING! LESLIE IS AMAZING...
HEHEHE
AH! IS THAT THE POWER OF FRIENDSHIP?
THE PHOTO ALBUM

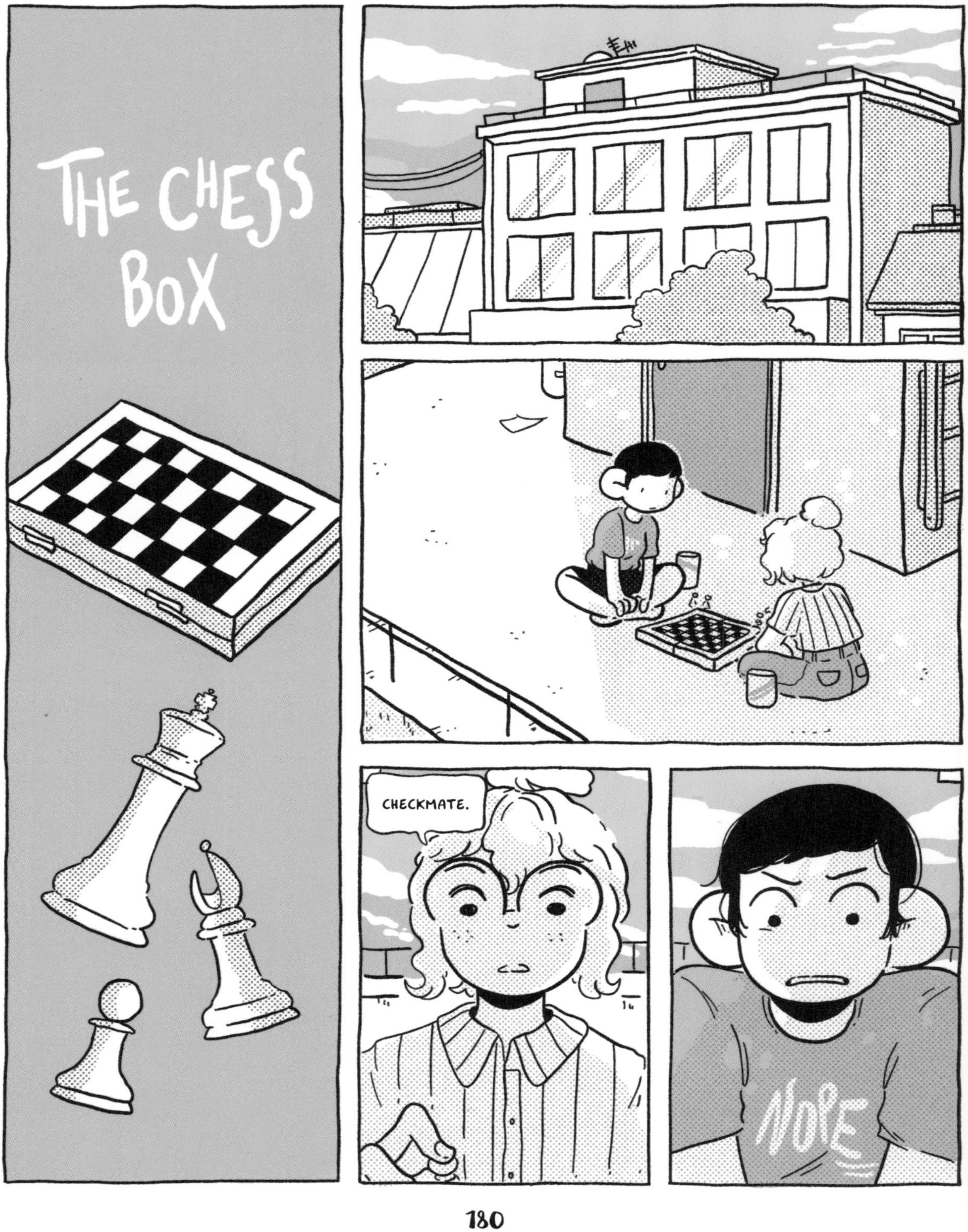
THE CHESS BOX
CHECKMATE.
NOPE

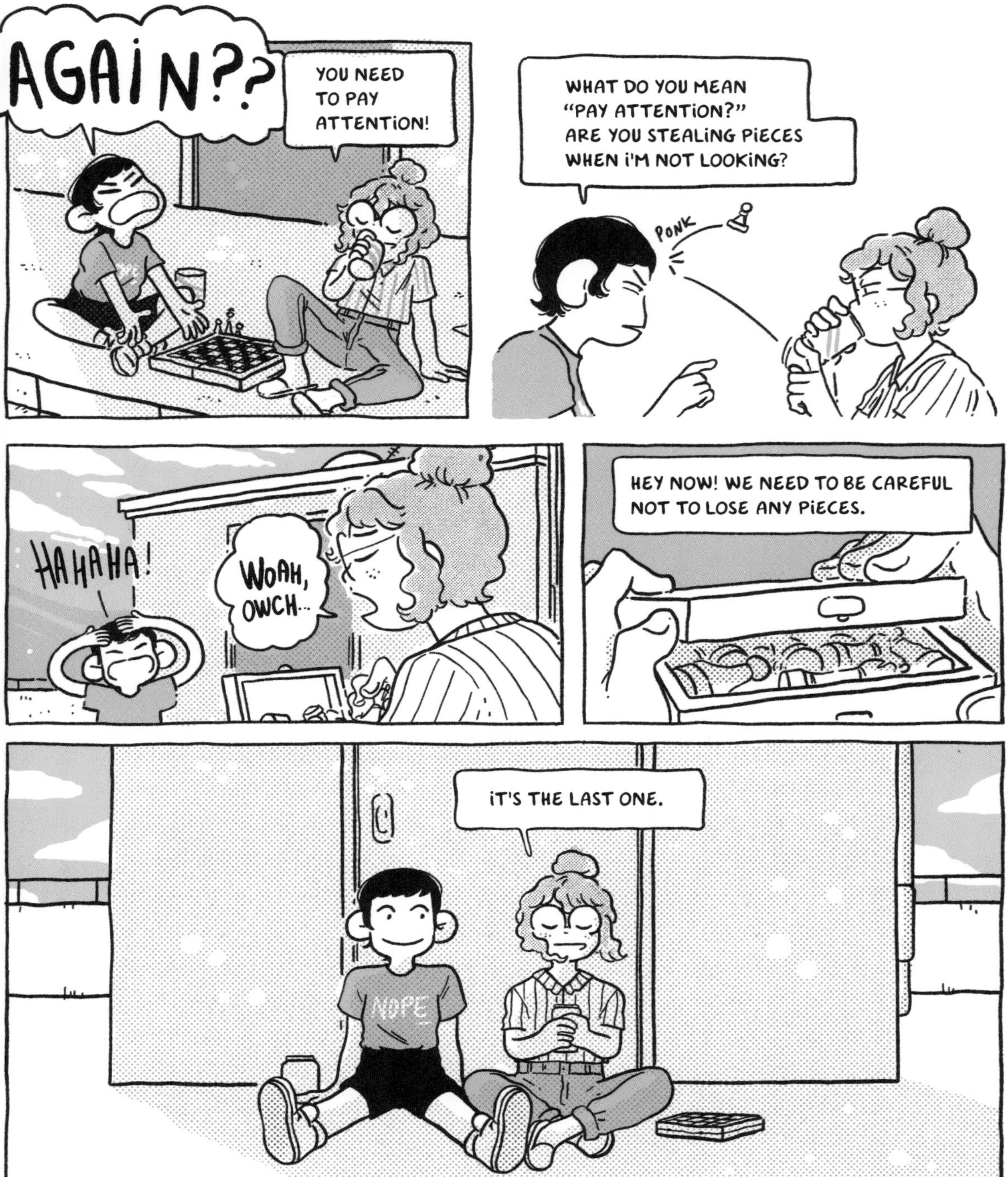
AGAIN??
YOU NEED TO PAY ATTENTiON!
WHAT DO YOU MEAN "PAY ATTENTiON?" ARE YOU STEALiNG PiECES WHEN i'M NOT LOOKiNG?
PONK
HAHAHA!
WOAH, OWCH...
HEY NOW! WE NEED TO BE CAREFUL NOT TO LOSE ANY PiECES.
iT'S THE LAST ONE.
NOPE

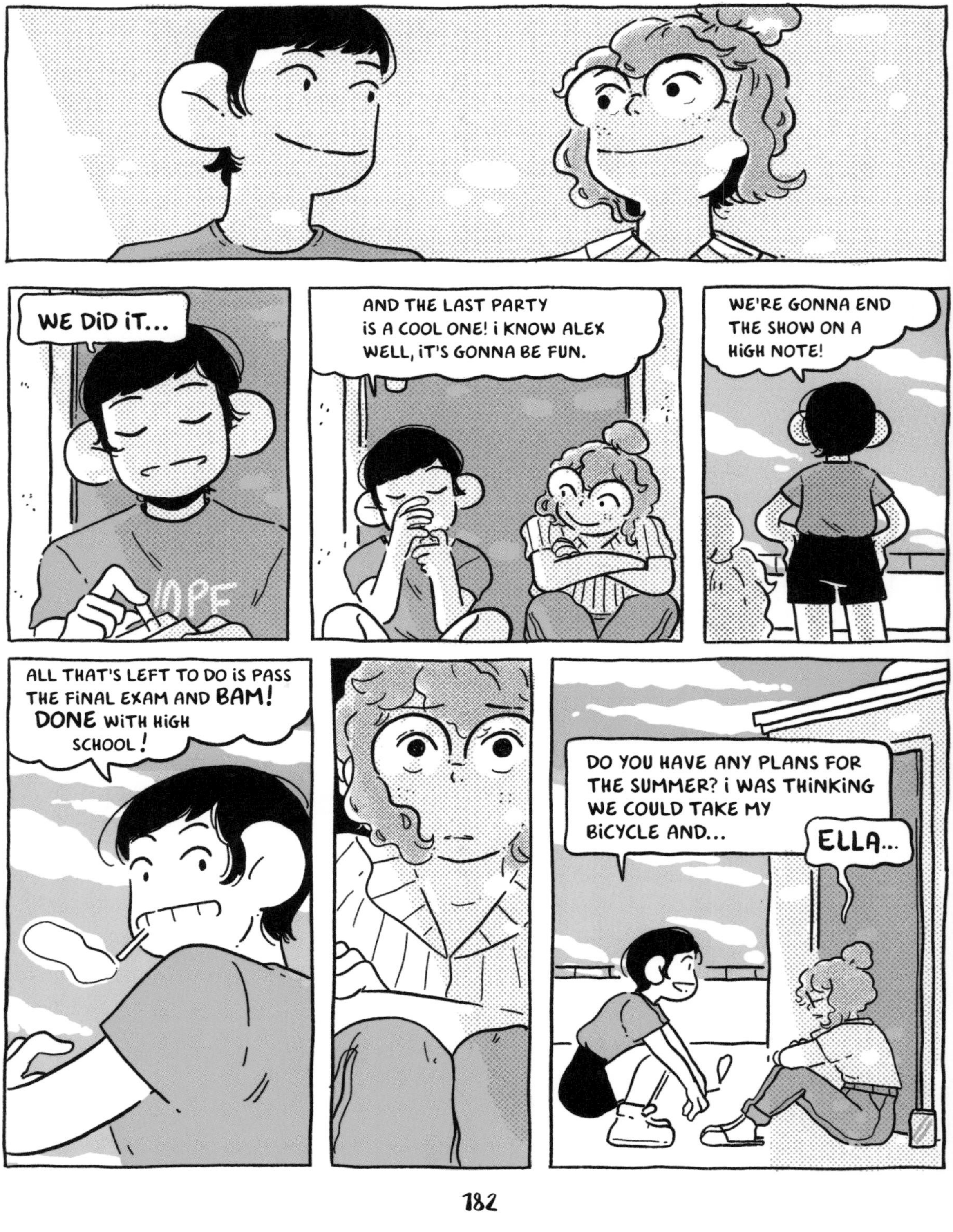
WE DID IT...
AND THE LAST PARTY IS A COOL ONE! I KNOW ALEX WELL, IT'S GONNA BE FUN.
WE'RE GONNA END THE SHOW ON A HIGH NOTE!
ALL THAT'S LEFT TO DO IS PASS THE FINAL EXAM AND BAM! DONE WITH HIGH SCHOOL!
DO YOU HAVE ANY PLANS FOR THE SUMMER? I WAS THINKING WE COULD TAKE MY BICYCLE AND...
ELLA...

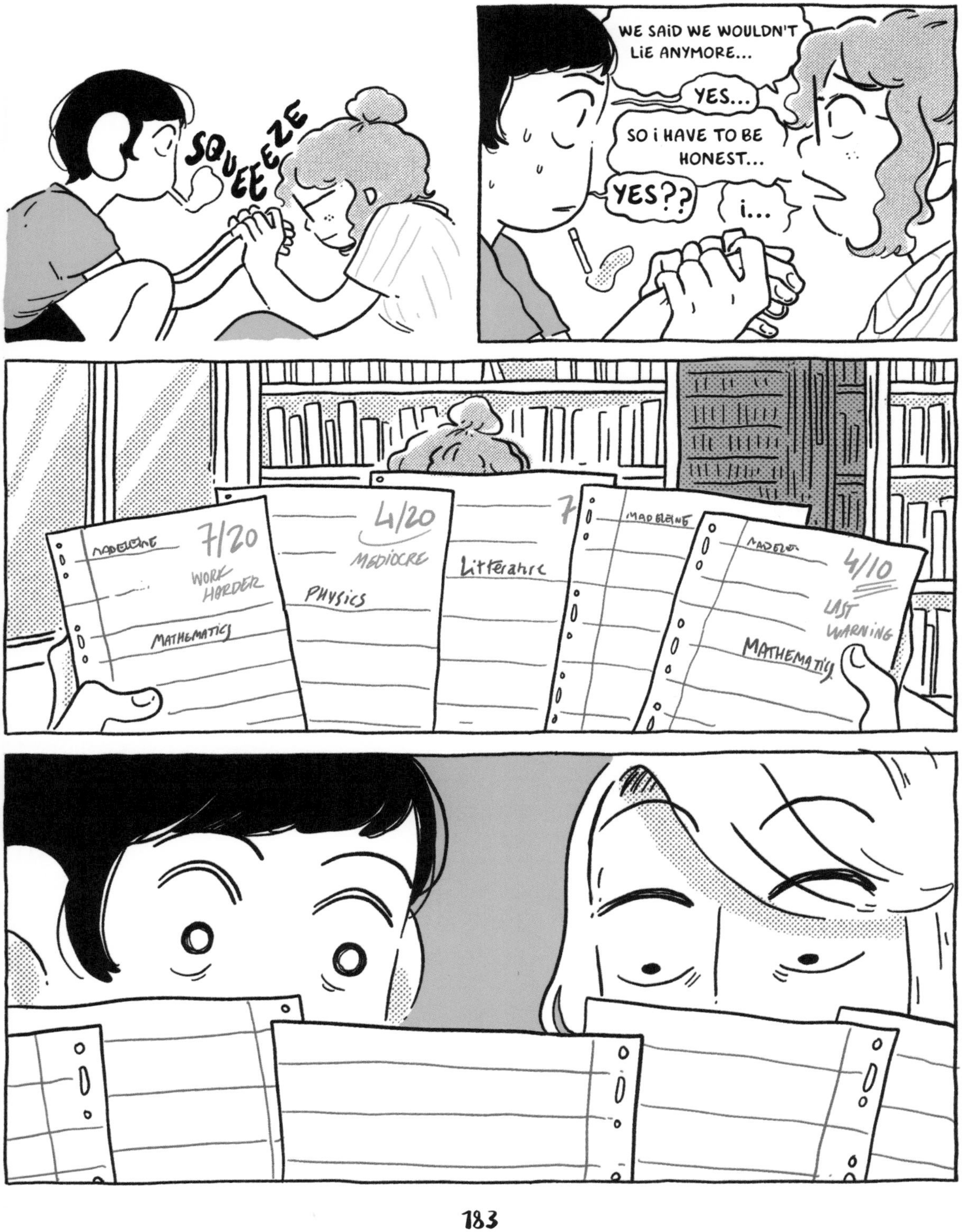
SQUEEEZE
WE SAID WE WOULDN'T LIE ANYMORE...
YES...
SO I HAVE TO BE HONEST...
YES??
I...
MADELEINE
7/20
WORK HARDER
MATHEMATICS
4/20
MEDIOCRE
PHYSICS
Litterature
MADELEINE
4/10
LAST WARNING
MATHEMATICS

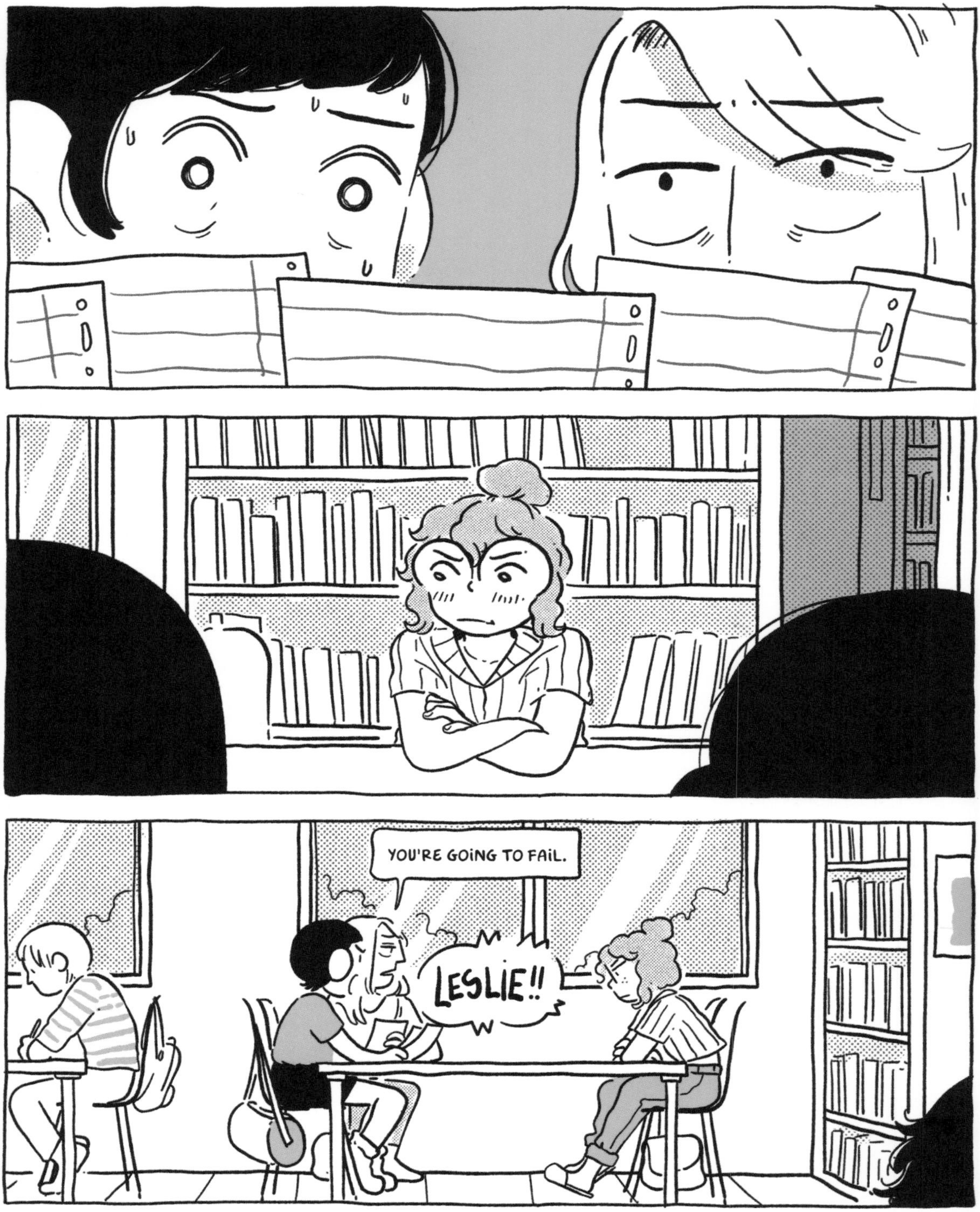

YOU'RE GOING TO FAIL.
LESLIE!!

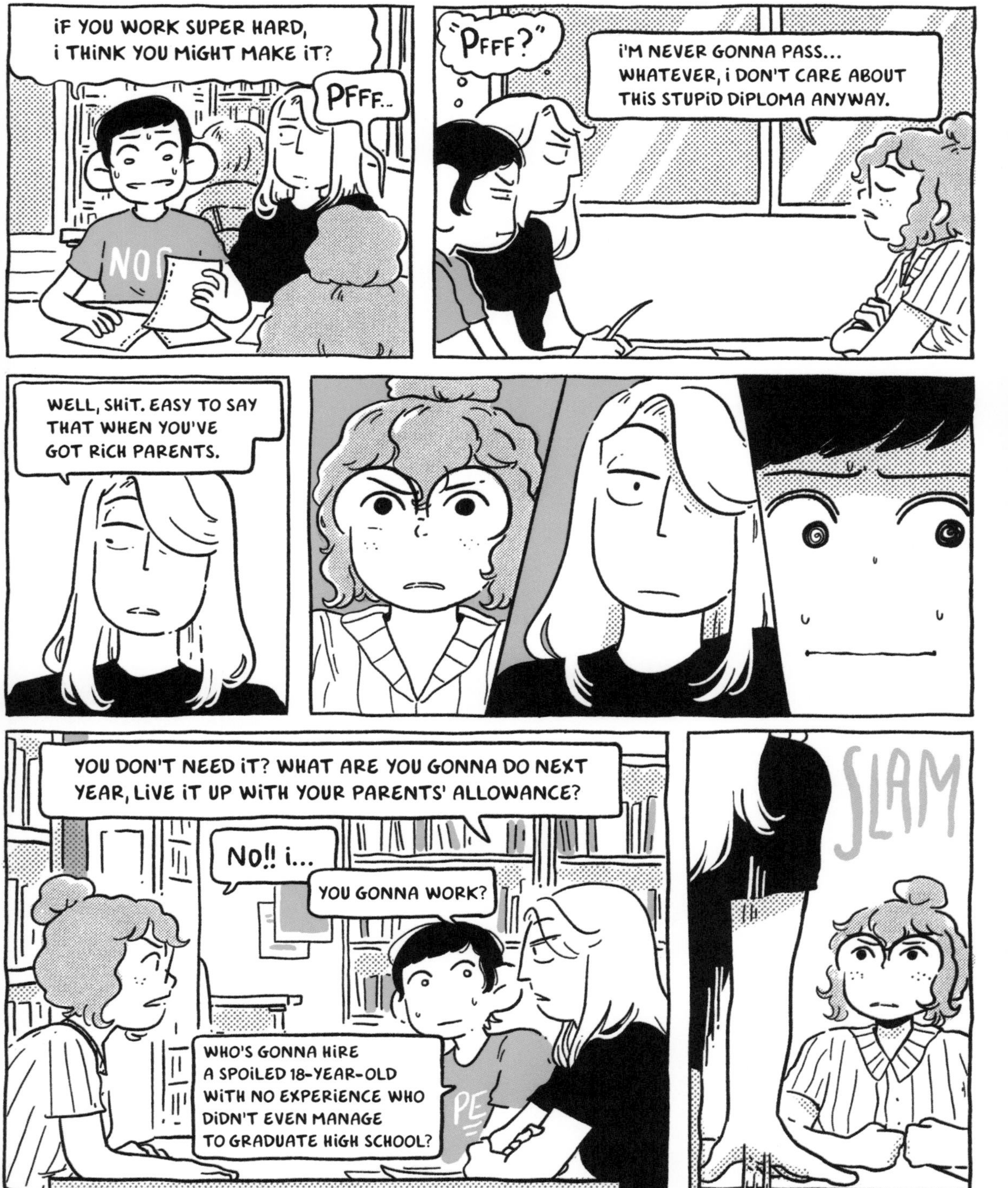
IF YOU WORK SUPER HARD, I THINK YOU MIGHT MAKE IT?
PFFF...
"PFFF?"
I'M NEVER GONNA PASS... WHATEVER, I DON'T CARE ABOUT THIS STUPID DIPLOMA ANYWAY.
WELL, SHIT. EASY TO SAY THAT WHEN YOU'VE GOT RICH PARENTS.
YOU DON'T NEED IT? WHAT ARE YOU GONNA DO NEXT YEAR, LIVE IT UP WITH YOUR PARENTS' ALLOWANCE?
NO!! I...
YOU GONNA WORK?
WHO'S GONNA HIRE A SPOILED 18-YEAR-OLD WITH NO EXPERIENCE WHO DIDN'T EVEN MANAGE TO GRADUATE HIGH SCHOOL?
SLAM

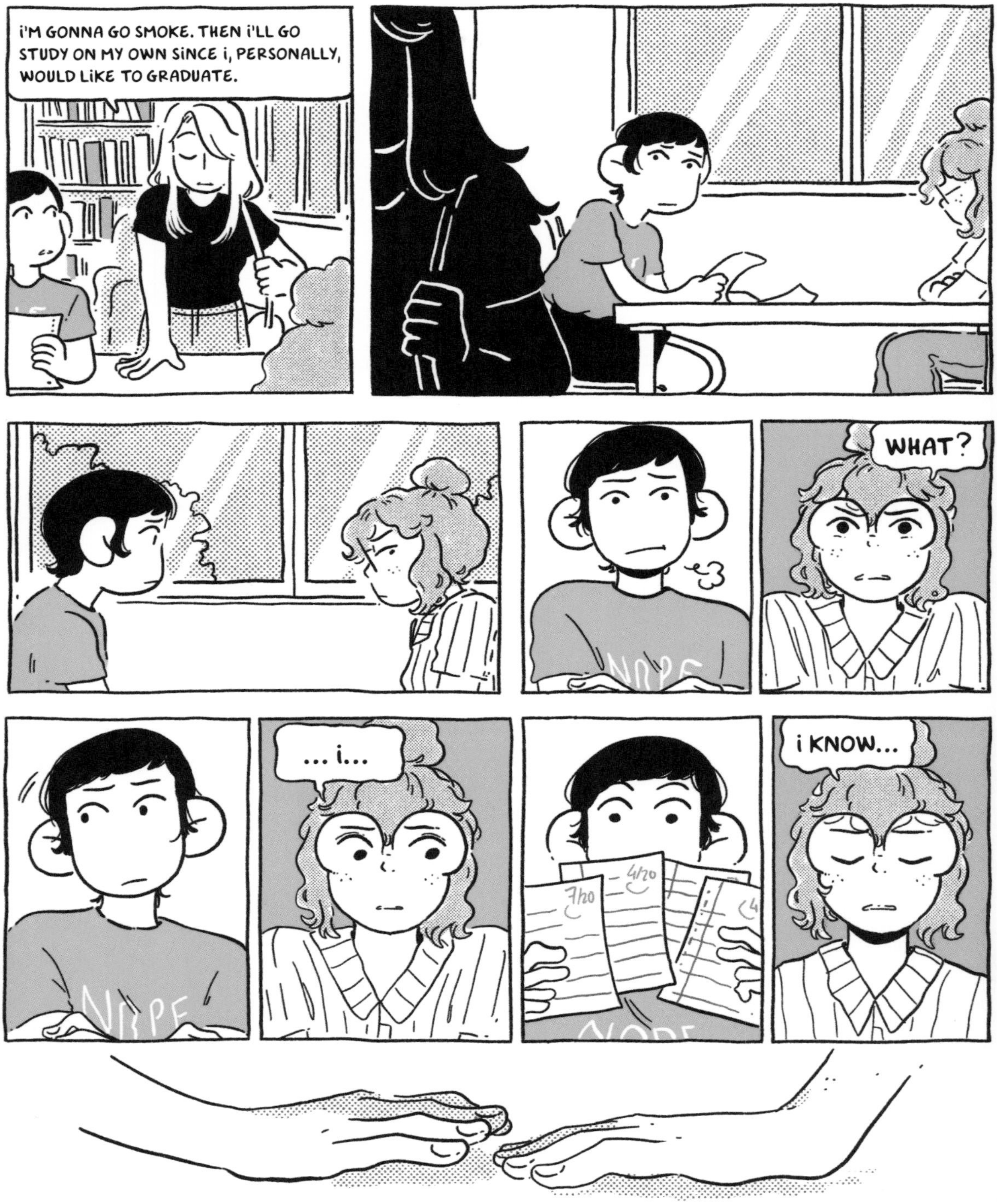
i'M GONNA GO SMOKE. THEN i'LL GO STUDY ON MY OWN SiNCE i, PERSONALLY, WOULD LiKE TO GRADUATE.
WHAT?
... i...
i KNOW...

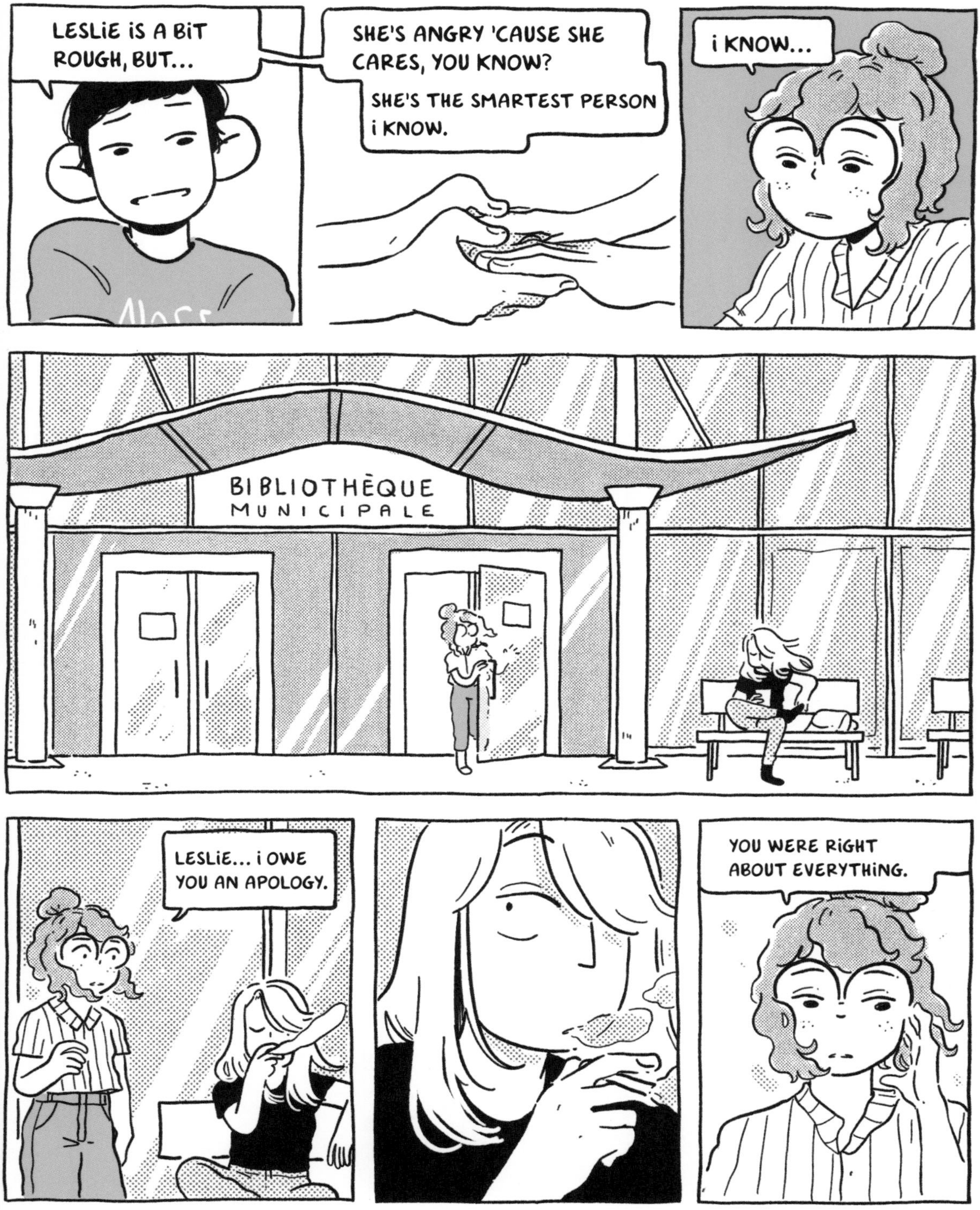
LESLIE IS A BIT ROUGH, BUT...
SHE'S ANGRY 'CAUSE SHE CARES, YOU KNOW?
SHE'S THE SMARTEST PERSON I KNOW.
I KNOW...
BIBLIOTHÈQUE MUNICIPALE
LESLIE... I OWE YOU AN APOLOGY.
YOU WERE RIGHT ABOUT EVERYTHING.

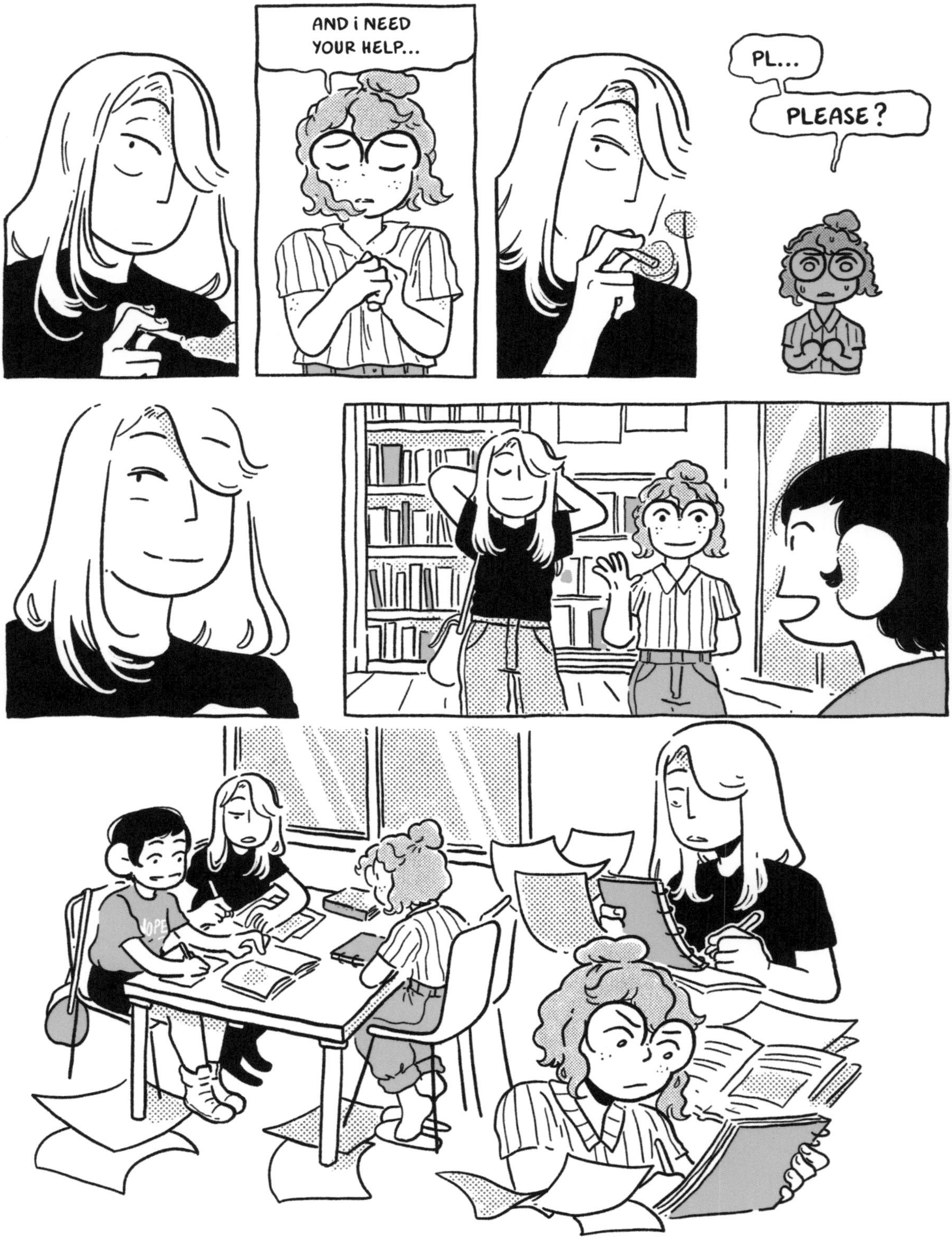
AND i NEED YOUR HELP...
PL...
PLEASE?

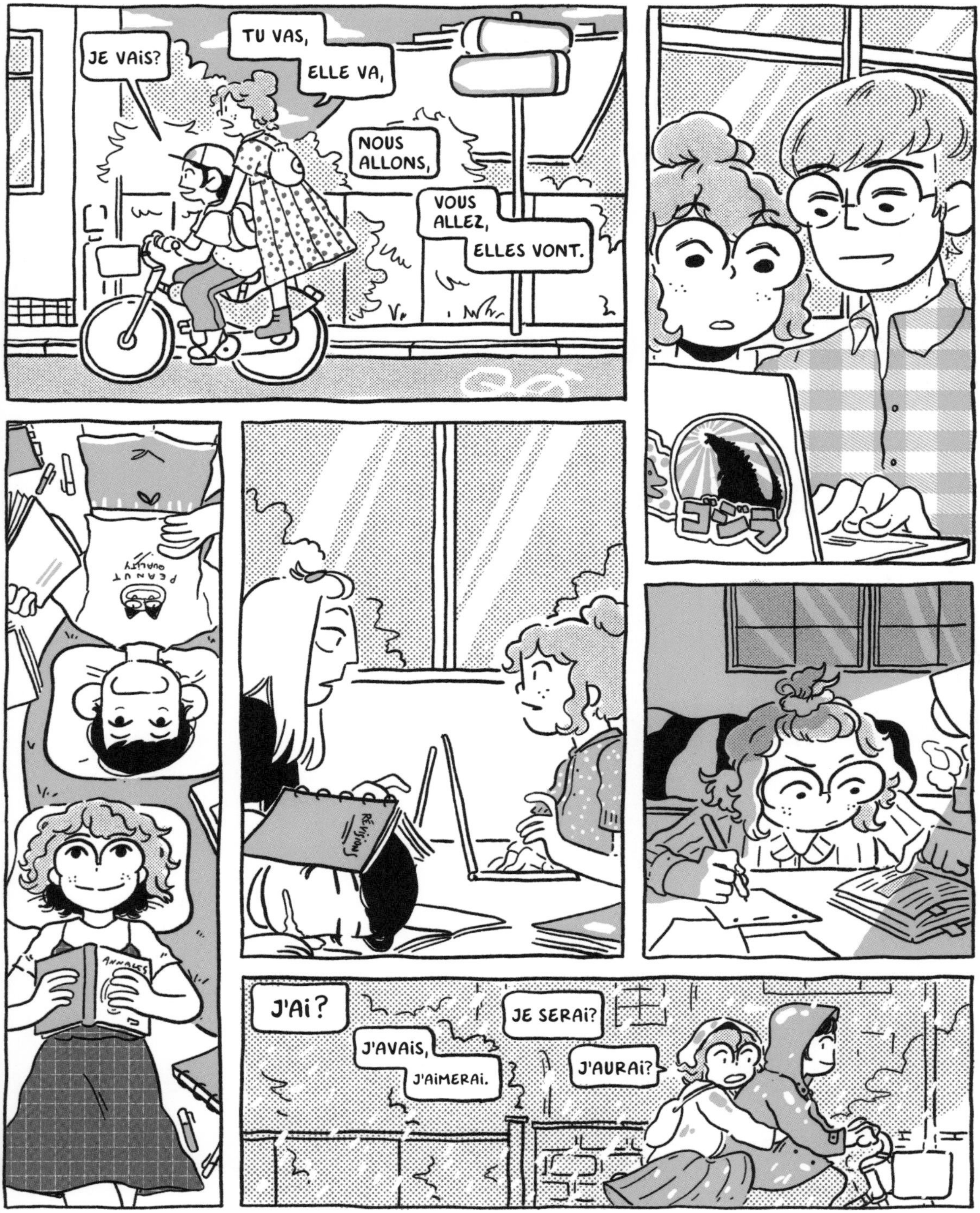
JE VAIS?
TU VAS,
ELLE VA,
NOUS ALLONS,
VOUS ALLEZ,
ELLES VONT.
PEANUT QUALITY
RÉVISIONS
ANNALES
J'AI?
J'AVAIS,
J'AIMERAI.
JE SERAI?
J'AURAI?

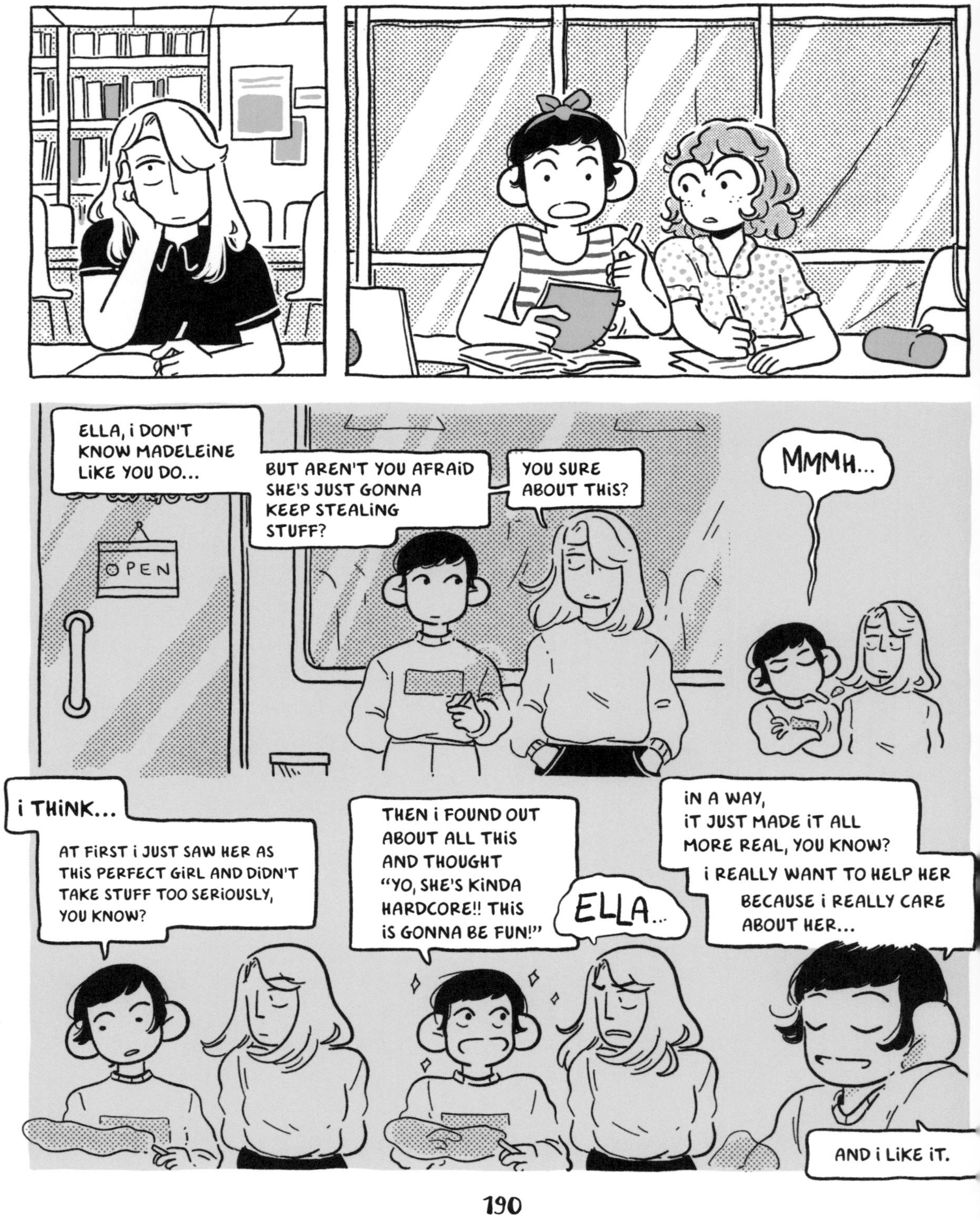
ELLA, i DON'T KNOW MADELEINE LiKE YOU DO...
BUT AREN'T YOU AFRAiD SHE'S JUST GONNA KEEP STEALiNG STUFF?
YOU SURE ABOUT THiS?
OPEN
MMMH...
i THiNK...
AT FiRST i JUST SAW HER AS THiS PERFECT GiRL AND DiDN'T TAKE STUFF TOO SERiOUSLY, YOU KNOW?
THEN i FOUND OUT ABOUT ALL THiS AND THOUGHT "YO, SHE'S KiNDA HARDCORE!! THiS iS GONNA BE FUN!"
ELLA...
iN A WAY, iT JUST MADE iT ALL MORE REAL, YOU KNOW?
i REALLY WANT TO HELP HER BECAUSE i REALLY CARE ABOUT HER...
AND i LiKE iT.

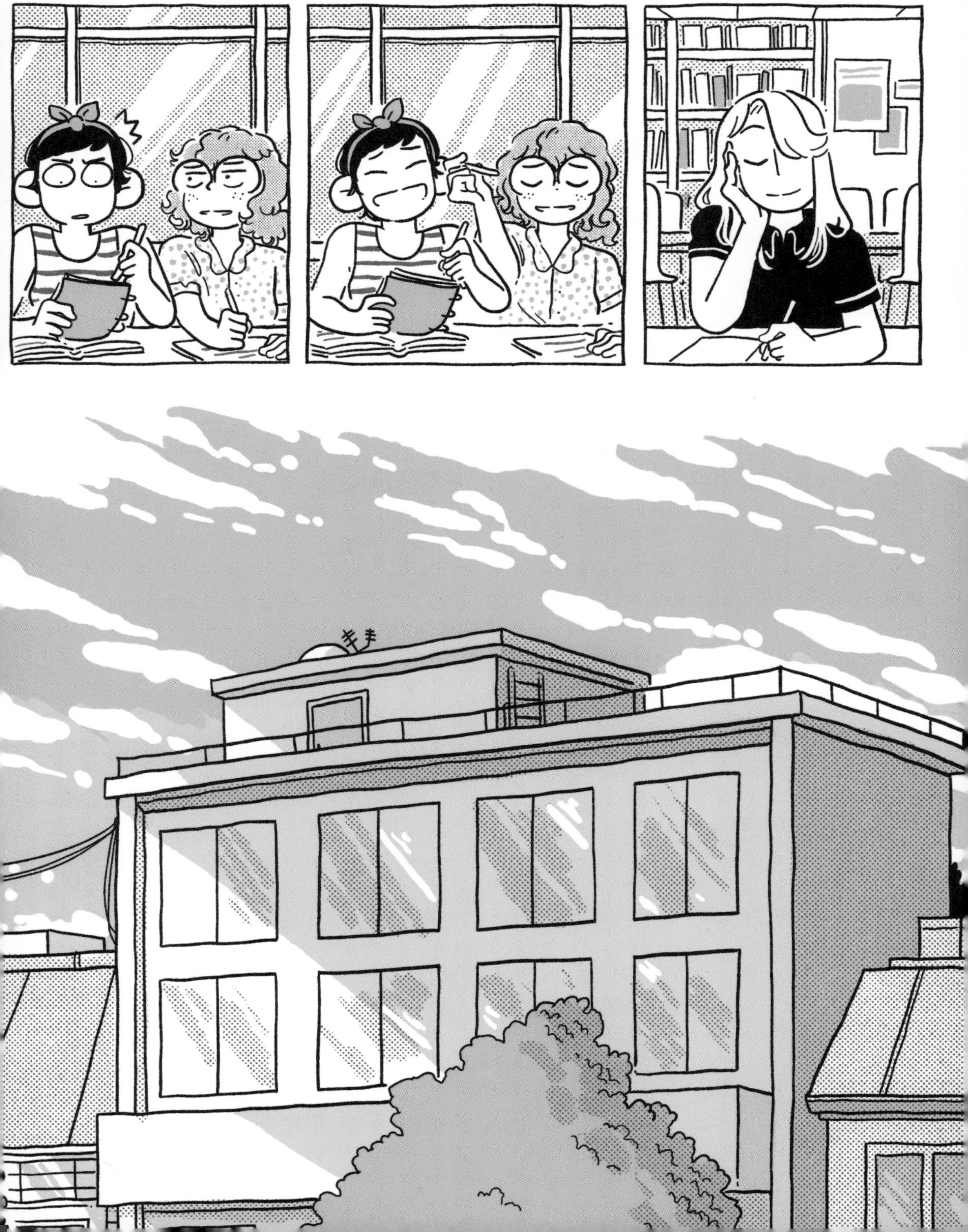

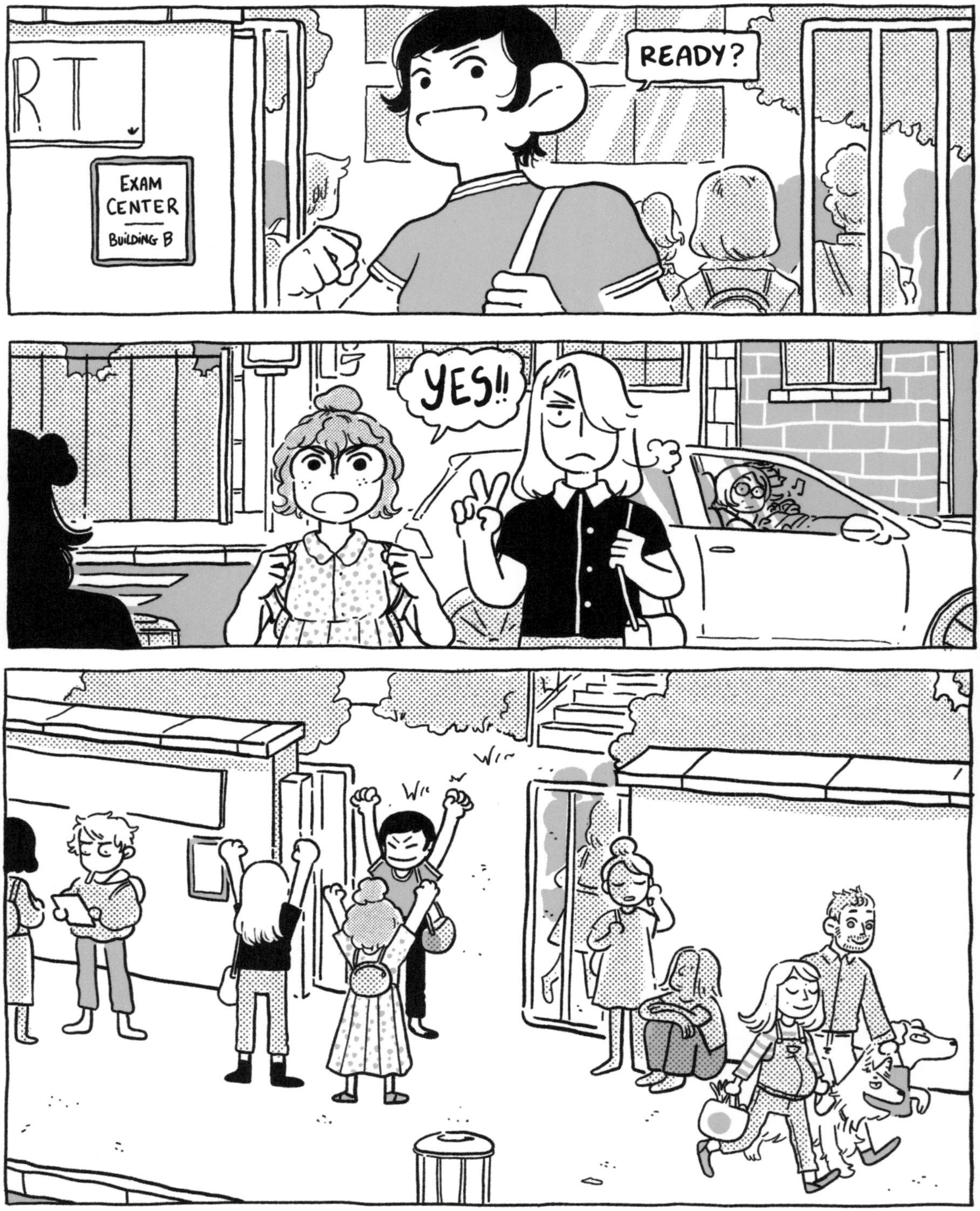
RT
EXAM CENTER
BUILDING B
READY?
YES!!

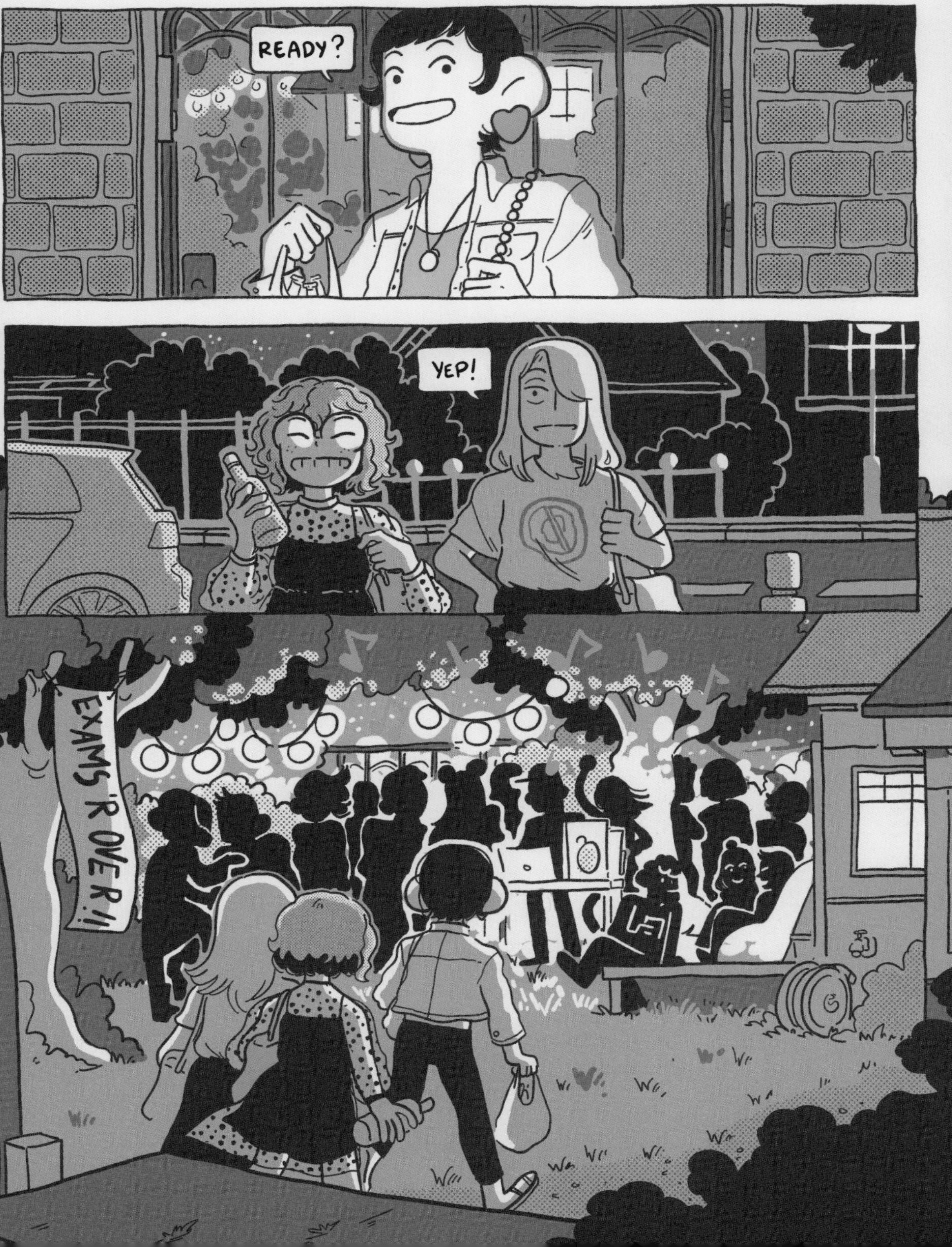
READY?
YEP!
EXAMS 'R OVER!!

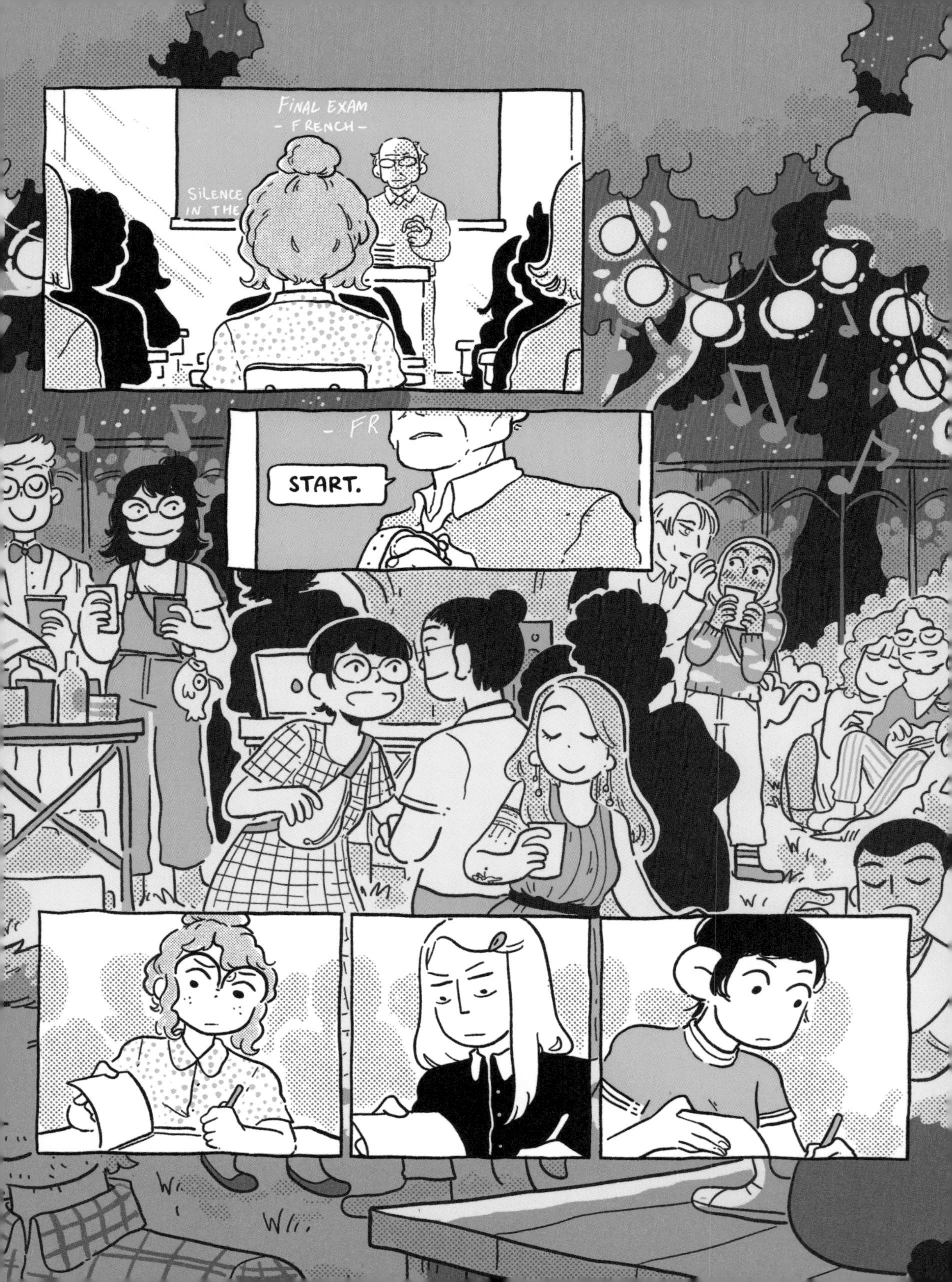
FINAL EXAM
- FRENCH -
SILENCE
IN THE
- FR
START.

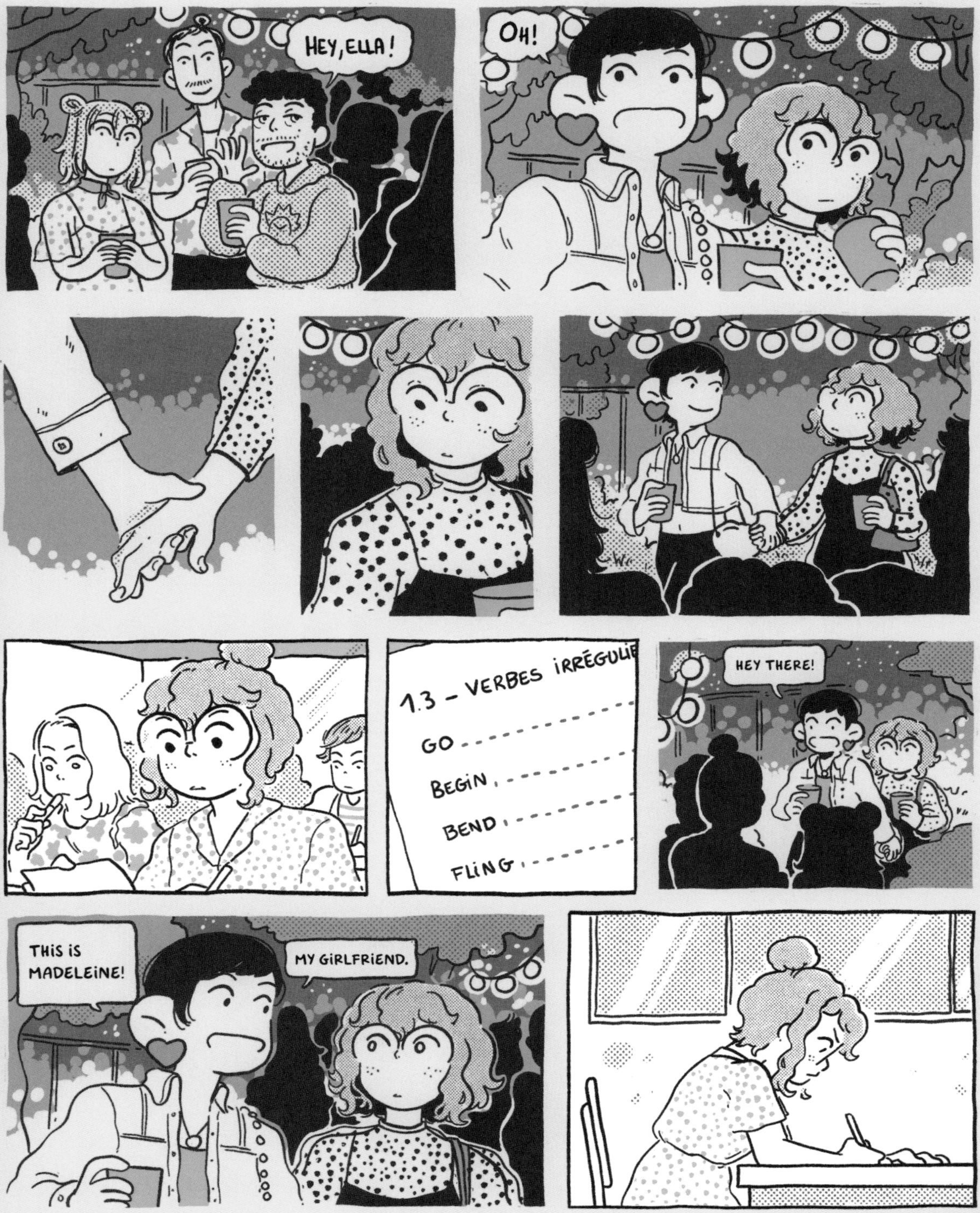
HEY, ELLA!
OH!
1.3 - VERBES IRRÉGULIE
GO
BEGIN
BEND
FLING
HEY THERE!
THIS IS MADELEINE!
MY GIRLFRIEND.

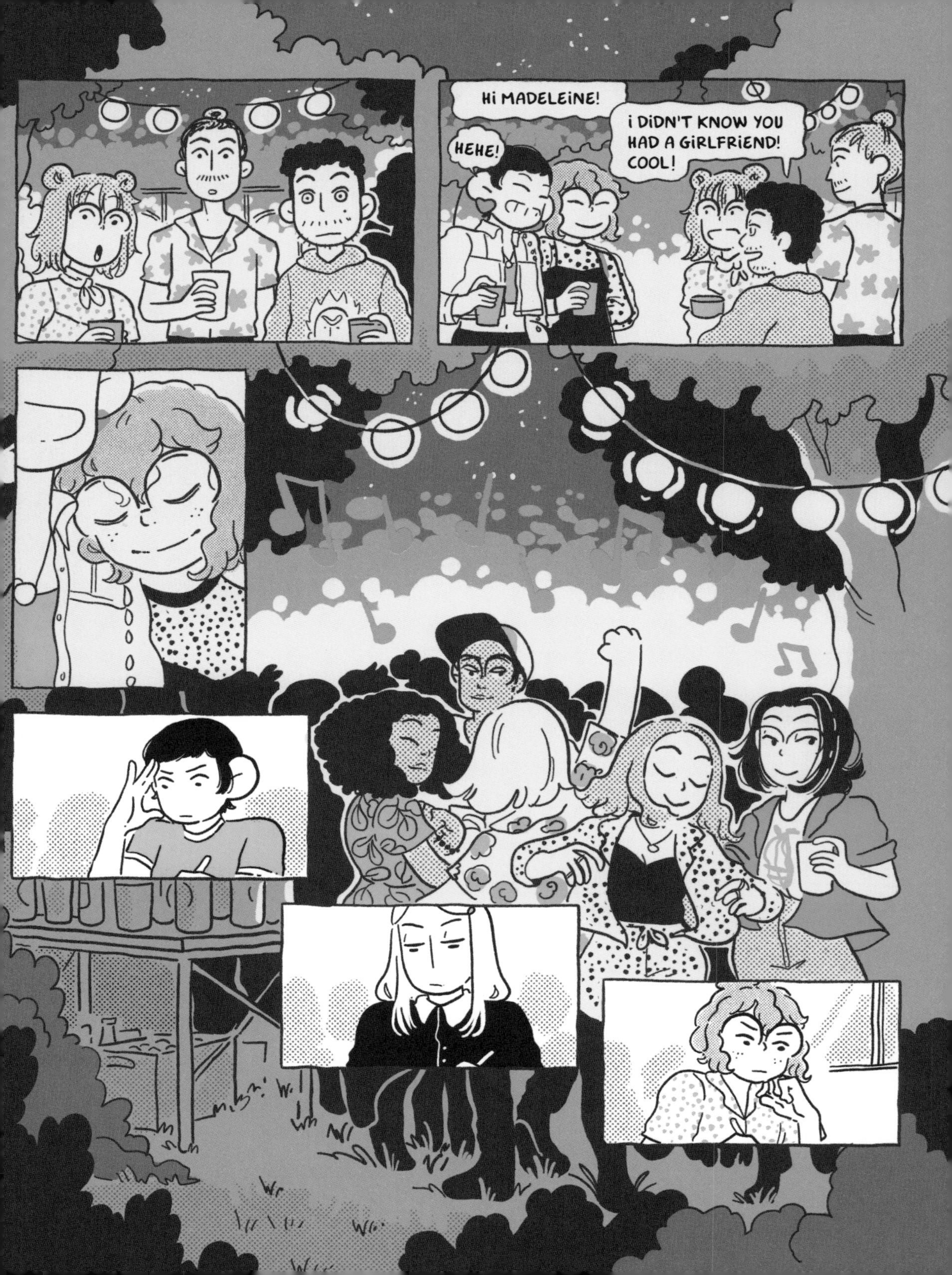
Hi MADELEINE!
HEHE!
i DIDN'T KNOW YOU HAD A GIRLFRIEND! COOL!

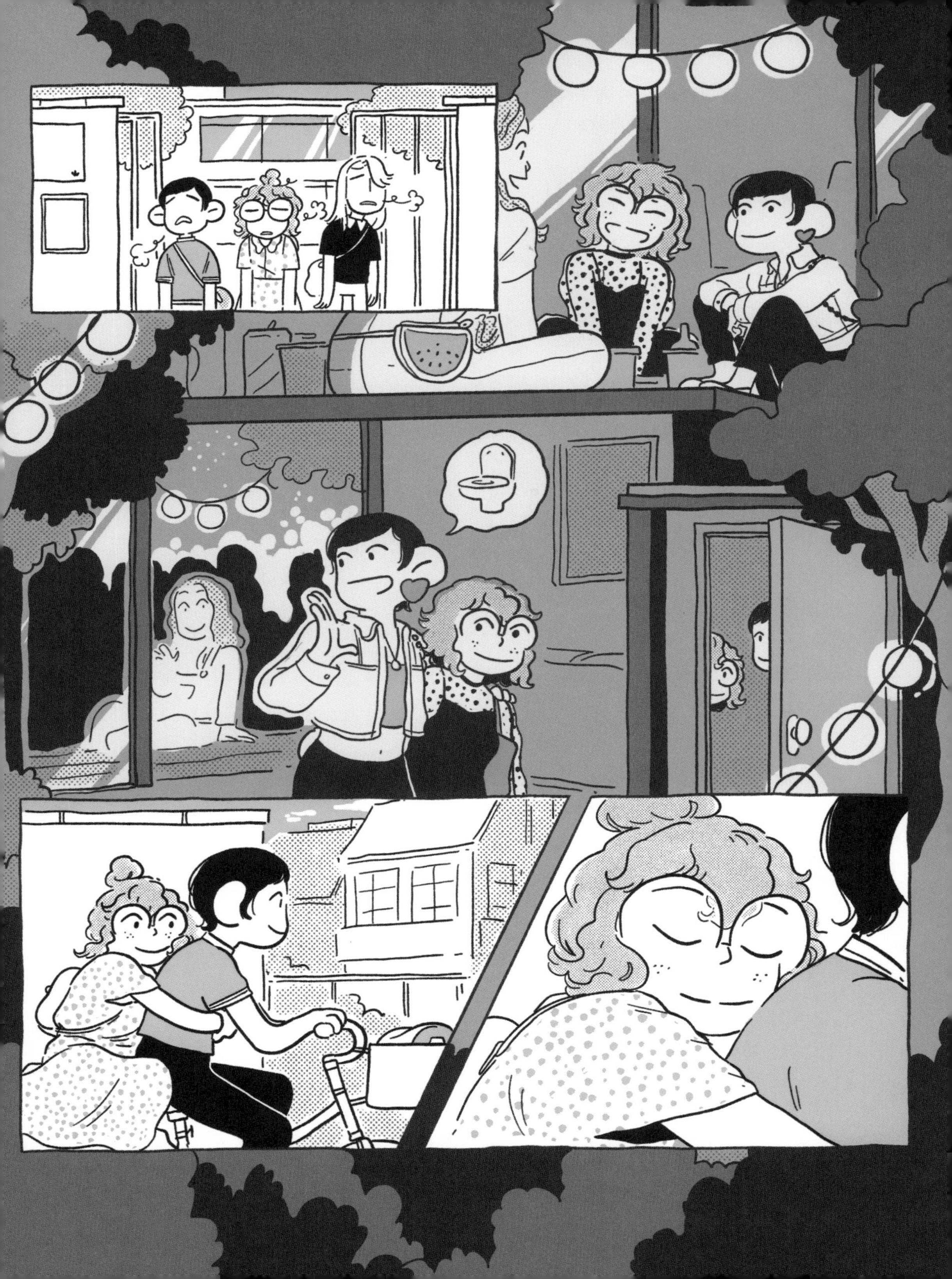

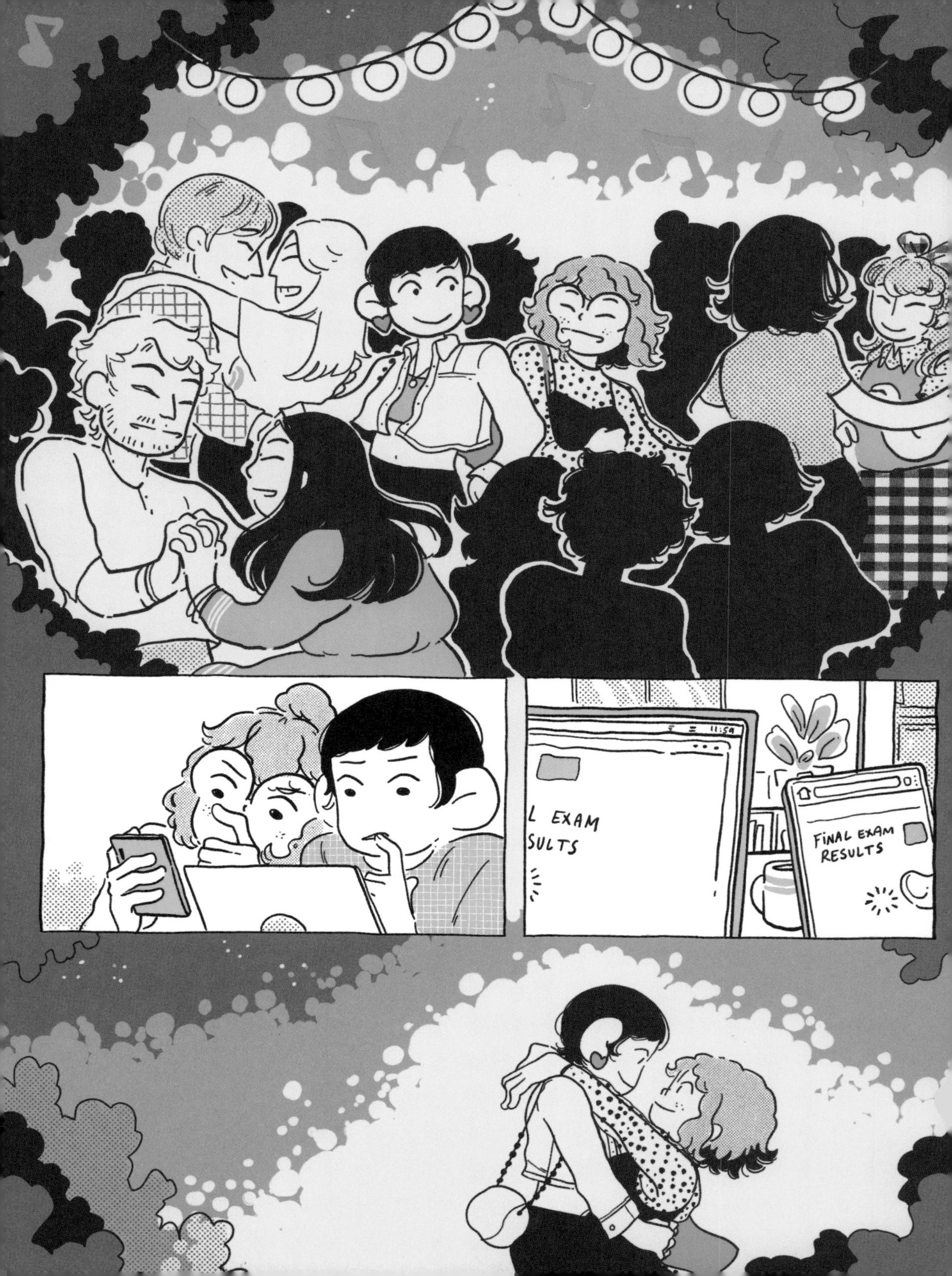
11:59
L EXAM
SULTS
FINAL EXAM
RESULTS

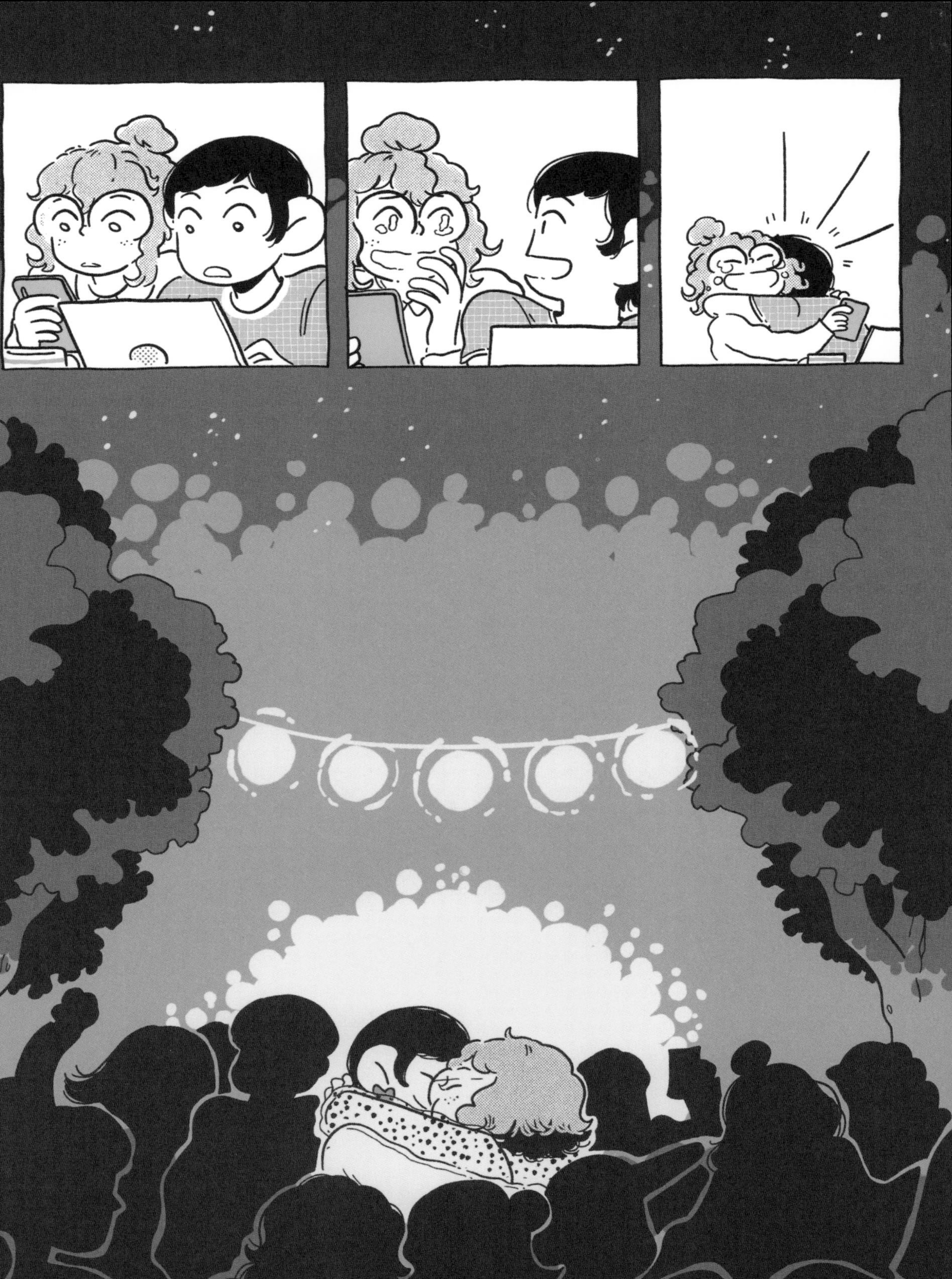

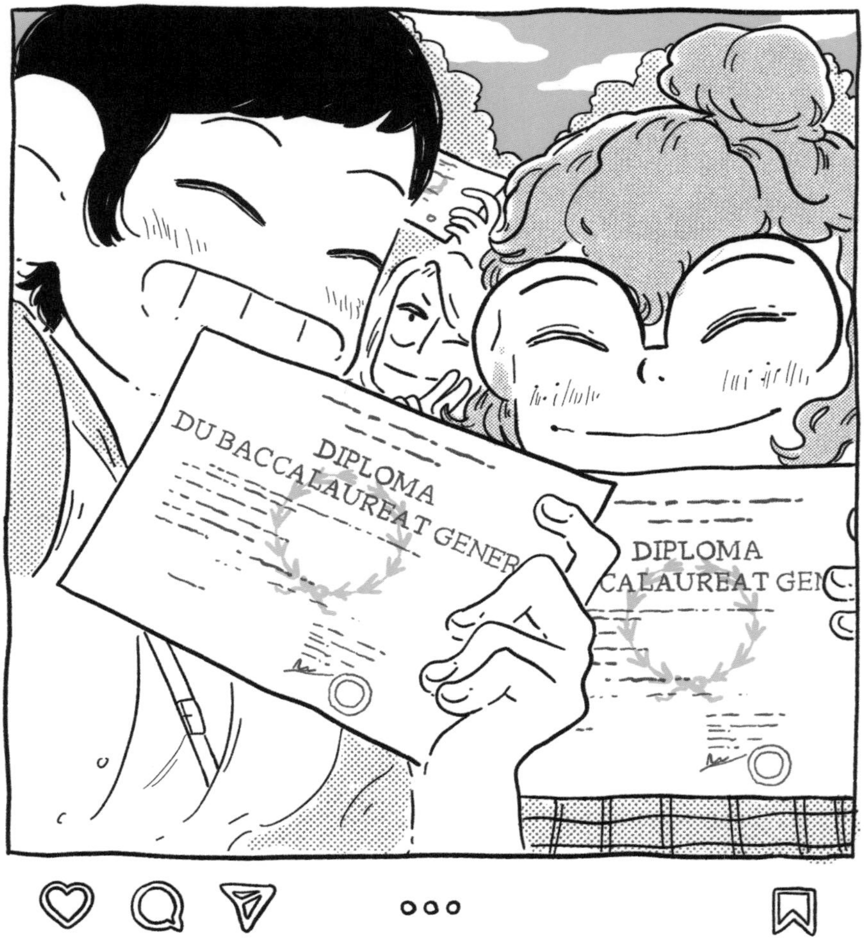
DIPLOMA
DU BACCALAUREAT GENER
DIPLOMA
CALAUREAT GEN

THE NECKLACE

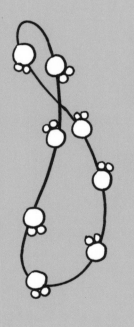

i THINK iT'S IMPORTANT TO DO iT.

BUT i DON'T WANT HiM TO HURT YOU AGAIN.

SO,
i'LL GO.
OK.

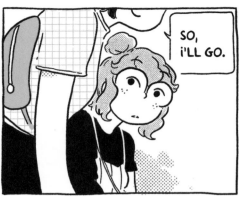

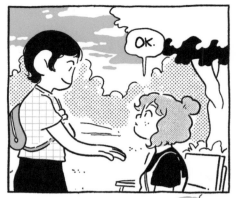

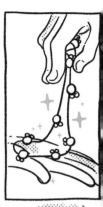

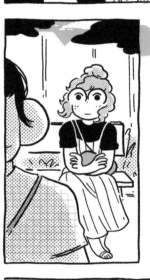

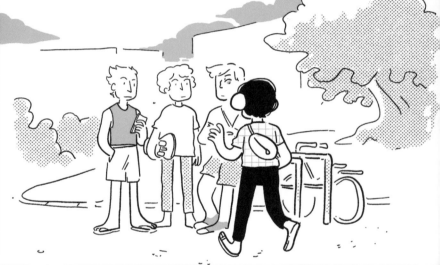

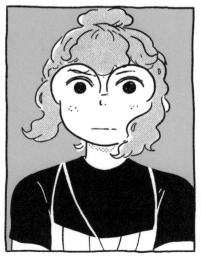

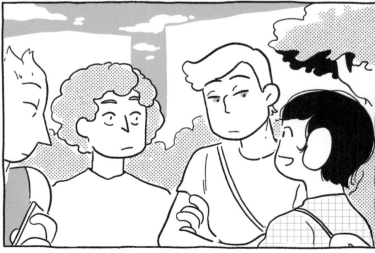

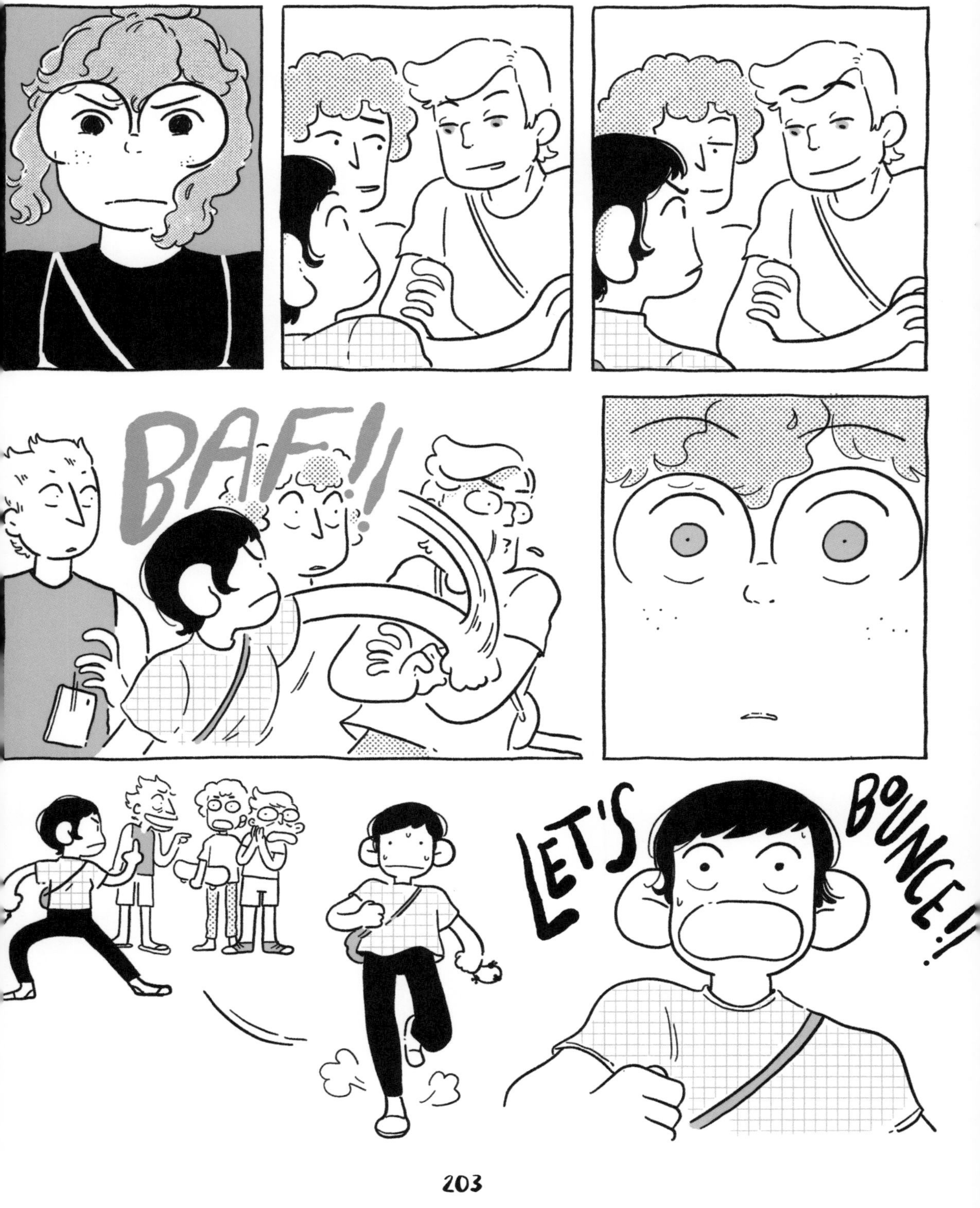
BAF!!
LET'S
BOUNCE!!

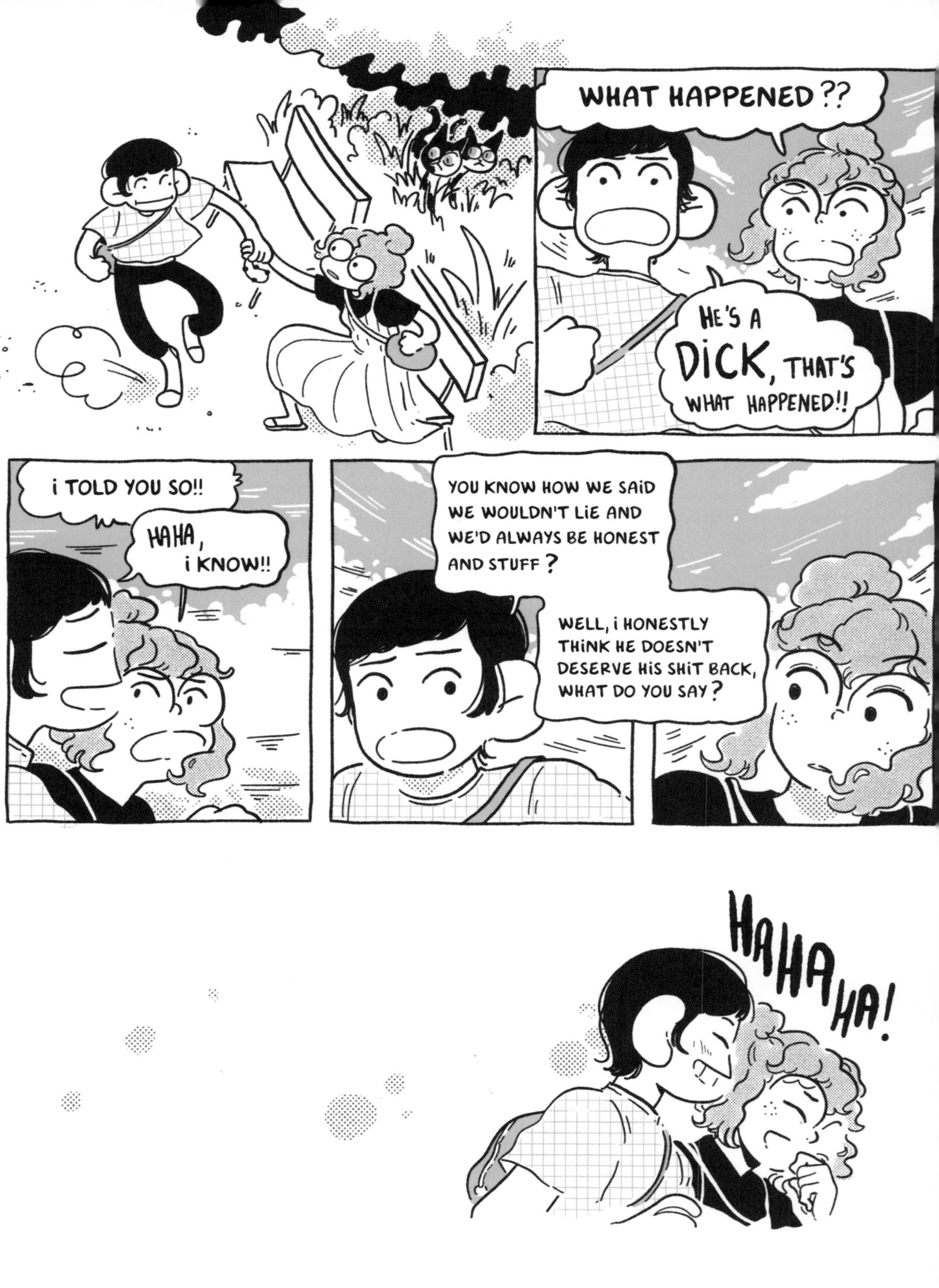
WHAT HAPPENED??
HE'S A DICK, THAT'S WHAT HAPPENED!!
i TOLD YOU SO!!
HAHA, i KNOW!!
YOU KNOW HOW WE SAiD WE WOULDN'T LiE AND WE'D ALWAYS BE HONEST AND STUFF?
WELL, i HONESTLY THiNK HE DOESN'T DESERVE HiS SHiT BACK, WHAT DO YOU SAY?
HAHAHAHA!

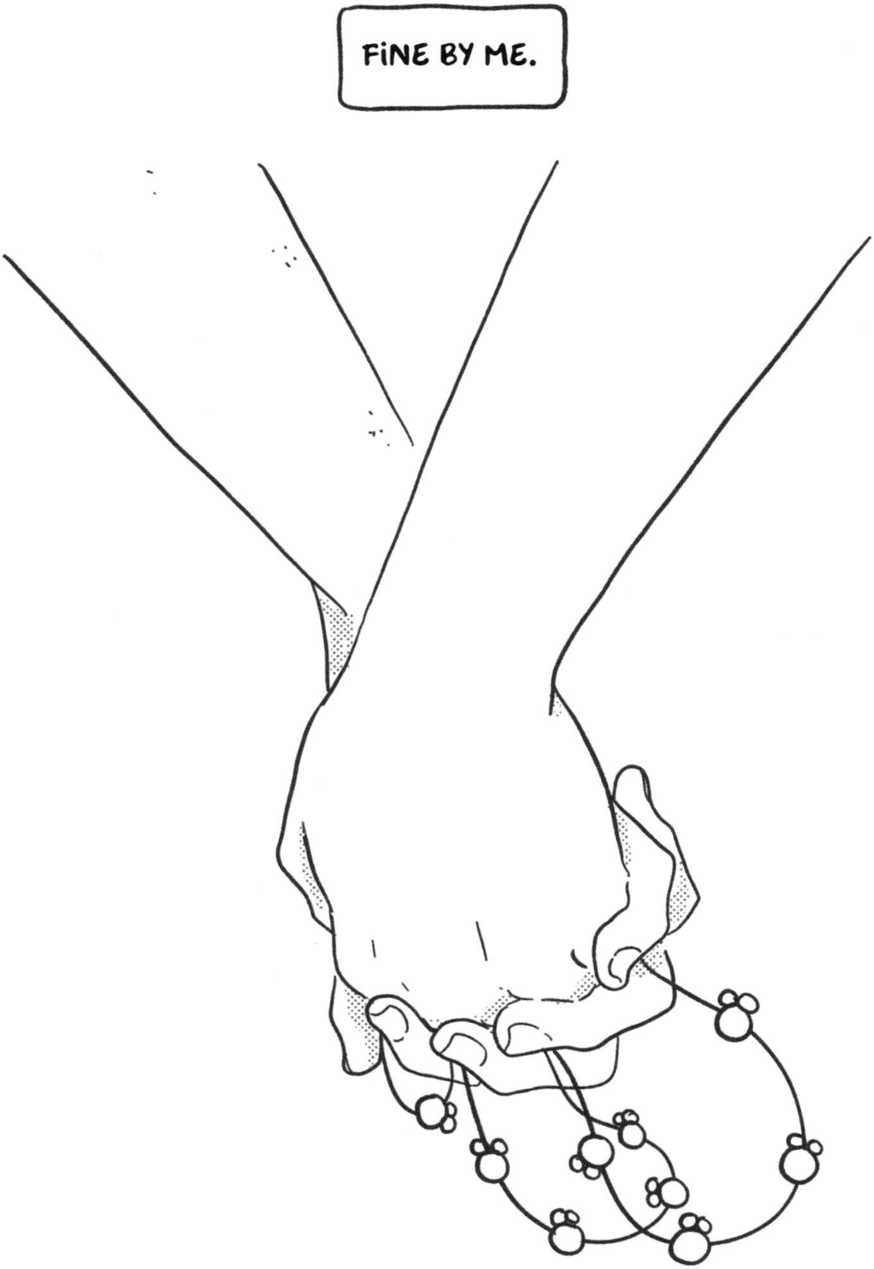
FiNE BY ME.

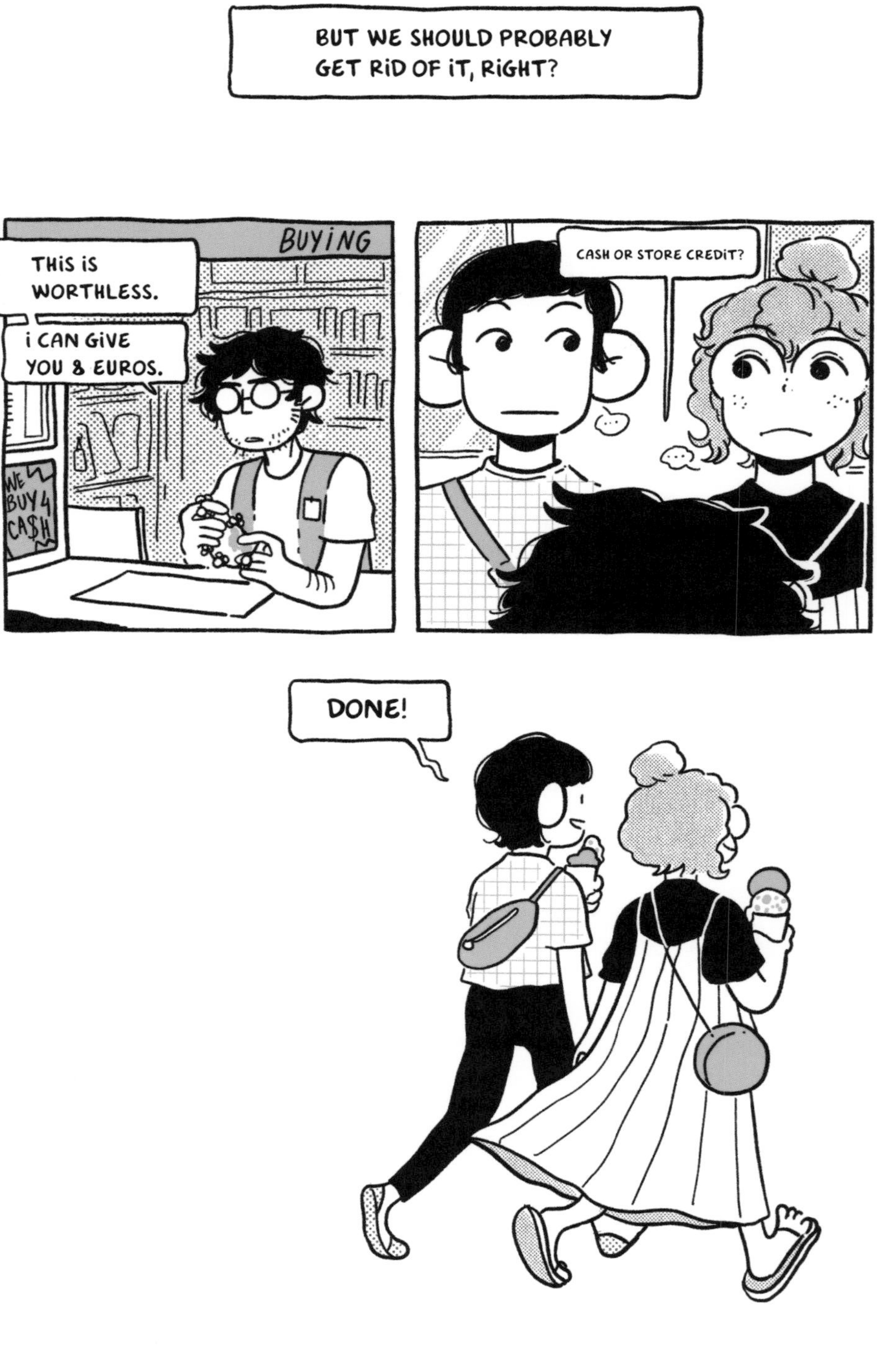
BUT WE SHOULD PROBABLY GET RiD OF iT, RiGHT?
BUYiNG
THiS iS WORTHLESS.
i CAN GiVE YOU 8 EUROS.
WE BUY 4 CA$H
CASH OR STORE CREDiT?
DONE!

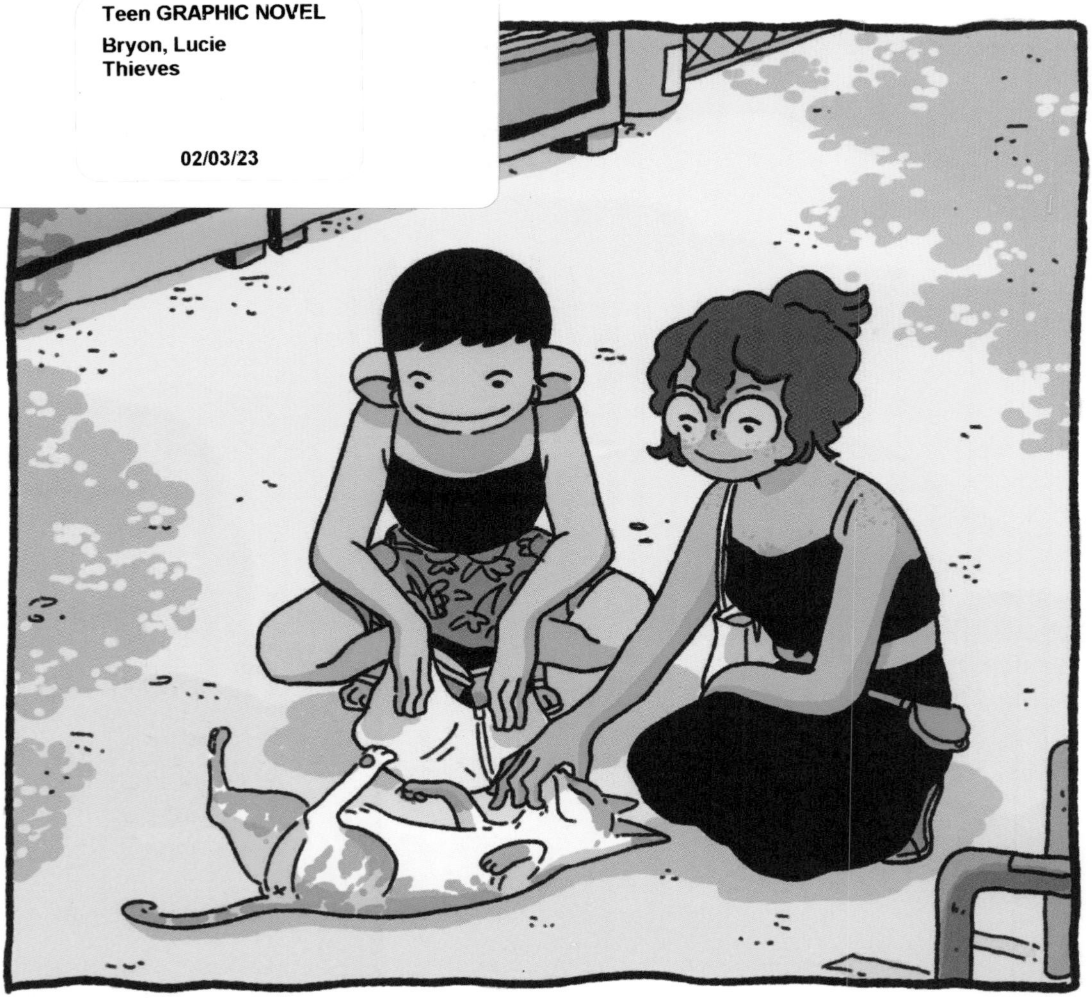

Thank you

To Max, Frédéric, Claudine, Marie, Noémie and the whole Sarbacane team
for their trust, support, work, an encouragements on this book.

To my family, for everything,

to Valentin, my first reader and biggest supporter,

to Peanut, the greatest desk mate,

to Zainab, for her friendship and advice,

to everyone who followed this book's creation on socials,
for their enthusiasm and lovely messages,

and to all the friends who sent me their picture to use as reference
for the last party scene, I'm glad I was able to invite you all.